The
Best Actors
in the World

Recent Titles in
Contributions in Drama and Theatre Studies

The
Best Actors
in the World

❧ ❧

Shakespeare and His Acting Company

DAVID GROTE

Contributions in Drama and Theatre Studies,
Number 97

GREENWOOD PRESS
Westport, Connecticut • London

Library of Congress Cataloging-in-Publication Data

Grote, David.
    The best actors in the world : Shakespeare and his acting company / David Grote.
      p. cm.—(Contributions in drama and theatre studies, ISSN 0163–3821 ; no. 97)
    Includes bibliographical references (p.) and index.
    ISBN 0–313–32088–8 (alk. paper)
    1. Shakespeare, William, 1564–1616—Stage history—To 1625. 2. Shakespeare,
William, 1564–1616—Stage history—England. 3. Shakespeare, William,
1564–1616—Friends and associates. 4. Theatrical companies—England—History—16th
century. 5. Theatrical companies—England—History—17th century. 6.
Actors—England—History—16th century. 7. Actors—England—History—17th century. 8.
Chamberlain's Men (Theater company) 9. King's Men (Theater Company) 10. Kemp,
William, fl. 1600. I. Title. II. Series.
PR3095.G76 2002
792'.0942'09031—dc21   2002016080

British Library Cataloguing in Publication Data is available.

Copyright © 2002 by David Grote

Library of Congress Catalog Card Number: 2002016080
ISBN: 0–313–32088–8
ISSN: 0163–3821

First published in 2002

Greenwood Press, 88 Post Road West, Westport, CT 06881
An imprint of Greenwood Publishing Group, Inc.
www.greenwood.com

Printed in the United States of America

The paper used in this book complies with the
Permanent Paper Standard issued by the National
Information Standards Organization (Z39.48–1984).

10 9 8 7 6 5 4 3 2 1

The best actors in the world, either for tragedy, comedy, history, pastoral, pastoral-comical, historical-pastoral, tragical-historical, tragical-comical-historical-pastoral, scene individable, or poem unlimited. Seneca cannot be too heavy, nor Plautus too light. For the law of writ, and the liberty, these are the only men.

Hamlet, II,ii,392–98

Contents

Acknowledgments

The germination of a project such as this necessarily lies so far back in time that it is impossible to identify, much less acknowledge, all of the people who have contributed to its current form. I am deeply grateful to George Butler, without whose interest and suggestions this volume would not exist. I am equally grateful to people such as Thomas Whitbread and Norman Farmer, who all those years ago gave me the love for the Elizabethan theater that ultimately led to this project. In the years between, the actors, students, and associates whose ideas, discussions, and arguments sharpened my thoughts would make a list longer than another chapter, and I can only beg their forgiveness for not trying to list them all. It is equally impossible to acknowledge the tremendous debt I owe to my wife, Susan, who served as support, challenger, historical adviser, and copyeditor extraordinaire, and who managed both to remain sane and to keep me sane during what became an obsessive focus on the manuscript.

Preface: A Note on Spelling and Citations

Spelling of Elizabethan names was wildly inconsistent. Shakespeare's variable signatures are of course well known, but the same kind of variation holds for all the other actors of the day. In general, I have used the form of the primary citation in E. K. Chambers, *The Elizabethan Stage* (Oxford: Clarendon, 1923), II, with the following exceptions: rather than Burbadge, I use Burbage, which in more recent years has become the more common usage; rather than Kempe, I use Kemp, which from his publications was apparently his own preference; and rather than Goughe, I use Gough simply because the final e looks more odd than in other instances where it is retained.

For Shakespeare's works, all citations to stage directions or to lines in original spelling are to *The First Folio of Shakespeare, 1623*, Ed. Doug Moston (New York: Applause, 1995), which uses the same through-line numbering as in the Hinman edition found in almost all libraries, and are designated as in (F1129). Citations in modern spelling are to the relevant New Arden edition as indicated in the bibliography and are designated in act, scene, and line as (I,i,1). Citations to the plays of Ben Jonson are to *The Complete Plays of Ben Jonson*, 4 vols., ed. G. A. Wilkes (Oxford: Clarendon, 1981), and plays of Middleton are to *The Works of Thomas Middleton*, 8 vols., ed. A. H. Bullen (Boston: Houghton, Mifflin and Co., 1886), both of which also use (I,i,1). Citations to Fletcher's plays, however, are to *The Works of Francis Beaumont and John Fletcher*, 8 vols., ed. Arnold Glover and A. R. Waller (Cambridge: Cambridge University, 1906–10. Repr. New York: Octagon, 1969), which has no line numbering, and thus are indicated only by volume and page, as (I, p27). Citations to all other plays are to (Act, scene, line) of the relevant critical edition in the bibliography; if this edition uses through-line numbering, then the citation is (1. 127).

Introduction

In the summer of 1594, William Shakespeare joined a company of actors who are known as the Chamberlain's Men. This is, without question, the single most significant act in Shakespeare's life and career; it is for the actors of this company that he would provide almost all of the plays that have made him the most important writer in the English language. This was not a company in the modern sense, but rather a group of specific men (and boys) who would work together every day, in many cases for the rest of their lives. Such proximity can only have exerted the most profound influence on Shakespeare as a writer. At the same time, despite the perennial presence of men such as Richard Burbage, Henry Condell, and John Heminges, this company, like all acting companies today, was in a constant state of flux. There were only two very brief periods of less than three years each in which the company did not make at least one major change in membership; not coincidentally, these were also Shakespeare's most productive periods of writing. Throughout all of the remainder of his career, the company changed personnel almost every season. Thus, a great deal both of the variety and the continuity of Shakespeare's output can be traced directly to the membership of the acting company for which he wrote. Nevertheless, the influence of the actors for whom he wrote and with whom he acted is one aspect of Shakespeare's life and work that has received little attention in the overwhelming body of Shakespearean study and criticism.

This book is an attempt to establish a unified and detailed history of Shakespeare's acting company, that is, the group of specific actors for whom his plays were written. It is a chronological history of the acting company known as the Chamberlain's Men and later known as the King's Men during Shakespeare's professional career. It begins with the company's formation in the summer of 1594 and continues until the burning of the first Globe in 1613, after which Shakespeare ceased to participate in company affairs. It deals with the actors in that company, including the boys, detailing their individual growth and decline, their retirement or death, and their replacement by new actors who themselves began to grow. It establishes as precisely as possible the places where these actors performed and the plays that they performed in each place, including those by writers other than Shakespeare. It tries to establish with equal precision when they actually performed, with careful consideration both to the numerous theater closures during plague outbreaks and to all known political suppressions.

To understand the life of any acting company, one must understand not only who was in it, but also what roles they played. Thus, the only way one can hope to understand the ways in which Shakespeare planned or modified his plays for specific actors is to attempt to cast all of the plays. In 1927, T. W. Baldwin, in a brief and somewhat casual portion of a much larger work,[1] made the only serious attempt to assign Shakespeare's original roles to specific actors. Because of the difficulties associated with many of Baldwin's conjectures, more recent scholars have assumed that sufficient evidence was not available to provide a detailed history of the acting company itself.

Nevertheless, a significant amount of factual data is available and when considered from a somewhat different viewpoint can provide a great deal of information. We know the names of almost all of Shakespeare's actors, including all the Sharers, many of his Hired Men, and most of the significant boys. From information in various court and legal documents of the day and from allusions in other literary works, we can date their stage service with some accuracy and determine the most critical factor in their casting assignments: their age. We can, with considerable certainty, also determine at what point specific actors had company shares, another critical factor in casting decisions. We also have a reasonably good idea of the general workings of the Elizabethan acting partnerships. Thus, once we consider the plays themselves chronologically, it is possible to cast not just one or two roles but in fact most of the Sharer roles in all of the plays. Each successful role assignment we make by process of elimination simplifies the casting of other actors in the company in all succeeding plays. Naturally, most contemporary interest will focus on the plays of Shakespeare. But the acting company performed the work of many playwrights, and the validity of our casting assignments can be demonstrated by the application of the same principles to the surviving plays by playwrights such as Jonson, Dekker, Tourneur, Barnes, and John Fletcher.

I have tried to use generally accepted dates for the composition of the plays of the era, where such general acceptance exists. However, as all Shakespearean scholars are aware, there are very few plays for which dating is universally agreed, and a surprisingly large number of these accepted dates—see *Macbeth, Much Ado About Nothing, As You Like It,* or *Hamlet,* for example—are based on almost no evidence other than general acceptance. Where no firm external evidence exists, almost all such previous attempts have been based on allusions within the plays and assumptions about stylistic growth and change, which are dependent on the individual critic's or scholar's sensitivity to a particular aspect of the material. It is impossible to write a chrono-logical history without sequence, so, by necessity more than by intention, this book has also become an attempt to firmly date Shakespeare's plays. Where my conclusions differ from the generally accepted, there are detailed arguments. The factor I have tried to introduce into the discussion is the composition of the acting company that would have performed the plays, which is rarely if ever considered in relation to such questions and which, when added into the equation, offers some surprisingly valuable evidence.

None of the specific data in this book will be unfamiliar to Shakespearean scholars. What is unusual is the attempt to arrange this information consecutively, to put what is usually treated in a generalized manner into a tightly specific order. When viewed from the perspective of the acting company itself, much familiar information takes on new meanings, and new light can be thrown onto a number of often intensely debated questions in Shakespearean criticism that cannot be resolved solely by textual analysis or from existing historical documents. For example, this volume suggests a new candidate for the missing *Love's Labour's Won* and offers a new approach to the dating of plays such as *All's Well That Ends Well*, *Troilus and Cressida*, and *Coriolanus*. It offers an explanation of the mysteries of Samuel Crosse, listed among the Principall Actors in the Folio although absent from all other partnership records, and of Lawrence Fletcher, the extra clown who unexpectedly appeared on the 1603 patent but is not listed among the Folio actors. It describes a history for the acting company and for Shakespeare that is far more complex than usually described, a history of both success and risk, planning and chaos, skill and luck.

Although I believe the casting assignments made in the course of this book are correct, they are only a means to an end. At one level, they validate the chronology, but more importantly, they help us to see Shakespeare (and the other playwrights of his era) in a new way. By putting names to the actors and their roles, we can at last begin to see Shakespeare the actor-playwright. We can glimpse the profound influence on his work of the specific actors for whom he provided material, year in and year out. In particular, we can begin to see the critical impact on his work of three particular adult actors—Richard Burbage, Will Kemp, and Augustine Phil-lips—and three stunningly gifted boys—Nicholas Tooley, William Ecclestone, and an otherwise unknown boy probably named Alexander. The nature of such influ-ences can only be sketched here due to limitations of space. But with a history of the acting company available, we can glimpse an aspect of Shakespeare that remains all but unexplored after centuries of study.

Chapter 1

Prologue

The acting company known as the Chamberlain's Men was first organized in the late spring or early summer of 1594. But no acting company starts from nothing. Many of the men in the company were established performers with ten or more years of stage experience, and they performed within a unique social and theatrical context that shaped their organization, decisions, and productions.

All of these groups were what we now call repertory companies. This meant that each group was a closed company with a fixed number of members who performed a number of different roles in a number of different plays. This was not a matter of choice so much as a matter of necessity. In a world in which a town of a thousand people was considered a metropolis, no acting company could hope to perform in one place for long. Hence, all the early actors had to tour to support themselves. Naturally, each company tried to keep its numbers as small as possible when touring. Records are necessarily incomplete and inconclusive, but surviving scripts from before the 1580s indicate that such companies carried no more than eight adults.[1] The men were partners in the company, sharing equally in the proceeds of each performance, and thus are usually known as Sharers.

This was the only form of company organization the actors had ever known, and so it continued to be the fundamental organization used even after some of the companies began to base themselves in London and to tour only irregularly. The practical effect of this system was that the Elizabethan acting company was a communal organization. All of the Sharers participated in all the decisions as well as in all the income. A share was in effect permanent. In one way, it was like tenure in a small college, requiring the vote of all the faculty. It was not given lightly, for the candidate would be with the group every day for the rest of his professional life. In another way, the company was like a marriage; legally, the Sharers of a company were joint tenants, sharing equally in all the assets of the group, with their shares reverting to the other company Sharers at their death. An actor might leave or might be thrown out, but if that happened the result was like a divorce, messy, disruptive, and possibly even life-threatening for the group. But as in a small faculty or a marriage, all decisions were made communally; at various times, some individuals might be more powerful and influential, but eventually, they would require the consent and cooperation of all the other Sharers for any decisions made on behalf of the company. This included both the selection and the casting of all plays.

English law authorized the immediate arrest of any masterless men. Touring actors thus were forced to travel under the nominal banner of some Lord, and the greater the Lord the greater the value of his protection. Even so, the noble sponsorship was more a legal fiction than a matter of subsidy. The various Lords were figureheads who, with very few exceptions, contributed no money and took no part in company decisions, including company membership. However, it is only through the Lord's name that companies can be identified, and our own modern need to identify groups for historical clarity has given perhaps undue emphasis to these patrons. Whatever the name used, the real authority in any acting company rested in its Sharers.

When touring, these companies usually performed in temporary spaces—the enclosed yard of an inn, a guild hall, or a large hall in a local landowner's house or castle. In London, however, there were actual theaters after 1576. These were necessarily not too different from the temporary spaces used outside London, but the simple fact of their existence had a profound effect on the way actors began to think of themselves and their material. The first of these was known simply as The Theatre, because it was unique when constructed in 1576 by James Burbage and his brother-in-law John Brayne. So successful was it that a second theater was soon built in the vicinity by a man called Lanham (perhaps with Burbage as a partner), known as the Curtain because it was in Curtain Close outside the city walls to the north. By 1587, the London demand for plays had grown so great that Philip Henslowe built a third theater, the Rose, on a site south of the Thames.

Within a few years of the construction of the Rose, a number of actors began to think of themselves and their profession in a different way. They began to see themselves as actors based in London who occasionally toured, rather than as actors who toured and occasionally visited London. How that change came about is largely undocumented and is still unclear, even in broad outlines. The one actor who seems to figure most prominently in that change is England's first real star, Edward Alleyn thought of today as the first Tamburlaine, Faustus, and Jew of Malta. In his youth, Alleyn joined a company patronized by the Earl of Worcester. But early in 1589, Alleyn walked out on Worcester's Men to join a new company patronized by the Lord Admiral. By 1590, he was in yet another company, whose patron is unknown. This company remained at The Theatre until May 1591, when Alleyn accused James Burbage of stealing part of the box office receipts and Burbage responded by insulting the Lord Admiral, after which Alleyn and part of the company walked out. Shortly afterward, Alleyn was at the Rose, or so we assume, because at about the same time he married the landlord Henslowe's stepdaughter. This company was known as Lord Strange's Men. Plague brought those performances to an end in the summer of 1592, and in early 1593, Alleyn organized yet another company with which to tour. This was also patronized by Lord Strange, although Alleyn claimed the personal patronage of the Lord Admiral.[2] The tour itself was unprofitable, or Alleyn tired of the road, and the actors shortly returned to London. During the first half of 1594, Alleyn reorganized, or returned to, the Admiral's Men, while most of the actors who had toured with him organized a new company. Since Lord Strange died that spring, they somehow obtained the patronage of the Lord Chamberlain. Alleyn took his company to the Rose, where they remained until Henslowe built them a new theater building, the Fortune, in 1600; there they remained until it burned down in 1621, thus becoming both the first permanent London-based company and the first company permanently based in a single theater building.

As Alleyn's early career indicates, these early London years, when Shakespeare arrived and began to participate in London theatrical life, were chaotic. Major companies were organized or re-organized during every year, most often as a result of Alleyn's defection or entrance. But other factors played their role in the chaos. The first attempt at a London company had been the Queen's Men, organized in 1583. But they had received serious blows in 1587, when their leading man, William Knell, was killed in a brawl with another actor while on tour, and again in 1588, when their chief clown, Richard Tarleton, died. Also in 1588, the Earl of Leicester died, throwing all of his actors out on the streets, so to speak. Many of those men will appear in later history, but their attempts to find work during 1588–89 may have been a major stimulus in the organization of more than one new company, especially the one patronized by Lord Strange. The Earl of Worcester died in 1589, shortly after Alleyn left the company; no one quite knows what happened to the actors who did not leave with Alleyn, and their need for a new patron further added to the confusion. The Lord Admiral's company and Strange's Men both had serious political problems related to the Martin Marprelate repressions, and Strange's Men (perhaps both Strange's and the Lord Admiral's companies) were officially closed down in November 1589. About the same time, a company sponsored by Lord Pembroke appeared on the scene, and in some way equally unclear, Shakespeare began to write for them, and we must assume, also to act with them. He provided them with two parts of *Henry VI* and *Titus Andronicus*, and perhaps a number of other plays as well. Where they played, and with what actors, remains one of the greatest of all mysteries in Shakespeare's biography.

The Theatre and its successors all appear to have had room for about two thousand spectators—which in turn meant that new material exhausted its audience with fewer performances, requiring ever more new material. Thus was born the professional playwright. On the road, the acting companies had only needed a handful of plays, because they would normally exhaust the local audience in one or two performances. Most of these plays would have been developed by the actors themselves over the years. London, however, devoured those plays in only a few performances. Thus, the actors came to depend on the writers, who expanded the actors' material, but also added enormously to the expenses of the company, with a playwright usually paid six or more pounds per script.[3]

At the same time, as London audiences saw more plays by more writers, they grew more demanding about their contents. Two actors, bare boards, and a passion no longer sufficed to attract the crowds. Although people still referred to hearing a play, most of the crowd expected to see something as well. As in our own day, spectacle and effects became an important part of the theatrical event. One of the most effective of spectacles is the crowd, but to play crowd scenes, a company has to have a crowd of actors. By the late 1580s, no company with a serious London presence could expect to survive on a diet of plays with only six or eight actors. All of the companies began to add new members known as Hired Men, actors who were not Sharers but were paid a small, fixed fee to swell the crowd and play the minor soldiers, messengers, peasants, citizens, and comic butts in the new kinds of plays. By the mid-1590s they were such a regular part of all play productions that they were hired for the entire London season and usually remained with a single company for years at a time.[4]

In the summer of 1592, plague returned to London, and for most of the next two years, London theaters were closed while the disease decimated London's population. During that time, all the earlier theater companies collapsed. Alleyn organized a touring company with a new license, as we have seen. Pembroke's Men also tried to tour but went broke. When they staggered back into London, they were forced to sell off a number of their properties and playscripts. Some of those plays also ended up in the hands of printers, which is how we came by the earliest printings of work by Shakespeare. Worcester's Men and the Queen's Men left London to tour permanently.

In December 1593, yet another new company appeared on the scene. Plague apparently had declined to a point where Henslowe could reopen the Rose. A company under the protection of the Earl of Sussex performed there in late December and January, including a performance of *Titus Andronicus* on January 24, 1594.[5] This company had last been seen in 1591 when it combined with the remainder of the Queen's Men for a few London performances before going on the road. They had obviously bought some of the Pembroke playbooks, such as *Titus Andronicus,* which suggests a large company. The company closed in February, probably because Lent began, and then performed for about a week in April. Henslowe's journal shows very respectable income for those performances; nevertheless, Sussex's company packed up and left the Rose and are not heard from again in London records. Shortly afterward, Alleyn rejoined the Admiral's Men and took over the Rose permanently.

The Strange's Men left behind by Alleyn should have become masterless men, but by June they had found a new patron: Henry Carey, Earl of Hunsdon, the Lord Chamberlain and one of Elizabeth's most trusted courtiers. It would have been hard to find a more powerful patron, because Carey was Elizabeth's nearest living blood relative, son of Mary Boleyn; given that Mary had been Henry VIII's mistress both before and after he married her sister, it was not inconceivable that Hunsdon was in fact Elizabeth's half-brother. Hunsdon had patronized a provincial touring company last recorded in 1589. It is unclear why he suddenly decided to patronize this new company. Nonetheless, he did. At that point, the company known as the Chamberlain's Men was formed.

Although many of the Chamberlain's Men had previously worked under the patronage of Lord Strange, this was a new acting company. The previous Strange company had been built around Edward Alleyn. With Alleyn gone, the remaining men were forced to rethink their organization and to find a completely new repertory. As a result of this reorganization, they added at least two comparatively unknown actors, William Shakespeare and Richard Burbage, who would shortly become the most famous and influential figures in the theatrical life of the era, and arguably in history.

Before we examine the detailed history of the new Chamberlain's Men, it is beneficial to meet all the original members of the company. If the Chamberlain's Men had a star in that first season, it was Will Kemp, the company's principal clown. He is first noted in the record as a part of Leicester's troupe in northern Europe during the mid-1580s, but by the early 1590s he was back in London and known as the most famous comedian in England. When Edward Alleyn put together his touring company in 1593, Kemp was that company's clown. Thus, by the time he joined the Lord Chamberlain's company in London in 1594, he had at least ten years of performing experience behind him and must have been thirty years old, probably older. He was famous as a clown and as a dancer, the master of that peculiar English specialty, the theatrical jig. (The jigs were performed after each play and featured some kind of comic routine at least in part set to music, usually involving either a man and a woman or two men and two women. Jigs were partly scripted and partly improvised, interspersing the jokes with specialty dances.) From other, later references, we know that Kemp was also a physically large man with a common touch, who preferred to play common man characters.

The most experienced serious actor in the company was George Bryan, who also had been a member of Leicester's touring company. He was back in England before 1590, when he probably joined Strange's company. He, too, toured with Alleyn during the 1593 tour. He retired in 1597–98 but was sufficiently well regarded to become a Groom of the Chamber sometime between 1598 and 1603, which position he continued to hold until his death in 1613. This was a relatively minor position, and technically, all the original members of the Queen's Men during Elizabeth's reign were so designated, as were all the King's Men when they served during the visit of the Spanish ambassador in 1604. But as far as we can tell today, Bryan is the only actor to have served as such with no background in a royal company—not even Edward Alleyn was ever listed as such[6]—which indicates he had unusual prominence both on and off the stage. In 1594, Bryan would have been about thirty-five years old.

Thomas Pope had also been with Leicester's company, and his name is continually linked with Bryan's in the early surviving records. He retired in 1600 and died in 1603. Ben Jonson later called him a "fat fool," but it is not clear whether Jonson was referring to him personally or to his performances. Other period allusions call him variously "Pope the player" and "Pope the clown," but no modern scholar has seriously argued that he was the company clown instead of Kemp.[7] In any case, it does seem clear that as his age increased, so did his waistline, and that he was noted for playing less serious characters.

John Heminges would eventually become one of the most famous names in Shakespeare studies, for he helped edit the first Shakespeare Folio. His first theatrical citation is on the 1593 touring license with Alleyn, but he must have had considerable previous experience in order to be included as a Sharer in such an all-star company. In 1588, he married the widow of William Knell, the Queen's Man killed in the duel at Thame, and moved into Knell's house in London. More than likely, then, Heminges was also an actor in the Queen's Men by 1588. This marriage indicates a man at least in his mid-twenties in 1588, so by 1594, he was an experienced performer of about thirty, roughly the same age as Shakespeare.

Augustine Phillips first entered the record in a play generally referred to as *The Seven Deadly Sins*, which was apparently a set of one acts illustrating each theme. The play has disappeared, but a summary of entrances, exits, props, and casting assignments, which the Elizabethan's called a "plot," has survived for three of those plays.[8] This plot is one of the major pieces of evidence about the early careers of many in the Chamberlain's men, for among the actors listed are Phillips, Bryan, Pope, and Richard Burbage, as well as a number of others who are discussed later. Unfortunately, the one thing the surviving copy lacks is a date. The play itself is assumed to have been written by Richard Tarleton, who died in 1588 and acted in the Queen's Men, but none of the actors listed have ever been tied to the Queen's Men. It was found among the papers of Edward Alleyn, but Alleyn's name is not included; two adult roles, King Henry and Lidgate, are uncast, but these are part of a narratorial frame, a dull and undramatic assignment for a star like Alleyn. For general purposes, scholars date it 1590–92, but this is not very helpful when trying to follow the careers of individual actors. Most important is Burbage's assignment to Gorboduc and Tereus, two leading roles of precisely the kind of characterization usually played by Alleyn. If it dates to 1590, then Burbage was much older than generally thought; if 1592, then Burbage's career makes more sense, taking over leading roles played by Alleyn before he walked out of The Theatre in 1591, but it is difficult to explain how the paper itself came to be in Alleyn's possession. Nevertheless, within the context of the full careers of the various actors involved, late 1591 or early 1592 seems the most likely date. Even with the unsettled date, it does provide valuable information about the kinds of roles assigned to particular actors, which will help us assign later roles in their Chamberlain's Men careers.

In *The Seven Deadly Sins*, Phillips played Sardanapalus, a historical character neither young nor old. However, William Sly, a man later identified as his apprentice, played adults in the same play and then went to the Admiral's company at the Rose in 1594; this means that Phillips had been acting for some time, or he could not have had a grown apprentice by this date. Thus, he too was roughly the same age as Shakespeare, perhaps a year or two older. Phillips published a jig in 1595, so he was at least an occasional dancer and could also play humorous roles when needed. He died in 1605 shortly after his retirement.

Possibly the youngest man in the company was Richard Burbage. His exact age is not known. Many years later his brother Cuthbert would say Richard had acted for 35 years, which is used to give him a generally accepted birth date of 1568–70. However, in 1590 Richard was hauled into court for beating up the representatives of the widow Brayne, who had come to demand the share of Theatre income owed to her late husband; in the surviving reports, he is described as a very young man, so he may have been only in his late teens at that date. He is in two surviving plots, playing a messenger in *Dead Man's Fortune*, usually dated 1590, and in *The Seven Deadly Sins* doubling two major roles. If the *Sins* plot dates to 1592, he may have been born as late as 1572, and Cuthbert's comment may have included some youthful apprentice years. In either case, in 1594, Richard was still in his early twenties, possibly very early.

Henry Condell was also in his early twenties, assuming he was the Harry who played one of Gorboduc's grown sons in *The Seven Deadly Sins*. Not much has been established about his early life, but he would live and perform in the company for a long time, retiring probably in 1619–21. He also helped edit the 1623 First Folio of Shakespeare's plays.

To this company was added William Shakespeare, thirty years old and perhaps looking a bit older. Both the notorious Droeshot engraving in the Folio and his bust in Stratford made while family members were still alive show a bald man, the hairline receding from the brow, which does not happen overnight. In 1594, he was probably not yet bald, but the hairline would have started to recede, which would have made him look a bit older than his thirty years.

The inclusion of Shakespeare in the company was a most remarkable step. When and how Shakespeare came to London and became involved in theatrical life is a matter of much debate. The first reference to him in London is Greene's deathbed attack on:

. . . an upstart crow, beautified with our feathers, that with his Tyger's hart wrapt in a Player's hyde, supposes he is as well able to bombast out a blanke verse as the best of you: and, being an absolute Johannes Factotum, is in his own conceit the onley Shake-scene in a countrey.[9]

The precise meaning of this has occasioned much argument, but it is clear that by 1592 Shakespeare was known in London as an actor. If Greene is to be believed, Shakespeare was a relatively minor player, the kind who does in fact have to do a little bit of everything in an acting company, but he was nonetheless experienced and well known for his performances. Perhaps because of Greene's charge, it has become a tradition that Shakespeare was not much of an actor. Certainly, during the plague years of 1592–94, Shakespeare seems not to have toured with any of the acting companies, for he somehow became attached to the Earl of Southampton. He wrote *Venus and Adonis* and *The Rape of Lucrece*, both dedicated to Southampton, as well as the bulk of his sonnets, generally assumed to have been addressed to the

Earl as well, and in the summer of 1594, he had not acted anywhere for at least two years. Even so, there can be no doubt that Shakespeare had a full share in his new company, for he was one of the three men to collect the court payment in early 1595.[10] For the other Sharers to be willing to include Shakespeare indicates that he was held in high regard as an actor and as a person by not just one or two, but by all the company. Thus, it seems clear that they regarded him as a man of considerable acting skill. While he was never a company leading man like Burbage—his age, more than anything else, would have made that difficult—he would turn out to be one of the company's most versatile and valuable performers, as we shall see in detail in the course of this work.

Shakespeare of course brought another skill, the ability to fashion plays for his company, and this too was important. If an acting company were to remain for long in London, it would need new plays on a regular basis. An acting company could tour for years with only two or three plays because they would never stay in one small town for more than two or three performances. London was large enough that any single play might draw audiences for six or more performances, but then something new would be needed. When the various early touring companies began to settle in London, they eventually required the services of the professional playwright. To modern readers, Marlowe is the giant of this early era, whose *Tamburlaine* in 1587 introduced Marlowe's mighty line of iambic pentameter, that became the voice of the age. Every play that followed from his quill was apparently a hit, and modern productions are still seen of *Doctor Faustus* and *Edward II*, while *The Jew of Malta* probably had a profound effect on Shakespeare's *Merchant of Venice*. But Marlowe was not alone; by 1587–88 when *Tamburlaine* was current, Greene, Kyd, and Shakespeare were all writing for the stage in London. Robert Greene, like Marlowe another MA from Cambridge, deserted his wife to live with the sister of the most famous thief in London and afterward identified himself as the first to make his living from the "penning of plays." There is no reason to doubt the claim, although he was also an energetic pamphleteer as well as a playwright. The earliest of his works to survive in print is thought to be *Alphonsus*, usually dated 1587, but the one most likely to still appear in modern textbooks is *Friar Bacon and Friar Bungay*, a wild mishmash that continued to be performed into the 1630s. Thomas Kyd's career was even more limited, although he probably wrote the two most popular works of the time. *The Spanish Tragedy*, probably 1589, was printed and reprinted at least eleven times before the Civil War and was performed by both of the great actors of the age, Edward Alleyn and Richard Burbage. The most prolific of these early playwrights, however, was a man who is rarely thought of as one of the first professionals, William Shakespeare. Nevertheless, the scholarly consensus today is that by the time Greene called him an upstart crow, Shakespeare had written *2 Henry VI*, *3 Henry VI*, *Richard III*, *Titus Andronicus*, *Comedy of Errors*, *Two Gentlemen of Verona*, and *1 Henry VI*, plus early versions of *Taming of the Shrew* and *King John*, with an early version of *Love's Labour's Lost* also a possibility. He is accepted by almost all as a major collaborator on *Edward III* and by a significant number as a collaborator on, and perhaps the sole author of, *Edmund Ironside*, which some think is even in Shakespeare's handwriting. He remains the only plausible candidate for *Arden of Faversham*, although the nature of the extant text makes it difficult to do modern textual analyses that might verify the assumption. With a minimum of eight works, possibly thirteen, not counting collaborations that may have disappeared, this would push the beginning of Shakespeare's theatrical career back to 1588, if not earlier. Most of these plays would eventually be revived by, and probably revised for, the Chamberlain's Men, so we need not devote time here to the arguments about the dating of Shakespeare's early plays.[11] The significant point is that Shakespeare was one of the founders of English playwriting; only the accident of the early deaths of the others from his generation has made him seem a writer from a later date. To a considerable extent, although laid on the foundation of Marlowe's iambic pentameter, the Elizabethan theater was fundamentally Shakespeare's own invention.

Greene's career was cut short by his sudden death, ostensibly of too much wine, in 1592. Marlowe was murdered in 1593 in what was long thought to have been a tavern brawl, but which more modern research suggests was an assassination connected with his other life as a spy.[12] Kyd was arrested for atheism in 1593, and the experience broke him; although he was later released, he quickly declined and died, so completely in disgrace that his parents refused to accept his estate. As a result, by 1594, Shakespeare was not only the most experienced professional playwright in the nation—he was all but the only professional playwright in the nation. (With Shakespeare tied to the Chamberlain's Men, the Admiral's men were forced to turn to the forty-year-old Antony Munday as their primary playwright, with help from Richard Wilson, who began by writing morality plays before 1580, and Henry Chettle, a pamphleteer who had not written for the stage before.) But Shakespeare could only do so much as a writer; three or four new plays a year would have been the maximum output anyone might expect. And no one could predict that his future plays would be popular. The company would obviously need many other writers if they were to be successful. Shakespeare the actor would be valuable every day. He was brought into the company as an actor; the playwriting was extra.

No London company could hope to be successful over the long term without men to play the crowds, so the new company eventually took on a set of Hired Men. Given the evidence of Shakespeare's plays, they must have hired a large number of them, although they may have waited until they had exhausted the audience for their smaller cast plays performed at Cross Keys before they started hiring. We cannot be sure of the exact number of Hired Men at any time; David Bradley has argued from detailed analyses of casting requirements that almost all Shakespeare's plays can be performed with a company of sixteen adults, which would indicate eight Hired Men.[13] The extant plot for *The Seven Deadly Sins* does seem to have eight (although the eighth, "Vincent," is a musician and might be a boy). My own practical stage experience suggests that they probably eventually had ten, at least from 1595 until Kemp's exit, which would give them a margin of safety when doubling roles and would also allow them to carefully distinguish the "funny-looking" Hired Men from the "serious" ones (see also Appendix A).

The comic Hired Men can be most clearly identified. In *Much Ado About*

Nothing, Verges is identified in both the quarto and Folio (F1997–2064) as Cowley. This would have been Richard Cowley, who would eventually graduate from Hired Man to Sharer in the company, listed on the company patent of 1603 and among the Principall Actors in the Folio. He was in the company that performed the *Seven Deadly Sins*, from the nature of his roles a Hired Man who also could act as a musician. He carried letters for Alleyn during the 1593 tour, and thus was known to many in the company but not a Sharer. The role of Verges is quite small, suggesting he was still a Hired Man as late as 1598, but it tells us Cowley was short and that he specialized in comic old men, although he was probably in his mid-twenties in 1594. In *A Midsummer Night's Dream*, we see Starveling, a very skinny man, Snout, a man with a funny nose, and Snug, a muscular man who plays the dim-witted characters so often associated with the very large. The company skinny man was John Sinklo, named in the quarto of *2 Henry IV* as the beadle insulted for his thinness (V,iv) and mentioned again in Marston's *The Malcontent* for a similar look. Such similar skinny characters as the tailor in *Taming of the Shrew* or the Apothecary in *Romeo and Juliet* indicate his presence over some years. A large man was also consistently used in very minor roles, such as Charles the Wrestler or Peter Bullcalf; slow wits almost always go with large bodies in comedy, so he also would have played roles like Snug and Dull. Two names, John Duke and Robert Pallant, seem possible. Both were in *The Seven Deadly Sins*. One of Duke's several small roles was Will Foole, indicating he did comic characters. Duke is listed by Jonson in *Every Man In His Humour*, and neither is mentioned in any other company until 1601, when both joined Kemp in a new company. Thus, one and probably both were in the Chamberlain's company in the years before 1600. Which was the big strong man is a toss up at this point; however, as we shall see, the only likely role for Duke in *Every Man in His Humour* will be for a tall, strong man, so he is the more likely choice as the strong man. In that case, the man with the funny nose may have been Pallant, or it may have been Cowley.

Other Hired Men names are more debatable. The Folio text of *3 Henry VI* indicates a Gabriel and a Humphry; the names may survive from the original Pembroke productions or indicate men in the Chamberlain's company when these were first revived. The only theatrical Gabriel in the historical record is Gabriel Spenser, who joined an acting company at the Rose in 1597 and was shortly afterward killed by Ben Jonson. The only Humphry is Humphry Jeffes, who also appeared in that 1597 Rose company along with his brother Anthony and who later made a modest name for himself among the Admiral's Men. There is a servant called Anthony in *Romeo and Juliet* who does not actually speak, so we cannot be certain an Anthony was in the company; nevertheless, if Humphry was a company Hired Man, Anthony probably was as well. As is seen later, there were some new hirings by the Chamberlain's Men during 1596–97, so it is plausible that Spenser and the Jeffes were Hired Men with Shakespeare's company and then left for greener pastures after a few years. There is a character in the Folio of *2 Henry VI* named John Holland, whose name also appeared as a Hired Man in the *Seven Deadly Sins* plot. This might mean he was also a Hired Man in the new Chamberlain's Men. One other possible name is

Robert Lee, who is listed on the plot for *Dead Man's Fortune* in 1590–92 with young Burbage. Nothing is heard of him again until he joins the Worcester company in 1603, much later than the original group that had included Kemp, Duke, and Pallant. He could have been anywhere in the intervening years, but the Chamberlain's company is at least a possibility. William Sly is often mentioned by modern scholars as a possible member of the original Chamberlain's Men, either as a Hired Man or even a Sharer. Although Sly would eventually join the company, Henslowe's mention of him on October 11, 1594, indicates that he was at the Rose with Alleyn at that time, and a later mention in 1598 of one of his costumes among the inventory of Admiral's Men assets further supports that assumption.[14] Thus, he could not have been a member of the original Chamberlain's Men in 1594.

As the least specialized reader knows, all the women's roles during this era were played by boys. Why the touring companies did not carry along their wives and daughters, as did the Continental commedia companies, is unknown. So far as we can tell from extant records, no women performed at any time during the sixteenth century. This was not a matter of legal restriction but of social custom. All men learned their trades not in schools but through apprenticeships. Actors had no formal guild with rules about apprenticeships, but taking an apprentice was the natural system of the country. Most of the theatrical boys, like most other apprentices, spent most of their apprenticeship as servants for their masters, but they also learned to act by acting, going on stage when needed. Usually the boys portrayed boys—pages, servants, and teenaged sons—but because they were smaller than the men and their voices had not yet broken, the boys also played the occasional role for a woman. By the 1590s, these female roles were beginning to expand, but so firmly established was the apprentice system that it seems never to have occurred to anyone to even consider training female performers. The boys were not members of the acting company as such. Each was apprenticed to a specific adult actor who in effect rented the boy's services to the company as needed.[15]

We can be relatively sure there were at least eight boys in the company, for there were eight adult full Sharers. Although most plays of the era use only three or four boys in clearly defined speaking roles at any one time, the company would have needed far more. Almost all Elizabethan plays have opportunities for pages, servants, and boys of various kinds without necessarily being identified as specific named roles. In general, Shakespeare habitually wrote for large groups of boys during all stages of his career. A play like *Hamlet*, with only three identified boy/women, is balanced by *Merry Wives of Windsor*, for example, with four women, two boys, and additional fairies, or *As You Like It*, with three women, young Jacque de Boys, the two singing boys, and the singers of the masque. *A Midsummer Night's Dream*, from 1595, demands at least nine boys: Flute, the four women, and four named fairies; if the Indian boy came on stage, the number was ten, not counting Puck, who was almost certainly played by an adult. *Richard III*, on stage in 1596–97, also requires at least eight: Anne, Margaret, Elizabeth, the Duchess of York, the two princes in the Tower, and Clarence's two children, plus at least one page who might be doubled. Nor was Shakespeare the only company playwright to make such demands; Dekker's *Satiro-*

mastix needs at least eight boys, and many of Beaumont and Fletcher's plays for the King's Men required as many, most as singers or dancers. Not all of these boys would necessarily be in every play, but they would be available. Their numbers might well be augmented by other boys apprenticed to the company's musicians.

It is important that we remember that boys means precisely that—boys. Perhaps because their roles are usually women, and in Shakespeare's work at least are often quite demanding, it has become almost automatic to think of them as having been played by particularly beautiful and/or effeminate young men, an assumption encouraged by the recent spate of productions casting drag artists or young men well into their twenties or even thirties. Nothing could be further from the record, where in every instance they are referred to as boys. In addition, we should remember that for various reasons, puberty strikes boys much earlier in our own day than it did in Shakespeare's time. The voice break and the change in musculature that we associate with the mid-teens occurred in general much later, meaning that most Elizabethan boys looked and sounded much younger than would boys of similar age today. The equivalent modern image is not the drag artiste but the English choirboy.

We cannot be absolutely certain of the specific ages of the boys, because there was no official guild for actors and even in the more formal guilds, rules were often bent. Elizabethan law set a minimum length of apprenticeship at seven years, and many guilds required ten. Most Elizabethan apprenticeships began around age ten, and the all-boy company that opened at the Blackfriars in 1600 recruited or kidnapped members as young as age 10, although some were as old as thirteen, and some apprentices in the more formalized guilds have been found as old as fourteen at the beginning of their bonds.[16] The adult acting companies probably used the same general parameters, for very practical reasons: It would take a few years to train a boy to speak properly, loudly, and expressively, while a boy whose voice had broken could no longer convincingly play non-comic women. Thus, it would be pointless to start a boy much later than thirteen, for he would become properly trained only around fifteen, when his master might begin to worry that puberty might strike at any moment and make him unfit to play women. Likewise, a boy under ten, due to his physical and mental limitations, would not make a plausible servant, much less a useful stage actor. Actors often make up their own rules, so this can only be a general guide; still, it seems most probable that the apprentices in the acting companies began between age ten and twelve and continued in apprentice roles until somewhere between seventeen and twenty, and in women's roles in particular until no more than about seventeen. Interestingly enough, this is precisely the pattern for the only boy whose career we can trace through cast lists that define actual roles, although his career lies outside our period. Robert Gough, whom we meet as an apprentice in the Chamberlain's Men, eventually had a son Alexander, born in 1614. Robert died early in 1625, but Alexander was apprenticed to someone in the King's Men. Alexander then appears in the company cast lists playing women from 1626 through 1632 (i.e., from the age of twelve to late seventeen or early eighteen). The earliest citations are for small roles, only 37 lines in *The Roman Actor* of 1626, expanding to the largest female role, some 357 lines, in *The Wild Goose Chase* of

1631–32. Afterward, his name disappears from the record.[17] Similarly, Ezekiel Fenn was born in 1620 and acted women's roles for Queen Henrietta's company, reaching the large roles of Sophonisba in *Hannibal and Scipio* and Winifred in a revival of Fletcher's *Wild-Goose Chase* during 1635, when he was fifteen. A poem celebrating his first adult role was published in 1639, which at the very least means he had moved to adult roles of some note before his nineteenth birthday. The poem was probably written before 1639, indicating Fenn quit playing women or boys well before age nineteen, and this may have been as early as age seventeen, when he was one of the company leaders called before the Privy Council on May 12, 1637. We also know of some exceptions—in 1626, William Trigg was apprenticed to Heminges for twelve years[18]—but for the most part, we should expect to trace the career of individual boys playing women for only five or six years, if that long, and can assume that we are seeing them from the age of twelve or thirteen through sixteen or seventeen. Illness, an apprentice's rebelliousness, and of course a general lack of talent all might make any individual boy's stage career even more brief.

Because of the unpredictable nature of puberty, it is logical to assume that many of the Sharers actually had two boys. A master would want to always have a stage-ready apprentice. As we have discussed, once a boy reached the age of seventeen or so, his performing life in women's roles was nearing its end, no matter how much time he might have left on his bond; meanwhile, it would take a year or two to prepare a younger boy to replace him. Thus, a wise master would look for a new boy about the time his older boy turned sixteen. At the Rose, Henslowe once noted payment to "Thomas Downton's bigger boy,"[19] and we can assume that several of the masters in any company would have a bigger and a smaller boy at any given time. If puberty was delayed for the old boy, the master might have two boys available on stage in relatively significant roles at the same time; if the older boy matured normally, then there was a new boy ready to replace him as soon as his voice broke. On the other hand, if a boy took sick, grew unruly, or displayed no talent, the master might find himself without a boy for several years until a replacement could be found and trained.

It is not clear what happened to the boys if the masters retired or themselves died. When Augustine Phillips died in 1605, he left a bequest to the boy James Sands to be paid only when the boy had finished his bonds. Because Phillips was dying, Sands must have been expected to finish his term with someone else, suggesting that another master in the acting company had taken the boy on. It is also possible that the various masters may have done some trading of boys. As is seen here, the various boys associated with Burbage had a remarkably sustained level of talent. A large part of Burbage's fame rests on roles interacting with complex women as varied as Juliet, Beatrice, Desdemona, and Lady Macbeth, who must have been played by several different boys. Burbage would have to have been a most remarkable talent spotter to so consistently identify such potential in boys of ten with no stage experience; thus, it is at least possible that he traded boys on occasion. As is seen later, in the first Jacobean decade, it often seems as if Burbage has all the boys, for we see a large number of new plays in which the women play scenes only with Burbage or with other women. Because that era will also be a period of high turnover among the adult Sharers, it is possible that Burbage simply began to accumulate the apprentices of members who retired or died. But that lies far in the future; in 1594, Burbage was only one among equals in his company, and all of the Sharers seem to have had at least one apprentice.

Where the boys came from is an intriguing question. The repertory actor's most valuable skill is literacy, for lines can only be memorized from written rolls if the actor can read. But parents who had gone to the trouble of schooling their boys would be unlikely to apprentice them to a career so disreputable as the stage. Two of the apprentices discussed later, Nick Tooley and Christopher Beeston, both performed under aliases, which suggests boys who have run away from home, and it is likely that others in the company did the same. In later years, many of the apprentices would be sons of actors, and Ben Jonson in a masque of 1616 has a costume woman brag about her boy who is sought by Burbage and Heminges. Richard Burbage, himself the son of an actor, probably began acting as an apprentice after his father James had retired from the stage. The shortage of names both of boys and of actors in earlier companies makes it difficult to identify such theatrical roots, but it seems more than likely that most of the boys had parents who either had acted or who worked around the theater in other capacities.

Thus, when the Chamberlain's Men began to perform in the summer of 1594, it consisted of eight Sharers: Bryan, Burbage, Heminges, Kemp, Phillips, Pope, Condell, and Shakespeare; and at least eight boys. At some time during the next year, they added some eight to ten Hired Men, including Cowley, Sinklo, Pallant, and Duke, and perhaps including Spenser, both Jeffes, Holland, and Lee.

If we are to begin to understand how Shakespeare fit into this company and how he shaped his plays for them, we must do more than simply name the actors. We must, of course, cast them. No surviving cast lists for this company identify both players and roles until long after Shakespeare's retirement, so this must to some extent be a matter of conjecture. But such conjecture need not be groundless. We have already identified the single most important points of repertory casting: the number of Sharers and their ages. Fortunately, the new Chamberlain's company made no known changes in the company of Sharers until about 1598, so we can begin with a fixed group over several years of work. Even more fortunately, we know what work they did during those years. In 1598, Francis Meres published *Palladis Tamia: Wit's Treasury*, which included his thoughts on contemporary English literature. Shakespeare was compared to Ovid for his poems, both published and unpublished, and to both Plautus and Seneca for his plays: *Gentlemen of Verona, Errors, Loue Labors Lost, Loue Labours Wonne, Midsummers Night Dreame, Merchant of Venice, Richard the 2, Richard the 3, Henry the 4, King John, Titus Andronicus,* and *Romeo and Iuliet.*[20] Although this is not a complete list of Shakespeare's theatrical works written before 1598, it does reveal that these twelve were current and recognized as Shakespeare's work. Hence, we must assume that they were known because Shakespeare's acting company had performed them in the period immediately before Meres wrote, between 1594 and early 1598. *Titus Andronicus* was published before the Chamberlain's Men were organized; although the company later performed it, the available text was intended for another company. Similarly, *Richard III, Comedy of Errors*, and *Two Gentlemen of Verona* are all generally thought to have been written for earlier companies, with printed texts that may or may not reflect modifications made for the Chamberlain's Men. With those exceptions, the remaining plays on Meres's list are generally accepted as either works written specifically for this company or, if initially composed earlier, works that were modified in such a way as to make the current text fit the Chamberlain's Men. (More detailed discussion of these issues follows as each individual play is discussed.)

It is critical to remember that casting for the Elizabethan actors was a different process from casting for modern productions. In contemporary plays, we start with a script and then look for the best available people to portray the characters. If it is a new script, it may be further modified during rehearsals to fit the actors cast, but the basic impulse is to fit actors to the script. For the Elizabethans, the acting company existed before the script. All productions started with the actors who then looked for a script they could perform. When old plays were revived—and many old plays were revived—they were often rewritten, at considerable expense, to fit the needs of the current company, even if the company already owned the old play. All new plays were commissioned, but more specifically, they were commissioned by the actors of a specific company for the actors of that specific company to perform. Thus, the basic impulse in Shakespeare's time was to fit the script to the actors. No playwright was paid until the actors themselves had approved the work.[21] And the actors were not going to approve payment for any work unless it had suitable roles for all the actors involved in the decision-making process.

What constituted a suitable role might vary from player to player and play to play, but certain fundamental factors would always be involved. First and foremost, we must assume that the Sharers did in fact perform in every play. There is considerable argument about this, but common sense dictates that none of the various Sharers would want to pay the others for not working. Nor would any of the actors volunteer to take days off; actors want to act and perhaps even more importantly want to be seen, and it would be absurd to think they might approve any new script unless they themselves had a role that matched their own opinion of themselves.

Second, but equally important, the Sharers would always play the largest roles. What constitutes a large role is of course open to debate, but as is seen in detail throughout the following pages, it is remarkable how obvious this distinction is in these plays, as in most plays performed later by the company as well. There are occasional complications caused by the fact that clown roles are much smaller in the more serious plays, but for the most part there can be no doubt (see also Appendix A). Some of the large roles are much larger than others, but it is almost always clear which roles belong to the Sharers and which to the Hired Men. As a general rule, the non-clown Sharer roles:

1. play a significant role in the plot,

2. appear in several different scenes, and

3. total about 4% or more of the overall line total.

For some of these plays on Meres' list we find that a significant character in several scenes may have a line count that drops into the 2%–3% range (e.g., Tybalt), but in most cases that character has a significant skill and makes a great impact, and often is in a position to double other significant roles to bring up the actor's total line count. Hired Men roles, by contrast, appear in only one scene (the rude mechanicals of *A Midsummer Night's Dream* are almost the only exception). They almost never reach 1% of the lines, although individual Hired Men of course may have played several of these small roles in the course of a single play. Given these very basic assumptions and the information we already have about the company members, an experienced stage director can easily determine the probable original cast for all of the plays listed by Meres.

As the principal comedian, Kemp would have played the largest clown roles, whatever their nature. There is a great deal of variety from Bottom to Launcelot Gobbo to Peter (assigned to him in the quarto of *Romeo and Juliet*), but theatrically these distinctions do not matter to an audience—the clown is the clown is the clown. That these roles are so varied testifies to Kemp's remarkable range. In general, the clown would have played any significant common men in the more serious plays as well, whether comic or serious, because the clown by his very nature and obvious identifiability would not be able to play nobles.

For the non-clown actors, however, the most critical casting factor is age. The Elizabethan theater had no makeup as we understand the term—they could of course black up with burnt cork, but greasepaint and latex were unknown. Modern commentators have usually assumed that wigs and false beards were available, but this does not seem to be supported by the evidence. Modern wigs made in the manner of late sixteenth-century wigs—by hand, with each hair individually threaded into a hand-woven mesh—cost $3,000 or more. For the Elizabethans the cost would have been equivalent in the terms of the Elizabethan economy, placing wigs among the most expensive and valuable assets of the company. Yet, Henslowe's detailed inventory of the Admiral's Men's assets in 1598 lists no wigs, even for the boys to wear while playing women. Neither does the actor Edward Alleyn's personal inventory made at about the same time.[22] We know from Bottom's comments in *A Midsummer Night's Dream* that false beards were available (I,ii,83–89), but we also know that they were shoddy, unrealistic, and considered by both the professionals and the audience to be old-fashioned and laughable. Even if we assume that wigs and beards were available, the smooth-faced young man might put on a false beard or wig to play older, but the bearded veteran could not do the same to look younger. The Elizabethan audience was very close, in bright daylight, and would know the difference immediately. Hats, of course, were commonly worn and might disguise the hair somewhat, but the extant drawings of *Titus Andronicus* in performance (see page 36) and of a performance at the Swan (see page 75) indicate that many of the actors performed without hats. And we need to remember that to the Elizabethans, age distinctions would have been much more obvious and pronounced than in our own time; the normal life span was much more compressed than in our own day, so that a man was old in his late forties, and middle age started for some in their late thirties. Naturally, there was some flexibility; no one checked IDs, so when we say an actor played his age, we mean that he played the age he looked. Shakespeare at thirty but with a sharply receding hairline might have started playing middle-aged roles well before he reached true middle age; similarly, fat men almost always played older than their true age. Stage age is also a relative factor—an actor of thirty could play twenty if the other actors around him all looked older, but he could not play twenty if the other actors on stage were all genuinely twenty. But day in and day out, the most mature men in the company would play the most mature characters. Thus, Bryan and Pope would have played the non-clown fathers, Burbage and Condell the young men often their sons. Because we know that Pope ran to fat and was perceived as more comical, he must have played the fathers of more genial appearance, like Baptista. In turn, that would mean that Bryan played the more stern or martial men of middle age, like Henry IV or Titus Andronicus.

Because Burbage soon became the major star of the Elizabethan stage, we must assume his talent was visible from the beginning. Although he may not have always played the largest role in the play, he would have played the largest role in his age group. Thus, we can securely assume he played Romeo, Bassanio, and Prince Hal. Condell, then, as the second non-comic young man, would have played the second young men. Modern casting traditions, in which all actors in major professional productions are always too old by a decade or more, have sometimes obscured the nature of this second young man, but it certainly includes Tybalt, the Dauphin in *King John*, and Richmond. Curiously, these three young men were unusually adept with a sword, although only one actually won his fight with Burbage. This adept swordsman, who nevertheless usually loses to the leading character, continues long after 1598, most vividly in Laertes. In the practical world of the stage, this means he was the company's best swordsman, for it takes great skill to be killed safely or (perhaps even more important) not to defeat the hero accidentally, a factor even more important in Shakespeare's day when the actors used real swords. Thus, we can be certain that Condell was this swordsman and pencil him in for later roles such as Laertes and Cassio that come after 1598. As it happens, in *The Seven Deadly Sins*, the actor named Harry fought on stage as Ferrex, and in fact lost his duel, so it appears Condell had begun to play this type of role well before he joined the Chamberlain's Men. We can also assume from these roles that he played young hotheads, even when there were no swords involved.

That leaves the three men in the middle, Heminges, Phillips, and Shakespeare himself. In these known 1594–98 plays, there is one consistent character type who is neither father nor son, nor is he a common-man clown. This is a man we might call the Motor Mouth or the Smart Aleck. He talks and talks and talks, sometimes with fancy like Mercutio, sometimes with poetry like Richard II, sometimes purely to hear himself talk, like Gratiano or Don Armado. Most curiously, he is often physically graceful and reasonably good with a sword. This is a most unusual combination—between Shakespeare's plays and *Cyrano de Bergerac* there are very few theatrical wits who are also good swordsmen. All the serious Sharers could at least hold a sword convincingly, for almost all appear in a battle scene at some point, but this man does more than simply keep from embarrassing himself. So rare is such a combination of skills that we must assume that all these roles were played by the same man. Shakespeare of course could be witty—after all, he wrote the roles—but there seems little room in his background for swordplay lessons. Heminges was probably a leading man when younger, so he may have been adept in both areas. However, I tend to lean toward Phillips, for four reasons. He was a man of some wit, the author of at least one published jig, and apparently an outstanding dancer, indicating somewhat greater than average athleticism. He was also something of a musician, as shown by the large number of musical instruments bequeathed in his will; ultimately, two of these Motor Mouths will sing—Jaques and Toby Belch. Third, in *The Seven Deadly Sins*, Phillips played the colorful and eccentric Sardanapalus; we do not have a script, but the fact that he played at least one scene "in a dress" would suggest that the play emphasized his more effeminate side, which usually indicates both a physical and a verbal grace and dexterity. Finally, the verbal pyrotechnics disappear rather suddenly in 1604, with Lucio possibly the last example, although he has no swordplay or musicality. Phillips retired sometime in 1604, while Heminges and Shakespeare continued. Thus, Phillips seems the most likely great talker. The roles played by Heminges and Shakespeare will take much longer to sort out and even then will be the most conjectural of our assignments.

I think it is also possible to cast the boys. As a general rule, we can assume that each boy played most of his scenes with his master. We know very little more about Elizabethan rehearsal practices than is told to us by Peter Quince; the little we do know suggests that most rehearsal was handled by actors running over their scenes together by themselves. It would have been awkward and inconvenient for an adult to find time to work alone with the apprentice of another master and would to a considerable degree defeat the purpose of the apprentice system if he were to do so. An apprentice was supposed to learn about acting from his master, and thus his master must have taught him his roles and performed in most of his scenes. This is most obvious in short roles, which often involve a single scene. Even in longer roles, if we see a long duet set piece, such as Richard's wooing of the Lady Anne, or Romeo and Juliet's balcony scene or sonnet scene, we can be certain this is a master and his apprentice working together, even if the boy has significant scenes with other adults. When playing women at least, their own age was irrelevant; as all the boys were the wrong age for the women they portrayed, there is no reason why older boys should have played older women. However, age was important in relation to the size of roles. Naturally, as a boy grew more experienced, he might play significant scenes without his master, and we can also assume that a boy would rate longer roles as he grew more experienced. However, there would have been no requirement to give the boys longer roles as they aged; a boy of twelve would be unlikely to play roles with three hundred lines, but a boy of sixteen might play roles of three hundred lines in one play and thirty in the next, depending entirely on the role played by his master and the dramatic requirements of the material. It is tempting to assign character types to the boys, but the urge should be resisted, just as it should be for the adult Sharers. Because the roles were written specifically for each boy at the time of original production, we must assume that, once the master was cast, then the woman required in any of his scenes would be designed by the playwright to fit the skill level and personality of the particular boy concerned. Naturally, Shakespeare (or any other writer) would not write characters he did not believe the available boy could play, but the repertory system demanded that the boys, like their masters, be able to play a number of different character types. We have some, although not all, of the names of the company's original boys. However, as the specific role assignments for each of these boys primarily will depend on the assignments of their masters, we will wait until we know more about the workings of the company before assigning specific names to each boy's role.

Beyond the comedic Hired Men whom we have identified, it is neither possible nor necessary to assign most Hired Man roles. Outside of the comic stooges, they were by definition nonentities (see Appendix A). As history develops, we will be able to trace some careers and identify some specific roles, but in the overwhelming number of cases, it does not matter who played which messenger. Sharers and boys are critical, because Shakespeare and all the other writers for the company wrote with each of them specifically in mind. We have at this point determined enough about the individuals to begin a more detailed chronological survey of the performing life of this company.

Chapter 2

From Cross Keys to The Theatre, 1594-97

The Chamberlain's Men first appear in the record in the summer of 1594. During June, they played jointly with Alleyn's new Admiral's Men at Newington Butts, an inn about one mile south of the Thames, operated in some way by Henslowe.[1] In his notes Henslowe does not distinguish between the two companies, but they apparently alternated days, for three of the plays recorded by Henslowe were performed at the Rose within the next eight days, whereas three others eventually surfaced in Shakespeare's company.

No further notice of the Chamberlain's company has been found until October, when their new patron intervened on their behalf. On October 8, 1594, Lord Hunsdon formally requested permission from the Lord Mayor for "my nowe companie of Players" to begin performing at an inn called the Cross Keys in Gracious Street.[2] The letter implies that they had been previously performing in the London area, but Henslowe's detailed and apparently complete records show no further performances at Newington Butts. Most likely, the company toured the small towns around London, using the time to learn to work together and to build a basic repertory of plays.

Although the arrival of Shakespeare's company in London is very firmly documented, it begins with a mystery. Cross Keys was an inn converted for actors in the traditional touring manner. Why didn't the company perform in one of the existing theater buildings? The Admiral's Men went to the Rose, but why then didn't the Chamberlain's Men go to The Theatre, particularly since it was operated by the father of the company's new leading young man Richard Burbage? Why instead go to a smaller, less practical inn within the potentially repressive jurisdiction of the Lord Mayor? The only plausible explanation is that some other company was in The Theatre. If it had been empty in October, surely James Burbage would have leased it to a company that included his son. Similarly, we must assume no other company would have been given the premises before October if James had known his own son's acting company might be needing it within a few months' time. Thus, Richard Burbage must have been a very late addition to the Chamberlain's Men, joining after the elder Burbage had already committed The Theatre to another company, possibly even later than the June performances at Newington Butts. (Who that other company might have been is unknown, although the Sussex company that had been at the Rose in January is most likely.)

Hunsdon's letter said his company would play at Cross Keys "this winter time," and there is no reason not to believe it. If there were another company at The Theatre, they would hope to play there until Lent at least. Thus, Shakespeare's company entered London rather like a modern fringe company, performing in a small, converted space rather than one of the regular theaters.

But unlike most modern fringe companies, they were an immediate success. They survived long enough to be called to court at Christmas, where they presented two plays for Elizabeth. They also were hired for the Twelfth Night celebration in January 1595, at the Inns of Court, where they presented *The Comedy of Errors*. This is such an obvious choice for such an audience that some have thought the play was written specifically for this occasion, but practical issues make this most unlikely. Elizabeth paid her performers a standard fee of ten German marks, which translated into a bit more than 6½ pounds, usually accompanied by a tip.[3] It is unlikely any other private performances would have been paid more. Because new plays cost a company six to eight pounds, the actors would have lost money on a unique private performance. *The Comedy of Errors* appeared at the Inns of Court because it was suitable material drawn from the company's existing repertory.

As such, it tells us a great deal about the company's first London season. It is short, Shakespeare's briefest work by some three hundred lines, requires little or no special staging facilities beyond two doors, and has a very small cast. It is, in fact, ideal touring material, precisely the kind of production we would expect to find from a company with its feet firmly planted in the inn yard or the dining hall. The other plays of that fall must have had similar characteristics, whether comic or serious. This points directly to *Two Gentlemen of Verona*, which many scholars date as new in this year, although others think it is an older play with some significant revisions made at this time, and still others argue it all dates much earlier.[4] It would be asking a great deal of Shakespeare to learn a full company repertory as an actor, participate in all the many Sharer crises associated with a new company, and still write a new play within a single month; logically, then, *Two Gentlemen*, like *The Comedy of Errors*, was probably a revival of a play written much earlier.

One of the fundamental assumptions of this work is that Heminges and Condell were able to verify the plays included in the Folio as Shakespeare's work because they had in fact worked on the plays with Shakespeare. Thus, inclusion in the Folio is accepted as demonstration that this acting company actually performed the play at some time when Heminges, Condell, and Shakespeare were all active. As with any other point in Shakespearean studies, there are serious, reputable scholars who disagree with that assumption in relation to some specific plays, and we discuss some of those reservations as the plays appear. Specific textual issues, particularly in the earliest plays probably first written for some other company, are questions for another work. However, the attempt by Heminges and Condell to print the plays "as [Shakespeare] conceived them" and "according to their first originall"[5] meant that they wished wherever possible to restore the earliest version available to them, which in turn would have been the version first provided to this company. In some cases, this may have been an earlier version with little or no modification, such as *Titus Andronicus*; in others, it may have been a revision made by Shakespeare on an earlier play that may or may not have been by him originally (see discussion on *Taming of the Shrew*). In the very late plays, as is seen here, they may even reflect revisions made by others. But whatever the nature of the text printed, it is assumed in this work to be the earliest available to Heminges and Condell after the summer of 1594, and to reflect to the best of their memory their understanding of Shakespeare's intentions for performers and performance at the time. Thus, the inclusion of *Two Gentlemen of Verona* in the Folio indicates the play was performed at some point by this company, whenever it may have been first composed, while its mention by Meres indicates the performance came before 1598. Both these points and its small cast size and simplicity of staging point to this first season, with or without some modifications that have not survived.

We can be sure that Kemp played Dromio of Syracuse and Launce, simply because he was the chief clown. Who played his twin is not so obvious. Most likely it is Pope, who was Kemp's age or older and large in size. We can also be sure that Burbage did not play either of the Antipholi, because the one from Syracuse is described as thirty-three years old (V,i,400) and Burbage was not yet even twenty-five. The company members of the appropriate age were Heminges, Phillips, and Shakespeare. Because Shakespeare was the least experienced of the trio, the twins were surely Heminges and Phillips. Bryan, then, as the eldest remaining Sharer, played Egeon. Shakespeare and the young Burbage and Condell played the smaller roles of various townspeople.

In *Two Gentlemen of Verona*, Heminges and Phillips would have repeated their pairing as near twins, playing Proteus and Valentine. Bryan would have played the more authoritative of the two fathers, the Duke of Milan, with Pope as the more conventional father Antonio, doubling the Host in Milan. Speed is clearly and often identified as a boy (III,i,257) and a "sweet youth" (II,v,2), which may mean he was taken by the still young-looking Cowley but more probably indicates he was in fact played by a boy; as all his scenes are in comedy routines with Launce, then he must have been Kempe's apprentice. Burbage was probably the brave and noble Eglamour who must fight several outlaws at once, with Condell using his sword skills as the chief outlaw to lose to Burbage, as he would continue to do for the rest of his performing career. Burbage probably doubled the servant Panthino, who disappears early, to provide the stage time suitable to his share. Shakespeare would then have been the ridiculous suitor Thurio, with his receding hairline and any remnants of his Warwickshire accent underlining his comic unsuitability for Sylvia.

In these two early productions, we can see a company still feeling its way. Both *Comedy of Errors* and *Two Gentlemen of Verona* are short, with 20% to 30% fewer lines than Shakespeare's later romantic comedies like *Merchant of Venice, Much Ado About Nothing,* or *Twelfth Night.* Both are extremely simple to stage, suitable for inn yard or dining hall, making no unusual demands for upper levels, extra entrances, trap doors, or unusual props and costumes. In both, the characters are long-established theatrical stereotypes with little of the complexity or subtlety we have come to associate with Shakespeare. Both place most of the burden of dramatic success squarely on the shoulders of the clown, who was in this case Will Kemp, the most famous clown in the nation, with most of the additional weight carried by a pair of physically similar romantic leading men. The roles for the new Sharers like Shakespeare and Burbage are still comparatively small and undemanding. Nor are there any significant demands for Hired Men, only the Outlaws in *Two Gentlemen* and the Gaolers in *Comedy of Errors.* This would seem to indicate that the company began in October 1594 with only two to four Hired Men, gradually adding new ones only as their position became more secure. Many of these characteristics, of course, may be the result of the plays' composition well before 1594. However, we must assume that the versions printed in the Folio reflect the plays that were familiar to Heminges and Condell as Shakespeare's work, and thus the extant text probably represents with reasonable accuracy the play as performed that first year.

The small Burbage assignments at this time may seem startling to some readers, but we must constantly remind ourselves that Burbage in the autumn of 1594 was not yet the greatest star of the era. When the company began, he was merely a talented young actor with not very much experience. The only documentary evidence of his previous career indicates he was still playing bit parts in 1590–92, as we have previously discussed. We can assume he was in the company at The Theatre in 1590–91, but that company was headed by Edward Alleyn, which would have meant Burbage played only supporting roles at best. In the summer of 1591, Alleyn and a number of the other actors left The Theatre after an argument about James Burbage's honesty, so we can be sure that Richard did not take Alleyn's side and follow him and the group called Strange's Men to the Rose. He may have performed with Pembroke's Men, a group about which little definite has been established, but the published plays associated with them offer few major vehicles for an actor of Richard's youth. And of course, during 1593 and early 1594, he did not act at all. That he obtained a share in the new Chamberlain's Men indicates that the other men saw some serious potential (although the fact that his father owned the finest London theater building, which Richard stood to inherit, may have affected their decision as well). The *Seven Deadly Sins* plot does indicate that by early 1592 he was at least occasionally playing major roles, but even so, in October 1594, he was still one of the youngest and least experienced men in the company. One of the major themes of our history will be the way in which Richard Burbage emerges from the group and engages Shakespeare's attention, but that will be a gradual process occurring over many years. In 1594, Burbage, like Shakespeare and the company as a whole, still had a long way to go.

Other plays in that first season can be identified with some certainty, but their texts have all disappeared. One was probably the play about *Hester and Ahasuerus* that had been presented at Newington Butts.[6] A German play called *Hester and Haman* is thought to have been adapted from an English touring play related to this, but it is so much changed by its German adaptor that no firm conclusions can be drawn.[7]

They may also have performed a version of *Hamlet*. This, too, had played at Newington and did not follow Alleyn to the Rose, but it was clearly not Shakespeare's version. Greene mentioned it as early as 1589, far too early to have been written by Shakespeare in its present form. No copy of this *Ur-Hamlet*, as it is usually called, now exists, but most scholars assume it was by Kyd. Shakespeare's company was still playing it in late 1595 or early 1596, when Thomas Lodge wrote about the "ghost which cried so miserably at The Theatre, like an oyster-wife, *Hamlet, revenge.*"[8] Thus, they may not have revived it until some months after this first winter. Because we know nothing more specific about this play than that there was a Hamlet, a ghost, and a Claudius figure on whom the ghost sought revenge, we can know little about the company's production. However, we can be sure that Burbage did not play Hamlet at this time; had he done so, there would have been little or no reason for Shakespeare to write his own new version later.

A version of *Taming of the Shrew* also was performed at Newington Butts, but both the quarto published in 1594 and the Folio version require much larger companies than the Chamberlain's Men appear to have been in the winter of 1594–95. Petruchio seems very much the kind of character Alleyn might turn to when he essayed comedy, and, if the most current datings of the Folio text are accurate, the play may well have been written originally for Alleyn in 1589–91.[9] But there are no hints of further performances of such a play at the Rose in succeeding years. Possibly the Newington Butts production was yet a third version that has completely disappeared. As is seen here, the peculiarly large cast of principals, the lack of allusions in other sources, and the disjointed nature of the Folio text itself all combine to make *Taming of the Shrew* one of the most difficult of all Shakespeare's works to place in this company's repertoire.

Another work sometimes suggested for this first season is a play about the early years of the reign of Richard II, usually referred to as *Woodstock*. The work exists only in manuscript (Egerton MS 1994) and has never been precisely dated. Chambers identified it as *1 Richard the Second* and thought it must have been performed by the Chamberlain's Men. If so, staging requirements that demand only a minimal within and no above would make it plausible for the Chamberlain's Men during the Cross Keys season. Despite the title given, Chambers made no suggestion that Shakespeare actually wrote it, although no other viable candidate has surfaced. Everitt has suggested that it is actually by the young Shakespeare, but the argument is predicated on strong stylistic similarities to other early plays such as *Edmund Ironside* that have not themselves been generally accepted as Shakespeare's work. If true, however, Shakespeare's authorship would all but certainly indicate the Chamberlain's Men did not perform it, for then Heminges and Condell would have included it in the

Folio. In *Woodstock*, Green is killed while he is very much alive in *Richard II*, which as Peter Ure concludes, in numerous other points "contradicts and overlaps [*Woodstock*] in a way no sequel would."[10] The significant disagreements between Shakespeare's version and the anonymous one only make sense if we assume Shakespeare was writing an independent play on the same topic rather than consciously preparing a sequel.

This does not preclude a Chamberlain's performance of *Woodstock*, particularly in the earliest days of the company. However, there seem to be too many (or too few) Sharer roles, with twelve characters appearing throughout the entire play, but only five of them exceeding one hundred lines; the sixth largest role, the governor LaPoole, has almost one hundred lines but appears in only one scene that makes it impossible for him to double any of the other principals. The largest roles are assignable to the known Chamberlain's Men, assuming that Burbage would have played the young Richard, aged twenty at the play's beginning; Bryan then would have been the obvious Woodstock, at some 600 lines the largest role by far, Pope the most probable fat, corrupt judge Tresillian, and Kemp the servant Nimble. But the other roles are much more difficult to assign given the known ages of the remaining Sharers. The enormous number of Hired Men playing commoners—nine in addition to the company Clown in a single scene (III, i)—plus Bagot and Scroop and the Osric-like Courtier who all appear in scenes that make their doubling of these commoners implausible if not impossible, all indicate a far larger company than in the Cross Keys season (or any later season of the company, even at its most prosperous). Thus, it seems most likely that, whatever Shakespeare's participation in *Woodstock* may have been, it came well before 1594, and that when the Chamberlain's Men took up the topic of Richard II in the next year or so, Shakespeare wrote them a completely new play.

The anonymous *Locrine* may also be tentatively tied to this season on grounds of its publication as "Newly set foorth, overseen and corrected, By W. S." in 1595. As the play was registered June 20, 1594, just after the Chamberlain's Men left Newington Butts, the work itself predated the formation of the Chamberlain's Men. Its printer and a number of close associations with *Selimus* strongly suggest the work belonged to the Queen's Men, who sold off a number of their plays during the plague of 1593–94, if not even earlier. However, the curious title page of the quarto suggests something more than the simple printing of an old play. A corrected quarto would seem to indicate the existence of an earlier printing that required correction. Curiously, the final speech of the narrator was clearly written in 1595, for it refers to Elizabeth's 38th regnal year (V,v,203), and other scenes, particularly for the clown, seem to postdate the play's registration in 1594.[11] The delay of a year or more between *Locrine*'s registration and printing, although not unique, does allow time for such an early printing in June or July 1594, with corrections in a second printing newly set forth a year later. Thus, the play was probably performed shortly after its initial printing, which performance in turn stimulated sales of the printing, and then led to a second printing amended to include material from the recent performance.

Such a performance only can have been by the Chamberlain's Men or the unidentified company we have assumed were in The Theatre, for there is no mention of the play in Henslowe's journals. The extant text is at least performable by the Chamberlain's Men at this time. The dumb shows are rather spectacular in costume, including a lion, a bear, a crocodile, and a snake, and numerous characters from classical mythology, but require a very small number of performers, and the company of course need not have performed the dumb shows in a revival. A trap door is essential because two different characters throw themselves into a river, but otherwise, there is no use of either a within or an above, which means that the play could have been easily presented on an inn yard stage. The casting, however, is not as obvious as for the other plays we have identified this season. The three fathers constitute the major problem, for we know the company had only two. However, if the balding Shakespeare played the invader Humber, who is generally portrayed as younger than the other fathers and whose son is both very young and a small role, then the remaining Sharer assignments are more than merely plausible (see Chart B). This casting is particularly tempting, because the scenes thought to have been added in 1594–95 involve Humber, the clown Strumbo, or both, and thus W. S., who played in those scenes, would have been the logical person to provide them to the printer in 1595, whether he wrote them or not. However, on the basis of current evidence, we can be no more than tentative in assigning such a production to the company at this time.

The Chamberlain's Men obviously made an enormous impact in its first months in London, for they were brought to court twice after only a few months. However, we must not make too much of this. Hunsdon was, after all, Lord Chamberlain and as such might be expected to favor his own company whenever possible.

In the first few months of the company's career, Shakespeare's writing would have been confined to relatively simple revisions, for he was busy learning his own acting roles. All of the plays we have identified in this first season are old plays that may have been selected in part because many of the company members had performed in them at an earlier time and already knew their roles. Shakespeare, as a man who was probably not a full Sharer in any company before 1592, and then took two years off, would have had to learn almost all his own roles from scratch. He may have made numerous revisions to plays by other writers as well, all of which have disappeared. But writing new plays would have required more time than he had available before Christmas, 1594. In their effort to establish the precise date for Shakespeare's plays, almost all scholars have focused on the date of composition rather than the date of production, and as a result have implied a speed and proficiency that verges on the supernatural. Shakespeare was noted in his time as a fast and fluent writer who rarely blotted a line, but even the most fluent writing takes time at a table. Before October 1594, Shakespeare was acting with the company on the road, and no one writes anything while being jounced around in an oxcart on rutted dirt roads. When the cart stopped, the company would have been involved in the complex business of setting up the stage and rousing an audience, so no new writing was likely until the company settled down in London in October. As an active performer, Shakespeare could only have written very early in the morning or late at night, when he would not have been needed at the theater for other duties. Even the physical act of writing itself was slow, for quills had to be dipped, cut, and trimmed constantly. Once the script was finished, the company had to consider it, ask for revisions, and approve the final draft. Then a fair copy had to be made to send to the censor, who sometimes demanded additional revisions and who was under no obligation to read a manuscript immediately. Once the censor approved, new copies had to be written out for the prompt book and for the actors' rolls. Then there was rehearsal, however minimal by modern standards. All of this takes time, which is one of the reasons why so many Elizabethan plays were written by collaborators who could split the plot outline in half and write twice as fast; even with collaborators, however, it would be remarkable if any play reached the stage within three to four months of its initial proposal.[12] Thus, it seems unlikely that Shakespeare could have written *Comedy of Errors*, for example, as a *new* play for this particular company before its known performance date.

However, as the company became more established, he would have both the time and the opportunity to write new material expressly for his new partners. Almost certainly, the first fully original work for this group was *A Midsummer Night's Dream*. Internal references to the unusual weather of 1594, a lion at the Scottish court in October 1594, and to Spenser's *Epithalamion*, published early in 1595, lead most scholars to date the play in 1595.[13] Because of the romantic themes and the final blessing of the house by Oberon, many have suggested a play commissioned for a noble wedding celebration. The most common candidate is Elizabeth Carey's wedding on February 19, 1596, in Blackfriars, although this seems a bit late for the allusions in the text. As her grandfather was the same Henry Carey who patronized the acting company, they almost certainly performed something during the celebrations, but there is nothing to connect *Dream* itself to the occasion. As discussed earlier, financial considerations rule out the idea that the play was commissioned for such a performance, even before we ask how appropriate might be a play that celebrates young girls who defy their parents and elope with young men of whom their parents disapprove. Thus, although it could have been modified for the Carey wedding some months later, it seems all but certain that *Dream* was written in the early part of 1595 and publicly performed shortly afterward, perhaps as late as actual Midsummer, June 24.

Modern productions have tended to make this one of the most spectacular of Shakespeare's plays, but the script we have is remarkably devoid of effects. It requires very little music, only the one fairy song (a second is given in the Folio at the end, but curiously all modern editors indicate this as a speech for Oberon, not a song sung by the fairies[14]). No off-stage music but a hunting horn is heard. The Elizabethan perception of fairies was quite different from our post-Victorian cuddlies, so we need not even envision any special costume requirements for the decidedly earthbound and specifically male fairies in Titania's service. It is also rather surprisingly short on crowds; outside of the comic Hired Men among the rude mechanicals, not a single line is spoken by an adult non-Sharer. Thus, it is remarkably well-suited to the small company that played *Comedy of Errors* in January.

Likewise, it is extremely well suited to the inn yard or hall. Neither Oberon nor Puck is required to go above (as is almost always done in modern stagings), which would simplify the staging of many scenes and eliminate the need for Oberon to announce his invisibility (II,i,186). Nor does the Folio suggest any within, for the young lovers fall asleep on the open stage where they are directed to lie in view on stage until Theseus at last awakens them (F1507).

A Midsummer Night's Dream is the epitome of the ensemble comedy. Roles are more evenly balanced than in any other Shakespearean work. Only Egeus and Philostrate are small roles, and the Folio confuses the two names (F1874), suggesting they were played by the same actor. Bottom of course was Kemp, most likely with his apprentice as Flute. The presence of a boy to play Speed in January 1595 indicates that Kemp's apprentice was already quite old and experienced, so he might very well look as if he had a beard coming. Duke, Sinklo, and either Cowley or Pallant were the other rude mechanicals, as previously identified. Burbage and Condell, the two young men, split Demetrius and Lysander, more closely balanced than the pair would ever again be in Shakespeare's plays. Bryan or Pope must have been Egeus; because it is all but impossible to envision a fat Oberon, then Pope was Egeus/Philostrate. Puck is the rude, vulgar, and often aggressive Robin of medieval lore, no child at all, so Phillips the verbal show off with a dancer's grace is the most likely casting, leaving Heminges, Bryan, and Shakespeare to sort out Theseus and Oberon. Because Theseus is portrayed as a much more mature and experienced man than we would otherwise expect for a bridegroom, Bryan seems to have been intended. Oberon has a large number of scenes with his obviously experienced apprentice playing Titania, which favors Heminges for Oberon, for Shakespeare's boy would have been most inexperienced at this date.

By process of elimination, that leaves Shakespeare as Peter Quince. This comes as something of a surprise, for one of the most persistent of all critical traditions is that Shakespeare did not like the clowns and did not like Kemp in particular. And yet, his first new work for this company provided Kemp with one of the largest roles in the play, one of the best ever written for a comedian, and then Shakespeare wrote himself into the clown team. We return to his relations with Kemp many times in later chapters, but it helps to remember this most unexpected development at the very beginning of Shakespeare's career with this company.

The women of *A Midsummer Night's Dream*, as the first roles written specifically for the boys of this new company, provide the first clear view of some important young males. One—Hermia—is unusually short, whereas Helena is somewhat taller than average, or unusually thin, or both. The short one is feistier, more impulsive in nature, or at least is able to project that persona. A third, Titania, is more regal, with a nice line in haughtiness that can be turned to comic effect in her scenes with Bottom. The fourth, Hippolyta, is not yet much of a speaker but is more Amazonian in appearance, muscular or stout. Titania, Helena, and Hermia are all obviously experienced boys, for they have one hundred fifty lines or more and play extensive scenes with actors other than their masters.

With Heminges cast as Oberon, Titania was almost certainly Alexander Cooke, who is known to have been apprenticed to Heminges. As an adult, his name shows up in a number of Jonson's cast lists, and he was listed among the Folio's Principall Actors. Although he died young, he was married by 1603, which means he was then an adult out of his bonds and probably in his mid-twenties. It is possible that Cooke was the son of an actor named Lionel Cooke, who had been one of the twelve original Sharers in the Queen's Men in 1583. Lionel disappears from the record of that company after 1588. This may mean nothing, for the membership of that company in the ensuing years is very uncertain, but it probably means that he retired or died shortly afterward. We do not know that Lionel had a son, but if he did, he would have apprenticed him to someone else only after 1588, when Heminges also would have been taking on his first apprentice, all of which would fit with what we know about Alexander's age. Whether Lionel's son or not, young Cooke was in his mid-teens by the time Shakespeare began writing *A Midsummer Night's Dream*, and as one of the more experienced boys, able to be trusted with long speeches and significant scenes with actors other than Heminges, such as played by Titania.

If Bryan was in fact Theseus, then Hippolyta was his apprentice, for whom no name is known. There was a very young boy identified as T. Belt in *The Seven Deadly Sins* who had a scene with Bryan. Nothing else is known about him, but we will see a boy fairly regularly associated with Bryan until about 1597, which would fit the hypothetical career of Belt.

This play alone does not allow us to identify the boys playing Hermia and Helena unequivocally, for Demetrius and Lysander both play long scenes with both girls, but the two physical types will be paired again. The other four boys playing the fairies are very young still, with only a speech or two, used primarily for their singing voices, and are thus almost certainly boys added new by their various masters during 1594 and now just beginning to test the waters on stage.

2 Henry VI probably appeared during the last few weeks at Cross Keys. This was not a completely new play, for a version of it had been performed during 1591–92, almost certainly by Pembroke's Men, and then printed in 1594 as *The First Part of the Contention betwixt the two famous Houses of Yorke and Lancaster*. It is now generally, if not universally, accepted that the Folio represents Shakespeare's original, written in 1592 or earlier, with *York and Lancaster* a bad quarto, a memorial reconstruction made by several actors who no longer had access to Shakespeare's written text.[15]

Neither Meres nor any one else mentions any of the Henry VI plays after 1594, but they all must have had at least some Chamberlain's Men performances, because they are included in the Folio. Precisely because Meres does not mention them, we must assume they were never presented as the intentional cycle implied by the Folio titles. The popularity implicit in such an undertaking surely would have attracted Meres's attention. Rather, the three Henry VI plays must have been played by the Chamberlain's Men at different times as separate, distinct plays.

The play we know as Part II has the most balanced ensemble of all Shakespeare's histories, with five roles near 10% of the total lines, pointing to an early performance before company stars had emerged. It may have entered the company rep while they were still at Cross Keys, for it is the only one of the Henry VI plays not to make extensive use of a balcony level. Nevertheless, it must have reached the stage only after the company was well established, for the work requires an enormous group of Hired Men, particularly among Cade's followers, and as we have seen, the requirements for Hired Men through *A Midsummer Night's Dream* were minimal both in number and in acting skill. Thus, its most likely production was in the summer or early fall of 1595, as the company was expanding its size and preparing to move into The Theatre.

This is the only Henry VI play in which Henry himself is in his twenties, so this was Burbage's role, but it is not the kind of role that leads to stardom. Duke Humphrey speaks of his great "age" (II,iii,18), so he was one of the oldest actors, most likely Bryan. Pope then would have played Old Clifford, perhaps augmenting his role by doubling Cardinal Beaufort, who disappears a full act before Clifford's arrival. Warwick is young and tempestuous, which fits what we have established about Condell's roles. Although there is no clown per se, Kemp surely played Jack Cade, for the common man role was always given to the clown. His captor Iden, described as larger than Cade (IV,x,46–47), would have been played by the company strong man Duke. Kemp probably doubled earlier, probably as the drunken armourer defeated by his apprentice, played by the experienced and relatively older boy who had played Speed. The fraudulent blind man Simpcox, supposedly blind and frail, is a brief Hired Man bit firmly in the line of old coots that would become Cowley's specialty, probably borrowing Kempe's younger apprentice for his wife. Suffolk has an attractive "proportion" (I,iii,54), which tells us little, because Heminges and Phillips were playing twins only a few months earlier; the number of scenes he has with Margaret suggests Phillips, whose boy has been somewhat more feminine than Heminges's apprentice. York is actually the largest role in the play, with far more lines than Salisbury, so his role probably went to Heminges, more experienced than Shakespeare. Although it may be generally agreed that this text is the original of the somewhat garbled Pembroke *Contention*, there is one strong hint that Shakespeare made at least some revisions in early 1595—the role we have assigned to Shakespeare by process of elimination, Lord Salisbury, is tripled in size from the earlier printed quarto.[16]

2 Henry VI is in many ways Margaret's play, her more than three hundred lines exceeding Henry's own role in size while making far more dramatic impact. It would be nice if we could actually identify this boy. Unfortunately, the best guess is the boy Ned, who played one of the women in scenes with Phillips as Sardanapalus in the *Seven Deadly Sins* during 1591–92. Nothing more has been found about this boy, and no Edward will appear in later records of the Chamberlain's Men.

The company may also have revived *Fair Em* at about this time. The first quarto was undated, but recent scholarly study argues for a memorial reconstruction in 1592–93.[17] That quarto was credited to Lord Strange's Men, who disappeared with Strange's death in early 1594. However, a large number of the original Chamberlain's Men had been in Strange's Company at some point, so the play could easily have been among the assets they brought to the new company. The extant text is very brief, less than 1,500 lines, as we would expect of a memorial reconstruction. Although the original in performance must have differed from the quarto in a number of details, the cast of principals would have been the same, and that cast fits very easily with the Chamberlain's Men at the time of *A Midsummer Night's Dream*. There are two fathers, the Danish King and the Miller, for Bryan and Pope; a commoner clown for Kemp and a much smaller role of a commoner father such as would become Cowley's specialty; three significant men neither old nor young, for Shakespeare, Heminges, and Phillips, and one role of an attractive lover for a full Sharer, suitable for young Burbage, and a second young man with a smaller role for Condell. Perhaps more significantly, as in *A Midsummer Night's Dream*, there are four significant women, although one, like Hippolyta, has only a handful of lines. Assuming the company revived the play at any time, such a revival is most likely in this first season, when the need for tested material was greatest and when the simplicity of staging would have been most attractive.

Even more tentative would be *Edward III*, registered December 1, 1595, and printed shortly afterward in 1596. This would suggest that it had been revived by some company during 1595. The most likely date of the text is 1589,[18] but the registration and publication dates would seem to indicate it was not sold by a company during the plague outbreak of 1593–94, in turn again suggesting a popular production during 1595. It was assigned to Shakespeare in a bookseller's catalogue and has been claimed at least in part for Shakespeare by careful scholars like Chambers. Fred Lapides, the most recent editor of the text, concludes, after some two dozen pages of evidence: "There is no evidence that eliminates Shakespeare as the author of *Edward III*; on the contrary . . . every examination . . . eliminates every other author but Shakespeare." Wells and Taylor regard it as the most likely candidate for inclusion in the canon, but were unwilling to commit fully on the basis of available evidence.[19] However, the more securely Shakespeare is tied to the text, the less likely is a Chamberlain's Men performance; a company performance of a Shakespearean work should have earned it a place in the Folio. And the script itself seems to be designed for a much larger company than the Chamberlain's Men at this time, with at least ten principal non-clown adult characters appearing in multiple scenes (as in *Woodstock*) that would make doubling of the roles all but impossible. It may well have been written by Shakespeare, but he does not seem to have brought it into the Chamberlain's Men repertory.

It is not certain how long the Chamberlain's Men remained at Cross Keys. According to Lord Hunsdon, the company intended to stay at Cross Keys all winter, and as we have seen, the plays datable to that winter all make very minimal demands on the space or on the size of the company. The plays datable from mid-1595 to mid-1597 all demand a much larger complement of Hired Men and a theater building with an above. Thus, the actors must have moved to The Theatre before the autumn of 1595. Most Elizabethan leases and rents were paid and expired on one of the quarter days; thus, Lady Day, March 25, or Midsummer, June 24, are the most plausible dates for leases to change. If the title of *A Midsummer Night's Dream* is related to its premiere date, then the company remained at Cross Keys until June.

When the Chamberlain's Men escaped Cross Keys, they moved into The Theatre where they would remain until the summer of 1597. Arguably, this is the most significant moment in Shakespeare's career. Although the great tragedies were still to come, these first two years in The Theatre introduced *Richard II, King John, Romeo and Juliet, Merchant of Venice*, at least one and possibly both parts of *Henry IV, Love's Labour's Lost*, a revival of *Richard III* that may have involved significant revisions, and a play known as *Love's Labour's Won* that I later argue has survived in an extremely popular form under another title. These should rank among the most amazing two years in the history of art. Had Shakespeare been killed in some tavern brawl before the Globe opened, he would still be regarded as England's greatest playwright. The Theatre was the building where Shakespeare learned to be Shakespeare, the performing space that profoundly shaped all his ideas about what could and could not be done on stage. When we consider that *Much Ado About Nothing*, and probably *Julius Caesar* and *Henry V* as well, were all written before the company finished building the Globe, it becomes clear that The Theatre, not the Globe, was Shakespeare's real psychological home.

The precise nature of the space in The Theatre has received comparatively little attention, with most research focused on the Globe. There is no extant description, and evidence in the surviving scripts is often contradictory. Although we all recognize *the* Balcony Scene, for example, there is no balcony indicated in any of the extant versions of *Romeo and Juliet*; the light "through yonder window breaks" (II,ii,2), and although the quarto identifies the morning-after scene at a window, the Folio merely says "aloft" (F 2032). Jessica is obviously at a window, and *Richard III* is most easily observed talking to the two bishops at a window. On the other hand, the scenes on the wall in *King John* seem obviously not a window. The nature of the within is even more confused. Nevertheless, it is obvious that The Theatre did provide Shakespeare and his compatriots with some kind of upper playing area and with some lower area that could be hidden from audience view when necessary. More importantly, once Shakespeare knew that such spaces were available, he made sure to use them.

A Midsummer Night's Dream and *2 Henry VI* probably played for at least a few performances in the new building. Some overlap of the Cross Keys plays and new plays would have been necessary to sustain daily performances. Although it is difficult for plays with complex staging requirements to work in a makeshift theater, it is no problem at all for plays with relatively simple requirements to be staged in better-equipped facilities.

The poor weather of 1594 continued in 1595, severely reducing crop yields throughout England. Rising food prices led to serious unrest in London, eventually resulting in the execution of five apprentices.[20] We know the theaters were closed, although we do not know the precise date of the order, because the Lord Mayor complained when they re-opened.[21] The Rose closed on June 27 and stayed closed until August 25,[22] so The Theatre probably closed at about the same time. It is often assumed that the Chamberlain's Men went on tour, but it seems unlikely; Heminges baptised a child on May 2, 1596, indicating he had fathered it in July or early August 1595 and thus must have been in London at that time.[23]

If nothing else, the unwillingness to tour indicates that the company had been unusually successful during the first half of the year, leaving the Sharers with so much money that they felt unworried by the prospect of a couple of months off.

Shakespeare may have gone back to Stratford for a visit, but if so, no record exists. If he did visit his family, he devoted much of the visit to writing. Sometime shortly after the summer hiatus, he provided the company with the first of an amazing sequence of new plays.

Richard II was almost certainly the first new work for The Theatre, although it was not registered for printing until August 29, 1597. The most plausible premiere is in the autumn of 1595, on the assumption that Sir Edward Hoby's invitation to Robert Cecil for a dinner on December 7 at which "K. Richard [would] present him selfe to your vewe" may refer to a private performance of at least part of the play. Because it makes significant use of Samuel Daniel's epic *The First Fowre Books of the Civile Warres*, registered October 11, 1594, and printed early in 1595, it was probably written no earlier than the summer of 1595. As we shall see, 1596–97 is so crowded with new plays that can be dated with some security that *Richard II* must have been written and performed during 1595.[24]

History plays, such as *Richard II*, offered several practical attractions. First, the plots came ready-made; with a copy of Holinshed's *Chronicles* and Edward Hall's history of the War of the Roses, the playwright need only select the relevant passages and supply dialogue. This meant new plays could be written quickly. Second, the sprawling nature of the history provided material for numerous Sharer roles of significance, as well as excuses for crowd scenes and other spectacles. *Richard II*, however, seems to be based on something more than the simple historical record. Its theatrical model surely lies in Marlowe's *Edward II*, published in 1594, but certainly seen (and possibly acted in) by Shakespeare several years earlier. Much of Richard's history ran parallel to that of Edward—his disregard of the general welfare while pursuing his own pleasures, his capture by an influential small coterie, and of course his defeat, capture, deposition, and murder—but Shakespeare's treatment of these scenes often seem a gloss on Marlowe's earlier versions of the same scenes, a point noted by many previous critics. In *Richard II* we see Shakespeare now improving on Marlowe. The language is more poetic and mellifluous, the characterizations far more subtle, the political themes developed with more depth. The play lacks some of the vigor of Marlowe, but in all other aspects is clearly superior. It is both Shakespeare's homage to the first master of English theatrical verse and his farewell. With *Richard II*, Shakespeare at last found his own voice.

Almost everything about *Richard II* is remarkable, including its very existence. No topic could have been more dangerous in the climate of the times. The increasingly withdrawn and erratic Elizabeth was often compared to Richard, her favorites to Bushy, Bagot, and Green. It was not too far in the future that Essex would try to become Bolingbroke in an open coup, his followers spurred onward by a performance of *Richard II.* How the play ever got past the censor is another of the many mysteries of Elizabethan theatrical history.

Once it reached the stage, however, it was immensely popular. Elizabeth herself complained about its forty performances,[25] almost certainly an exaggeration on her part not to be taken literally, but still indicative of her feeling that it was everywhere and refused to go away. When printed in 1597, it ran through three editions in little more than a year and continued to be printed and apparently revived three more times in Shakespeare's lifetime. As such, it can stake a claim to being his greatest hit. It was also the first play to be printed with Shakespeare's name on it (Q2 in early 1598), a factor perhaps not unrelated to its popularity.

The modern tendency has been to see the play as a bit talky, so it has usually been revived only when there was a famous star eager to take the role of Richard. This has led to an assumption that Richard must have been intended for Burbage. However, although Richard is the largest role, there is a crucial and very large role for a younger man, Bolingbroke. Not only is he a son of one of the other characters, which means he must have looked significantly younger than most of the other actors, but he is reminded by Richard that Richard is the elder (II,iv,204–5), despite their being historically the same age. Thus, the only possible Bolingbroke is Burbage, the company's young leading man. In 1595, Phillips was precisely the age Shakespeare gives to Richard, older than Burbage/Bolingbroke, younger than York or John of Gaunt, and we have already seen his strong verbal skills. Curiously, in 1601, when the company was in serious trouble over the revival attended by Essex's men, it was Phillips who was called to answer the charges (see p. 107). This is most unusual because by that time, Shakespeare was known as the writer, the company star was Burbage, and Heminges was their regular business representative before the court. This can only mean that Phillips took a very prominent role in that revival. Because that revival was presented very quickly, the remaining Sharers must have all played their original roles; the most prominent role of course is Richard. Thus, Phillips is the most probable Richard. In the first production, Bryan and Pope would have split the two principal fathers York and Gaunt, each with apprentices to play their Duchesses; with Burbage as Bolingbroke, then Condell played the other young man Aumerle. Of the remaining significant roles, although Mowbray claims to be forty (I,iii,159), he is clearly younger than York or Gaunt; the most likely actor is Shakespeare, only thirty-one but able to play older due to his receding hairline. He may also have doubled Carlisle, who does not enter until Act III, leaving Heminges as Northumberland. Kemp and probably his apprentice played the only common man characters in the play, the gardeners. It will be important that we remember this, for much twaddle has been written both about Kemp's enormous ego and Shakespeare's use of the clowns to pander to the pit. Surely, had either of these been true, there would have been some longer and funnier pandering in this most wordy of all Shakespeare's historical tragedies.

Before Shakespeare's next great new hit arrived, the Chamberlain's Men revived one of his most popular older plays, *Titus Andronicus.* Although printed in February 1594 as a Pembroke company play, and thus written even earlier, and performed at

Newington Butts in June 1594, it must have been revived by the company during late 1595. Lord Harington brought the company to his house for a private performance of the play on January 1, 1596,[26] and there is a drawing of a scene (known as the Peacham drawing) that appears to be dated 1595.[27] The drawing is not necessarily accurate, but it indicates the artist saw *Titus* in 1595. The Emperor enters "aloft" (F333) with Tamora, coffins are placed in a tomb, which must be a within, where one of the banquets is also discovered (F1451), and a trapdoor is fundamental, all indicating a fully equipped theater rather than a temporary inn yard. Bryan, now identifiable as the more dynamic and serious of the two fatherly Sharers, was surely Titus. Marcus, his brother of similar age, then would have been Pope. Aaron the Moor would have gone to Phillips, the company's most dynamic and verbal player. Titus's eldest son Lucius, about thirty with a son of ten or more, and Saturninus were split between Heminges and Shakespeare, with Demetrius, the eldest of Tamora's sons, played by Burbage and his brother Chiron by Condell. The clown role for Kemp is very brief, as is common in many of the tragedies later. Young Lucius actually plays all his scenes with Marcus, so he must have been an apprentice of Pope.

One of the most striking aspects of Peacham's drawing of *Titus* is that although kneeling, Tamora is as tall as most of the men standing around her. This may be amateurish drawing, although the other figures are all properly proportioned and the armor is unusually accurate.[28] Or it may mean that Tamora was so tall that the artist, drawing from memory, misjudged her comparative height when kneeling. If so, it indicates that one of the boys, although still young enough to look and sound feminine, was also as tall as, if not taller than, many of the adults in the company. Tamora has most of her scenes with Saturninus; assuming that the Emperor was played by Heminges, then Tamora would have been Cooke. Thus, despite his youth, Cooke had grown to be taller and perhaps stronger than not only the other boys but also many of the adults in the company, a factor that will become significant in several of Shakespeare's other plays to come.

No matter how successful Shakespeare's plays may have been, the company must have staged numerous new plays by other writers during this season, but all have disappeared. On the strength primarily of Shakespeare's plays, the company had become the first among equals in the English theater. During the Christmas celebrations of 1595–96, they appeared five times before Elizabeth. All in all, it was an amazing achievement for a company that had begun with few plays and no place to perform barely fifteen months before. But the next eighteen months would be positively astonishing.

By the time *Richard II* and *Titus Andronicus* reached the stage, Shakespeare and his partners had been working together for more than a year. In that time, they had become both a cohesive and a popular company, with a repertory of plays that allowed each of the Sharers his moments of glory. Shakespeare the writer, sharing the same experiences as Shakespeare the actor, had learned how to use the various skills of each actor in a wide variety of roles. But he had also had time and the perception to see potential in many of these men that had gone untapped. The stimulus of available and stable talent allowed him to follow *Richard II* with a most amazing and unusual play, *Romeo and Juliet.*

Although printed in a bad quarto in 1597 and seen at the Curtain in 1598, the play is universally agreed to have been written earlier. The consensus is that the play was written during 1595, and thus was probably on stage as early as the winter of 1595–96.[29] Most scholars actually place it early in the year, before *A Midsummer Night's Dream,* but its fundamental demands for a much larger company and a much more sophisticated theatrical space with both an above and backstage space for a large bed and a tomb indicate it must have come later, after the company had moved to The Theatre.

Romeo and Juliet has been so popular for so long that it is easy to overlook its revolutionary nature. It is Shakespeare's only romantic tragedy, and as far as I can tell from surviving texts, the first such play in England. It is arguably the only romantic tragedy in history in which the principals are not forced to chose between love and honor. It is a tragedy about commoners; the two warring houses are not York and Lancaster but two extremely successful Veronan businessmen. Even though one sometimes feels Shakespeare himself would have sided with Capulet, the play expresses seriously and passionately the nature of young love, something treated only in comedy by his contemporaries and usually only in a series of stereotypes. Something very remarkable must have stimulated Shakespeare to take such a risk. In the modern world we would turn for an explanation to some passion in his private life, as did the film *Shakespeare in Love,* but the other Sharers were also involved in the commission and the risk. That stimulus must have been something in which they all shared.

One answer lies in the most remarkable aspect of the play, and one little noticed today: Juliet. Juliet has well over five hundred lines, almost one fifth of the total. This is a gigantic jump in prominence for a boy; outside of Shakespeare's later work, only the early anonymous *Arden of Faversham* and Webster's *The Duchess of Malfi* (written almost two decades later) provide any role for a boy comparable in size. Shakespeare's source material was very old, Arthur Brooke's translation in verse of *The Tragical History of Romeus and Juliet,* in print since 1562, and it is followed unusually closely, so it seems very likely that the story was chosen primarily because it provided the potential ideal role for a specific boy.

The most striking aspect of Juliet, after her very existence, is that Shakespeare goes to a great deal of trouble to specify her age as thirteen (I,iii,16–21). This is triply remarkable because the source says she is sixteen,[30] a much more marriageable age; because it is unnecessary—he never tells us the age of Portia or Rosalind or Viola, and marriageability is all the plot requires; and because Burbage, who must have played Romeo, was well into his twenties, which could easily have made their scenes look more like child molestation than passion. Something made the boy look so young as a woman that Shakespeare felt obligated to go out of his way to explain it. It was not the boy's own youth, for the boy playing Juliet's mother was probably younger, and in order to take on a role as enormous as Juliet, the boy must have been quite experienced. The only factor that could explain this is that the original

Juliet was unusually small. Juliet must also have been apprenticed to Burbage. During the previous year, we have seen another unusually small boy playing romantic scenes with Burbage, Hermia in *A Midsummer Night's Dream*. Thus, they must have been played by the same boy.

We know the name of one of Burbage's apprentices at this time, Nicholas Tooley, but he does not seem suitable for the role. He was apparently a most loving and contented apprentice, for he continued to live with Burbage until the great actor's death, then moved into the household of Cuthbert Burbage where he stayed, un-married, until his own death. Phillips left Tooley a small bequest as a "fellow" in 1605, indicating that he was no longer an apprentice by that time. He was not listed, however, in Ben Jonson's cast lists for 1598 or 1599, implying that he was still an apprentice at that late date. Tooley provides a serious problem, for in his will he admitted that his real name was Nicholas Wilkinson, for whom a baptismal record has been found dated February 3, 1575. This in turn has led many to believe he was the Nick playing women in *The Seven Deadly Sins*, when he would have been fifteen to seventeen. This seems most unlikely, because Nick plays no scenes in that production with Burbage. As we see here, Tooley almost certainly did not obtain a share until 1613–14, and all the evidence available indicates that he retained only a half share for the rest of his life. It would have been most illogical for the company to grant even a half share to an actor who was already thirty-eight years old, an age when full Sharers might start thinking of retirement, and to force him to wait for a share through almost twenty years as a Hired Man would have been a cruel insult that makes his obvious love and admiration for Burbage very difficult to explain. Thus, it seems most likely that Tooley was a different Nick and a different Wilkin-son, who finished his bonds between 1600 and 1604, probably closer to the later date. Perhaps he took the stage name of Tooley to avoid confusion with the other Nicholas Wilkinson. Unfortunately, this means he also could not have played Juliet, for he would have been far too young and inexperienced in mid-1595, when Shake-speare was writing the role.

However, there is another possibility. In *The Seven Deadly Sins*, a boy called Saunder played six of his seven scenes with Burbage. He played two significant roles, Gorboduc's Queen and the beautiful Procne who is raped by Tereus. We do not know the actual size of the roles, so Saunder might have been as young as thirteen; the important point is that he was obviously Burbage's boy. Assuming the plot was made in 1592, then this Saunder would have been around sixteen in 1595, the age at which we would expect to see him assigned his largest roles. Juliet is Shakespeare's (and the Chamberlain's Men's) attempt to take full advantage of what must have been his considerable talents. (As was seen earlier, this was not Alexander Cooke, who was about the same age but apprenticed to Heminges. This was also not the "Sander" in the quarto of *The Taming of A Shrew* played by Pembroke's Men before 1593, as is sometimes suggested, for the Sander in that script was obviously the company's adult clown.)

The rest of the cast seems obvious, based on what we have already established about the company. Burbage as the leading young man was of course Romeo, with

Condell the hot-tempered young swordsman Tybalt. If the company favored Capulet as the genial party-giver of Act I, then he would have been played by Pope, with Bryan then as Friar Lawrence; if they favored the stereotype of the fat friar, Pope would have been the priest, with Bryan as Capulet. Interestingly, we rarely see Romeo's father, whom we would expect to carry some dramatic weight roughly equivalent to Capulet. Instead, he is relegated to little more than a walk-on, indicating that the role was designed for a Hired Man because the company had run out of more mature Sharers. Mercutio illustrates Shakespeare's desire to provide something flamboyant for his swordsman-speechmaker Phillips. In its way, Mercutio is a role almost as surprising as Juliet, but as we have seen Phillips already in major roles, we can understand the desire to show the actor to best possible effect, even at the risk of overbalancing the first half of the show. Heminges then would have been County Paris, who must also use his sword but not as well as Mercutio. Benvolio is rather sketchily provided in the source material by Brooke, and rather sketchily filled out by Shakespeare, more than likely for himself to play, his own maturity helping to explain the character's self-control.

Perhaps even more surprising than Juliet is the Nurse. She is such a large and juicy comic role that it is hard not to assume that Kemp donned a dress to play her. Unfortunately for that theory, the second, good, quarto very clearly indicates that Kemp played the servant Peter, who enters as the Nurse exits (IV,v), so he could not have played both even if he shaved his beard. Thus, the Nurse must have been played by one of the boys. This is all but certainly Kempe's older apprentice, whom we earlier saw as Speed. Since Speed is a large role, the boy who played him must have been quite experienced by the winter of 1594–95. Since Flute the bellows-mender in the summer of 1595 was expecting a beard soon, he must have been the same boy, and if he also dueled with his master in *2 Henry VI*, he was also growing quite large by the time of that revival. The Nurse is such a large and interesting role that the boy who played him deserved a name. The only apprentice in the record for Kemp before 1594 is Daniel Johns, but Johns was performing in Denmark with Kemp during 1585–86 and, as he was known by name, he must have been fairly advanced in age and experience at that date, meaning he would have been in his mid-twenties by the time *Romeo and Juliet* was being written. We know Kemp had a relatively inexperienced apprentice in 1592, when he played in *A Knack to Know a Knave* at the Rose. As printed, the play shows only eight lines for the kitchen Maid, who appears in the scene with Kemp and his stooges, so this clown boy was apparently still a novice at that date and most unlikely to have been Johns. Logically, Kemp would have begun training a replacement for Johns around 1590, perhaps a year or so earlier, making this replacement only twelve or thirteen when *A Knack* first appeared. Such a new boy would then have been around sixteen or seventeen in 1595–96, with both the age and experience to play even the Nurse. Kemp had a "servant" named William Bee who accompanied Kemp on his dance to Norwich in 1600.[31] We do not know how old Bee was at the time, but he must have been no longer a boy. A William Bee is found later performing with the Lady Elizabeth's Men, so it is at least possible that William Bee was a performer. (Bee was arrested in Norwich while touring in 1624, so this may not have been Kemp's William Bee but his son.) This does not necessarily prove that Bee was Kemp's apprentice during the 1590s, but his is the only name available, and for convenience, we will refer to this comic apprentice as Bee.

The nature of Kemp's participation in the Peter scene has led to much critical argument and even more abuse for Kemp's skill and reputation. Peter is a very small role very late in the play, consisting of a set of tasteless jokes that jarringly destroy the mood of the scenes around them. People who should know better have even claimed that they must be Kemp's improvisations, since Shakespeare would not write such material, conveniently ignoring the appalling bad taste of Lavatch's jokes or the dramatic pointlessness of the clown in *Othello* or *Antony and Cleopatra*, all written long after Kemp's death. Similarly, many point to this late appearance in the play as proof that Shakespeare tried to minimize Kemp's participation, ignoring the rather large contribution the company clowns make in the earlier parts of this play. Big Kemp and one of the Hired men, such as the little Cowley, must have been large Sampson and small Gregory, the comic cross-talk team who open the play. Kemp was also surely the comic servant who mixes up the letters, a routine he would repeat as Costard, and whom the audience, who had no printed programs, would have seen merely as Sampson returning. Those two scenes already give him a more substantial role than in any other tragedy during this era. Peter himself is most confusing, for the same name is used in II,iv for the servant accompanying the Nurse and again for Romeo's servant in the last act (F2874, ff.). Peter was something of a generic servant's name for Shakespeare, used in *2 Henry VI, Merry Wives of Windsor*, and *Taming of the Shrew* as well as *Romeo and Juliet*, but the name itself is very rare in other records of the era, falling out of fashion precipitously after Henry VIII broke with Rome. Even more curiously, Shakespeare used the name only once after 1600, as a typical Catholic name for a friar in *Measure for Measure*. This suggests that there was a Hired Man named Peter in the company who left around 1600. The most plausible explanation is that this Hired Man played the Act II scene with the Nurse, but the company was not satisfied, for whatever reason, with the way he did the Act IV scene that was also intended for him. Kemp was moved into the scene at the last minute, explaining why his name was simply inserted in the Q stage directions without revising the speech headings.

Not one actor named Peter has yet been found, underscoring the rarity of the name, but also making it difficult to be certain the actor Peter existed. However, there is one other clue—as written, Peter is supposed to sing, which Kemp is not otherwise known to have done. During these early years, the Chamberlain's Men had an accomplished singer, who is most obvious as Amiens in *As You Like It*. He can be seen also as Silence in *2 Henry IV* and Balthasar in *Much Ado About Nothing*, and the anonymous singer of "Who Is Sylvia?", "Tell me where is fancy bred," and of one of the songs at the end of *Love's Labour's Lost*. This singer was not one of the Sharers, but did occasionally speak lines, so he must have been one of the Hired Men. He disappeared around 1600, when the new clown Robert Armin took over all the singer's duties in new plays. No other name is available, so this Peter is at the least the most plausible candidate.

Romeo and Juliet displays an acting company at the height of its fame and prosperity. The stage is full of crowds, with guests attending the party, servants running in and out, and two public brawls. Significant minor roles like Montague, Escalus, and the Apothecary indicate the emergence of Hired Men who can be trusted as more than messengers or stooges. It also displays a playwright at the height of his powers. Although Shakespeare's later tragedies offer greater depth, never again would he write a non-comedy so efficiently and effectively constructed; even *Othello* circles back on itself for most of Act IV. *Romeo and Juliet*, once set in motion, sweeps along all but effortlessly. At the same time, it has room for some of the finest lyrical poetry ever spoken on a stage. This once, we can believe that Shakespeare never blotted a line.

We should not be surprised by this. There is a tendency to think of the plays of this era as youthful plays, because we know that *Hamlet, Othello*, and *King Lear* are still to come. But the Shakespeare who wrote *Romeo and Juliet* was no youth. At thirty-two in the spring of 1596, he was not only entering what the Elizabethans thought of as the downward slope to middle age, but he was also the oldest and most experienced playwright alive in England. Marlowe, Kyd, and Greene, the other giants of his generation, were all dead. By this time, Shakespeare had already written at least ten plays without a collaborator, probably more, and he surely also participated in a number of early collaborations where his hand can only be conjectured by modern critics. This is a far larger body of work than is known for any of those three early giants. *Romeo and Juliet* may seem youthful because of its youthful plot line and its energy, but the play is the work of the era's most mature and experienced playwright.

Shakespeare's next play, *King John*, was a return to English history, although there is much argument as to how much of the play was actually new at this date. A two-part *Troublesome Raigne of John, King of England* was printed in 1591, credited to the Queen's Men. Most critics think this a source for Shakespeare's version, although others think it a version based on Shakespeare's original, and still others think they are both versions of an earlier play that has disappeared. Various modern analyses of verse and vocabulary indicate the play is most similar to *Richard II, Romeo and Juliet*, and *1 Henry IV*, which would strongly indicate 1596, the date accepted by the most recent editors,[32] and as the timeline in Chart A shows, there is a conveniently blank period after *Romeo and Juliet* opened in which Shakespeare would have had time to write it. The *King John* in the Folio seems clearly to be tailored to fit the Chamberlain's Men of 1596. Most obvious is the prominence given to the Bastard, who has more lines than John himself. Because the Bastard is a young man, this can only have been Burbage, with the hot-headed Lewis Dauphin played by the other young man Condell. Given their ages, Bryan and Pope would have taken King Philip of France and the Papal Legate Pandulph. Philip is "a good blunt fellow" (I,i,71) of "large composition" (I,i,88), who thus must have been played by Pope, leaving the smaller Bryan as the villain Pandulph. King John, Hubert, and Salisbury are all significant characters neither young nor old, suitable for Phillips, Heminges, and Shakespeare. Kemp as the comedian may have played the nice bit as the abusive citizen of Angiers, but the Miles Gloriosus figure of the Duke of Austria is more likely; if the company did perform *2 Henry VI*, as suggested earlier, they already had a model of Kemp's head in the prop room to serve as Austria's head. We can probably see the skinny Hired Man Sinklo as the legitimate Fauconbridge, with "legs like riding-rods"(I,i,140) but almost no lines.

Despite the large role for Burbage, the most striking character is Arthur, who has almost five percent of the lines. Although his three-foot grave (IV,ii,101) is probably an exaggeration, there is no doubt that Arthur is very short. But the actor was not himself unusually young; the part is too large and demanding. This is a role for a boy who can be trusted, an experienced boy, so experienced that his death scene is a soliloquy, something that Shakespeare allowed even the adults only rarely. Much of this role is present in *The Troublesome Raigne*, but Shakespeare's decision to keep and even expand the role indicates there was an accomplished short boy in the company. This was not Saunder, for Arthur has no scenes with Burbage. Nor is it likely to have been Cooke, who seems to have been both taller and stronger than the other boys at this time. The boy plays most of his scenes with Hubert, which means Hubert could not have been played by Heminges, Cooke's master, and this in turn means he must belong to either Shakespeare or Phillips. Assuming Shakespeare even had a boy, he would have been still quite inexperienced for such a large role, suggesting that Arthur in fact was the apprentice of Phillips, and that Phillips therefore played Hubert. In this case, he probably also doubled the Citizen of Angiers, as assumed by many editors of the play, and the long speeches of that minor character certainly could reflect the verbal dexterity we have seen from Phillips elsewhere.

We know the names of three different apprentices who learned their craft with Phillips. One, James Sands, was still under bonds in 1605, when Phillips died, so he can be eliminated from plays produced in 1596. The other two, Christopher Beeston and Samuel Gilburne, were probably both in the company at this time. Born Christopher Hutchinson, Beeston eventually had a long and dubious career as actor and manager in the Jacobean theater. Some have identified him with "Kit" in *The Seven Deadly Sins*, but that Kit played two soldiers, indicating he was an adult in appearance well before the Chamberlain's Men were formed; if he was an adult in 1592, he would have been more than sixty-five years old when Beeston died in 1638, a most remarkable age for a man still active in the theater. Beeston was with the Chamberlain's company in 1598, listed in Jonson's *Every Man in His Humour*, but he was no Sharer, for he moved to Worcester's Men by 1601. That Phillips left him a bequest even though he was in a different company suggests he had been an apprentice who maintained good relations with his old master, underlined by the fact that he named his first son Augustine. However, to leave the company while Phillips was still active means he must have finished his bonds before 1601, and probably had quit playing women before 1598, when Jonson remembered him.

Thus, he was much older than Gilburne, probably about fifteen or sixteen years old in 1596, and thus must have been the short boy who played Arthur.

With Beeston cast as Arthur, the other leading boy playing Constance must have been Cooke, the eldest and most experienced of the remaining boys, continuing the queenly bearing we have seen in Titania and Tamora. (Given his comparative height in relation to the other two experienced boys Saunder and Beeston, he had probably been Julia who wears male disguise in *Two Gentlemen of Verona* as well.)

Although 1595 had been a year of almost uninterrupted success for the Chamberlain's Men, the theatrical world of 1596 returned to its more typical state, moving from crisis to crisis. Sometime during late 1595, Frances Langley had built and opened a new theater building, the Swan, on the south side of the Thames near the Rose. This meant there were four dedicated theaters in London. The Swan was the "largest and most distinguished" theater, able to hold three thousand people, according to a continental tourist who also left a drawing of its interior.[33] Fortunately for the Chamberlain's Men and the Admiral's Men, the Swan had everything but a theater company, so Langley resorted to other entertainments, such as fencing displays, bear baiting, or wrestling matches.

During that spring, Shakespeare provided a new, or at least partially new, comedy for the company that proved to be unexpectedly popular. *Love's Labour's Lost* was printed in 1598, its title page reporting it had been seen by Elizabeth at Christmas in 1597. However, the title page also noted that this was a corrected version, indicating that it was a second edition of a work that had appeared previously in a bad quarto that was somehow incomplete or inadequate but that had nonetheless been so popular it had sold out. This in turn would suggest that the first quarto had been printed at least a year earlier, if not more. We also know that there was a sequel, which Meres called *Love's Labour's Won*, that was also printed, although all copies have disappeared. Both were familiar to Meres before September 1598. There were a large number of unauthorized printings of Shakespeare's plays in 1597, which makes that the most likely date for both these missing quartos, and in turn means that the first play of the sequence must have appeared in 1596 at the latest.

Stylistically, the play seems to most scholars to have been written about the same time as *A Midsummer Night's Dream*, and the Russian disguises are usually thought to reflect the Russian pageant at Gray's Inn during the Christmas festivities of 1594–95. However, the choice of Russian disguise may mean nothing more than a desire to re-use some exotic costumes in storage that had been acquired for some other play in 1595 (or perhaps even purchased from Gray's Inn after their pageant). The early feel to the play[34] probably comes from the fact that much of it was written very early, around the time Henri III of France was killed in 1589. The only time when such an abrupt ending for a romantic comedy would have made any sense would have been when the news was current and the writer knew he had no choice. If written completely new at any later time, the play could have ended quite happily. The year 1589 is also the most likely time to name a comic ineffectual Spaniard Armado. How much of the play was revised in 1596, if at all, is not known. If it was written anew, or significantly revised, it would fit into Shakespeare's writing schedule after *Romeo and Juliet*, either just before or just after *King John*, in either case putting it on stage in the summer or autumn of 1596.

Berowne's actual age is arguable from the confusions in the text, but it seems obvious that he must have been played by Burbage. The only other likely candidate would be Phillips, who far more plausibly played the more grandiloquent Armado. Heminges, in this year playing most of the Kings, was probably Navarre. Condell must have played Dumaine or Longaville, and the other can only have been Shakespeare, who was at least no older than Heminges. That Kemp played Costard is obvious, which in turn means Bryan and Pope must have split Holofernes, Nathaniel, and Boyet. Holofernes has a thin face, subect of numerous jokes (V,ii), so he must have been the thinner Bryan, and curates are rarely portrayed as fat and prosperous, so portly Pope must have been the flatterer Boyet. This leaves Nathaniel the curate, smallest of the multiscene roles, to one of the Hired Men, probably Cowley. Jacquenetta was obviously played by Kemp's boy, but the role is very small; as his older boy was playing large, independent roles such as Juliet's Nurse at the time, this was probably a much younger new boy. The major boy's role of Moth, probably pronounced Mote at the time, was obviously intended for a very short boy with a lot of experience, exactly like the boy Beeston whom we have already identified as Phillips's apprentice. The Princess would have been Heminges's experienced and regal but tall apprentice Cooke, underlined by Costard's identification of her as the "tallest and thickest" woman present (IV,i,46–52), a most unusual description of a beautiful princess that can only have been included because it reflected the actor's actual appearance. The witty Rosaline obviously was played by Burbage's apprentice Saunder. The other two ladies were played by Condell's apprentice, whom we previously saw as Helena, and by Shakespeare's boy, now old enough to take on small roles.

The company was perhaps as surprised by the play's popularity as have been most modern critics, who tend to see the work as far too elegant and refined for the crowds in the pit at The Theatre. But popular it most certainly was. Not only did its success lead to an unauthorized printing, which in itself was so popular that Shakespeare released a corrected copy for a second edition within a year, but it also spawned a sequel, known to Meres as *Love's Labour's Won*. However, it would take some months before Shakespeare could get that sequel written, and we come to it later.

The tall and thick Princess suggests another revival or revision at this time, the play we call *1 Henry VI*. The play is generally assumed to be the *Harry the vi* recorded as new by Henslowe at the Rose in 1592, but there is nothing more than Henry's name to tie the two together. There is strong evidence in contemporary allusions that a play about brave Talbot was popular in 1591–92, but it seems likely that Henslowe would have indentified such a work as *Talbot*, just as we would today had not the Folio chosen to identify all the histories by the reigning King's name rather than their true subject matter. Modern analyses of vocabulary suggest composition about the same time as *Titus Andronicus*. Such analyses have also suggested that it is the work of at least two hands, and Gary Taylor has in fact argued for four, with most of the play actually written by the author of *Locrine*.[35] Unfortunately, the passages in *I Henry VI* assigned to Shakespeare by Taylor constitute less than one full act, hardly sufficient to merit inclusion in the same Folio that excluded plays such as *Pericles* and *Two Noble Kinsmen*, in which Shakespeare's hand is far more visible. Obviously, Heminges and Condell thought Shakespeare wrote it, which means they either must have had a copy in Shakespeare's hand or must have participated in a performance under Shakespeare's auspices. If it was a revision, then that revision must have been made after 1594. Our question here is when that revision, and performance, occurred.

Part I significantly differs from the other Henry VI plays in a relatively high proportion of rhymed couplets and an almost complete lack of prose, much closer in this aspect of style to *Richard II, King John*, and *Merchant of Venice* than to the other histories, which points to 1596. Given the importance of Talbot, who is both a dynamic middle-aged man and is called a "shrimp" (II,iii,22), he must have been Bryan, for we know Pope was not small. In turn, this means it must have been performed before Bryan retired in 1597. Joan appears on the walls and Talbot's men scale the walls with ladders, so it would require a substantial above as at The Theatre, which means it must have appeared after mid-1595. Perhaps most importantly, it requires two unusual and very experienced boys. Joan La Pucelle is not the frail icon of modern times but a large, masculine young woman able to handle a broadsword as well as any of the men in the cast, quite literally beating the Dauphin, the best swordsman among the adults, down to the ground.[36] The other is King Henry himself, who is very young, often referred to not as a boy but as a "child" (III,i,133; IV,i,192), even though his is also one of the largest roles in the play. Neither boy is closely tied to any particular master, which also points to their great experience, but may also indicate an earlier composition for the bulk of the play. Joan can only have been the tall Tamora and Princess of France, young Cooke, while the boyish Henry probably was Burbage's Saunder, the more experienced of the two shorter boys. The comparative lack of physical strength in the other boys can be seen in young Talbot, who has an effective moment or two but actually fights and dies off stage; he was certainly Bryan's apprentice, whom we also see prominently in the plays of this brief period. Margaret is little more than a cipher with only thirty-three lines, appearing only with Suffolk, and thus probably Phillips's younger boy Gilburne.

As with all the histories, there are a large number of adult roles that may have required some doubling. With Bryan as Talbot, Pope then played Winchester, the uncle of Gloucester. Plantagenet/York refers to his "young years" (II,v,107), so this was probably Burbage, with Condell in the much smaller role of the young, sword-fighting Dauphin. Phillips, Heminges, and Shakespeare split Suffolk, Gloucester, and Mortimer, the last of whose single, long scene may have allowed him to double elsewhere. Kemp might have played the only significant common man, Joan's shepherd father, but this was more in Cowley's usual line; all the Frenchmen are to some degree ludicrous to English eyes, so Kemp might have played someone such as the boastful and ineffectual Reignier, so much like Austria in *King John*. There remain an unusually large number of roles for Hired Men of considerable significance.

The fact that Meres did not mention the play does raise a serious question about this dating of company performances. Some play about Talbot had been extremely popular in 1590–92, and it seems unlikely his story would have lost its popularity in only four or five years, so it is difficult to explain the title's omission from Meres' extensive catalogue. Still, Heminges and Condell have more authority in this area than does Meres, and the omission may simply mean that Meres did not like the play. There is no mention of any Talbot play by this company, or any other, during later years, which might mean the interest in brave Talbot had run its course and the production was not much of a success; alternatively, the normal performance schedule was interrupted in that summer, which could have closed down even a popular play after only one or two performances. Although we cannot be as sure about the dating of the production as we have been with other plays in the Folio, on the basis of cast requirements, this still seems the most plausible date for a company performance.

In the early summer, the plague returned. The Privy Council ordered all theaters closed on July 22, 1596. The Rose remained closed from July 23 to the last week of October. In a double blow, on the same day as the closures began, Henry Carey, the Lord Chamberlain and company patron, died. The Chamberlain's Men decided to go on tour, visiting Feversham on the road to Canterbury in late July.[37] This suggests that they did not feel as financially secure as in previous summers. However, they may also have simply removed themselves from the immediate view of the local authorities while waiting to see if Carey's son George would continue the patronage. George did in fact become their new patron, and for those concerned with precision, since he was the new Lord Hunsdon but not the Lord Chamberlain, the company became Lord Hunsdon's Men.

At about the same time, Shakespeare's son Hamnet died, buried on August 11 in Stratford. Shakespeare probably did not even know of the illness until it was too late to return, for any messages sent to him would have had to catch up to the company on tour.

The new Lord Hunsdon may have been the company patron, but he soon revealed that he was no serious supporter. Stimulated by the building of the Swan and the coming expiration of the lease on The Theatre, James Burbage had bought a hall in Blackfriars that was technically outside the jurisdiction of the Lord Mayor and thus could be used for performances. At considerable expense, he converted it to an indoor theater space, the first such in the nation. The residents in the vicinity, however, were not delighted by the prospect of a theater that would draw large crowds to the neighborhood and demanded that Burbage not be allowed to open, using most of the standard NIMBY arguments still used today to block new construction. One of the signatures most prominent on the petition against the Blackfriars theater was that of George Carey,[38] who had a house nearby. With such influential objectors, the project was squelched, leaving Burbage with an enormous white elephant of an empty building and a crushing debt.

Even without competition from the Swan, audiences were much reduced. The famines of the previous year continued with more bad weather. London was flooded with the unemployed while food prices soared, severely reducing the amount of disposable income available for entertainments like the theater. Henslowe's journals show a marked decrease in income during the first half of 1596, and in the fall even that reduced income was cut in half. When the theaters reopened in late October, attendance was much reduced. When this happens, plays change more often, because they exhaust their audience more quickly. At the Rose, the Admiral's Men premiered six new works in only eight weeks during December and January, twice as often as in the previous spring.[39] Although the Chamberlain's Men may have been somewhat more popular, they too must have found themselves in search of more new material than they had in the pipeline from various playwrights. The company was beginning to take young Burbage much more seriously after his success as Romeo, by far the largest role he had yet played, almost 20% longer than the Bastard in *King John* and much more varied and dramatically demanding. Thus, it is not so surprising that in the circumstances, Shakespeare rummaged around in his trunk and dug out one of his oldest plays, *Richard III*.

Most modern scholars agree that Shakespeare first wrote *Richard III* before 1593, although the precise date is much debated.[40] Registered August 29, 1597, it was apparently printed in a great hurry in a bad quarto, suggesting a wish to take advantage of the popularity of current public performances. We consider some of the complex issues raised by this particular printing in chapter 3; the significant point here is that, in order to be printed in the late summer of 1597, the play must have been on the stage in the winter–spring of 1596–97. Given the reduced audiences of that season, it may well have been thrown on stage purely as an emergency stop gap when newer works failed to sustain their appeal. If so, it was a most fortuitous emergency, for the play was an explosive hit, just as it has continued to be for four hundred years. Richard became the king of villains, and Richard Burbage became the king of the Elizabethan theater.

Even more than Hamlet, Richard was the role that defined Burbage in the popular imagination. In the Cambridge student play known as *The Return from Parnassus*, a character named Burbage is asked to audition a would-be actor. The young man stoops over and begins to recite, "Now is the winter of our discontent . . ." (p. 197–98).

Although not originally written for this company, *Richard III* was probably staged with little revision, for there are numerous opportunities for the Sharers we have established. Richmond, who should be dramatically equivalent to Bolingbroke in *Richard II*, is a relatively minor character; as a young man good with a sword, he must have been Condell. Given his late appearance, he must have doubled someone else of signficance: Brakenbury or Tyrrell, or both, are practical and plausible. Buckingham, the second largest role and given to bombast and verbal obfuscation, would then have been Phillips. Stanley and Hastings, both older men, fell to Bryan and Pope, but the one who played Rivers may have doubled another role as well. The two elder brothers of Richard, Clarence and Edward IV, were split by Heminges and Shakespeare; given Heminges' somewhat more regal previous assignments, Shakespeare was probably the man drowned in a butt of Malmsey. There are no obvious clowns in the play, but the two murderers have something like the Sampson–

Gregory cross-talk routine, so they must have been played by Kemp and the same Hired Man who had played Gregory, with Kemp as the larger and stronger First Murderer, single-handedly lugging Shakespeare's body off the stage.

The women's roles indicate a play originally written for a much different company. Four of them are actually larger roles than any of the men's except Richard's and Buckingham's, in itself not a problem. The difficulty in identifying them is that they all seem to have all their scenes with Richard or with each other. We can be relatively certain that the passionate Anne was the boy who played Juliet, for example, but there are no clues to help identify the others. Given their long speeches and their independence, they must have been experienced boys, and thus we can be sure that Cooke and Beeston played two of them, but which two must be a matter of guess-work—very old women tend to seem very small, so Beeston has a slight edge for Margaret. The fourth one was probably Robert Gough, who was apprenticed to Pope.

We have, to this point, seen little of Pope's apprentice, although he is known to have had two at this time, Robert Gough and John Edmans or Edmunds. Gough, named in Pope's will in 1603, is usually assumed to be the "R. Go." who played Aspatia in *The Seven Deadly Sins*, and because he played many of his scenes with Pope, this is more than plausible. On February 13, 1603, he married a sister of Augustine Phillips, so he was definitely an adult before that date, and obviously was also well known to Phillips, indicating he had continued to act with the Chamberlain's Men in some capacity. Edmans split all Pope's arms and apparel with Gough but appears in no other acting records. He was also entering adulthood by the time Pope died, for he married Pope's principal legatee, Mary Clarke, in 1604. Pope retired about three years before he died, so it is not incontestably obvious when either of the boys finished his apprenticeship. It is unlikely the company would have continued to use the apprentices of a master no longer active, so both were probably in their late teens or older when Pope retired in or around 1600. As Gough was all but certainly in *The Seven Deadly Sins*, then he must have been sixteen or older in 1596; that we have not seen him in large roles previously reminds us how much the boys' careers depended on the roles played by their masters. It also underscores how many plays are missing from this period, from which we know only Shakespeare's work.

Richard's success in that winter almost certainly led to a revival of *3 Henry VI* as well, probably known at the time as *Richard Duke of York*, the title used in its earlier printing. (With such a title, Meres would have overlooked it, seeing it as merely Part I of a single work about Richard III.) No one has ever settled the issue of the play's relation to the two *Contention* plays, printed in 1594 and 1595 as belonging to Pembroke's Men, so although most scholars think otherwise,[41] it is at least possible that Shakespeare made some significant revisions at this time. Certainly, the seven significant adult principals fit his current company far better than would seem likely without such revisions. Richard is the same man who would eventually become Richard III, in many ways even more interesting and villainous, ultimately murdering Henry VI, so he would obviously have been played by Burbage. Two mature principal characters, Warwick and York, fit Bryan and Pope very nicely. Three men in their thirties, King Henry and Richard's elder brothers, Edward and Clarence, fit Phillips, Heminges, and Shakespeare. Both York and Clifford die early, so they may have doubled Lewis and the undependable Somerset, who make strong impressions in brief later scenes. The boy Cooke, now growing quite old and muscular for women, would have been the young and martial Prince of Wales, and Lady Gray would have been Phillips' apprentice. Margaret, however, is something of a mystery because she has scenes with everyone, but Saunder is still the most experienced of the boys available. As in most of the histories, there is no major role for any of the clowns.

Given the popularity of *Romeo and Juliet*, it is most odd that there was no sequel. The young lovers were of course dead, so we cannot look for a *Romeo and Juliet II*. But surely, with the play's phenomenal success (still playing, or revived successfully, two years later and popular enough to be stolen by someone for a printing) and the company's need for crowd pleasers in a time of reduced attendance, it must have occurred to the Sharers that Shakespeare should write another romantic tragedy for young lovers. But there is no *Pyramus and Thisbe*, no *Hero and Leander*, no *David and Bathsheba*, and no *Tristram and Isoud*. Shakespeare's attention turned instead to a much different kind of love story. For the first time in company history, a boy was given the largest role in the play—Portia. Almost all critical attention to *The Merchant of Venice* since Hitler has focused on Shylock, but it is Portia with 60% more lines who must carry the play. She is something new for Shakespeare, an attractive, desirable, intelligent, witty female who is yet so curiously a-sexual that she can successfully appear as a boy or young man. So effective was the boy that we now think of her type as the quintessential Shakespearean female. This is a boy to whom Burbage does not object, who plays the bulk of his scenes with Burbage, and in fact often outshines Burbage; the only possible available boy is Burbage's apprentice, the same Saunder who had played, and who was apparently still playing, Juliet.

The Merchant of Venice is one of the few plays that can be dated within a very specific and very limited period. Registered July 22, 1598 and mentioned by Meres at about the same time, it must have been on stage no later than 1597–98. Salerio's "wealthy *Andrew* docked in sand"(I,i,27) is now understood to be an allusion to the Spanish *St. Andrew* run aground during the Essex raid on Cadiz in 1596. News of this did not reach London before the end of July, when the Chamberlain's Men were on tour, so that particular line must have been written shortly after the company returned, probably no earlier than October.[42] The play also makes important use of an above, indicating that it was written for The Theatre, which the company left at the end of April 1597. Thus, the play was most likely new on stage in the winter of 1596–97.

The play is closely related to an Italian source, although no one has yet found an English translation or printing. If Shakespeare knew it directly, then he had to work much harder than he had done with *Romeo and Juliet* to adapt it.[43]

There can be no doubt that Burbage played Bassanio. *Merchant* requires two young male lovers, two middle-aged men, three significant men in between, and a major comedian with a minor stooge who plays old coots. The Hunsdon company had two young men, two middle-aged men, three men in between, and a major comedian with a regular stooge who seems to have specialized in old coots. It would be hard to find a script more carefully tailored to the company requirements. Were Burbage to play Shylock, simply because we think of that as the star's role today, someone from every age group in the cast would have to move to a role for which he was physically unsuited, ultimately leaving either Bryan, Pope, or the balding Shakespeare as Bassanio. The only way the casting could work would be Burbage as Bassanio, with Condell as the supporting Lorenzo, Pope as Antonio, Bryan as Shylock, Phillips as Gratiano with his "airy nothings," and Heminges and Shakespeare splitting "the salads," Salerio and Solanio, with the latter probably doubling the Duke.

One of the most interesting aspects of Portia is her male disguise. In twentieth-century criticism, much attention has been given to the sexual, social, and political implications of Shakespeare's women disguised as men, but most of this discussion has missed an obvious point. The actors who played Portia, Rosalind, and Viola were not pretending to be boys—they *were* boys. The pretense came when they put on the dress, not when they took it off. Although the disguise plot provides numerous comedic opportunities, it also solves a very serious practical problem for Shakespeare and his associates: what to do with a leading man whose leading woman was on the verge of manhood. Almost a year later than when Juliet was written for him, Saunder was about seventeen. At any moment in the near future, his voice was going to break. No one knew when that might occur, but there was no way to ignore the possibility. If Shakespeare intended to write a romance with Burbage as the leading man—and because Burbage was the company's young leading man, there was no choice in the matter—then he would have to find a way to use Saunder in that romance. Burbage's other apprentice was only about twelve and far from experienced. Putting the boy in male disguise for a significant part of the role turned a problem into an advantage; there was no difficulty believing Portia's disguise in the courtroom, because the boy the audience saw looked exactly like the boy he was. Interestingly enough, Shakespeare was so happy with this solution that he used it for all of the boys in the play. Nerissa plays most of her scenes with Portia, suggesting that the boy was also fairly experienced, but the scenes she has with adults are with Gratiano. This points to Beeston, another of the older boys often playing boys, such as Moth and Arthur, rather than women. Jessica also goes into male disguise, rather unnecessarily in a dramatic sense; Portia and Nerissa might need disguise to get into the courtroom, but Jessica could elope just as easily whether dressed as a woman or as a man. She plays most of her scenes with Lorenzo, and thus must have been Condell's apprentice, for whom we have no name. As we have seen, although this boy was probably a couple of years younger than Saunder, he was taller when they played Hermia and Helena together. It certainly would not have hurt anything to put him in boy's clothes as well.

Even with the declining audiences and the plague closures of 1596, the Sharers were making money. In May 1597, Shakespeare finalized the purchase of New Place, the second largest house in Stratford, and spent a good deal on major remodeling during the succeeding year,[44] which means he had earned a significant amount of income from his theatrical activities. Shakespeare probably earned more than the other Sharers, of course, because he was paid for writing as well as for acting, but all the members of the company would have shared in a similar prosperity.

The Christmas season of 1596–97 was the peak of the company's success. Even though their patron was no longer the Lord Chamberlain, the company played at court six times during the Christmas season of 1596–97, and they were the only company invited. Never again would they monopolize a court season, even when they were the King's Men in later years. All of Shakespeare's contributions in this season had been hits, which was fortunate because in the spring of 1597 the Chamberlain's Men entered a year of crisis that would have destroyed most other companies.

Chapter 3

The Crisis Years, 1597–98

Shakespeare and his partners could be forgiven if they chose to spend the pre-Lenten season of 1597 congratulating themselves. In little more than two years, they had gone from just another new acting company to the premier company in the nation. The combined success of *Richard III, Romeo and Juliet,* and *Merchant of Venice* had led to consistently packed houses, and the presence of Shakespeare as a regular playwright as well as an actor promised more such hits in the future. They monopolized the winter performances for Elizabeth. No acting company had ever known such success, nor held such bright hopes for further wealth and glory to come. But life in the theater is often more melodramatic than the life depicted on the stage. Within only a few months, the company would face extinction.

In January 1597, James Burbage died, which passed ownership of The Theatre and the Blackfriars building to his sons, Richard and Cuthbert. In other circumstances, this would have provided a permanent home in London for the company. On March 17, George Carey assumed his father's old position as Lord Chamberlain, so the company would have seemed to be secure at court. Unfortunately, the Burbages leased rather than owned the land under The Theatre, and on April 13, 1597, the Burbages lost their lease. It came as no surprise, the lease simply expiring after the traditional twenty-one years. This may explain why James Burbage had bought the Blackfriars before his death.

Their landlord, Giles Allen, did not like actors; he announced he would prefer to put the property "to some better use," and threw the company out. After April, the Chamberlain's Men had no theater. It matters little if you are the finest company in the land and honored with powerful patrons if there is no public place for you to perform. Logically, they should have moved to the Swan, the newest and largest space in the city. Unfortunately, the Swan was no longer available. After lying empty for more than a year, it had found a tenant in February 1597, when Pembroke's Men had returned from the provinces and had taken out a year's lease on the Swan.

Thus, the Chamberlain's Men had no choice but to move into the Curtain. It is unclear who owned the Curtain. Although the Curtain was near to The Theatre and James Burbage at some point had probably had some interest in the building, he seems to have given up that interest, for Cuthbert Burbage in later legal documents never mentioned it as a part of their inheritance. Built only a year after The Theatre, the Curtain's original lease of twenty-one years would also expire sometime in 1598, or so we must assume. In any case, its age meant that the Chamberlain's Men could not count on it as a permanent home. The Curtain had always been seen as a secondary space, used irregularly, and in such circumstances, it is common for landlords to allow property to become dilapidated. Nor was the Curtain itself particularly suitable to the company's requirements. We know very little about the Curtain's practical facilities, but it is obvious that the Burbages thought they were inadequate—despite access to the Curtain, the Burbages immediately embarked on negotiations with Allen to return to The Theatre.[1] They would not have done so if they had considered the Curtain to be an adequate substitute as a performing space.

At about the same time, the company faced its first serious political crisis at court. This grew out of another of Shakespeare's new plays, and another big hit, now known as *1 Henry IV*. As with so many of Shakespeare's plays introduced since early 1596, *1 Henry IV* was a revolutionary script that allowed a company actor to do something he had never done. *1 Henry IV* introduced the character now known as Falstaff, who can only have been played by the company clown, Will Kemp. Like Juliet or Portia, Falstaff is now so firmly established in the Western imagination that we may easily forget what an amazing creation he is. Although Kemp had already played large roles such as Bottom, he had never done anything like Falstaff. Nor had any other clown. Falstaff is more than twice the size of any other Kempean role, and in *2 Henry IV* the role will be even larger.

Falstaff is so unusual that more than one critic has suggested that Kemp could not possibly have played him.[2] Yet, if Kemp did not, who did? Burbage was automatically Prince Hal, the great young star of the company playing the most popular star/king in English history. Hotspur is the epitome of the hot-headed young man who is the mirror of Burbage and good with a sword, yet loses his final duel with Burbage, so he must have been played by Condell, who has played all such roles previously. Once again, as in all the new plays discussed thus far, we find two major roles for middle-aged men, Henry and Worcester, who must have been played by Bryan and Pope. Shakespeare, Phillips, and Heminges then doubled all the important men in the middle. The simplest doubles are Poins, Northumberland, and either Ross or Lord Bardolph doubling Vernon, Mortimer, the Archibishop, and Douglas. The Hired Men took Gadshill, the Carriers, and various travelers, messengers and soldiers, with perhaps the more trusted ones playing characters like Blunt or Lord Bardolph who appear often with almost no lines. Kemp can only have played Falstaff.

And there can be little doubt that Falstaff was designed for this performer, for

Falstaff is a wholly invented character. Although the name comes from the historical sources, the characterization is completely new.[3] Nor does he appear in the early Queen's Men play *The Famous Victories of Henry V* (which has a large role for a clown, but one very different in action and personality). Shakespeare made him up. This is something Shakespeare did only rarely. Almost all of his plays are based on other material, and although he compressed events and characters for dramatic purposes, he only added original material when the sources did not offer a good role for one or more of the actors available. But even in these cases, he rarely worried about the clowns. They make very small appearances in most of the histories. But obviously Shakespeare saw something in Kemp that had not yet been tapped and decided to invent a role that allowed Kemp to play a far more complex character than any clown had previously attempted.

Unfortunately, although the character was wholly invented, Shakespeare did not invent his name. In the original version, the character was named John Oldcastle, historically a friend of Hal. Oldcastle, however, was the antithesis of Falstaff, a brave soldier of tenaciously upright moral character who was ultimately martyred as an early Protestant. He was also the first Baron Cobham, and his descendants, now the Brooke family, were powerful and influential still. William Brooke, tenth Lord Cobham, had been Henry Carey's replacement as Lord Chamberlain in 1596. The Brookes did not take kindly to this travesty of the family founder's name, and they complained vociferously. Shakespeare changed the name, borrowing the name Falstaff from the same sources. There were no influential descendants of Falstaff, so the name stuck.

The question is when all this occurred. The explanation of the name change was not understood until the discovery of a letter written in 1625,[4] which does not help date the events. However, William Brooke was Lord Chamberlain from July 1596 to March 1597. Had the play appeared during that time, he would have had no need to complain to someone; he simply would have banned the play himself. Even had the Master of Revels somehow dared to pass the play for performance, the Lord Chamberlain carried an authority exceeded only by Elizabeth herself and perhaps Lord Burghley, and he surely would not have hesitated to use it to punish an insult to his family's honor. As is often seen in the career of Ben Jonson throughout this era, playwrights who upset powerful nobles could be jailed and their plays removed from the stage and even completely destroyed. Shakespeare changed the character's name, but there is no hint of any actual punishments given to Shakespeare or his companions. Thus, it seems obvious that the play must have appeared after William Brooke's death in March 1597, when his heir, Henry Brooke, although still wealthy and powerful, would have lacked the political clout to override the protection provided by George Carey, the new Lord Chamberlain and patron of the acting company.

This was the date assigned to the play by all major scholars through Chambers, but in 1931 Leslie Hotson threw all previous attempts to date the play into chaos. Hotson described a feast to honor new inductees into the Order of the Garter that had occurred in Whitehall on April 23, 1597, one month prior to their formal induction at Windsor. Because one of the inductees was George Carey, the patron of Shakespeare's company, and another inductee was Count Momplegard, from one of the German states, who seems to be reflected in the jokes about the German, and because there is a speech to ask the fairies to bless the Garter chairs, Hotson argued that *Merry Wives of Windsor* not only must have been played at this feast, but that it had actually been written expressly for the occasion.[5] This in turn would mean that *1 Henry IV* must have been playing considerably earlier. Since Hotson's book appeared, his arguments have been widely accepted, although with curiously little examination of the ramifications concerned. Because these ramifications are so important to our history, we must make a brief digression to deal with Hotson's arguments.

Despite the general acceptance,[6] there is no practical way in which this dating can be plausible. *Merry Wives* includes Pistol, Bardolph, and Nym, all in scenes that can only be explained as the revival of characters already popular with the audience from previous plays and known to be associated with Falstaff's milieu. The Bardolph in *1 Henry IV* is Lord Bardolph, a completely different character, and in the quarto it is clear that in the original version the character was called Harvey. The characteristics that made Bardolph famous would not be introduced until *2 Henry IV*, where Pistol also first appears. Nym is not introduced until *Henry V*. Thus, if *Merry Wives* is dated in April 1597, both parts of *Henry IV* as well as *Henry V* must be dated during 1595–96, bringing Shakespeare's total for this already miraculous year to a minimum of eight plays, more than one fifth of his total output. Had such output been possible, Meres should have noticed. Surely he would have mentioned a play about Falstaff or Oldcastle alone; there is no way anyone could mistake *Merry Wives* for a play about Henry IV, who does not even appear in it. Similarly, although Meres might see *1 Henry IV* as a play about Henry IV, if the complete sequence existed through *Henry V*, he would automatically identify it as what it is, a sequence about Henry V, not Henry IV.

Even if we somehow can squeeze the play into the calendar, Shakespeare's company did not have the actors to play it in April 1597. First and foremost, *Merry Wives* has no role for Burbage at this date. Although Ford, the largest Sharer role after Falstaff, may be younger than Page, there is no way he could be thought to be in his mid-twenties, as Burbage was at the time. Mrs. Ford "is not young" (II,i,109), and thus neither can be Ford. If Burbage is not Ford, his only other plausible casting is the minute role of Fenton. We could of course cast Burbage as Ford anyway, but then this would leave one of the two middle-aged Sharers, Bryan or Pope, without a role. The third largest adult role is Evans, the meek Welsh priest; the only Welsh accent in previous plays is Glendower, apparently a Hired Man role. Similarly, Slender is the fifth Sharer in size—the known skinny man is Sinklo, a Hired Man who has never had more than twenty-five to thirty lines and must have been nearing thirty years of age. The company's comic old man specialist was Cowley, who was also a Hired Man otherwise playing roles like Old Gobbo, less than forty lines per play. What playwright would write a play as a commission for the company patron to be played before the Queen herself and leave Burbage at home while giving three of the largest roles to Hired Men?

Once we begin to question any of Hotson's argument many of his points become considerably less convincing. For example, Carey was not the only inductee at that feast with an acting company; Pembroke was also an inductee, and we know his acting company was in London and trying very hard to make a big splash at the Swan. Furthermore, are we seriously to believe that, to celebrate the induction of a number of men into the Order of the Garter, Shakespeare would write a play that called one of those men a horse thief? It is true that Momplegard, the German, was not actually present, but it would be a very brave man indeed who would risk upsetting Elizabeth's foreign policy maneuvers by insulting in her very presence a man she was trying to honor. Similarly, Hotson suggested that Ford's alias, sometimes printed as Broome, sometimes as Brooke, was a satirical dig at the Brookes who had caused him such problems. But surely it would lead to even more trouble if Shakespeare suggested to Henry Brooke's face (for he was also an honoree at the banquet) that he would pay someone else to sleep with his wife. This would hardly mend the writer's fences with that powerful family. And other questions arise: When did Shakespeare gain his local knowledge of Windsor, which is unusually accurate? The company probably marched in the parade when the inductees came to Windsor, for Hunsdon brought about two hundred men to swell his train. But that was a month *after* the supposed play performance, not a month before. Finally, Hotson could find no reports of this feast that actually mention a performance, nor are there any unexplained payments to actors in any of the Chamber Accounts of the year.

Thus, despite the widespread agreement, we must conclude that *Merry Wives of Windsor* was not written and performed in April 1597, and that Hotson found a curious set of coincidences, nothing more. With *Merry Wives* no longer dated so early, we can begin to make some sense of the whole Falstaff sequence, with the first play, *1 Henry IV*, appearing in the late spring of 1597.

One other practical factor supports the dating of *1 Henry IV* in the late spring of 1597. It is one of a sequence of about a half-dozen known company plays that make no use of an above. The only possible use of the within is the sleeping Falstaff behind the arras, which can be and usually is staged with Falstaff off stage. Although one might of course write a play at any time with simpler technical requirements than available, this simplicity does seem to suggest that Shakespeare was writing for his company after it had lost The Theatre.

As we would expect in a play primarily concerned with civil war, the female roles are quite brief and undetailed. But this may also reflect a changing of the guard, so to speak. The boys whom we have been able to identify in previous plays all began performing before the plague years of 1593–94 and thus were sixteen or older when Shakespeare was writing *1 Henry IV*. It would have been risky to write major female roles for Cooke, Beeston, Saunder, or Kemp's older boy. But most of these boys had a replacement in place. Although the Hostess is certainly garrulous like Juliet's Nurse, she is a familiar comic stereotype that need not be tied to any particular boy's skills. The role itself is very brief, scarcely forty lines, suitable for a still young performer, and thus is more likely to have gone to Kemp's newer boy, who will grow along with the size of the role in the sequels. Cooke was almost certainly Prince John, a teenager with only slightly more than a walk-on but physically large enough to be a plausible combatant in the field, whereas Beeston, Gough, and perhaps even Saunder are simply invisible. Percy's wife, in two of the most charming and loving scenes Shakespeare would ever write for a married couple, performs only with Hotspur; with Condell playing Hotspur, then this was the same boy who had played Nerissa. Francis, the servant boy always shouting "anon," performs with Poins and Hal, and thus was probably Shakespeare's boy, but might well have been Nick Tooley, Burbage's younger boy who would have been ready for small roles at this date.

During this same spring, the Chamberlain's Men also faced some new competition. The new Pembroke Company that had leased the Swan in February 1597 began to perform after Easter. Thus, as the Chamberlain's Men moved into the inadequate Curtain, a new company in the largest and fanciest theater building in the city stood ready to steal a large part of their audience.

Faced with new competitors and the loss of their theatrical home, the Chamberlain's Men's thoughts rather naturally turned to sequels. Many of the company's previous hits of course could not be cloned: Romeo and Juliet were dead, Portia married and Shylock banished, Richard II fully deposed and dead. For *Richard III*, there was a pre-quel, which probably had already been put on stage, and *1 Henry IV* was as close to a sequel *Richard II* as they were likely to find, which helps explain why Shakespeare took up the subject to begin with. The surprise hit of the previous year had been *Love's Labour's Lost*. Unlike most comedies, it had concluded with the lovers' union unconsummated, so there was an opening in which to expand the play to a second part. Thus, it should come as no surprise that Meres reported a *Love's Labour's Won*. Shakespeare would have begun writing on it as soon as he finished *1 Henry IV*, but before he knew that Hal and Falstaff would merit a sequel of their own, which means it would have reached the stage in the late spring or early summer of 1597.

There has been much speculation about this play. We know that it was printed, for the title was eventually found on a bookseller's list of works for sale in 1603. One possibility of course is that it simply revived all the original characters and dealt with their meeting after the men had spent their year in monastic life. But if such a play existed and had been sufficiently popular to be printed, whether in a good or a bad quarto, it is difficult to explain how Heminges and Condell could have omitted it from the Folio. Thus, most scholars believe the play has survived, perhaps much revised, under a different title. Many candidates have been offered, including *Taming of the Shrew, Troilus and Cressida, Much Ado About Nothing,* and *All's Well That Ends Well.*[7] However, there is a much more obvious candidate that has received remarkably little attention. It requires both the male and female principals to undergo a serious labor before they can be united, the only such instance in all of Shakespeare's works. As in *Love's Labour's Lost*, the major characters are noble, the plot is clearly a part of the pastoral tradition, the upper class characters speak with both wit and graceful poetry, the play ends with a masque, and events are set in contemporary

France (the forest known as the Ardenne). This is, of course, the play we now know as *As You Like It.* The casting relationships are even more detailed. Both require six boys. One of these is a witty tease for the leading man, known by the same name in both plays, Rosaline/Rosalind. Another is a countrified low girlfriend for the Clown—the only instances in all of Shakespeare's works in which the Clown's inamorata is actually seen on stage. Among the adults, *As You Like It* is remarkably easy to cast in early 1597. Burbage would have been the young leading man Orlando, the largest male role, with Condell as the other young lover Silvius. Bryan is the obvious noble Duke, with Pope as the genial and mature Corin. Phillips repeated his verbose philosophizing Armado as the verbose but morose philosophizer Jaques. Heminges and Shakespeare then would be the villains of intermediate age, the usurper Frederick who is younger than the Duke and Orlando's brother who is older than Burbage. Charles the Wrestler is an obvious role for the company big man Duke, and Martext was probably the skinny Sinklo. No play in the Folio, except perhaps *Merchant of Venice*, fits this company more snugly. As is seen shortly, it is almost impossible to cast the roles with the company of 1600, where *As You Like It* is usually dated.

One other factor that points to this particular date is that it is the only time when the most probable Rosalind would be shorter than the most probable Celia. Shakespeare makes a point of the character's height, identifying Rosalind at court as shorter than Celia (I.iii,262), and again repeating that he is shorter than Phebe (III,v,118). This is most remarkable, for when two women go into disguise, we would normally expect the taller of the two to play the boy. Rosalind is of course a much larger role than Rosaline, but there can be little doubt they were played by the same boy, the same boy who played Portia, who also had the largest role in her play. The one physical fact we know about Saunder is that he was shorter than the other boys his age, but it is also clear that he was quite old. Hence, Rosalind spends almost all of the play as a boy. This would be his last hurrah, so to speak, for the boy who had acted with Burbage in *The Seven Deadly Sins* would have turned eighteen around 1598, and we will see no more roles for him as a woman; in 1600, when the play is usually dated, he would have been an adult and may well have left the company. Celia's actor is a little less clear. We know that Condell's boy was taller than Saunder, but he would have been occupied as Phebe. Heminges' boy Cooke was also taller and had played the Princess of France, but he had been the tallest and thickest boy almost a year earlier, which would have made the female disguise look silly beside Saunder's male appearance. Celia rarely speaks to any of the other adults, so she may also have been played by Gough, Pope's very experienced apprentice who must also have been sixteen to seventeen years old at this time. Jaques de Boys had just finished his schooling and was now a "young man" (V,iv,165), so he was probably played by Beeston, who was another boy in his late teens. The Hired Men filled out the court and the Duke's foresters, whereas the younger apprentices who begin to emerge in future leading roles performed the masque of Hymen and sang for Touchstone and Audrey.

Tradition has assigned Jaques to Burbage, but it seems unlikely either in 1597 or

1600. It is a much smaller role for a man who is much older than Burbage and who sings, which Burbage does not do in any other known role, whereas Orlando is the largest male role, macho enough to wrestle, who also gets the girl at the end, the only possible role for a company leading man. A more firmly fixed tradition from the Restoration says Shakespeare played Adam, but this too seems unlikely.[8] The most important physical aspect of Adam is that, like Cordelia, he must be small enough for Burbage to carry easily. Cowley was small, he specialized in old men, and although Adam appears in several scenes, the role is within the size range of a trusted Hired Man who would shortly gain a share of some kind in the company. The man who played Glendower is also a possibility; in *Merry Wives of Windsor*, the man with the Welsh accent is short enough to disport among the fairy children, and as we see here, he too was in line for a share in the near future. Adam could not possibly double either Frederick or Oliver, nor are those roles the size we have seen given to Hired Men in the past. It would have been counterproductive at best to cast Shakespeare as old Adam. If the Glendower actor played Adam, then Cowley played Kemp's country stooge William; if Cowley did his old man routine for Adam, then Kemp's older apprentice, now almost an adult, played William (which may be reflected in the character's name).

If the relationship between these two plays is so obvious, we might well ask why the connection has not been made more often.[9] First, a play called *As You Like It* was registered in the summer of 1600. It was not printed, so we do not know its contents, but the existence of that registration has curiously satisfied almost all scholars that it was also written in 1600, even though similar registrations for other plays have not prevented arguments that they were written years earlier. Similarly, all have assumed that this title was never changed, even while often arguing that other extant plays had begun life as the missing *Won* and had later been given a new title. But the most common reason has been the persistent critical distaste for Will Kemp.

For at least a century, critics have distinguished between Shakespeare's clown, personified by the Peter scene in *Romeo and Juliet*, and the fool, personified by Lear's fool.[10] Will Kemp was replaced around 1600 by Robert Armin, so it has become a commonplace to assume that Armin played all the fools, who were intelligent, sophisticated, and satirical, whereas Kemp played only vulgar, crude, common buffoons. Because Touchstone is described as a "motley fool" (II,vii,13) and is first seen at a ducal court, the usual deduction is that he must be a fool and not a clown, and thus the play must have been written for Armin, not Kemp. There are so many problems with such an assumption that it is hard to know how it could have become so widely accepted. First, throughout the Folio text, Touchstone is merely identified as Clown, as are almost all of Shakespeare's comedians when not given a character name; Touchstone is his disguise, like Rosalind's Ganymede. Second, long after Kemp's era, the crude vulgar clown continued to appear regularly—note Pompey Bum, the clowns in *Othello* and *Antony and Cleopatra*, Autolycus, or Mouse in the company's *Mucedorus*—so the clown's vulgarity was obviously not forced on Shakespeare by Kemp. Nor was Kemp confined to brief roles of gross vulgarity, as we have already noted in his resumé thus far. Third, getting slightly ahead of our story, Armin was known as a fine singer, and once he joins the company, almost all songs fall to his character. Touchstone not only does not sing a note in Shakespeare's most song-filled play, but he also remains on stage silent while little boys serenade him and Audrey. Fourth, the registration date of *As You Like It* in 1600 may well have preceded Armin's actual entrance into the company (see page 85). Fifth, in no later play does the Armin type of clown have scenes with a character who might be played by an apprentice or a Hired Man stooge, whereas *As You Like It* is full of such scenes for Audrey, William, and Martext. Finally, Touchstone's role is actually composed of variations on routines Kemp has done in previous plays: Audrey duplicates Jacquenetta's appearance as well as Launce's jokes; the cross-talk scene with William is standard stuff for Kemp and his stooges or apprentices; Touchstone's duel nonsense is but another variant of Sampson's and Falstaff's attitudes. There is nothing in the role Kemp had not already done elsewhere, and nothing required that he could not do, whereas there are almost none of the components regularly associated with Armin. Thus, there can be no reason why Kemp could not have played Touchstone or why the play itself could not have begun life as *Love's Labour's Won.*

When the Pembroke Sharers had moved into the Swan, they rather foolhardily gave personal bonds of one hundred pounds to Langley to secure the lease.[11] As a new company with a very large debt hanging over their head and playing in a very large theater building, they needed to make a splash very quickly. This would have required a number of exciting *new* plays. For one of these, they turned to Thomas Nashe, one of the most active and colorful of the Elizabethan pamphleteers who only occasionally wrote for the stage, and to a sometime bricklayer and ex-soldier named Ben Jonson, who had found a minor place in the new and expanded Pembroke company during the spring and was willing to try his hand at playwriting as well as acting. The result was a satirical comedy about life in London called *The Isle of Dogs.* The play was a spectacular hit. It was also treasonous, or so Elizabeth thought, and her opinion was the only one that counted. We have no idea what was in the play, because it was immediately banned and all copies were confiscated and destroyed. Nashe left town, but Jonson was slow off the mark and ended up in jail, along with two other actors, Gabriel Spenser and Robert Shaw.

Henslowe closed down the Rose on July 19 but tried a couple of performances in the next week,[12] so the initial Pembroke arrests apparently occurred on July 18 or 19. By July 28, the crisis had far outgrown simple suppression of the Pembroke's Men. On that date, the Privy Council ordered all theaters not merely closed but torn down.[13] I cannot stress enough the seriousness of this crisis. Elizabeth was so angry that she tried to remove all theater from the face of the English earth. It was the greatest crisis ever faced by the English theater, for plagues would eventually end and even Cromwell did not tear down the theater buildings. Technically, Elizabeth's order was never rescinded, although obviously the theaters were not razed. But they were most definitely closed for a long, indefinite period.

To all the actors in all the companies, this edict must have been devastating because it was so unexpected and apparently so permanent. Pembroke's company was all but destroyed, its members scattered if not threatened with execution. During the following winter, a much-reduced group went back out on the road, while Langley exhausted himself over the next few years in pointless lawsuits trying to collect the bonds from men who had no money.[14] The Admiral's Men, as far as we can tell completely innocent in the affair, were devastated. Some of their Half Sharers and Hired Men had already left to join Pembroke's in February, and after the *Isle of Dogs* crisis hit, several other key members deserted. When they tried to perform in the winter, at least seven new men were listed in Henslowe's records.[15] Most importantly, the company star Edward Alleyn retired.[16]

Theatrical tradition has long held that Alleyn retired because he could not stand being less of a star than Burbage. Even more often, tradition has assumed that Alleyn represented the old bombastic, stereotypical style of acting and Burbage the new, more "natural" and complex style. Although a feud is certainly plausible—competing stars rarely are friendly in any period of theatrical history—there is no evidence of any kind to suggest that Alleyn and Burbage represented different styles of performing. Alleyn is often associated with the pre-Shakespearean world because almost all of his known roles to survive were written before 1594. The Admiral's Men did a much better job of keeping their material out of print than did the Chamberlain's Men, and Alleyn in particular guarded his material jealously. The only Admiral's Men plays to be published are by Chettle, Dekker, or Drayton, and all date to years when Alleyn did not perform.[17] Any hope of publication of their old plays after Alleyn's death disappeared when all the company promptbooks burned in a fire at the Fortune in 1621. As a result, we know absolutely nothing about Alleyn's repertory at the Rose, despite the long list of titles in Henslowe's diaries. Any attempt to compare the two actors or the two companies would be like writing a history of British television without any tapes of ITV productions. Alleyn was born in 1566, which made him younger than Shakespeare and only a few years older than Burbage. He seems so much older to us today because he acted in Marlowe's plays, but Marlowe was Shakespeare's age and his early plays were written simultaneously with Shakespeare's early plays. Alleyn grew up in the same theatrical world as did Shakespeare and Burbage, and there is no evidence whatsoever to suggest that Alleyn personified a different or cruder style of acting. In 1597, Alleyn was thirty-one, hardly an old man by any standards, and Burbage had not yet played Hamlet or Othello or Lear, so any jealousy would have been on Burbage's side, not Alleyn's.

There was also a story that Alleyn had been frightened off the stage by the Devil himself, who was conjured up by accident in a performance of *Doctor Faustus*. The two allusions to the event say it occurred at The Theatre, where Alleyn last performed in 1591, or the Bel-Savage Inn, whose only known use as a performance space was before 1590. There was a single performance of *Doctor Faustus* in Henslowe's Diary for 1597, but that came in October and oddly enough has no income recorded. Given Alleyn's absence from all further records that winter, this was probably Alleyn's farewell performance, staged as a benefit for Alleyn himself.[18] The legend stands as testimony to Alleyn's skill and power to convince his audience, but little more. If there was any single reason why Alleyn chose to retire in 1597, it was because he had become a very wealthy man and did not wish to risk losing that wealth, and perhaps his life, in the theatrical climate that followed *The Isle of Dogs.*

Nor were the Chamberlain's Men untouched by *The Isle of Dogs.* Initially, they used the actor's traditional first resort in time of crisis—they got out of town. Records have been found of performances in Dover and in Bristol during September,[19] indicating a fast-moving company. Before they left town, they apparently tried to distance themselves from any possible political repercussions. Shakespeare changed Oldcastle's name to Falstaff (not that it mattered much if they could not perform again) and they dropped *Richard II* from the repertory. It was registered on August 29 and printed shortly thereafter (but without the deposition scene). This was an extremely good quarto, so clear that it can only have come from someone with access to Shakespeare's papers,[20] indicating that it was a printing authorized by the Sharers or Shakespeare or both, further underlined by the addition of Shakespeare's name on the second printing. According to Augustine Phillips, it was never performed again until the Essex fiasco in 1601, despite a popularity that led to three editions within a year. Thus, the printing must have been intended to signal to the court that the company had no plans to perform the play again. Although it did not eliminate the play from memory, it at least shifted the onus to the printer and confined its potential influence to the literate and wealthy minority.

During 1597–98, an unusually high number of Chamberlain's Men plays appeared in print in bad quartos. *Richard III's* bad quarto was registered on October 27, 1597. At about the same time, unauthorized versions of *Romeo and Juliet, Love's Labour's Lost,* and *Love's Labour's Won* appeared, although only copies of *Romeo* have survived. The simple existence of these four bad quartos tells us that Shakespeare's plays had become immensely popular. But they also indicate some serious changes within the company itself.

The most widely accepted explanation for most of the bad quartos is that they were memorial reconstructions, texts put together from memory by one or more actors who were, at some point, involved in a performance of the play. Because printers then as now were most likely to be interested in popular, *recent* work, actors were most likely to reconstruct work shortly after they had been involved with it. An actor who was an active member of a company might well lose his job if it were learned that he had supplied such a reconstruction, for a play once printed could be performed by anyone. Thus, the most likely sources for these printings were actors who were no longer acting in their previous company. This was almost certainly the reason for the printings of *Titus Andronicus* and memorial versions of other early Shakespearean plays during 1593–95, when many actors were jobless due to the plague and almost all the companies reorganized, leaving former Hired Men without hope of further employment with the same company. Which at last brings us to our point: the sudden appearance of such a large number of the reconstructed versions of plays belonging to the Chamberlain's company at this time must indicate that one, probably several, Hired Men had been let go.

It would help if we knew precisely when the two *Love's Labour* quartos were printed, but because both have disappeared we cannot be more precise than sometime in 1597. It is often argued that the *Romeo and Juliet* quarto, although unregistered, was printed in March because it identifies the company as Lord Hunsdon's, and Hunsdon became Lord Chamberlain on March 17.[21] If it was in fact printed at this time, then at least one of the sources for the reconstructed text was probably Gabriel Spenser, one of the probable Hired Men introduced in chapter 1. He was gone from the Chamberlain's Men by February 1597, when his name is found in the newly expanding Pembroke company at the Swan. However, he could not have been on tour with the Pembroke company before February. A particularly contentious fellow (he eventually was killed in an argument with Ben Jonson), Spenser was cited by a coroner's court on December 3, 1596, for killing a man; he was apparently acquitted on grounds of self-defense. Because he was under arrest awaiting his trial, the Chamberlain's company would have needed to replace him on stage in December, and because he went to another company after his aquittal, that replacement must have been permanent.

Spenser may well have been aided in his reconstruction by Humphry Jeffes, whom we earlier identified as a probable Hired Man in the Chamberlain's Men. Jeffes is not known to have been in the Pembroke company during the spring of 1597, but those records are necessarily incomplete. He had definitely moved to the Admiral's Men by October, where later transactions indicate he originally held only a half share,[22] exactly what we would expect for a new member whose previous stage experience had been confined to Hired Man roles (and income). He and his brother Anthony may have left about the same time as Spenser, or may have moved during the chaos of the summer. The sale of *Richard III* in October would have provided him with at least some of the capital needed to obtain his Admiral's share. Two of the new Hired Men added to replace them will be introduced in detail later, but we should note here the addition of a new man with a pock-marked face, who will be seen most vividly in the lower class Bardolph of the coming years.

Of course, these personnel changes would not have mattered if the theaters had in fact been torn down. No one knows why or when, but at some point Elizabeth's fury over *The Isle of Dogs* calmed and she relented. Jonson was released from jail on October 8, so official ire must have been somewhat mollified by then. Henslowe's diary shows some new performances beginning October 11, but these were very tentative, totaling only four for the entire month. His daily journal stops on November 5 in the middle of a page, suggesting erratic performances at best. From that point, he shifts to notations of weekly receipts into March 1598, and every week shows some income.[23] However, until February, only Christmas week provides him with more than fifty shillings income, amounts that during the previous year were earned with as few as one or two performances. Thus, it seems clear that the Rose was not in daily use during most of the winter. This would seem to indicate a tentative testing of the official waters that prevented the Admiral's Men from performing a regular full schedule of six performances a week.

We must assume a similarly tentative and abbreviated return to the stage by the Chamberlain's Men. To some degree, all the actors had been forgiven by Christmas of 1597–98, for the Admiral's Men without Alleyn twice performed at court. The

Chamberlain's Men were seen four times. One of those four was *Love's Labour's Lost*, and probably *As You Like It/Love's Labour's Won* was another. Given the problems with the Brooke family, we can assume they did not bring *1 Henry IV* as well, no matter how popular Oldcastle/Falstaff might have been. But the lifting of the legal restrictions against performances would not help the company much if they could not soon find a suitable theater in which they could regularly perform.

As the year 1598 began, the company's primary concern was to get back on stage somewhere on a regular basis. Apparently, the Chamberlain's company were still in the Curtain, because a performance of *Romeo and Juliet* was seen there by John Marston about this time,[24] one of Saunder's final appearances as a woman. However, Marston identifies the play and the Curtain, but not the performers, and because the play had been published in 1597, another company may have been performing it. Certainly, by early 1598, both Saunder and Burbage were growing awkwardly old to be continuing their original roles. If the Chamberlain's Men were at the Curtain, they were still unhappy about it, because the Burbages were still negotiating with Giles Allen to re-open The Theatre in the spring.

It is probable that at some time in early 1598, the Chamberlain's Men revived Marlowe's *Edward II*. Originally printed in 1594 and again in 1595, the work received a new quarto during 1598, the most likely stimulus for which would have been new performances. A later quarto identified the play as belonging in 1622 to the Queen's Men, but their predecessor company, Worcester's Men, did not exist in London before 1600. Nor were any performances recorded at the Rose by Henslowe at any time. Thus, the Chamberlain's Men are the only company likely to have produced it in this decade. Although we cannot know how the printed quarto was modified, if at all, for the actual performance, we can be sure Burbage would have taken Edward, one of the great starring roles of the era, designed for a performer about the same age as Burbage. Phillips would have been a powerful Mortimer, with Condell a most plausible Gaveston. Isabella, who spends far more time with Mortimer than with Edward, was probably Beeston, forced by the demands of the role to put on a dress one more time, while Phillips's much younger boy Gilburne played Isabella's young son, Prince Henry (see also Chart B). Of course, it is also possible that the new edition may have been stimulated by the great popularity of the quartos for *Richard II*, which had many parallels to (and perhaps borrowings from) Marlowe's play. Hence, we can at this point claim the play only as a probable, but not certain, part of the company's repertory.

During that winter, the company released *1 Henry IV* to a printer, registered on February 25, 1598. This quarto is all but identical with the Folio, a draft in Shakespeare's own hand,[25] and can only have come from Shakespeare himself, with the agreement of the other Sharers. Both the timing and the quality of this edition indicate that, as with *Richard II*, the, Chamberlain's Men had decided to avoid all potential political problems by washing their hands of the play. The text shows numerous signs of hasty, and clumsy, revision, with many jokes about the name Oldcastle and similar name confusions for Bardolph/Harvey and Peto/Russil. Given that Oldcastle jokes were still current for years,[26] it is altogether likely that the character was called Oldcastle on stage until the theaters closed in mid-1597. In that case, the name was changed to Falstaff solely for the printing.

That Falstaff was never seen on stage during 1597 under that name in Part I is underscored by the curious epilogue of *2 Henry IV*. There the audience is reminded that "Oldcastle dyed a martyr, and this is not the man" (F3348). That information would have been unnecessary if the audience had seen Part I with Falstaff rather than Oldcastle; had that been the case, the epilogue should have been added to the end of Part I.

What seems to have happened is that Shakespeare and his partners completely withdrew Part I after *The Isle of Dogs*, sending it to the printer with the name Oldcastle changed to Falstaff and only minimal further revision. Nevertheless, Oldcastle/Falstaff had been far too successful a character to abandon completely, particularly because the company had faced considerable financial difficulties due to the recent closures and the loss of their regular theater. Thus, as soon as Part I was taken off the boards, Shakespeare began writing a replacement. This appeared very early in 1598, for by February 28, Essex wrote to a friend ridiculing Henry Brooke as "Sir Jo. Falstaff."[27] Apparently, the printer did not notice that the play on stage was different from the one being printed, for the title page of Part I identifies it only as "The Historie of Henry the Fourth."

2 Henry IV was a most unusual sequel in Elizabethan terms. The logical follow-up historically would have been to see Hal take the throne and then invade France; instead we see the mopping up of the civil war, with Hal not even appearing until II,v. Part II is not so much a sequel as a rewrite of Part I, with new tavern scenes, new quarrels with the Hostess, a new exposure of Falstaff's lies, yet another scene in which Hal disappoints his father, a new war in which Falstaff tries to avoid fighting, and a new scene in which he claims a victory he did not earn. This is not the pattern for Elizabethan sequels, in which the succeeding parts of the story are often very different in plot and/or tone (see the two parts of *Tamburlaine* or *The Spanish Tragedy*). It is not so much *Falstaff II* as *Falstaff Redux*. The new play did not mention Oldcastle at all, thus solving the problems with the Brookes. Just to be sure the Brookes were mollified, Shakespeare added the curious epilogue.

One other point should be mentioned about the epilogue, for it provides a valuable insight into Shakespeare's and his partners' attitudes to playwriting. Despite the stunning rejection of Falstaff in the last scene, neither Shakespeare nor the company intended it to be final. The epilogue reassures everyone in the audience, telling them the rejection was purely for public show, just as Falstaff claimed, and that Falstaff will return in the true sequel, which will deal with Hal's wars in France (F3345–47). At the very least, this indicates that Shakespeare was already beginning to plan *Henry V*. It also indicates that neither Shakespeare nor his partners had intended Falstaff's rejection to have the dramatic weight it has assumed in recent years, preferring to keep all commercial options open.

2 Henry IV also gives us some of the clearest insight into both Shakespeare's and the company's desire to use all the Sharers effectively. At the end of Part I, Hotspur, Blunt, Douglas, and Worcester were dead, and Glendower had simply disappeared.

Thus, at least four Sharers and a major Hired Man needed new roles for the sequel. Interestingly enough, we see five significant new characters in Part II. First, Prince John becomes a major character. This may of course have been the boy Cooke, but Condell, who often played Burbage's brother and was good with a sword, now needed a role, which John fulfills perfectly. Both the Lord Chief Justice and the Archbishop now become major roles. The Justice's appearance is particularly odd, because there was a famous historical instance of young Hal striking him which did not appear in Part I. Now the Justice has a wholly invented scene with Falstaff. Pope, who played Worcester, and Heminges were both free. Northumberland is quite mature, but the role is remarkably brief given his historical importance, both signs pointing to the Hired Man who had played Glendower. This still left Phillips, the most probable fiery Douglas of Part I, with nothing to do. Enter a flamboyantly verbose and fiery lower class character, Ensign Pistol, a comic inversion of Douglas without a sense of honor or a touch of bravery. It is a comparatively small role, but it had a major impact on the audience, as indicated by his mention on the cover of the first quarto of Part II. His introduction here is doubly revealing because, like the Chief Justice, he should have been in Part I as well. But in Part I, Phillips had something else to play. Not until Phillips needed a role did Shakespeare decide to invent Falstaff's colorful comrade.

Finally, there is Justice Shallow. We know that Cowley played comic old coots like Verges and Old Gobbo, and Justice Shallow is the very epitome of the comic old coot. He plays all his scenes with Falstaff, so we would automatically turn to a member of Kemp's comic team, where Cowley has been since 1594. But Shallow is an enormous role, well over two hundred lines, and Cowley has to this point played only roles of a size suitable for a Hired Man; there are also the multiple scenes with Davy, the performer's apprentice, which Cowley as a Hired Man would not be likely to have. It is at this point that we may notice Shallow lives in Gloucestershire, just over the county border from Shakespeare's home in the Cotswolds, and sharing much the same accent as Shakespeare would have spoken off the stage. We may also recall the tradition that Shakespeare had played old Adam, another very old man far older than any of the Sharers might in fact be. We have seen no particularly significant role in *2 Henry IV* that must have been played by Shakespeare; Poins, whom he probably played in Part I, disappears from the sequel with plenty of time to allow Shakespeare to change and to sprinkle white powder in his hair. And, as we shall see, Shakespeare is the only Sharer who might be free to repeat the role in *Merry Wives of Windsor*. Thus, when all things have been considered, Shakespeare seems the only likely nominee. The remaining cast members continued in the same roles they played in Part I, as we would expect in a sequel (see Chart B).

At some point during the winter of 1597–98, George Bryan decided to retire. No one has previously established a precise date, but it is universally accepted that he was gone before 1599. In a rep company, the loss of a Sharer threatens to throw the entire company out of work. Unless someone is on hand to step directly into all that actor's roles, the company simply does not have any material that can be put on stage and must either reorganize the company or reorganize the repertory. If relations with the retiree are friendly, he can minimize problems by giving notice and then gradually phasing himself out of performances. He would continue to play his usual roles in extant work, but in all new plays, the company would commission no roles for him. Thus, when they reached the last performances of his old material, he could withdraw fully, sell up his share, and retire.

Ideally, the company would also look for a replacement and gradually insert him into the company, first in new roles in new plays, then perhaps taking over some of the retiring Sharer roles in more long-lasting plays. In a company as carefully balanced as the Chamberlain's Men, they would naturally look for a replacement who at least looked mature, to maintain some balance in ages within the company. He should not be as old as Bryan, for then he might himself grow ill or retire suddenly, but he should be old enough to play characters older than Heminges or Shakespeare, men now in their mid-thirties. We can identify just such a person in the plays we have dated from the spring of 1597.

At that time, a Hired Man appeared with a most unusual identifying skill, a Welsh accent, first seen in Glendower. Shakespeare rarely specified unusual accents for his characters; with the exception of Dr. Caius, the only ones to come readily to mind are the Welsh accents of Glendower, Fluellen, and Evans. Scotsmen such as Douglas of course may have had accents, but there is no hint in the text itself of any attempt to require it. (Curiously, although everyone makes fun of Don Armado's verbosity, no one mentions his Spanish accent.) The last such requirement in company records is Rees ap Vaughan, the second largest role in Dekker's *Satiromastix* of 1601. Glendower with his single scene is too small a role for a Sharer in 1597 or earlier, while Evans and Vaughan are far too large for a Hired Man later, so this must have been someone new who began as a Hired Man but became a Sharer rather quickly, and then disappeared from the company by the time Queen Elizabeth died. He also obviously looked mature, for Glendower has a married daughter.

This new man is, I believe, Samuel Crosse. He is listed among the Principall Actors in the Folio. That list is more than a little confusing, for at least three of the men listed joined the company after Shakespeare quit writing. It is obviously not arranged in order of either age or size of Share. However, the first eight names can be demonstrated by other evidence to have been in the original company, whereas the last eleven can be shown to have joined after 1610. The ones between are mixed rather randomly, as we shall see in more detail, but their placement does seem to indicate they were second-generation Sharers, joining after the original Sharers of 1594 but before the late group. Crosse's name sits in the middle of that group, but he is not cited in any of the 1603 Sharer lists. Thus, he apparently entered the company later than 1594 but retired or died before early 1603. Nothing definite is known about Crosse. In 1612, Thomas Heywood mentioned him as someone famous "before my time,"[28] and implied he was in the Queen's Men, although his name is missing from the surviving records of that company. If Crosse was in the Queen's Men, then he had probably been touring with that company since 1590 or earlier, making him an experienced and mature actor by the mid-1590s. The Queen's Men had passed through London briefly in the summer of 1595, taking on some new players that included Henslowe's brother,[29] which would indicate that some old players left. This would have been the logical moment for Crosse to retire from that company. Why he did not stay in retirement can only be conjectured—perhaps he fell on hard times and was given a chance to return to the stage by one of the several members of the Chamberlain's Men who might have worked with him in the Queen's company before Heywood's time. At any rate, we see a very mature man become obvious among the Hired Men with Glendower, one who very soon rises to Sharer roles that disappear after 1602. He need not have actually been Welsh, for the accent does not appear in every play; on the other hand, an experienced actor would have learned to suppress an accent that most of his audience thought comical whenever it was not needed for effect. Crosse is the only likely candidate, the only listed Principall Actor who could conceivably have been of the right age at this time.

That Crosse was intended for a Share from the moment he joined the company is indicated by the fact that the actor playing Glendower also has an apprentice. Glendower's daughter speaks only in Welsh to him, which Shakespeare leaves to the pair to improvise, a scene that would only have been possible between a master and his apprentice. It would have been most odd for a career Hired Man to have an apprentice, and I have found no other indications of any boys tied to Hired Men, but it is perfectly plausible for an experienced actor who is only temporarily acting as a Hired Man while waiting for a Share to become available. (Later, in *Merry Wives of Windsor*, the actor with the Welsh accent will do another foreign language routine with his apprentice, young Page's Latin lesson.)

By 1598, Bryan was, very possibly, the oldest actor alive in England, and he must have known his roles would only grow smaller each year as his partners began to mistrust his memory and his stamina. If he had any doubts about his future, the jailing of the three Pembroke actors in the summer of 1597 would have tipped the scales. However, his relations with the other Sharers were still pleasant, so he probably continued to perform at least his older roles during early 1598 until finally surrendering his share. Bryan's portrayal of the dying Henry IV thus probably marked his last appearance with the company, his retirement becoming final at the last performance of Part II.

When he retired, Bryan would expect to be reimbursed for his share. The company was much more successful than in 1594, with a large repertoire of scripts and a collection of costumes and props, all of which Bryan had helped pay for. A new Sharer would have to be not only of suitable age and experience but also have some capital. The company Hired Men, although serving faithfully since 1594–95, would have had little chance to accumulate any capital, and most of that would have evaporated during the closures of the previous year, when they had had no work at all. Given the size of the roles that are seen in the next few years, it is most likely that Bryan's share was split in half. One half of the share went to Crosse, whose roles increase dramatically in size during 1599.

The other half of Bryan's share probably went to a new man who can be first seen in a Hired Man role in *2 Henry IV*. In that play, we see two unusually thin men, Shadow, thin as "the edge of a pen-knife,"(II,ii,262) and Feeble the tailor. Sinklo, the company's skinny comic Hired Man, could not have played both, for they are on stage together. Thus, during the closures of late 1597, the Chamberlain's Men added a second thin actor. In succeeding years, we see Sharer-sized roles for a thin, youngish but not attractive man with a wispy beard—Slender, Aguecheek, and Horace in *Satiromastix*. As these roles indicate, advancement to Sharer-sized roles would come quickly for this actor. Sinklo, the company skinny man, might have taken some of these later roles, of course, but he was never mentioned on any of the Sharer lists or among the Principall Actors. On the other hand, William Sly was. Sly is not only named in the Folio but was also a Sharer of sufficient prominence and wealth to eventually hold a share in the Globe. The surviving portrait of Sly does not show a particularly thin face, but it was painted years later, when he was more mature and more successful. Given the options, Sly is the only plausible candidate.

Sly is assumed to have originally been an apprentice of Augustine Phillips, but by the time of *The Seven Deadly Sins* plot, he was old enough to play young adults, such as one of Gorboduc's sons; assuming that the Harry who played the other son was Condell, then Sly was roughly the same age as Condell. In 1594–95, he had been listed by Henslowe as some form of Sharer in the Admiral's Men, but he was not among the members of the new Admiral's company indicated by Henslowe after October 1597.[30] The Admiral's Men had been as stable as the Chamberlain's until 1597, so it is clear that Sly changed companies during that year, almost certainly during the *Isle of Dogs* closure when all the groups were trading members. Sly, having sold out some form of share when he left the Admiral's Men, would thus have had the capital necessary to buy out half of Bryan's share.

We have no irrefutable proof that Shakespeare's company offered any half shares, but there is a great deal of evidence to indicate that half shares were common in the period,[31] not to mention Horatio's joke to Hamlet about them (III,ii,272–3). The Lady Elizabeth's Men in 1611–13 even had "three-quarters sharers."[32] The common practice was for the Sharers to meet after the performance, pour all the money onto a table, and divide it up. The smallest English coin of the day was the farthing, a fourth of a penny, and daily financial transactions thus would be most easily conducted in multiples of four. As noted earlier, the old touring companies seem to have most often consisted of eight Sharers, and this company clearly began with eight shares, and it is most unlikely that the remaining Sharers would have voluntarily reduced their income from all future performances. It would thus have been both simple and traditional to split both income and expenses into eight equal portions and then, if there were more than eight Sharers, have two people split one of those portions in half. If the company were successful, such a half-share holder would still earn far more than a typical Hired Man.

Thus, in July 1598, the company consisted of nine Sharers: Burbage, Condell, Heminges, Kemp, Phillips, Pope, and Shakespeare with full shares, Crosse and Sly with half shares.

It is from this season that we see the earliest extant new company play not by Shakespeare, Ben Jonson's *Every Man in His Humour*. Perhaps because of his *Isle of Dogs* problems, Jonson set this satire in Italy, but no one was much fooled. By the time it appeared in his folio, the scene had been returned to London, where it is placed in all revivals.[33] In that 1616 printing, Jonson included a cast list identifying players but not their roles. The list included Shakespeare first, with Burbage, Phillips, Heminges, Condell, Pope, and Kemp following. "Will. Slye" marks the first notice of his membership, and John Duke and Christopher Beeston conclude the list. Crosse is not mentioned, nor are significant comic performers such as Cowley or Sinklo, but that need not be taken to prove that they were not participants; many of Jonson's other lists are significantly incomplete. The play itself has at least a dozen significant adult males who cannot be doubled, so there were several important players in addition to those listed. Jonson's list actually dates from many years after the fact, after Sly, Duke, and Beeston had all become famous names in the Elizabethan theater whose mention would help increase the status of Jonson's material. Both Beeston and Duke deserted the company for a risky new one within a couple of years, which they would have been unlikely to do had they held even half shares in the far more prosperous and stable Chamberlain's Men. Their inclusion here can be taken as solid evidence that they did perform in the play, but does not prove they were Sharers or that they played large roles.

All Jonson's plays appear at first glance to be more difficult to cast from our perspective, simply because they are *different* from Shakespeare's work, on which all our initial analysis has been based. Jonson's comedy depends on satirical comic types, and thus pays little or no attention to the ages concerned. And there are some questions about the relative size of roles because some of the plays are known to have been revised by him before printing (see *Sejanus* and *Every Man Out of His Humour*), although the length of most others indicates either similar unadmitted post-production revisions or extensive pre-production cuts (see *Volpone, Catiline*, and perhaps *Alchemist*). Using Jonson's list, and the other actors whom we can be sure were present but not mentioned by him, we can cast *Every Man in His Humour*; however, the existence of multiple versions of the play, both of which are a little long in relation to the other known comedies performed by this company, means we cannot be quite as certain about the actual size of certain roles that should have been played by Half-Sharers in the original production. Kemp played either Cob the water carrier or Bobadilla the braggart soldier, similar to Falstaff, but since Cob is a commoner with a comic wife, suitable for Kemp's apprentice who had played Jacquenetta, Cob is far more likely. In that case, Pistol/Phillips played Bobadilla. Justice Clement is a merry old judge, which points to Pope. Thorello/Kitely, the jealous husband, is the largest role, quite suitable in age for Burbage and the first of many such insanely jealous husbands he would play in both comedy and tragedy, with his younger apprentice Nick Tooley as his wife Biancha. Several years later Jonson would write a brilliant, mercurial servant called Mosca, very similar in character to Musco/Brainworm in this play, and there is strong evidence that Mosca was specifically designed for Condell; thus, there is a very strong likelihood that Condell also played Musco here. Lorenzo Junior rarely speaks to his father but does play several significant scenes with Bobadilla, suggesting Beeston, the old apprentice of Phillips who was by this time about eighteen. As we have seen, the company had no genuinely young Sharers at this time, with everyone the same age as Burbage or older; such a large role as Lorenzo Junior would be most unlikely for an adult Hired Man but would not be at all unusual for an experienced boy. Giuliano/Downright is several times described as "a big, tall man" (IV,ix,53), which fits what we know of Duke, and the role, although significant, is very brief, so this seems his most probable assignment. Of Jonson's list, we still have Shakespeare, Heminges, and Sly uncast. There is a guilty pleasure in thinking of Shakespeare portraying the bad poet Matteo, but the larger role of Prospero/Wellbred is equally likely, given his age, and his boy has played only very brief roles that fit with the size of his sister Hesperida. The country cousin Stephano/Stephen, who desires a duel and generally gets everything wrong, would have been plausible for Sly, whom we will later see playing the similar Aguecheek. Since Lorenzo Junior was still a teenager, Heminges or even Crosse could have been his father, but the size of the role favors Heminges, leaving Crosse as the city gull and poetaster. Both Matteo and Stephano are relatively long roles for Half-Sharers, but they are also the two roles that could most easily be trimmed in performance.

Jonson's play probably did not reach the stage until late summer, for we know that a German tourist had his pocket picked at a performance around September 20, 1598.[34] Thus, it was contemporary with one of Shakespeare's most popular comedies. *Much Ado About Nothing* was not mentioned by Meres, but it was registered on August 4, 1600, and quickly printed in a good quarto. As life for the Chamberlain's Men would become rather confused in early 1599, the second half of 1598 is *Much Ado*'s most likely production date.

Benedick is so large a role, and Claudio so comparatively small, that there can be no doubt that Burbage played Benedick, with Condell as Claudio. Benedick is also an invented character not in any of the probable sources,[35] tailored precisely for the actor who would play him. Burbage's apprentice Tooley must have played his love interest Beatrice, for Saunder was far too old by this time. As discussed in chapter 2, Tooley was apparently brought in to be Saunder's replacement, meaning he was fourteen or so in 1598. Although Beatrice is a witty, intelligent woman, it is clear that she is a woman, not a girl; there is something about her that makes her seem much older than the other women of the play, a spinster rather than an ingenue, quite different from the witty Portia, Rosaline, and Rosalind who had earlier partnered Burbage. There will be something more mature about Burbage's females over the next few years. This may indicate something physical about Tooley, although it is unlikely he was fat, the usual way to indicate female maturity; most likely, his voice was a little heavier than that of the other boys, so that he sounded less girlish in relation to them. Condell's apprentice then would have been Hero.

Dogberry and Verges are identified in the Folio as Kemp and Cowley (F2000, ff.). Verges is nonetheless a very brief role, so it is likely that Cowley was still a Hired Man at this late date. The same funny-looking Hired Men we have seen since *A Midsummer Night's Dream* filled out the rest of the watch, augmented by the pock-marked Bardolph actor. Borachio is Spanish for drunkard, so Phillips, the man who played the drunkard Pistol, seems most plausible. Leonato is the only father, so that must have been Pope. His brother Antonio is a very small role suitable at most for a Half-Sharer like Crosse, leaving Sly as Conrade, the other significant Half-Sharer sized role. Don Pedro and the villain Don John remain for Heminges and Shakespeare. Heminges, in general, seems to have played more handsome roles in the past, so Heminges is slightly more likely as Pedro, leaving Shakespeare as the villain John. On the other hand, Shakespeare's receding hairline would have made him look older, so we can not be absolutely certain.

The Folio lists Jacke Wilson in a stage direction for the scene in which Balthasar sings "Sigh no more, ladies" (F868). There are two John Wilsons known in the era. One was baptized April 24, 1585, making him thirteen when *Much Ado* premiered. He was a professional musician as an adult, mentioned as a member of a town band in 1621. The other, born April 5, 1595, was also a musician, a famous lutenist and composer who wrote songs for the King's Men as early as *Valentinian*, usually dated 1614. This would make him seventeen when *Much Ado* played at court in the winter of 1612–13, and thus equally plausible, if the Folio direction comes from that production. Balthasar has a previous scene flirting and dancing with Margaret, however, which makes it clear that Balthasar was not a boy's role. Thus, it seems most probable that Jacke Wilson was not Balthasar but was inserted in the directions to be the accompanist for Balthasar. As both the Jacke Wilsons were lutenists, the stage direction could date from either production, and it is even possible that Jacke Wilson in the premiere was replaced by Jacke Wilson in the revival. Balthasar was thus almost certainly the same singer who had played Amiens, the Hired Man we have tentatively identified as Peter.

Burbage's next comic role was probably the least romantic of all lovers in dramatic history, Petruchio. Modern scholars have yet to agree on a date for *The Taming of the Shrew*, although all believe it was one of Shakespeare's earliest works.[36] A play called *The Taming of a Shrew* was printed in 1594 and attributed to Pembroke's Men. Fortunately, we need not resolve the relationship between the two plays here, where our concern is the date at which the Chamberlain's Men may have actually performed the play. A second printing of *A Shrew* appeared in 1596, which would suggest a performance of a Shrew play in that year. However, Shakespeare's *Shrew* has always been one of his most popular plays, and there can be little doubt that it was extremely popular in his own day as well. But if the play were as popular as its later history indicates, then Meres should have listed the play in 1598 as one of Shakespeare's comedies. So significant is that lacuna that for many years, *Taming of the Shrew* was thought to have been the missing *Love's Labour's Won*. Because Meres did not mention the play, we must assume the first Chamberlain's Men production came after mid-1598, after Meres had finished his work. On the other hand, *Taming of the Shrew* has an enormous role for a traditional company clown of the type often played by Kemp; it is extremely unlikely that the Sharers would have opted to revive the play during 1599, when their relations with Kemp were most strained and unpredictable. Thus, the last half of 1598 seems the only plausible date, on the same grounds as are universally accepted for the dating of *Much Ado*.

The text is notoriously confused in many places, suggesting revisions and modifications that may have crept in over any number of years.[37] Nevertheless, all modern critics and all modern verbal analyses indicate the play is an early work, and it would be difficult if not impossible to argue on stylistic grounds that it was written, even in part, between *Much Ado About Nothing* and *Julius Caesar*. The knock-about routine for Petruchio's servants is unique to Shakespeare's version, and since it fits so neatly with the comic Hired Men in Dogberry's Watch, it does seem probable that this was in fact new in 1598. But with that one exception, the play was probably revived rather than newly written.

In fact, the play may well have been cut in performance. As the Folio text stands, there are too many Sharer roles for any date from 1594 to 1607, when it was almost certainly revived. That problem, however, disappears if the Sly scenes are cut. When that happens, one of the two fathers, Vincentio, becomes a half-sharer role, as does the Pedant, while Christopher Sly himself, another half-share role, is completely eliminated. The Sly scenes altogether total just over 300 lines; their removal would leave a play of well over 2,400 lines, longer than *Comedy of Errors, Two Gentlemen of Verona*, and *The Tempest*, and such a cut was relatively common in productions until fairly recently.[38] Baptista, the more genial and ineffectual father with a full sharer role is suitable for Pope, with Crosse then as the half-share Vincentio. Petruchio and Lucentio would be Burbage and Condell. The Pedant is left by default to Sly, who is too young to impersonate Condell's father, although his thinness would be in the center of the stereotype for academics in the same vein as Holofernes. But Tranio, actually the second largest role, Hortensio, and Gremio are three men of very different ages. Gremio, the old pantaloon, is a caricature, and thus playable by anyone with powder in his hair and a funny stoop; if Shakespeare did in fact play Shallow, then he would certainly have also played Gremio at this date. Heminges and Phillips have always played men visibly older than Condell or Burbage, so Tranio comes as something of a surprise for either, but both would be suitable for Hortensio. There is a plausible Kate, Burbage's boy Tooley who had played the shrewish but more witty Beatrice, whereas the other women have such small and stereotypical roles that they could have been played by any of the younger boys. Only Biondello stands out; he is identified numerous times as a boy who should still be in school, so he must have been played by an apprentice, and because most of his longer scenes are played with Baptista, this must have been one of Pope's apprentices. Because Gough was already quite old at this time, Edmans is more likely. Kemp was obviously the principal clown, Grumio.

Although the company had a number of popular successes during 1598, it is unclear where the Chamberlain's Men were actually performing. As we have seen, they began the year in the Curtain but were not happy about it. Cuthbert still hoped to make a deal with Giles Allen, but that collapsed around Michaelmas in late September, when Allen announced his intention to tear down the building despite a Burbage offer to double the rent.[39]

The situation was desperate. Obviously, the Curtain was unsuitable, or they would not still have been trying to get back to The Theatre. The only other option was the Swan, whose landlord was even more cantankerous and contentious than Allen.

The court seemed to love the company, the populace certainly loved them, every play they touched seemed to turn to gold; life would have been perfect if they could just find some place to perform.

There is a possibility that during the summer, they did in fact move to the Swan. Shakespeare himself had some business relationship with Langley, for both were named during November 1596 in a lawsuit by one William Wayte for sureties of the peace, something like a modern restraining order.[40] What that relationship might have been has never been explained, nor why it also included the two women also cited, but the connection is clearly there. The Swan was new, it was large, and it was certainly available, for Pembroke's Men were long gone. In February 1598, the Privy Council formally suppressed an un-named "third company" in London.[41] The most likely candidate for that suppression is the reformed Pembroke group; if so, then they were definitely gone no later than Lent of 1598. Surely the Chamberlain's Men at least considered the possibility of the Swan.

Curiously, in *Much Ado About Nothing*, Borachio tells Conrade to "Stand thee close, then, under this penthouse, for it drizzles rain" (III,iii,101–02). As it happens, we have a sketch of the interior of the Swan, copied from one made in 1596 by a visiting Dutch student named Johannes de Witt, which seems to show just such an overhanging balcony across the rear of the stage. I say seems because the sketch is amateurish and unclear. Perhaps no drawing in history has led to more dispute among scholars. So, all in all, it cannot be used as inarguable proof in this question.

There are good reasons why the company would have wanted to try the Swan, even had The Theatre not been well and truly out of reach. Not only was it the most modern performing space in the city, but it was also well beyond the reach of City authorities, on the south bank of the Thames. One of the least examined questions about the decision to build the Globe is why the company did not simply lease the Curtain instead and then remodel it to fit their needs, which would have been cheaper and would have maintained access to their traditional audience. Before the Globe, the Chamberlain's Men had been the northern company. Any move across the river would risk the loss of most of their regular audience, for whom south bank access was inconvenient, expensive, or both. The decision to build the Globe across the river on the south bank of the Thames would have seemed far less risky if the company had in fact tested the waters, so to speak, by performing successfully for some period at a south bank site. The only one available at this time was the Swan.

We know they lost the Curtain at some point, because a new company appeared there. But the date when this happened is unsettled. Lord Strange had patronized a company in which many of the Chamberlain's Men had performed prior to 1594; shortly after the Chamberlain's Men had been organized, Strange's heir, William Stanley, now the Earl of Derby, patronized a new company that spent most of its time touring in the provinces. In February 1600, they received payment for a performance at court. They would only have been invited if they had a current London presence, so they must have been performing regularly in the town for some time during the previous year of 1599. Platter, the same tourist who saw *Julius Caesar* at the Globe in September 1599, saw another play the next day at what from his description of the location "in Bishopsgate" can only have been the Curtain.[42] He does not name a company, but Derby's is the only likely candidate. Obviously, they moved into the Curtain when the Chamberlain's Men vacated. Records exist of this company on tour in October 1598; since they were also on tour in October 1599,[43] they most likely established the London reputation that brought them to court at some point between those two tours, perhaps as early as the autumn–winter of 1598–99.

If the Chamberlain's Men did move to the Swan, they were as unhappy there as they had been in the Curtain. The Burbages in particular had grown desperate. Because the Blackfriars could not be used, the brothers were in effect bankrupt. When Allen claimed that the lease gave him rights to any improvements on his land and threatened to tear down the building, the Burbages saw what little remained of the family estate evaporating. Richard in particular was not one to calmly surrender family assets, as his attack on the Widow Brayne in 1590 indicated. Richard and Cuthbert concocted a daring plan; over the Christmas holiday season of 1598–99, while Allen was at his country property, they brought in a crew of carpenters and stole The Theatre, post by post. According to Allen's later lawsuits, they

. . . then and there armed themselves with divers and many unlawful and offensive weapons, as namely, swords, daggers, bills, and axes, and such like, and so armed . . . in very riotous, outrageous, and forcible manner . . . attempted to pull down the said Theatre . . . then and there pulling, breaking, and throwing down the said Theatre in very outrageous, violent, and riotous sort, to the great disturbance and terrifying not only of your subjects, said servants and farmers, but of divers others of your Majesty's loving subjects there near inhabiting.[44]

The courts eventually ruled in favor of the Burbages, although it was a moot point by then.[45] At the time, however, the whole affair was a case of cutting off a nose to spite the face. They may have kept Allen from getting the building, but they owned nothing more than a pile of lumber. The Burbages needed income, and the Chamberlain's Men needed a home. The only solution to both problems was for Cuthbert and Richard to build a new theater.

❧ Chapter 4 ❧

The Globe and Kemp's Exit, 1599–1600

The new theater building was, of course, the Globe, which in our time has become synonymous with Shakespeare's work. A large building holding more than two thousand spectators, it was constructed on the south side of the Thames, an area technically outside the legal jurisdiction of the Lord Mayor of London, and already home to the Rose, the Swan, a bear pit, and a large number of taverns and brothels. It stood on a site owned by Nicholas Brend, to the east of the Rose and the Swan. Audiences coming from London proper had to cross the river by boat or walk across the only bridge, on the site of the modern London Bridge. (The modern reconstruction is west of the Rose, somewhat further from the bridge.)

It has become a convenient shorthand to say that the Chamberlain's Men built and owned the Globe. A closer study of the record indicates a somewhat different arrangement. Because Richard Burbage was a member of the Chamberlain's Men, the company became in effect a permanent resident, but the Globe was no more "owned by the Chamberlain's Men" than was the Rose or the Fortune owned by the Admiral's Men, who played in them equally uninterruptedly.

The confusion is caused by the unusual way in which Burbage financed the building's construction. Theaters then as now were very risky ventures. If a company was successful, a landlord who took a share of the box office would make a great deal of money. But if there were no hits, there was little income. And if the theaters were not able to open—due to plague, politics, or the lack of an available company—there was no income at all. Henslowe's diaries indicate a profit of perhaps sixty pounds a year between 1592 and 1597, after deducting normal expenses and the remodeling he paid for.[1] That looks like a substantial income only because it does not include his initial cost of construction; he may never have recovered his original investment. The Burbages owned a perfectly suitable indoor theater from which they had derived no income for years, and the *Isle of Dogs* affair had demonstrated to all potential investors that the Elizabethan theater had no secure future. In addition, the Burbages had a terrible business reputation. Dismantling The Theatre was a colorful exploit, but it was unlikely to encourage investors to trust them to honor their financial agreements in future.

As a result, the Burbages turned to the only investors willing to risk a new theater, the members of the Chamberlain's Men who were desperate for a theater space. On February 21, 1599, a consortium signed a lease for land owned by Nicholas Brend. Shortly afterward, using the lumber taken from The Theatre, they hired Peter Streete, the contractor whose crews had dismantled the old theater, to build a new one, to be called the Globe. But it was not a partnership of equals—Cuthbert and Richard Burbage retained half as their share. The other half was split among five actors, Shakespeare, Pope, Phillips, Heminges, and Kemp.[2] Thus, it included most of the full Sharers in the acting company and looked like an acting company project, but in practice, the arrangement was completely separated from the acting company. First, it included only those members of the company with enough capital to invest, apparently about a hundred pounds in cash for each. There were no half shares and no inclusion of the actor Half-Sharers we have identified, nor curiously, was Condell included. More significantly, the shares were immediately converted from joint tenant shares to tenancy in common. This meant that the shares could be sold outside the Chamberlain's Men or passed on to heirs who had nothing to do with the company.[3] Most were passed to nonactors within a very short time. Had the Globe been an acting company project, then the shares in the building would have been passed along new actors as part of their company membership. Most importantly, however, the two Burbages retained 25% of the building each. Thus, the Burbages with their 50% were in actual control. They could not take unilateral action without the agreement of at least one of the other partners, but even if all five of the others banded together, they could not force a decision without Burbage agreement (see Chart F). To maintain that control, the Burbages were willing to borrow a large sum at what Cuthbert claimed were ruinous interest rates.[4] The need for a theatrical home may well have been a major motivation for the five investors, but the Globe itself was a Burbage real estate project too expensive to build without additional capital from associates. Because Richard was an actor, his associates were actors. But in no way should the deal be interpreted as a theater built and owned by the Chamberlain's Men.

Once the decision to build the Globe had been taken, it would have been very difficult for them to perform in any other space. What landlord would rent to them, knowing that they intended to leave at a moment's notice? As noted earlier, Derby's Men were quite probably in the Curtain by this time as well, closing off that option for a performance space.

Nor does it seem likely that the Chamberlain's Men might have gone on a tour that spring, as has been suggested to explain the brief bad quarto of *Henry V*.[5] While the Globe was under construction, the partners would be needed to supervise the construction. No Elizabethan builders worked from blueprints. At least one of the partners would need to be available on almost a daily basis both to answer questions and to make sure that the workmen were in fact erecting what had been agreed. This would have been very difficult to do if they all had to perform every day, and impossible if they were performing in the provinces. Cuthbert, of course, was no actor, so he would naturally deal with most of the construction problems, but even so, precisely because he was no actor, the other partners would want to be kept up to date.

All of these factors point to an end of company performances no later than February 1599. When the other theater companies began to play again after Easter, the Chamberlain's Men were standing around in the English spring rains waiting for the contractor to finish the job. Most of the partners had committed all their capital to the project, and no one had any income. The later success of the Globe has obscured the desperation with which it was built. The partners in the building were all mature men who had staked most, if not all, of the capital they had accumulated over a long performing career. Since the summer of 1597, despite the acting company's popularity, the actors themselves had been living hand to mouth without a regular, dependable London home; and due to the combination of politics, Lent, and the search for a theater, they had not performed at all for about half of the previous two years. If the Globe should fail for any reason, most if not all of the men would be bankrupt. And there were any number of ways in which the venture could fail: Elizabeth could close the theaters again, without warning or even reason; the builder could run into unexpected delays that prevented the opening for months; the company's old audience might decide it was too far to walk to come see the plays on the south bank; the new plays commissioned might be failures; some actor might suddenly fall ill or be killed in a duel or a tavern brawl. Should any of those things have happened during 1599, the acting company would most likely have been broken up, with Richard Burbage taking the remnants on tour to escape the bailiffs. As a man with property outside of London, Shakespeare would have been able to return to Stratford with some financial stability, but we would never have had *Hamlet*, *Othello*, *Macbeth*, *King Lear*, or *The Tempest*. Much was at stake as the company waited for the Globe to be ready for an audience.

There must also have been considerable tension. Although we cannot identify the precise arguments and crises of this spring, we can guess they existed, because they always do in the course of major construction. But we also know they existed because the apparently comfortable family of the acting company cracked up. When *Henry V* reached the stage that summer, Falstaff was gratuitously killed offstage and Kemp was nowhere to be seen. Because Kemp had invested in the Globe in February, he obviously had intended to remain a part of the company in the new building. It must have taken a major disagreement to have driven him out.

More than likely, the argument had been festering for some time. As we have seen, within the past two years, the company had developed two stars, Kemp and Burbage. Very few companies can survive with two stars, even if one is comic and one serious. In general, scholars have laid the blame on Kemp, partly through the general scholarly distaste for clowns and partly because he was the one to leave. But Burbage was the man with the muscle in 1599, and if any particular conflict grew into a crisis, Burbage must have been a major contributor. Richard Burbage may have been the most trustworthy and sincere of partners; no one at this distance *knows* otherwise. But then, the assault on the Widow Brayne's representatives in 1590, who had merely tried to collect money legally due to her, and his "theft" of The Theatre would seem to indicate that compromise and problem solving were not high on his list of personal priorities.

Whoever was at fault, it is obvious that there was an explosion that resulted in Kemp's exit at precisely the moment it could have done the most damage to the company, only a few days before the Globe was ready to open.

When the Globe was ready is still a matter of much debate. We know it was in operation before September 21, because, as noted earlier, a tourist named Thomas Platter saw *Julius Caesar* there on that date. A surviving inventory of Brend's property shows "de novo edificata" on May 16,[6] but there is no practical way it could have been completely finished so quickly. When Streete built the Fortune later in 1600, he promised seven months but took much longer; because the Globe was Streete's first theater, it certainly would not have been built significantly faster. Construction would not have begun until the lease for the land was signed in late February, for the Burbages had learned from their experience with Giles Allen not to build on another man's land without written guarantees. Thus, using the Fortune timetable, it would have been August or September before the building was ready. However, as John Orrell has indicated from his detailed study of the Fortune's construction, most of Streete's time was spent in obtaining and hewing the timbers; once they were available, the building itself rose in about three months.[7] Because the Burbages had a pile of timbers already cut to order, it was thus at least possible for Streete to get the Globe in shape for use within little more than three months. This would make early June the earliest possible date of the opening.

Steve Sohmer has recently argued on the basis of complex astronomical and astrological computations that *Julius Caesar* first played June 12, 1599.[8] Despite the detail of this argument, I find it hard to accept that, in the midst of simply trying to make sense of his material in a dramatic fashion, Shakespeare took time out to fill it with astrological codes that would either be incomprehensible to the audience (and invisible to all readers for four hundred years) or, if comprehensible, would make nonsense of the second and all succeeding performances. Although we can certainly believe that Shakespeare or someone in the company arranged astrological readings that might designate June 12 as the ideal opening date, it is far more difficult to believe that the vagaries of the weather, the capriciousness of the Master of the Revels, and the usual habits of building contractors all managed to be suspended so that everything finished on a schedule that allowed them to open on that day.

Far more likely is that the building opened about the same time as the premiere of *Henry V* in July or very early August. The Chorus in *Henry V* congratulates Essex on his great success in Ireland (V,30–32), which is only explicable in July, for by August everyone knew Essex had made a mess of the war again.[9] However, the

Prologue/Chorus is missing completely from the bad quarto printed in 1600. Because this is obviously a memorial reconstruction made by minor actors,[10] it indicates that the Prologue/Chorus either was not actually performed or at the most was performed only once on the opening day and then dropped from all further performances, thus making it impossible for the minor actors to hear his speeches often enough to reconstruct them. *Henry V* is precisely the kind of play one would expect to be used to open a new theater—intensely patriotic, vividly spectacular with large crowds and battle scenes and numerous brilliant court costumes, celebrating arguably the greatest moment in English history. It also included a popular role for the company's leading man, Richard Burbage, playing a character he had already established with great success. And it offered a chance for another appearance of the phenomenally popular Falstaff character, as promised in all the performances of *2 Henry IV* during the previous season. Nothing could have been more carefully calculated for the opening of a new building.

Unfortunately, Falstaff did not appear in *Henry V*. Falstaff dies in the most traumatic way possible for an actor—offstage. Many textual scholars are convinced that this was a last-minute decision, as large chunks of dialogue too numerous to detail here seem to have been written for Falstaff and then simply reassigned to different characters.[11] These confusions are present in the bad quarto of 1600, even more garbled but easily discernible, so we can assume that no version containing Falstaff ever reached the stage. The principal beneficiaries of this revision seem to have been the actors playing Pistol and Fluellen, now among the very largest roles in the play. With Phillips repeating a popular characterization, Pistol's increase would have been a crowd pleaser, whereas the expansion of Fluellen indicates the respect in which Crosse with his Welsh accent was held, despite technically holding only a Half Share. Burbage of course was Hal, the star of the play, with his French counterpart the Dauphin another hothead with a sword suitable for Condell to play. The only father figure is the French King, so that must have been assigned to Pope. Shakespeare and Heminges in their mid-thirties seem the only likely Canterbury and Exeter, which leaves the French Constable to Sly. The only Sharer in a position to double the Chorus is Canterbury, who disappears after Act I, and it is certainly attractive to think that Shakespeare the writer was also the narrator. However, he could not have spoken the Prologue as well, for Canterbury enters on the heels of the Prologue's exit, which may explain why the narrator has two different names; if Prologue and Chorus were two different speakers, then the Prologue was almost certainly Phillips, who as Pistol is the last of the full Sharers to appear on stage. Slow, silent Gower would have been taken by the strong silent Duke. The cocky Nym was probably one of the shorter players; of the Hired Men, the most trusted was obviously Cowley, who was short and sufficiently mature to be a Corporal. All the female roles but the Hostess are brief and bland, with the lovely Katherine primarily characterized by her fractured English, suggesting Crosse's boy who seemed to have a knack for languages, or at least accents. However, Katherine also has a lady-in-waiting, a much smaller role more suited to Crosse's boy, leaving Tooley as the most likely Katherine. The largest boy's role is actually Pistol's boy who, although playing a lad disgusted by his master, must have belonged to Phillips, indicating he was played by Samuel Gilburne, the boy who replaced Beeston. We have seen him previously in relatively brief roles, but by 1599 he would have been fourteen or so, more than ready for more fully developed characters.

In all likelihood, then, Shakespeare actually wrote the play during 1598, just as he had promised in the epilogue of *2 Henry IV*, with a substantial role for Falstaff. Once the Burbages decided to build the Globe, the company Sharers, recognizing it as an ideal play for the new theater building, postponed its opening. Then, as the official opening of the building drew near, tempers flared and Kemp walked out. Shakespeare made a hurried rewrite and the company performed the play without Kemp.

One of the plays alternating with *Henry V* all but certainly was the anonymous *A Warning for Fair Women*. It was printed in 1599 as "lately diverse times acted by the right Honorable, the Lord Chamberlaine his Servantes." There is as usual much argument about its dating, with many tracing the script back to about 1590.[12] Even if true, it is clear from the quarto that the Chamberlain's Men had the work on stage very shortly before its printing. However, as we have seen, the company was in the inadequate Curtain for most if not all of 1598, and *A Warning for Fair Women* makes some enormous demands on a stage's technical facilities. A tree grows up out of the ground in view of the audience (ll. 1266–70), the dumb show reveals a banquet table from behind curtains (ll. 778–80), and the character Browne is hanged on stage, indicating both a trap door and some place overhead where the rope could be attached. Assuming that the printed text, whatever its original date of composition, reflects the work as actually staged by the Chamberlain's Men, then this can only have happened in the new Globe. Given the relatively late start to the Globe performances and a printing in 1599, the play must have been one of the earliest productions to reach the Globe stage.

A Warning for Fair Women is a *domestic tragedy*, a modern term used for dramatizations of lurid current events of the day. In practice, this usually meant wife murdering husband, as in *Arden of Faversham*, the primary model for all of these works, or husband murdering wife or child, as in the company's later *Yorkshire Tragedy* or Heywood's more famous *Woman Killed with Kindness*—almost always with adultery as a motivation. It is a genre generally thought to be beneath Shakespeare's talent, although *Othello* follows all of the conventions except an English setting. *A Warning for Fair Women* is not a particularly great play, but it serves to remind us that the company produced more than English history and elegant comedy. In the details of Captain Browne's romance with the married and reluctant Anne Sanders and his eventual murder of her husband, we see for the first time the company members playing average people from the everyday world of modern London. Burbage of course would have been Browne. Only one truly middle-aged character has any prominence, the boisterous Old John, who seems to have a very personal relationship with his buxom boisterous maid, suitable for Pope and a chubby apprentice who must have been Edmans. (The lack of a second middle-aged role for the retired Bryan underlines the dating of 1599.) The second largest male role is Roger, Anne's servant, who has served her for seven years "man and boy" (140) and thus should be no older than his mid-twenties. No one among the Sharers was so young, but Condell usually played the foils to Burbage, and Anne actually has more of her scenes with Roger than with Browne, suggesting she was played by Roger's apprentice. The murder victim Sanders and his neighbors Barnes and James are all mature men, suitable for Heminges, Shakespeare, and Phillips (Barnes and James feel very much like one original role split in half for two Sharers). In that case, then the brave servant John Beane would have been played by Sly and the Lord Justice by Crosse, both suitable roles for Half-Sharers. Browne spends far more time with Anne Drury, the conniving neighbor who dabbles in witchcraft, than he does with Anne, so this must have been Burbage's boy Tooley, who as we have previously suggested was able to project more maturity than the other boys of the time. As with so many of the older scripts revived in this era, we can not know if the dumb shows so popular in the plays of the 1580s were included in the revival production. These at least seem possible, because they are spoken almost exclusively by boys, with the principal narrator Tragedy quite a substantial role. The brief scene for the two commoner carpenters is the kind of thing Kemp did regularly, with either Cowley or perhaps the old apprentice who was now an adult, but it is also the kind of scene that could be taken at short notice by two Hired Men. Thus, it is one of the few plays that have survived from this season in which Kemp could be quickly replaced without major revisions of the script.

One early Shakespearean work may also have been thrown into the breach. Both parts of the *True Contention* plays were reprinted in 1600, suggesting some production of plays on the subject during 1599–1600. These of course need not have been by the King's Men, but the company did have versions in their repertory. One of these, *3 Henry VI*, featured no significant role for Kemp, so it is an obvious candidate for revival during the emergency of the first couple of weeks after Kemp left. Burbage would have been the only genuine personification of Richard Plantagenet for Elizabethan audiences, which would have certainly been an additional attraction for the Sharers (see Chart B). We might argue that this was the company's first production of the play. Earlier, I suggested that the play was introduced in 1596–97, when Meres might have thought of it as one part of a play sequence about Richard III, but it is possible that Meres did not mention it because it was not introduced until after 1598. Whether first revival or second, the fact that it could be played without Kemp if necessary makes the 1599 performances all but certain.

Many scholars think that after Kemp was written out of *Henry V*, he never returned and that he never played at the Globe at any time.[13] However, this seems unlikely, to say the least. Most obviously, if he left irrevocably in the summer of 1599, his partners would have been forced to buy out both his acting share and his Globe share. However, the costs of the Globe had been so great that few of the other Sharers would have had enough cash on hand to make such a buyout until the company had been playing for some time. Second, Platter seems to have seen Kemp on stage. After the performance of *Julius Caesar*, he saw "two in men's clothes and two in women's" dance what was probably the jig, although he described it as "extreme elegance." Without Kemp, the company had no clown for the jigs, and in September Kemp's eventual replacement, as we shall see, was still performing at the Curtain with a different company, where Platter saw him as well.[14] One of those Globe dancers was most probably Kemp. Third, *The Return from Parnassus*, staged at Cambridge sometime during the academic year 1600–01, portrayed Burbage and Kemp as partners, friends and members of Shakespeare's company. The author was sufficiently informed about London theatrical life to mention the War of the Theaters (see p. 111), so he should have noticed if Burbage and Kemp had not performed together for eighteen months or more. And finally, anyone in the company could have delivered the dramatic report of Falstaff's death. That the Hostess did so, who had previously been twice played by Kemp's apprentice, would certainly suggest that the company had not yet broken cleanly with Kemp.

Nor is there any evidence that the company was able to replace Kemp in 1599. Because the Chamberlain's Men did eventually find such a replacement, the difficulty in doing so is often glossed over rather casually. To replace a comic is hard enough, for the comedian needs very special and specialized skills. But to replace a star comic means that you must find another star comic. In 1599, there were only three possibilities in the nation, John Singer, George Attewell, and Robert Armin. Singer and Armin were both working, Singer with the Admiral's Men, and Robert Armin at the Curtain. Both would be unlikely to want to change companies at this point, for they had established themselves with routines, associates, and regular audiences where they were. Attewell, who had been with Strange's Men in 1591 and had authored and/or performed the most famous published jig of the day, had a house in London by 1599, suggesting he had retired from touring and might have been available. If the Chamberlain's Men talked to Attewell, he turned them down, for he is listed in no records of the company at any time. Singer was already around forty and on the verge of his own retirement in 1602–03; to change companies at such an age would have been an absurd career move. That left only Armin. However, Armin either hesitated or resisted, or perhaps was not even approached in July 1599. He published two joke collections, *Foole Upon Foole* and *Quips Upon Questions* a year later during 1600, and both identified him as the Clown of the Curtain,[15] so he was rather obviously still there long after the Globe opened in the summer of 1599.

Even a temporary loss of Kemp would have placed the company in a difficult position. They had ordered a number of new plays for their new theater building, most of which would have had significant roles for Kemp. The majority of their most successful past material, including all the romantic comedies and the Falstaff plays, demanded Kemp. Even had Armin come immediately, he would have provided no easy solution to this problem, for he was everything Kemp was not. Kemp was large, normal in facial feature if common in his routines, and a famous dancer; Armin was very short, ugly, a wit with a much greater verbal than physical arsenal, and one of the finest singers of the day.[16] If the Chamberlain's Men somehow convinced Armin to come, it would require the complete revision of *everything* in the company repertoire, which if nothing else would mean a great deal of money paid to writers at a time when the financial resources of the Sharers were nearly exhausted. Since we know Armin was not with the company until at least a year later, and as we shall see, because we can identify very plausible Kemp roles in some plays later than July 1599, it seems likely that Kemp and his nemesis, whoever that may have been, "kissed and made up" as actors are famous for doing.

Kemp's return is in fact strongly supported by the evidence of the plays actually performed by the Chamberlain's Men during the autumn of 1599. All the other new plays performed in that year have very obvious requirements for a clown of the physical size and performing style of Will Kemp. It is true that Ben Jonson does not list Kemp in his cast list for *Every Man Out of His Humour*, which is usually offered as evidence that Kemp was gone for good, but, as we shall see, Jonson neglected to list a number of other members of the company, including Shakespeare, and there is an obvious Kemp role in that work.

There is no clearly identified Clown role in *Julius Caesar*, on stage in September, but there would have been plenty for Kemp to do in the play. The "serious" Sharers had much to do among the nobles in the large cast, most doubling characters in Rome and on the battlefield; thus the company needed all its "commoner" Hired Men and Clowns to appear more than once. The various Plebeians speak about 5% of the lines, an unusually high proportion for commoners in Shakespeare's work, with another 10% of the lines scattered among soldiers, servants, and minor noble and military Romans. The jokey cobbler in Act I was almost certainly intended for Kemp, whereas the senile poet who appears in Brutus's tent is a bit for Cowley as the old coot; but there were plenty of other characters in between to keep Kemp and all his stooges busy.

Burbage was Brutus of course, but the real fascination is Cassius, who has more than five hundred lines. Lean of look, slightly older than Burbage, and a most convincing speaker, this can only have been Phillips. Pope was the oldest man available, so he would have been Caesar himself. Antony, however, is more difficult to cast, because the company had no Sharer who was younger than Burbage. Still, Condell usually played the handsome mirror of Burbage, so he is our best guess. Given what we have established previously about appearances, Heminges was probably the martial Messala, doubling one of the smaller conspirator roles such as Decius. This would have left the largest remaining conspirator role of Casca to Shakespeare (which perhaps coincidentally allowed the writer with "little Latin and less Greek" to say "it was Greek to me" [I,ii,281]). Crosse and Sly, Half-Sharers still, doubled or tripled, with Sly probably as Pindarus.

Brutus' wife Portia, although a brief role, would have been Tooley, with the small boy Lucius probably Tooley's future replacement making a very young first appearance. Calpurnia would have automatically gone to Pope's younger apprentice Edmans. Cooke, Gough, and Beeston were for all practical purposes adults, whether they had finished their bonds or not. Cooke thus probably played Octavius, the youthful adopted son of Caesar who has only about fifty lines, whereas the others filled out the Plebeians and soldiers. We have no idea what happened to Saunder after he quit playing women; if he was still in the company, then he was probably Strato, the servant who helps Brutus commit suicide.

Every Man Out of His Humour was registered on April 8, 1600, and then printed almost immediately. To have exhausted its run so that it could be printed at that date, it must have been popular several months earlier. However, Jonson's play also alludes to *Histriomastix*, written in 1599, which in turn had alluded to *Every Man In His Humour*, so *Every Man* must not have appeared before the Globe opened. As a result of his murder trial following the duel with Spenser, Jonson had seen his property confiscated. He had been forced to return to brick-laying in April 1599, so he had not yet been paid for the play at that time; Henslowe recorded payments to him and Dekker in August and September for *The Page of Plymouth*,[17] the first of several works for the Admiral's Men. Thus, it seems likely that Jonson finished *Every Man Out of His Humour* between April and August, after which he ceased to write for the Chamberlain's Men. This in turn would suggest the play reached the stage in September, about the time Platter saw *Julius Caesar*.

In his folio edition, Jonson noted a cast of Burbage, Heminges, Phillips, Sly, Condell, and Pope. Kemp was not listed, but then neither was Shakespeare. Because the play has at least eleven male principals with more than one hundred lines in multiple scenes that make doubling implausible, it seems safe to say that the original production included more than the six Sharers Jonson listed. However, with Jonson there is always the possibility that the printed text includes much material that was not performed. The cover of the first quarto claims to contain "more than hath been Publickly Spoken or Acted," so some significant cuts were made before performance (or additions were made expressly for publication). The play has well over four thousand lines; assuming Shakespeare's comedies were the typical performing length, then more than 1,500 lines must have been cut in rehearsal, a substantial chunk of the play. This means we cannot be sure of the comparative size of the various roles, making it very difficult to spot the two Half-Sharers in particular. We can, however, be relatively sure that Cordatus and Mitis, prologue and commentators who expound Jonson's theory of comedic humours, were not performed at such length, if at all,[18] and there are very suitable roles among the remaining characters for all the known full Sharers at this time, including the actors Jonson did not name.

The largest role probably was not taken by Burbage, for it is the comedian's role of Buffone. Buffone is a joker, a drunkard, a large "banquet beagle . . . (who) will swill up more sack at a sitting than would make all the guard a posset"[19]—in other words, a Falstaff. He has a long knock-about scene in a tavern with a set of comic commoners, another of the long line of routines with stooges that Kemp had performed since *A Midsummer Night's Dream*, and he dances. The only possible casting is Kemp, demonstrating both that the role was written for Kemp and that he must have returned to the company in time to play it.[20] Next largest are Macilente, the scurrilous troublemaker, and Fastidious Brisk, the slave of fashion. Macilente is a "lean bald-rib" (V,iv,21), certainly the same lean and hungry look of Cassius; Brisk plays the viol, which would seem to point to Phillips, who left a large collection of such instruments in his will. However, if Phillips is Brisk here, then the lean and hungry actor must have been Burbage, meaning Burbage played Cassius, which would overturn everything we know about Burbage. Brutus has always been understood to be the star's role, the tradition running unbroken all the way back to Betterton, and major Burbage roles in later years, such as Hamlet and Macbeth will feature much the same combination of nobility and vacillation, so we must assume that he was always intended to play Brutus. Thus, Phillips must have portrayed Macilente and Burbage Brisk, with the viol playing done badly for a joke, as the lines about untuned strings indicate. There is only one father, Sordido, who is described as a "boisterous whale" (I,iii,68) and thus must have been Pope. The temperamental swordsman and bandit Shift is a character type who would normally be played by Condell, but it is the smallest of the principal roles, and he is a bandit who is all bark and no bite; he is also approaching forty, for he served in Holland "in my Lord of Leicester's time" (III,vi,50–1) and his obsession with becoming a "tall man" (V,iii,60) indicates the pugnaciousness of the short, all of which point away from Condell and toward Crosse. There is another very important role for a man of about thirty, the besotted husband Deliro, who also has an experienced apprentice as his wife Fallace. Condell's apprentice was now the most experienced of the boys in the company, and had usually played beautiful women such as Hero, so he and Condell seem more likely as the Deliro/Fallace pair. Shakespeare and Heminges then split Puntarvalo, a stiff-necked man of inappropriate seriousness, and Sogliardo. Sly then would have been Sordido's son Fungoso, in the printed text a larger role than we would expect for a Half-Sharer, but with many of the characteristics of Aguecheek, whom he will play in the future. The other significant female, Saviolina, is obviously Brisk's apprentice, indicating Tooley.

One other new play further underlines Kemp's continued presence, *Thomas, Lord Cromwell*, registered and printed in August 1602. Although it is sometimes suggested that this is a revision of a much earlier work that predates the formation of the Chamberlain's Men, the most recent scholarly analysis dates the extant text in 1599–1600 from a number of topical allusions.[21] As might be expected from its title, the work features an enormous role for Cromwell, with more than a quarter of all the lines in a brief text, certainly portrayed by Burbage. However, the second largest role is Cromwell's servant Hodge, an obvious clown role, who begins the play as a blacksmith. This can only have been Kemp, for his eventual replacement Armin, given his small size, could never have been a plausible blacksmith. Thus, it seems clear that Kemp was still performing in highly visible roles throughout this first Globe season. There are numerous roles in *Cromwell* for the whole company, perhaps with several Sharers doubling as they did in *Julius Caesar*. Cowley is obvious as Hodge's ridiculous father, but because of the brevity of the extant text, we cannot be as certain of the size of roles, making other Sharer assignments extremely tentative (see Chart B).

Cromwell's primary interest today is that its cover claimed "Written by W. S.," and most studies focus on the authorship question, in search of some plausibly dull and incompetent author to whom we might assign blame to remove this blot from Shakespeare's record, with little attention paid to the contents of the play itself. The text is brief, garbled, and simplistic and is almost certainly a memorial reconstruction, although no scholar has yet bothered to try to firmly establish this. The clarity of the scenes with Hodge stand in sharp contrast to the other scenes, reminiscent of *The Merry Wives of Windsor* bad quarto reconstructed also in 1602, where Kemp's scenes seem far better remembered than those involving other actors, Burbage in particular. Such a reconstruction would not necessarily show Shakespeare's hand any more clearly than does the *Merry Wives* quarto, and if Shakespeare only revised a few scenes of an earlier work, then his hand would be even less obvious. Nor would there be any particular reason to include it in the Folio.

Cromwell introduces one other minor but significant addition to the company's assets—a model of Burbage's head displayed after Cromwell's execution. It must have been an expensive investment, so it comes as less of a surprise that in a while we will rather gratuitously see Macbeth's head on a pole as well.

Given what we know about actors in general, it seems all but certain that after his return Kemp would have expected a new starring vehicle to replace the lost Falstaff role in *Henry V,* perhaps even demanded it as a condition of his return. Once Kemp was back in the fold, the Sharers would have wanted Falstaff to come back to life as well, for he was an exceedingly popular character. Thus, it would have fallen all but automatically to Shakespeare to devise a Falstaff play as quickly as possible. Because Falstaff was dead in the history sequence, Shakespeare could not turn to Holinshed for help; instead, he turned to comedy of a type that would become a staple in the English theater, a sex farce in which the sex is never consummated.

We know the play as *The Merry Wives of Windsor.* Legend has it that the play was written in two weeks, because Elizabeth wished to see "Sir John in love."[22] Although unsupported by any evidence from the era, the tradition certainly fits the slapdash feel of the script. The text is loosely constructed even by the standards of the day, with characters and subplots appearing and disappearing for no discernible dramatic reasons, and no logical connection between the Falstaff sequences and the traditional young lover plot. It looks very much like a set of new Falstaff scenes grafted rather clumsily onto some other play.

However Shakespeare may have fabricated the concoction, the important question here is when all this happened. As discussed in some detail previously, the April 1597 date proposed by Hotson is most unlikely. But all of the objections noted in chapter 3 disappear if we place the premiere in the winter of 1599–1600. Even the legend that Elizabeth requested the play becomes believable; because all productions known to have played before Elizabeth occurred between Christmas and Lent, the most logical time for her to make such a request would be in the winter, leading to a very hurried production. *Every Man Out of His Humour* and *Thomas, Lord Cromwell* indicate Kemp was still active at that date. The rest of the cast now fits the extant adult company like the proverbial glove, exactly as we would expect to find in a comedy thrown together quickly for a rep company. Phillips and Shakespeare simply repeated their earlier turns as Pistol and Shallow, as did the Hired Men who played Nym and the pock-marked Bardolph. Ford was obviously Burbage's role, the largest male role after Falstaff and a jealous husband of about Burbage's age of thirty or so. Both the size and the accent of Evans' role makes far more sense, now that we have seen Crosse play Fluellen. Hot-headed swordsman Condell would have played the hot-headed duelist Caius, sporting a comic French accent, perhaps not too different from his French accent as the hotheaded Dauphin in *Henry V*. Slender is left for Sly, which makes equal sense because we saw him enter the company as a thin man and he had at least a half-share as well by this time. The tiny role of young Fenton would then have gone to one of the former boys, probably Alexander Cooke, out of his apprenticeship but not yet a Sharer requiring longer romantic scenes.

Normally, the father role would fall to Pope automatically, in which case Heminges would have played the Host. However, the stereotype of the tavern owner throughout all of history has been a genial fat man, which points to Pope. Page is the father of a daughter of marriageable age, so he need not be as old as would the father of a son in a similar situation; Heminges could plausibly fit. In the past, we could turn to the apprentices to help resolve this question, but the boys raise an interesting problem in themselves. Mrs. Ford was Tooley, Burbage's experienced boy; she is "not young" (II,i,109), and Tooley has shown a tendency toward mature women in his casting assignments. Mistress Page is one of the best-kept secrets in Shakespeare, the ninth largest role he wrote for a woman, longer than Viola, Lady Macbeth, Cressida, or Juliet's Nurse. (If Queen Katherine in *Henry VIII* is counted as Shakespeare's work, then Mistress Page is the tenth longest female role.) It is such a large role and such a unique character—the only comic mother in all of Shakespeare's work—that it could not have been written for an untried boy. It can only have gone to an experienced boy who could also suggest middle age. The surest sign used on stage to indicate female middle age is fat, and we have identified a comedic fat boy who by this time would have been able to take on roles of more than two hundred fifty lines—Kemp's second apprentice. As it happens, Mrs. Page rarely even speaks to her husband, playing most of her scenes with Mrs. Ford or Falstaff, or both, which would make Kemp's boy the only plausible choice.

It may be possible to identify this particular boy. Within the next ten years, a new clown called William Rowley would grow prominent among Shakespeare's competitors. Little is known of Rowley's early life, but he is assumed to have been born around 1585, which means he would have begun an apprenticeship around 1595, precisely when Kemp would have been looking for a replacement for Bee. Rowley later became famous as both clown and playwright, best known today for *The Changeling* and *The Witch of Edmonton*. The first plays on which he collaborated were performed in 1607 by Queen Anne's company, the royal version of Worcester's Men, where Kemp took himself and his apprentice when he left the Chamberlain's Men. In 1609, Rowley joined the Duke of York's, indicating he was a young man with no more than a half share in Queen Anne's Men. Even more importantly for our question, he was famous as a very fat clown. Rowley's identification as Kemp's fat, second apprentice lacks documentary evidence, but it is nevertheless strongly circumstantial; Rowley was the right age with the right appearance, he first appeared in the right company, and was a clown very much in the Kempean manner, who must have apprenticed with a Kempean clown to learn his craft. Kemp is the only likely master.

With Rowley as Mrs. Page, it would mean that Mistress Quickly was not played by the boy who had played Quickly in the *Henry IV/V* plays. Shakespeare goes to considerable effort to place her in Caius' household, so we must assume that, despite the name, she was understood to be a completely different character played by a completely different boy. The question is: What boy? It is a very large role, and she plays scenes with almost everyone in the company, both indicating considerable experience and maturity. Both factors would seem to point to John Edmans, who had played Pope's boisterous and buxom maid in *A Warning for Fair Women*; the initial version may have included more material for her with the Host, who was played by Pope. If Anne led the fairy singing, as some editors surmise although the Folio assigns no soloist, then she was played by Crosse's boy; however, he is far more likely to have played William Page, who does the Latin lesson with Evans. In that case, Anne Page could have been just about any boy.

Although probably not written specifically for a Garter ceremony, *The Merry Wives of Windsor* would have been popular material for private performances. It is colorful, hilarious, easily cuttable to fit various circumstances, and makes no serious demands on stage technology, with no above or within required. The Garter speech might well have been inserted for a performance before new Garter inductees in April 1600.[23]

With these new plays added to the repertory and Kemp returning to the regular performing company, the first six months in the Globe were a rousing success. The company played three times at court that winter, verifying their continued popularity and artistic standing. The Sharers were making money, and the partners in the Globe were making even more, as evidenced by their eventual decision to buy out Kemp. Even so, there were two major problems to be dealt with in the winter of 1599–1600. One was the festering situation with Kemp. He may have been persuaded to return to the company to get them through the first Globe season, but as the new year began, it must have grown obvious that the crisis had only been postponed, not resolved. The other was Pope's decision to retire, which is generally accepted to have occurred no later than 1600. As we saw with Bryan, the preferred approach to retirement would have been for Pope to continue playing existing roles but not to have roles in any new plays, so that the company could prepare for a smooth change-over when he was gone. Eventually, his Globe partners honored the bequest of his shares to a young woman with no connection to the theater, so he seems to have retired amicably. He was certainly older than forty in 1600, and his Globe investment meant he could look forward to a steady income, so it should come as no surprise that his thoughts should turn to retirement. The question is, when did he actually decide to leave? He was obviously still playing major roles in the summer of 1599, and we have identified significant characters of his age and type among the revivals we can trace to that year. However, in March 1601, Heminges and Richard Cowley collected the payment for the company's winter performances for Elizabeth, indicating that Cowley now had a share of some sort. Thus, *The Merry Wives of Windsor* probably marked Pope's last new play with the company, after which he arranged the transfer of at least half of his share to Cowley.

Records of Cowley go back to *The Seven Deadly Sins*, in which company he was clearly a Hired Man. His first child was born in 1596, suggesting a marriage in 1595, about the time we began to see him as a regular among the clownish Hired Men of the company, and indicating he was in his mid-twenties when the Chamberlain's Men were first organized. Identified in the Folio as Verges, he probably played the other comic old men, such as Old Gobbo, as we have discussed previously, and since Verges is short, he probably played other shorter characters as well. Most of those roles have been in the thirty- to forty-line range, perfectly suitable for a Hired Man. For the most part, there will be no significant increase in the number of lines in roles we can assign to Cowley in the immediate future, but his name will appear in all the Sharer lists of 1603–04 and among the Principall Actors in the Folio, so he must have attained at least a Half-Share before 1603; his collection of the court payment in March 1601, must mean he had obtained his share before that date.

Given the continued brief nature of Cowley's future roles, it seems clear that the he only managed to obtain half of Pope's share. The most logical use of the other half share would have been to promote one of the former apprentices, such as Cooke, but there is no sudden increase in prominence of roles for very young men. Beeston would shortly leave the company, which he would not have done had he held a share of any size. Both Cooke and Gough eventually appear among the Principall Actors, but neither is in any of the several Sharer lists of 1603–04. Thus, the other half of Pope's share apparently went to Crosse, whose large Welsh-accented roles in *Henry V*, *Merry Wives*, and in future plays all point to a full Sharer.

When all the shuffling ended, the Chamberlain's Men still had, as noted earlier, eight full shares split among nine partners: Burbage, Shakespeare, Heminges, Kemp, Phillips, Crosse, and Condell had full shares, while Sly and Cowley held half shares.

During that same winter, Kemp concocted a most amazing scheme: He decided to morris dance all the way from London to Norwich.[24] To modern eyes, this is nothing particularly striking—the basic morris steps are little more than walking, and traders and travelers walked from London to Norwich all the time. But the feat seized the Elizabethan imagination, and by the time he finished the jaunt, Kemp was one of the most famous men in the kingdom. He took many wagers (and many of the bettors disappeared when he came to collect on his return). This would seem to indicate, at the very least, that he had not yet sold his Globe shares, for the hundred pounds or more from that transaction would have negated any need for new cash. The dance happened during Lent, so it need not have interfered in any way with Chamberlain's Men performances. Likewise, the decision to go during Lent (February), when the weather was usually at its worst in the east of England, would indicate that he had other commitments that prevented an attempt during more pleasant weather later in the spring. The dancing took nine days, but bad weather meant the whole trip took more than three weeks.

However, any plans to continue performing with the Chamberlain's Men seem to have crashed suddenly during that spring. Kemp's pamphlet about his dance was registered on April 22, but when it reached print it contained a brief and very angry epilogue. Most of this epilogue is concerned with his attempt to track down the "ballad-makers" who had been circulating satirical reports of his feat. He found his man, but not before he had died, and the matter would hold little modern interest had he not addressed this epilogue to "my notable Shakerags." Although there is nothing that connects Shakespeare with these ballads, that address does more than suggest that Kemp was very angry with Shakespeare about something. He continued, "I William Kemp . . . am shortly God willing to set forward as merily as I may; whether I my selfe know not."[25] That would seem to indicate that he had now severed all ties with the Chamberlain's Men. If this break had occurred before his dance or before the registration, he would have had no need to make the epilogue a separate section. It must have been added after the main body of the text was registered. If the company did in fact perform *Merry Wives* for the Garter feast on April 23, then Kemp was certainly still present at that date. He may have added the epilogue at any time after that date; nevertheless, it must have taken at least a few weeks after Kemp's return around Easter for the various ballads to be circulated, for Kemp to search for his nemesis, and then for the ballad-maker to die. Thus, the major clash probably occurred during May or very early June, after which Kemp stormed out.

This time, however, the other Sharers were ready. They had had a year to accumulate capital to buy him out of the Globe as well as the acting company. They had also had plenty of time to start negotiations with Armin and to think about new play topics that need not include Kemp. So after this breach there was no attempt to smooth things over. What part Shakespeare played in all this is unknown, but Kemp obviously felt that Shakespeare in particular had betrayed him.

According to legal testimony many years later, Kemp sold his Globe share to Shakespeare, Heminges, and Phillips. They in turn laundered that share through one Thomas Cressey, who resold it to Shakespeare, Heminges, Phillips, and Pope. (That Pope was not present when the first deal was made underscores the assumption that this all happened after Pope had retired.) Thus, the Globe ownership was now constituted with half in the Burbage hands and equal shares of one eighth for the other four partners (see Chart F).[26] No mention was made of Kemp's acting share. It was eventually taken by Armin, but there is no evidence that Armin was standing outside the door waiting for Kemp to leave. Rather, the Chamberlain's Sharers probably bought Kemp's share and held it in reserve for the new clown, whoever he might be and whenever he might be able to join the company (see Chart E).

The company may have dug out some very old material to tide them over the emergency caused by Kemp's exit. *Titus Andronicus* was reprinted in 1600, with the Chamberlain's Men added to the long list of companies which had performed it. The probable casting of a *Titus Andronicus* revival is somewhat problematical; although Crosse could certainly take over Bryan's role of Titus, and his apprentice would have been able to handle Lavinia with little difficulty, Burbage's age and stardom made it difficult for him to play the small son's role he had first taken. But then, revisions may have been made that we know nothing about, since the quarto simply reproduced the old Pembroke version. It is equally possible that the reference to the Chamberlain's Men refers to their earlier production in 1595.

Once Kemp was gone for good, the Sharers began dumping the Hired Men who had worked in his comic routines. By the time of *Twelfth Night*, which has numerous opportunities for a comic guard like Dogberry's Watch, the comic bit parts are gone, never to return in any of the company plays. Shakespeare's later plays will often have large casts, but the Hired Men roles will be soldiers, messengers, and lords who walk on and get off as quickly as possible. A brief distinctive bit for a Barnardine is the exception rather than the rule. Because it was the comic Hired Men who obviously went missing from later plays, it looks very much like a real purge. Once Kemp had left, the Sharers decided to make a clean sweep and get rid of any players who might feel any allegiance to Kemp. This was not necessarily all spite, of course. With Kemp gone, there was very little for his stooges to do: If there is no Dogberry, who needs a comic Watch?

But the cost was enormous. At one fell swoop, the Chamberlain's Men lost almost all their comedic repertory. Once Armin arrived, he might pick up some of the roles, of course, but the tiny and cynical Armin could never play Bottom or Cob or Buffone and certainly not Falstaff. Nor could anyone else in the company; the other fat man, Pope, had retired as well. Although most of these productions had run their course at the moment, they were valuable properties with potential for further revivals. But without the same actors, or replacements of similar types and skills, the plays were useless without extensive, and expensive, revisions.

Naturally, with so many long-serving Hired Men and former apprentices thrown onto the streets, there were some disgruntled actors more than willing to provide printers with versions of Chamberlain's Men hits. The remaining Sharers acted quickly to thwart such potential thefts. They arranged on August 4 for Thomas Pavier to register *Henry V, Every Man in His Humour, Much Ado About Nothing* and a play called *As You Like It* "to be staied" (i.e., to prevent someone else from publishing them). On August 23, a different printer re-registered *Much Ado About Nothing* and added *2 Henry IV*. On October 8, *A Midsummer Night's Dream* was registered as well. (To this list we might also add *Merchant of Venice*, stayed in July 1598, and then re-registered in October 1600.)

Although the staying registration worked for most of these, it came too late for *Henry V*, which was already at a printer and put on sale before August 14. This was clearly a bad quarto, now generally credited to the actors who played Exeter and Gower.[27]

If nothing else, this list tells us which plays the company considered to be most valuable, and the corresponding magnitude of Shakespeare's responsibility for the company's commercial success. But it also indicates how serious this break-up had become.

Curiously, even though the staying registrations worked to keep bad quartos out of the bookseller stalls, they did nothing to prevent publication of some very good versions of *Much Ado About Nothing, A Midsummer Night's Dream, Merchant of Venice*, and *2 Henry IV*, which were potentially more damaging to the company itself. Precisely how and why these good quartos came to be made available requires a discussion that is far too complicated and argumentative for this work, which is concerned with various textual questions only as they relate to the acting company's history. However, every one of these good quartos had the name William Shakespeare prominently displayed, which should provide some hint as to the source of their various manuscripts.

One of the most curious aspects of these registrations is the play that was not registered. If the purpose of the staying registrations and/or Shakespeare's later printings was to prevent Kemp or the Hired Men from printing unauthorized versions of hits, then why was *Merry Wives of Windsor* not protected in the summer of 1600? Whether written in the previous winter as I have argued, or in 1597 as Hotson argued, the play was surely as popular if not more so than the other Falstaff plays, yet no one seems to have been worried that some version might find its way to a printer. That it could be stolen is demonstrated by the fact that it was, but only some two years later. At the same time, the company went to some trouble to protect *As You Like It.* If this were *Love's Labour's Won,* as I have argued, then it needed no protection, for it had been stolen and printed already in a version that has disappeared in our own day. If, as others have argued, it was a new play written for Armin, then it cannot have been yet written while Kemp or his comedy team were in the company; thus, it would have needed no staying registration to protect it from an unauthorized reconstruction.

The most obvious solution to the quandary is that the play registered as *As You Like It* is not the same play called *As You Like It* in the Folio. The Elizabethans were rather casual about titles in general, and Shakespearean comedy titles are no exception. Except for *Taming of the Shrew,* the romantic comedies written for this company could trade titles almost at random. Any of them might be "All's Well That Ends Well," or "What You Will," or "As You Like It," and all are "Much Ado About Nothing." As only *Much Ado* was printed before the Folio, we have no way of knowing how most of the comedies were actually identified by their original audiences, who had no printed programs and usually referred to plays by the name of the most interesting characters. Later citations would identify *1 Henry IV* as *Hotspur* or *Much Ado* as *Benedicte and Betteris.*[28] *Twelfth Night* was apparently called *What You Will* until Marston printed a play of the same title, forcing a change when Shakespeare's play was registered for the Folio. The 1600 registration of *As You Like It* may even refer to a work not by Shakespeare, the title of which was re-used by Heminges and Condell (or by Shakespeare). It is certainly curious that no later productions of a play called *As You Like It* are known, even among the numerous revivals for James's court where it would have fit nicely, nor are any other titles that might apply—no *Rosalind,* for example (see also p. 207). Most likely, however, is that *As You Like It* was the rather cynical title originally given to the slap-dash *Merry Wives.*

As such, the registration protected the play for about eighteen months, until someone hit on a way around the stay—a new title that more accurately described its contents. Thus, on January 18, 1602, a John Busby registered "A booke called An excellent and pleasant conceited comedie of Sir John Faulstof and the merry wyves of Windesor." This was so obviously what the play was about that no one thought to connect it to the nebulous old title of *As You Like It*. Under this new title it reached print. It may also have reached the stage of Kemp's new company, Worcester's Men, for whom Henslowe noted a play about Oldcastle. The continued public confusion of Oldcastle and Falstaff and the earlier appearance of a play about Oldcastle by Drayton and others makes Henslowe's notation less than conclusive as to the precise play performed.[29] This quarto was a much garbled version, even though Shakespeare was credited on the title page. The Chamberlain's/King's Men themselves revived the play in 1604–05, where court records simply called it *Merry Wives of Windsor*, but another revival in 1612–13 was called *Falstaff*. By 1623, Heminges and Condell accepted common usage and printed it in the Folio as *The Merry Wives of Windsor*.

This scenario is of course purely conjectural without a copy of the missing *Love's Labour's Won*. But it does offer a plausible explanation of the 'disappearance' of the very popular *Love's Labour's Won* and the peculiar failure to stay *Merry Wives*. It might also explain why *As You Like It* was given a new registration for the Folio in 1623 as one of the plays "not formerly entred to other men"[30]: As far as Heminges and Condell were concerned, it had not been registered previously, since the 1600 registration with that name had actually referred to a different play.

The exodus of Kemp and the Hired Men comedians was the single most significant event in the life of the company during Shakespeare's career. In the summer of 1600, the Chamberlain's Men started over. For all practical purposes, they became a new company, for which they had to find a new repertoire. This was first and foremost a new repertoire without Shakespearean comedy.

From 1594 until the Globe opened, Shakespeare wrote ten securely datable new plays. Five were comedies: *Love's Labour's Lost*, *Love's Labour's Won*, *A Midsummer Night's Dream*, *Merchant of Venice*, and *Much Ado About Nothing*. Two others were histories in which a comic character had the largest role, the two Falstaff plays. In addition, in 1594–98 he revised or perhaps completely rewrote three more comedies—*Comedy of Errors*, *Taming of the Shrew*, and *Two Gentlemen of Verona*—and at least two of those stayed in the active repertory for years. Of the completely new material written for this company, only *Richard II*, *Romeo and Juliet*, and *King John* were not comedic, and *Romeo* has far more comic scenes than all the later tragedies put together. Until Kemp left the company, the company's strength was comedy, and Shakespeare came very close to being exclusively a writer of comedy. After Kemp left, all that changed.

Some of the comedies have leading roles for Kemp, whereas in others he is clearly a supporting character, but they all share something that is missing from all the plays written after Kemp was gone. They are, for want of a more precise term, genial. The comic characters in general, and Kemp's roles in particular, have an enthusiasm for living that turns even the cruel melodrama of Shylock into something altogether surprisingly positive and happy. To compare the sour taste left in the mouth by *Measure for Measure* or *All's Well That Ends Well* with the audience's pleasure at the conclusions of *Merchant of Venice* or *Much Ado About Nothing* is to recognize the difference immediately. Helena's plight is not all that different from Hero's, nor

Isabella all that different in personality from Portia, and yet the later plays are bitter and problematic for most viewers, whereas the earlier comedies have been hits in every generation.

How much of the openness and geniality of the 1590s comedies comes from Kemp and how much from some aspect of Shakespeare's own personality that later changed may be open to debate, but there is certainly no doubt that a change in tone followed Kemp's exit. Shakespeare's last popular comedy would be *Twelfth Night*, written only shortly after Kemp left and before Shakespeare knew his replacement Armin on a personal level.

With Kemp gone, the balance of the company changed. Burbage was now both the star and the landlord. Before Kemp's exit, the Chamberlain's Men had been an ensemble company, with dominant roles shared from play to play by several different actors, even including a boy on occasion. After Kemp left, it became Burbage's Men. Not only would Burbage's role be consistently the largest role in almost every extant company play over the next decade, but also his role would usually be twice the size of any other Sharer's, with very few exceptions. Shakespeare's plays in particular would come to focus all but completely on Burbage. In the era before Kemp left, the company had been not Kemp's company or Burbage's company but Shakespeare's: He provided roughly three plays a year, every one a hit. After Kemp left, Shakespeare's output not only slowed down but also lost its box-office magic. His last big hits, *Hamlet* and *Twelfth Night*, appeared in 1600–01 and had perhaps already been written at least in part before Kemp left. After that, Shakepeare seems to have lost his touch. The peaks were incredibly high—*Othello, Lear, Macbeth*—but the valleys were incredibly low by his previous standards—*All's Well That Ends Well, Troilus and Cressida, Timon of Athens, Pericles*, or *Cymbeline*.

The detail is still in the future of this history, but it is important we notice this closing of an era. The traditional view of Shakespeare's and the Chamberlain's Men's career is best summed up by Bernard Beckerman: "[The Globe's] construction initiated a glorious decade during which the company achieved a level of stability and a quality of productivity rarely matched in the history of the theater."[31] In fact the Globe's construction marked the conclusion of the most stable and productive era for both the acting company and for Shakespeare. The opening of the Globe initiated a period of chaos, instability, internal bickering and backbiting that eventually resulted in the complete remaking of the company, the loss of more than half its most popular repertory, and the conversion of the company from a quasi-medieval group of equals into a quasi-modern star-dominated organization. The company purges of 1600, followed by the political turmoil still to come surrounding Elizabeth's death, the return of the plague, and further deaths and retirements within the company would mean that rarely a year went by without a major change in the Sharers, the boys, or both. In the process, these changes came very close to ending Shakespeare's career as a playwright. For Shakespeare the writer, the first Globe decade would be a period of confusion, box office failure, and constant changes of direction. For Shakespeare the actor, the first Globe decade would be an era of chaos, complication, and economic peril.

All of this chaos and confusion are dealt with in the following chapters. At this point, it is important to note that the Globe opening and the subsequent expulsion of Kemp and his stooges mark the end rather than the beginning of Shakespeare's most productive era.

Chapter 5

Life Without Kemp, 1600–03

Kemp's exit could have destroyed the Chamberlain's Men, particularly as it was accompanied by a number of external crises as well. But luck is often as important in the theater as skill or talent, and during 1600, the Chamberlain's Men received a number of lucky breaks that combined to avert disaster.

The first crisis was new competition from Henslowe, who decided to try to nullify the Globe's impact by building his own new theater. To maximize its impact, he chose to build it north of the City, near the former site of The Theatre, in a blatant attempt to lure away the Chamberlain's Men's old audiences north of the Thames. In January 1600, he and his son-in-law Edward Alleyn hired Peter Streete to build the Fortune, with a contract that has survived but given much frustration to modern research, for it required that it be "finished and doen according to the manner and fashion of . . . the Globe,"[1] without specifying many of those Globe details. Had the Fortune been built as quickly as the Globe, opening in April or May just as the Kemp crisis hit, the effect could have been devastating to the Chamberlain's Men. Fortunately for them, Streete was much slower than when he built the Globe. Henslowe's diaries indicate a growing frustration over delays and broken promises that are all too familiar to homeowners dealing with modern builders. As a result, the Admiral's Men were not able to move to the new space until November,[2] after the Chamberlain's Men had had time to bring in Armin as their new clown and build a new repertory. The Admiral's company continued at the Rose when possible, but with Alleyn retired and the building now comparatively dilapidated, they were not as strong a threat as they had been or as they should have been in the present circumstances.

The decision to build the Fortune backfired on Henslowe and Alleyn. Much

concerned about "the multitude of the [play] houses and the misgovernment of them
. . . and disorders that doe thereupon ensue," the Privy Council on July 22, 1600,
ordered that there should be no more than two theaters and two theater companies
in London. If the Fortune opened, the Rose (and the Curtain as well) were to be
closed and torn down. Such restrictions, of course, would not harm the Admiral's
Men or the Chamberlain's Men, but it did cut off one source of Henslowe's personal
income. However, both acting companies were seriously threatened by another portion of the same order. Once the Privy Council decided to intervene in theatrical
questions, they were not satisfied with limiting theaters; they also decided to limit
performances to "twice a weeke and noe oftener."[3] Under normal circumstances,
this would have been cataclysmic, reducing the company income by two thirds
without a corresponding reduction in expenses—rents, maintenance, production
expenses, and new scripts took no similar reduction, and the Sharers could not cut
the already low pay of Hired Men and musicians so severely without risk of losing
them altogether. But coming at a moment when the Chamberlain's Men were extremely vulnerable, the edict actually served to protect them from competition,
blocking the organization of a new company by Kemp or a London visit from one
of the touring groups. It also all but eliminated one of their biggest problems, and
greatest expenses, at precisely the right moment. With only two performances a week,
new plays would last far longer, giving the company the breathing room necessary
to rebuild a Kemp-less repertory. (This may also help explain why Jonson, Dekker,
and newcomers like Marston began writing for the children's companies; the adult
companies did not need their new work often enough to provide a living.)[4]

As with most attempts to suppress theatrical activity in this era, the Privy Council
order was eventually ignored or forgotten. By the fall of 1601, there were far more
adult performing groups than the city could possibly support. But the 1600 edict
postponed most of that competition until Burbage's company had reorganized and
rebuilt its repertoire.

Perhaps frustrated by the Fortune delays as well as disturbed by the legal problems,
the Admiral's Men went on tour in the summer of 1600 for the first time since *The
Isle of Dogs* affair. There is no similar record of the Chamberlain's Men outside of
London.[5] Later baptisms indicate Condell and Heminges both fathered children
during that summer.[6] Coupled with the presence of some of the company members
in town for the various August print registrations, this would indicate the Chamberlain's Men never left town and thus had a monopoly on audiences at the precise
moment they would have been most vulnerable to competition.

The June regulation probably solved their clown problem for them as well. During
1600, Robert Armin published two pamphlets in which he was still identified as the
Clown of the Curtain. But after the edict of June 22, the Curtain was shut down,
and Armin was out of work. If the Chamberlain's Men had previously tried to lure
Armin away, then this would have made up his mind for him. If they had not yet
made overtures, then Armin may have come to them. Either way, they now had a
chief clown to replace Kemp, with no competition elsewhere from Kemp himself,

and with a reduced performance schedule that provided the time to find new material, or revise old material, for Armin.

Although there was little or no adult competition, there were still competitors. The schoolboys at Paul's, who had been regular court performers in the 1580s, resumed public performances. The precise date is not known, though it may have been as early as 1598. Their early productions had been no serious threat, but by 1600 they had acquired some talented new playwrights such as Marston and Dekker and were sufficiently successful to be invited to court for a performance on January 1, 1601. Because they were a school giving private performances, they were apparently exempt from the June decree. So successful were the Paul's Boys that a second, competing children's company appeared, connected in some way to the old Children of the Chapel. This company was organized by the rather unsavory Henry Evans, who filled out the company by the simple expedient of kidnapping promising young boys. Most remarkable, however, was their performing space. Evans rented the disused Blackfriars indoor theater from the Burbages on September 2, 1600, and began performances sometime afterward, apparently using the claim that these private performances were not covered by the previous ban on use of the Blackfriars for a theater. (Evans's initial associate was his son-in-law Alexander Hawkins, a man of whom almost nothing is known; he is, however, with the exception of Alexander Cooke the only Saunder in theatrical records of this era. This of course does not demonstrate that he was Burbage's Saunder, who should have been in his very early twenties at this time, but the possibility is tempting as an explanation of the long-lasting trust by Burbage of Evans, who from the record was devious [or incompetent] even by Elizabethan standards.)

Over the next few years, this company would be known by many names, but for simplicity we will refer to them throughout the following as the Blackfriars Boys. Because of the "little eyases" comment in *Hamlet* (II,ii,336–38), much has been made of the threat these boy companies posed to the adults.[7] This was not a threat that bothered Richard Burbage, who was the Blackfriars landlord. In September, Burbage would have seen the deal as a salvation, for he would at last be receiving some income from his father's white elephant. Moreover, the cash would come at precisely the moment he most needed it, when the Globe performances had been reduced and just before Michaelmas, the traditional Elizabethan date for quarterly payments on loans, such as the ones he had taken to build the Globe. With only two performances a week, and with the Admiral's company in limbo between theaters, the Chamberlain's Men could be relatively sure that they would be well attended, even if the boys did perform. The Blackfriars space had room for only six to seven hundred people, which made admission expensive, and the boys performed only once each week,[8] so the general audience demand for entertainment would not be seriously depleted as long as the edict stayed in force. In the next year, when so many adult competitors had reappeared, the boys might well have had a serious effect, but during the autumn of 1600, their impact was almost nil, except as a fashionable novelty.

The Blackfriars Boys may not have been on the stage at all until the end of 1600.

Although Evans' lease was to take effect on September 29, he was still trying to find boys as late as December 13, when he made the mistake of kidnapping young Thomas Clifton, whose father had connections at court.[9] Evans may of course have simply been building up his numbers, but the fact that he resorted to kidnapping a gentleman's son would suggest that he was still desperately shorthanded of literate and well-spoken boys. As a practical matter, it would have taken three or four months for any writers to provide new plays for the company. The earliest known play performed by them is Jonson's *Cynthia's Revels*, printed sometime after May 23, 1601. Jonson's folio claims it was "first acted in the yeere 1600," which may mean any time before March 25, 1601.

The survival of the Chamberlain's Men during this year of crisis had been much aided by the introduction of one of Shakespeare's most popular plays containing one of Burbage's most famous roles. Curiously, of all the many debated aspects of *Hamlet*, there is little disagreement about its dating, with almost all scholars placing its composition during 1600.[10] Nevertheless, it may be possible to date the composition more precisely. It seems clear that the play, if written, was not a part of the regular repertory before August; had such a well-known and popular work been performed during that spring, the company would have thought it necessary to register it along with the other plays to keep a reconstructed version away from the printers. On the other hand, there is no role for Armin. After all, who replaced Yorick at court? There are numerous points at which a jester figure might be introduced—Osric's first scene, for example, could easily be a "fool's" scene, as could the introduction of the players done by Polonius, or a court fool might even replace Rosencrantz and Guildenstern as Claudius' spy. This absence of the jester more than suggests that Armin was not a part of Shakespeare's thinking when the script was put together. This in turn would indicate its completion before August 1600.

Even considering Hamlet's anti-clown comments, we should note that there is in fact a Kempean clown role in the play—the gravedigger is dead center in the mainstream of lower class comedians that had been Kemp's stock in trade since 1594. Cowley may have taken over the role after he obtained his half share—the gravedigger is also an old coot—but it is unlikely it was written for Cowley, who neither before nor after would see such another solo turn. Thus, it seems likely that Shakespeare began writing *Hamlet* during the winter–spring of 1600, just after he had finished *Merry Wives*, but that it did not reach the stage until after the big blow-up of the late spring.

If nothing else, *Hamlet* marks the triumph of Burbage. With some 1,500 lines, more than 37% of the total, *Hamlet* was Shakespeare's gift to Burbage, a present that at times seems more capitulation than gift. It certainly distorts the idea of a repertory company as a partnership of equals. *Hamlet's* soliloquies add up to about two hundred lines, one seventh of *Hamlet's* total lines, and that does not include those soliloquies only minimally disguised as dialogue, such as "Alas poor Yorick" or "Speak the speech" or "The rugged Pyrrhus," which easily add another one hundred fifty or more to the total of such lines. To put that in perspective, *Hamlet* has almost the same number of lines in *monologues* as Shylock has in all of *Merchant of Venice*.

Curiously, *Hamlet* was not technically a new play. The Chamberlain's Men had played some version in 1594–96, to considerable success, but with someone other than Burbage playing Hamlet (see chap. 2). That play, usually called the *Ur-Hamlet*, has disappeared, apparently never printed, although it is usually assumed to have been written by Kyd. In 1600, the Sharers decided to revive the old work. For some reason, however, they decided to authorize a complete rewrite, something rarely if ever done during the era; the accepted pattern indicated by Henslowe's diaries and surviving plays for which we have revisions, such as *Mucedorus*, was to pay a writer (or writers) for new scenes that used the company's new actors, but to try to retain as much as possible of the old material that was already paid for. Without any text of Kyd's version, we can not even guess why Shakespeare made a complete revision, but it seems obvious that he did; not even the most meticulous analysts have found hints of anyone's hand but Shakespeare's in the versions we have today. (Of course, because *Hamlet* is the touchstone on which all such stylistic analyses are based, no one would dare to suggest it was not Shakespeare's work *in toto*.) The only likely explanation is that when Burbage decided to assume the role, he wanted it much expanded, and one thing led to another until Shakespeare had a completely new work.

Condell, usually cast as Burbage's alter ego with a sword, was surely Hamlet's alter ego with a sword, Laertes. Crosse, now the oldest man in the company, would have been Polonius. Tradition says Shakespeare played the Ghost,[11] and this is not as unlikely as most other of these traditions; white powder and the helmet's beaver would have disguised his own face and age, and the play is carefully constructed to make this minor character with relatively few lines seem like a major character, precisely what we would expect a master playwright to do with his own role. (The traditional double for the Ghost is the Player King, which would not have been possible for Shakespeare if he wore armor in the Ghost's bedroom appearance; however, Q1, based on performers' memories, says the Ghost wore "his nightgown" for this entrance,[12] which could have been thrown over the Player's costume much more quickly than he could have returned to his suit of armor.) This would leave Phillips and Heminges to play Claudius and Horatio, initiating the tradition of the absurdly old college chum. Either, although obviously older than Burbage, would have been a very young uncle. Given the broader range we have identified for Phillips, he is the more likely Claudius. Cooke, a young adult now but still only a Hired Man, would then have been young Fortinbras, a major character with almost no lines. Half-Sharers Sly and Cowley then must have played Rosencrantz and Guildenstern.

The women indicate the play's roots in an earlier version. Gertrude is the mother of a grown son, the only such character between Richard III's mother and Volumnia, and Ophelia goes mad, the only such instance for a woman, other than Lady Macbeth's sleepwalking, in all of Shakespeare.[13] This need not mean that Shakespeare retained any of Kyd's lines for them, but it does hint that he probably did not invent their characterizations. Gertrude, although married to Claudius, actually has more of her scenes with Hamlet, and thus was almost certainly Nick Tooley, whose tendency toward the mature would make him a plausible mother. Ophelia sings—the mad scene is more sung than spoken—which would suggest Crosse's boy; however, Ophelia actually spends far more stage time with Hamlet or Laertes than with Polonius. Because Burbage's apprentice was playing Gertrude, then Ophelia must have been Condell's boy; he would have been around sixteen or seventeen, so it is just possible he could still play a convincing girl. It may at last be possible to give this boy a name. An actor named Robert Beeston appeared in the new patent list for the Worcester's/Queen's Men in 1604. Nothing more is known about Robert, but we have seen that Christopher Beeston was one of Phillips' apprentices before 1600. Beeston was Christopher's stage name, so the congruence may mean nothing; nevertheless, it was also a relatively rare name, unlikely to appear twice by coincidence in such a small group. Christopher went to Worcester's Men in 1601, but Robert did not join for another two years, which would suggest he was at least two years younger, or at least under bonds for two years longer, both of which would fit the career we have thus far described for Condell's boy.

Hamlet and Burbage were an immense hit. It became one of his signature roles, played for years. With a hit like this, in a limited production schedule and with almost no competition, the Chamberlain's Men survived the loss of Kemp and had time to commission some new plays. But they lost their position at court as the undisputed leader of English acting companies. During the winter, they played only twice at court, a figure matched by the Admiral's Men and by the boy companies; they also participated in some joint production for a Twelfth Night celebration honoring a visitor from Italy.

As that visitor was named Orsino, Leslie Hotson has argued the play must have been *Twelfth Night*. Lord Hunsdon himself noted a special conference to select the play; although he did not mention a title, he did mention that it should have "rich apparell, have great variety and change of Musicke and daunces, and of a subject that may be most pleasing to her Majestie" (and also, one assumes, would not make great demands on an important guest's command of English). Orsino's letter home described a "mingled comedy, with pieces of music and dances," not at all like *Twelfth Night*. Court payment records list a show that night performed by three adult and two children's companies working together, which would have been a massive spectacle.[14] *Twelfth Night* has one of the smallest casts of any Shakespearean play, no place for groups of children, only minimal use of music sung by a single person, and no dancing whatsoever. Given that one principal is a Puritan, another is in mourning, and a third is in disguise as a man, there is little opportunity for visual splendor. It would be difficult to find a play less likely to have played on this occasion than *Twelfth Night*. (On the other hand, Jonson's *Cynthia's Revels*, written for the Blackfriars Boys, would have been all but perfect, with its two masques, dances, and numerous songs.[15])

This does not necessarily demonstrate that *Twelfth Night* had not been written by this time, only that it was not seen at court on January 6. It is certain that the play was seen at the Inns of Court almost a year later, when John Manningham entered a detailed description of its plot in his diary for February 2, 1602.[16] But that need not indicate the play was new at that later time— *Twelfth Night* has one of Shakespeare's smallest casts and simplest stagings, ideally suited to touring or to adaptation for private dining halls, and thus it may have been brought out of moth-balls solely for this single performance.

There can be no doubt that Feste was intended for Robert Armin to play, for the role is almost everything Kemp was not. Will Kemp was a common man clown, whereas Feste is a fool in the tradition of courtly fools. Kemp was a great dancer, but Feste sings, and sings often, some of the loveliest of all Shakespeare's musical insertions, including the epilogue. In comparison to Kemp's usual cross-talk routines, Feste is a man of wit and subtlety, and a soloist. Feste even dons a disguise as Sir Topas and puts on a funny voice, something missing from all Kemp's surviving roles. For the comedian, Feste is a dream part that displays all in one place a full range of skills that would otherwise be seen, if at all, in half a dozen different plays. It is a gift role, all but certainly purposely designed to showcase the company's new clown as effectively as possible.

The oddity is that Feste seems to have no part in the plot itself. He simply wanders from scene to scene, from household to household, with no fixed role in the action. Most obviously, he is missing from the central box tree scenes with Malvolio, even though he later quotes lines he never overheard; his place is taken, without expla-nation or introduction, by Fabian. What this suggests is that Feste was a late mod-ification, inserted after the main body of the play had been completed, taking over some other character's lines in some scenes and speaking newly written material in others. If we assume Shakespeare began writing *Twelfth Night* immediately after he finished *Hamlet*, then he would have been almost finished in August 1600, when Armin transferred to the company. The actor most probably affected was the man who played Fabian, who was replaced in the long Act I drinking scene with Toby and Aguecheek, but who was allowed to keep the box-tree scenes so he still had some significant stage time.

The rest of the play is relatively easy to cast, using the *Hamlet* company. Malvolio is the logical casting for Burbage; although both Belch and Feste are larger roles, they are clearly not Burbage roles, and Malvolio is an ideal role for the serious star of the company in a comedy. That Malvolio was seen as the star role is underlined by Manningham's single-minded focus on the character in his plot summary. Toby shares a number of characteristics with Pistol, another quick-tempered braggart and drunkard, and he is good enough with a sword to fight on stage, so he was most probably Phillips, despite our modern tendency to think of Toby as fat. Sly would have taken Aguecheek, repeating and expanding a characterization he had played as Slender. Condell, still youngish and noble in appearance, would have been Orsino. We might think that Cowley, not needed as a stooge for Armin, would have been assigned the servant Fabian, but Shakespeare, Heminges, and Crosse all outranked him and needed roles. Crosse of course had done comedy and might do so again, but Shakespeare seems marginally more suited to Fabian, given his early comedic roles. As the author, he was also the Sharer most likely to surrender some of his lines when it became necessary to make room for Armin. Thus, Antonio and the Captain/ Officer 1 were probably doubled in that manner by Heminges and Crosse respectively, leaving Cowley only the very minor Curio and either the Second Officer or the Priest.

And then there is Viola. Although we think of her as a woman disguised as a boy, to Shakespeare he was a boy disguised as a boy. For all but one very brief scene, Viola is in fact a young man. And Shakespeare is very clear that she is a young man, not a boy, for he is so sexually attractive that Olivia thinks him marriageable (and does marry his twin). The plot demands a boy who is no longer a boy, and we should assume that this was precisely what Shakespeare's company put on the stage. Shakespeare had of course written similar boy-women for Burbage's boy Saunder, but as we have seen, Saunder by this time must have been past twenty and far too old for even the brief female scene of this play (assuming he was still in the company at all). If Burbage was playing Malvolio, then his current apprentice Tooley would have played Olivia, whose large set pieces are with either Viola or Malvolio. There was, however, another very experienced boy at this time, Condell's boy Robert Beeston. Viola is quite independent, playing significant scenes with almost everyone in the cast, but her duet scenes tend to be with Orsino. By late 1600, Beeston was certainly in his late teens, so he would have had no difficulty portraying a convincing older boy. Maria plays almost all of her scenes with Sir Toby and thus must have been Gilburne.

Viola's twin then must have been Cooke. The role is carefully written for a very special and unique person—someone close enough in age and size and general appearance to pass for a beardless boy who is Viola's twin but who is nonetheless adept with a sword. Despite the relatively large number of Sebastian's lines, Cooke is the only real possibility. Shakespeare and Heminges, both now at least thirty-six, and Crosse, even older, would have been absurd, as would Cowley and Sly, who both were approaching thirty and were not athletic in appearance. The large size of Sebastian's role suggests that the company intended Cooke to soon take on a share. If so, something occurred to prevent this, for he is on no Sharer lists for years, and the size of his roles drops back almost immediately to those of a Hired Man.

As we have indicated, the company was missing a number of its most identifiable Hired Men in this autumn, and *Twelfth Night* is certainly a play without significant Hired Men. No more than eleven lines are not assignable to either Sharers or boys. It is a play written for a company stripped down to its absolute minimum. This may well indicate that, after a few months of limited performances, the Sharers decided to dump even some of the non-comedic Hired Men.

It is probable that this stripped down company also revived one of the most enduring hits of the era, the anonymous *Mucedorus*. The history of this play is much debated, but its first performances probably were before 1590, even more probably by the Queen's Men. The earliest surviving printing was in 1598, suggesting a popular revival in 1597–98, most likely by the Pembroke company, whose bankruptcy after the *Isle of Dogs* would have encouraged the sale of a version to a printer. Sometime afterward, it entered the repertory of Shakespeare's company, with additions included in a printing of 1610. When the additions were made is highly debated—a printing in 1606 suggests a popular revival at that time but did not include any new scenes, whereas a number of the additions of 1610 include satirical shots at Jonson that must have been part of the War of the Theaters in 1600–01.[17] Thus, the most likely date of a Chamberlain's revival and revision would seem to be at about the same time as Armin joined the company. The additions, when finally printed, are very brief and possibly memorial, simply inserted into the old printed text,[18] but they are significant because of their nature. First, they expand two roles, Mouse the clown and Mucedorus. In 1600–01, the Chamberlain's company were in desperate need of starring material for a new clown who was small in stature and for a serious leading man named Burbage. Second, the additions add two new characters, expanding opportunities for the comparatively large number of Sharers in that company while all but eliminating any need for Hired Men. Unfortunately, with so dubious a text, we cannot be certain of the size of all the Sharer roles (see Chart B).

There must have been other fare as well, which has disappeared. But being limited to two performances a week, the company would need only a few plays such as *Hamlet*, *Twelfth Night*, and *Mucedorus* to sustain them through the winter of 1600–01.

And then came the Essex affair, when the Chamberlain's company was at its luckiest. Since the autumn of 1600, the Earl of Essex had been back from Ireland, pouting and plotting in his house in the Strand. During the first week of February 1601, some of his followers paid the Chamberlain's Men to stage a revival of *Richard II*, which took the stage at the Globe on Saturday, February 7, 1601.

The next morning, Essex, with a group of about two hundred followers who had been to the play, took to the streets of London to rally the citizens for his coup, but the citizens resolutely refused to rally. Essex and the major ringleaders, including Shakespeare's former patron the Earl of Southampton, were arrested that evening, and Essex and Southampton were tried and sentenced to death. Southampton's sentence was commuted to the Tower, and most of the other noblemen who were convicted were released with heavy fines, but Essex was executed on February 25.

On February 18, the day before the trial began, the Privy Council interrogated the actors. Curiously, Phillips rather than Shakespeare or Burbage was called. He claimed that the actors had known nothing about the political plot. They had, he claimed, even tried to refuse, arguing that it was a very old play that they would have little time to prepare and for which there would be no audience. Their resistance was overcome, however, when the gentlemen offered to guarantee two pounds over and above any ticket takings, and so they succumbed.[19]

This was almost certainly codswallop. That Shakespeare had ties to Southampton was well-known since the days of *Venus and Adonis*. Likewise, everyone in the city knew the potential parallels between Richard's situation and Elizabeth's, which was one reason the Chamberlain's Men had stopped performing the play years earlier despite its popularity. As the goal of the coup was the deposition of Elizabeth, Essex's men must have insisted on the inclusion of the deposition scene that historically justified their plan and made the performance significant. Only a fool could have failed to recognize the implications of such a performance in the tense political climate of the day, and there is no evidence whatsoever that Shakespeare, Burbage, Heminges, or any of the others were political fools. In addition, Phillips claimed that the request for the play performance was literally overnight, that the gentlemen rowed over on the evening of February 6, the play was performed on February 7, and the revolt came on the 8th. This means that in roughly eighteen hours, which included time for sleep and food, all the old members of the original cast refreshed their memories of a play they had not performed for almost four years, that replacements were found for Bryan, Pope, Kemp, and *almost all* the Hired Men (of which the company was short-handed at the time), all of whom managed to learn their roles overnight, and that the play previously announced was taken off, another substituted, and somehow the entire city of London alerted to the change before noon the next day. Such a schedule is ludicrously implausible, even for a promised bonus of two pounds. Much more likely is that there was an earlier meeting not admitted to the council during which the plan for such a performance was first developed; the meeting on the 6th merely gave the green light to the performance already prepared. The actors may have agreed to do the performance purely for financial reasons, as Phillips claimed, but they did so with far more than eighteen hours of warning, in the full knowledge that something desperate was afoot. Yet, their luck held. Elizabeth and her councillors were in a merciful mood and chose to wink at the story Phillips fed them. In one of the many brutal ironies of Elizabethan political life, the acting company whose performance signaled Essex's coup was brought to perform for Elizabeth on February 24, the night before Essex's execution.

Paradoxically, it was the Admiral's Men once again who were most damaged; they had taken no part in the affair, but the Fortune was closed as well, just when it was new and fresh in the public eye. All of the theaters must have been closed on February 9, when militia patrolled the London streets to prevent any public gatherings in support of Essex,[20] and this closure certainly continued throughout Lent.

Some of the problems of the Chamberlain's company at this time are reflected in Jonson's *Poetaster*, written for one of the boy companies. Jonson's play was registered December 21, 1601, but *Satiromastix*, which comments on parts of *Poetaster*, was registered on November 11, so Jonson's play must have reached the stage several months earlier during the spring or early summer of 1601. In *Poetaster*, Captain Tucca meets starving actor Histrio, who comments that all the companies but his own are "on the other side of Tiber," and that "all the sinners in the suburbs come and applaud our action daily" (III,iv,168–71). Even with this suburban audience, the company is in desperate financial straits. Tucca promises to provide them with a hit and offers two talented boys to replace the weak apprentices in the company. At this particular time, the Globe was the only "suburban" theater in regular daily operation, with all the other companies across the Thames on the city side. Thus, Jonson seems to be referring to the financial and artistic difficulties of the Chamberlain's Men. This is a satirical exaggeration, of course, and perhaps even a certain amount of wishful thinking because the Chamberlain's Men had dispensed with

Jonson's services as a writer. But it does indicate that even Shakespeare's company was feeling the effects of the earlier restrictions and new competition.

By the time the theaters reopened after Easter, 1601,[21] and the June edict was beginning to be ignored, the Chamberlain's Men were in shape to take on almost any kind of competition. Armin was established in the company, and new Hired Men had been added from a combination of old apprentices now out of their bonds, such as Cooke and Gough, and a handful of new adults. One of these new men may even have been Shakespeare's brother Edmund, who left no records in Stratford after his birth but was buried in Southwark on December 31, 1607. A (bastard) son of "Edward Shackspeere, a Player," was baptized in London on August 12, 1607, so Edmund seems to have become an actor in London. In 1600, when the company had room for some new men, Edmund was twenty, just the age to leave home. Where else would Shakespeare's brother seek work on stage but in Shakespeare's company?

Few, if any, extant plays by Shakespeare have been securely dated to the years after *Twelfth Night*. The only work usually placed between 1600 and 1604 is *Troilus and Cressida*, and even this is not so certain as is often assumed, as is seen later. One possibility, however, is *All's Well That Ends Well*, which is almost always linked with *Measure for Measure*, performed in 1604. Most critics who link these two works argue that *All's Well* is the earlier play,[22] which would mean it would have been written for performance before the long plague break of 1603. The practical problem with this earlier date is that it would be very difficult to cast the text as it exists. Most obviously, the two Lords are identified not as 1 and 2 but as E and G. As we have seen in great detail, there are no company Sharers during 1601–03 with the initials G or E. Even if we ignore G and E, on the assumption that they were character names Shakespeare never got around to filling out, the rest of the play does not fit very well with the other Sharers of 1602. There are two older men, Lafew and the King, which perhaps might be taken by Heminges and Shakespeare, but then Burbage would have to play Bertram, a *much* smaller role and a bit too young for the thirtyish Burbage. If Burbage did not play Bertram, the most logical candidate is Cooke, who was not yet a Sharer. For Crosse, the third older man in the company, no role at all can be found.

However, *All's Well* as a text has seemed to many critics to be much revised. Its ratio of rhyme to blank verse is nearly one to five, matched only by *Romeo and Juliet*, *A Midsummer Night's Dream*, and *Comedy of Errors*, and surpassed only by *Love's Labour's Lost*, while its percentage of run-on lines is about the same as *Hamlet*, all pointing to a date even earlier than 1601; at the same time, the number of broken-ended speeches matches the plays dated after 1606, and various other vocabulary tests place it as late as 1608.[23] As seen in chapter 7, the Lord G and E passages may well be explained as a very hasty revision made for new Sharers in 1608. At that time, several of Shakespeare's plays may very well have been much modified to adjust for Burbage's shift from young men roles to mature roles. The logical revision at that later date would have been to reduce Bertram's role and expand the King's, and to replace some older characters in Italy with young soldiers. *All's Well* is slightly longer than most of Shakespeare's comedies, almost 3,100 lines in the Folio, but not so long that we can confidently claim to separate the early scenes from the later ones, as we can with some other later works.

However, if we assume that the major later expansion was in the King's role, then it is at least possible to conceive of a company production in 1601–02 with Burbage as a Bertram with a larger number of lines and Tooley as Helena, Armin as Lavatch, Phillips as another of his long-winded characters Parolles, and Shakespeare as the King. The rest of the scenes would have been much altered later, so we can only guess at the remaining role assignments (see Chart B).

By the early summer of 1601, the political restrictions of the previous year had lapsed. Not only were the two authorized companies playing more often than twice a week, but also some new and very serious competitors had appeared to challenge the dominance of the Chamberlain's Men. The Admiral's Men at last were able to perform in their new theater, the Fortune. Buffeted by politics in which they had taken no part and trying to fill an expensive new theater building, they lured Edward Alleyn out of retirement, offering him a share of the income without requiring him to pay a share of the expenses. Alleyn's return seems to have revitalized them as much as the new building. Over the next year or so, Henslowe's diary is filled with payments to writers for revisions of company plays to take advantage of Alleyn's return.[24] Elizabeth herself supposedly wished to have Alleyn on stage again, but if so, she was not eager to actually see him perform; his company was called to court for only one performance in the following year.

The Earl of Derby's company was also in town. They had been called to court in January 1601, as we have seen, so they must have been performing regularly in the city during that winter and spring. How long they remained in London is unclear, but the next notices of this company in the provinces do not appear until the winter of 1601–02.[25]

Competition far more potent even than Edward Alleyn arrived in late summer. Will Kemp had been seen in Italy during the spring of 1601, but by September 2, he was back in England. Within days, he was in a new company patronized by the Earl of Worcester. Although Worcester's Men had been seen in the provinces since at least 1555, this was obviously a newly organized London company. Its Sharers now included Kemp, Duke, Christopher Beeston, and Pallant, all former Chamberlain's Men, as well as Thomas Heywood, who had been writing plays for Henslowe since at least 1596. They leased the Boar's Head, a small inn converted originally by Frances Langley shortly after he built the Swan and then remodeled about this time. Just outside Aldgate, it lay practically on the doorstep of the London audience. Worcester's Men were an immediate success, invited to court in January 1602. In March 1602, the Privy Council accepted circumstances and issued a new order limiting London to three companies, Chamberlain's, Admiral's, and Worcester's, rather than the previous two. By September 1602, Worcester's had outgrown the Boar's Head and moved to the Rose. It was a phenomenal opening year.[26]

Obviously, by September 1601, the legal limitations established little more than a year before had completely collapsed. We must assume that not only were there more companies but also that the adult companies were performing more often, probably back now to their normal daily schedule. With the boy companies added to the mix, there was far more theater than even London could possibly support. As the Paul's Boys usually played on Monday and/or Sunday and the Blackfriars' Boys played only on Saturday,[27] there was of course no single day on which all the companies were playing simultaneously. Even so, with the Globe, the Fortune, the Boar's Head, the Curtain, and the Rose available, as well as the two indoor houses for the boys, there were spaces for eight to ten thousand spectators on any given day. No Renaissance city could possibly support that much theatrical activity for any sustained period, not even one as large as London.

This may account in large part for the so-called War of the Theaters. Much attention has been given to this feud between Marston and Jonson, which has been interpreted as not only a literary feud but also as emblematic of much more profound divisions, such as "private" versus "public," "court" versus "city," "boy" versus "adult," "literary" versus "popular," or "classical" versus "modern," in Elizabethan literary life. Many of these interpretations may have some validity, but as the "War" was primarily Jonson versus Marston, who were writing for the two children's companies, it was first and foremost a feud between Paul's and Blackfriars, with little or nothing to do with the repertoire or the audiences of the larger adult theaters.

This War, when coupled with Rosencrantz's comments, has led many to see the children's companies as major threats to the adults, which does not seem to be supported by the record. It was, after all, the boys who collapsed. It was also the boys who changed their repertory. After *Poetaster* and *Satiromastix*, the War was over. Even the Paul's boys were aware they were performing "musty fopperies,"[28] and the surviving repertoire of 1602 and later shows a change to comedies about daily life in London. At Blackfriars, the primary manager Henry Evans was negotiating with possible new partners for more capital before October 1601, and although that deal fell through, another finally materialized in April 1602. Financial difficulties continued, leading to arguments among the partners and complaints of fraud that forced Evans to temporarily leave the country.[29] This is hardly the record of a successful enterprise. Even Jonson deserted the boys, after September writing new scenes for *The Spanish Tragedy* and for a new play about *Richard Crookback* for Alleyn at the Fortune[30] and then returning to the Globe.

The movement of Jonson back to the adults was symptomatic of all the relations between the adult and the boy companies. The adults seem to have viewed the boy companies much the way Americans view Off-Off-Broadway or the English now view the Fringe, as a training ground for new talents and a place to develop more unusual material. A new generation of talented playwrights appeared there, with Marston, Middleton, and Chapman establishing their reputations in these early years, and Beaumont and Fletcher repeating the process a few years later. But all of these writers moved to adult commissions as soon as such commisions became available. Similarly, the boys' companies themselves provided an alternative to an acting apprenticeship within the adult companies. Of the eleven Principall Actors listed in the Folio who became Sharers after the boy companies began to graduate young actors, at least five—Benfield, Taylor, Field, Underwood, and Ostler—were trained in the boy companies rather than through adult company apprenticeships. The adults even picked up plays that had potential for a wider audience and gave them new, more visible productions, as we shall see shortly, much as we might see a play move to Broadway or the West End today.

The Chamberlain's Men seem to have had a close relationship with the Paul's Boys in particular. The most obvious sign is *Satiromastix*, the final shot in the War of the Theaters, performed according to its title page by both Paul's and the Chamberlain's Men. This was no joint production, such as at the Orsino feast, because the number of boy actors required is the same standard eight common to the Chamberlain's Men for most of their history. Thus, it seems to have played at Paul's before its registration on November 11, 1601, and then been revived, and perhaps revised, for the Chamberlain's Men before the printing dated 1602. Although the quarto credits Dekker, many scholars find Marston's hand.[31] If true, then Dekker's contribution was perhaps the sections unrelated to the satirical attack on Horace/Jonson. Most striking of the characters, almost certainly expanded for the Chamberlain's Men, is the second largest role, the voluble, middle-aged Welshman, Sir Rees ap Vaughan. This must have been the same actor who portrayed Fluellen and Evans, Samuel Crosse. Horace, a "thin bearded" (l. 564), "starved rascal" (l.586), must have been the same actor who played Anthony Aguecheek and Slender, William Sly. There is only one father role, Sir Quintillian; with Crosse as the Welshman, this probably fell to the balding and aging Shakespeare. There is no clown as such, but the venomous Asinius Bubo, named for the swollen glands of a plague victim, must have been played by the small and ugly Armin. The serious question is whether Burbage played the bombastic Tucca, the largest role, with some 22% of the lines. The character is more in the line of Pistol and Sir Toby. However, the only other conceivable Burbage role in age is the depraved King, who with only 155 lines seems far too minimal for Burbage. Tucca is described as "exceeding tall" (l.1272), which has been said of neither Phillips nor Burbage, although leanness sometimes suggests more height than in fact exists. However, it is possible that this particular line is merely a leftover from the Paul's version where he would have been played by the most experienced and tallest boy, and although printed would not have been spoken on stage by the adults. Given Phillips's portrayal of the decadent Claudius, the King is at least plausible casting for him, allowing Burbage to continue to dominate stage time as Tucca. The only plausible sincere lover Terril would be Condell, leaving Heminges as Crispinus, the stage version of Marston, and Cowley in the much smaller Half-Share sized role of Demetrius, based on Dekker. The boys roles are unusually bland. Only the widow Mrs. Miniver has a glimmer of personality, in appearance and type similar to the buxom Maria in *Twelfth Night*. However, she has no scenes at all with Phillips, but shares most of her scenes with ap Vaugh and Quintillian, suggesting either Crosses's or Shakespeare's boy, both of whom would now be near the end of their bonds, and both of whom have been identifiable in few significant roles during previous years. Celestine, the ingenue pursued by the decadent King, has most of her scenes with Condell, suggesting he now has a second apprentice who is ready for identifiable roles. The others are merely young females and thus barely distinguishable one from the other.

The baldness of several actors and the weakness of the boys in general suggest another play not usually dated to this period: *Coriolanus*. The potential tie to 1601–02 is the appearance of the tribunes Sicinius and Brutus, who are more than once both called bald old men (II,i,12; III,i,164). In this period, the company had one definitely bald Sharer, Shakespeare, plus the much older Crosse, for whom we have no picture but who had played a long succession of mature character roles for which baldness would have been an asset. The entire cast of *Coriolanus* fits more easily into 1601–02 than any other date of the company's history. At this time, Burbage was still in his early thirties, making Coriolanus far more suitable as a new role for the man who had just finished Hamlet than he would be later when Burbage was approaching forty. Aufidius is about the same age as Coriolanus, which fits Condell's usual role, particularly as he must yet again fight with and lose to Burbage. There are four major characters who ought to be older than Coriolanus, and four full Sharers who always played older than Burbage: Phillips would fit nicely with the "humorous patrician" Menenius (II,i,46), and with Shakespeare and Crosse as the two bald plotters, Heminges would have been the experienced general Cominius. Only one significant character might be younger than Coriolanus, Titus Lartius, but with only a relative handful of lines, he would have been suitable for Cooke, who had not yet attained even a half share. As seen in chapter 7, such casting assignments are much more difficult to make in 1608, the date toward which most modern scholars lean.[32]

The women's roles point even more clearly to this earlier date. To modern post-Freud audiences, the most interesting scenes are those between Volumnia and Coriolanus. Most of these speeches are taken with few modifications from North's translation of Plutarch,[33] but Shakespeare must have felt that he had a boy who could carry off the long confrontation scene, or he would have shortened it considerably. The only non-comic mothers of grown men that Shakespeare wrote after the early *Richard III* are Gertrude and Volumnia, so it seems more than merely possible that he wrote them for the same boy to play, young Tooley, who was also Burbage's apprentice. Volumnia is roughly twice as large a role as Gertrude, as we would expect if intended for the same boy with a year or more of additional performing experience. At the same time, Shakespeare seems to have eliminated most of Plutarch's reports of Coriolanus's wife Virgilia. She is now a woman of "gracious silence" (II,i,174), surely intended for a young, very inexperienced apprentice, apparently also apprenticed to Burbage, intended to be Tooley's future replacement.

As Chambers noted, "there is practically no concrete evidence as to date" for Coriolanus,[34] and there is nothing in the play itself that could not date to 1602. Its primary source is Plutarch, in North's translation printed in 1579, 1595, 1603, and 1612. The one significant variant lies in the "fable of the belly" told by Menenius at great length (I,1,95–153), which seems to reflect Camden's *Remaines*, published in 1605.[35] This work, however, begins with an epistle dated 1603, so the book itself was probably written in 1602. As the *Remaines* also contain an admiring mention of Shakespeare, there is the strong possibility that both men were friendly and were familiar with each other's work prior to publication; Camden may even have echoed Shakespeare's phrasing. The other factor usually thought to indicate 1608 or later, the "coal of fire upon the ice" (I,i,172), is part of a series of obvious contradictions and may have nothing whatsoever to do with the frozen Thames during the winter of 1607–08. As both these are in the same scene, they may also in fact demonstrate an addition made during a later revision (see p. 176). However, there is no doubt that the verse characteristics of *Coriolanus* are far more like those of the plays written after *Macbeth* than of those written before.[36] Nor has anyone previously made any serious arguments for later revision by either Shakespeare or a collaborator. Thus, barring further evidence, we cannot prove a version of *Coriolanus* first appeared at this time, but the hypothesis seems to me more than merely possible.

In his diary for March 3, 1602, John Manningham recorded:

Upon a tyme when Burbidge played Rich. 3. there was a citizen greue soe farr in liking with him, that before shee went from the play shee appointed him to come that night unto hir by the name of Ri: the 3. Shakespeare overhearing their conclusion went before, was entertained, and at his game ere Burbidge came. Then message being brought that Rich. the 3ᵈ was at the dore. Shakespeare caused returne to be made that William the Conqueror was before Rich. the 3. Shakespeare's name William.[37]

The date might mean only that Manningham had finally heard a very old joke. But if the joke was new, it indicates that *Richard III* was back in the active repertoire. This should come as no surprise. Burbage was the company's great star, and Richard was one of his greatest vehicles. With Alleyn reviving his own vehicles like *The Spanish Tragedy* at the Fortune[38] and Kemp heading a company with growing success at the Boar's Head, Burbage's great star turn would have been an obvious choice, although the three demanding women's roles may have been much simplified for the weak complement of younger boys reflected in all the new plays of the day. It would also indicate that the company's corps of Hired Men had been replenished, which would make the earlier production of *Coriolanus* even more plausible.

The 1601–02 season must have been remarkably successful, for Shakespeare had a great deal of cash that summer. On May 1, 1602, he bought the freehold to more than one hundred acres of land at Old Stratford, for the sum of 320 pounds. On September 28, he bought a small cottage in Stratford, around the corner from New Place, although the price is not recorded.[39] Such purchases indicate that he had accumulated a great deal of cash since his investment in the Globe.

During 1602, the company presented at least two of the works in the Apocrypha, plays printed during the seventeenth century with attributions suggesting or directly naming Shakespeare but not included in the Folio. Almost none of these apocryphal plays are now accepted as Shakespeare's work, even in part. For our purposes, however, we need not establish authorship in order to demonstrate their place in the Chamberlain's Men repertory.

The most popular of these apocryphal plays, and apparently one of the company's greatest hits for more than a decade, was *The Merry Devil of Edmonton,* first ascribed to Shakespeare many years after his death. Although there are allusions to it in Middleton's *Black Book* printed in 1604,[40] the theaters were closed for most of 1603 and early 1604, so the most likely date of *The Merry Devil's* performance is 1602.[41] This is arguably the most vivid and entertaining of all the anonymous plays of the era to survive into our day. Even in the garbled state of its text, one can easily understand why Jonson called it a "deare delight" of audiences as late as 1616[42] and why the printed quarto went through at least seven editions before the Restoration. One can also understand the urge to attribute it to Shakespeare, merely on the grounds of its obvious entertainment value. Whether Shakespeare collaborated cannot be proven, but the fact that the magician Fabel in the ostensible subplot is the largest role and is of precisely the right age and manner for Burbage suggests that someone very familiar with Burbage's requirements was involved.

The extant text totals only 1,501 lines, extremely short for a popular comedy (Shakespeare's briefest is *Comedy of Errors* at 1,918 lines in the Folio; most of his comedies are between 2,200 and 2,800 lines long.) It is almost certainly a memorial reconstruction made about the same time as the work was registered, in October 1607. An allusion in Middleton's *A Mad World My Masters* of 1608 makes it clear both that the play was on stage again in 1607 and that several of Smug the clown's scenes are missing from the printed version, and textual evidence points to a number of other missing scenes for other characters.[43] Thus, the surviving text may be a corrupt memory of the 1607 or the 1602 original.

Burbage would have been Peter Fabell, the largest role. There is also a very clear clown role, Smug, for Armin. Because of textual brevity, we can only in a general sense determine the comparative importance of the more minor characters. However, most of the character types have obvious matches in the company of this date. Shakespeare, Heminges, and Crosse cover the two major fathers and the talkative Host. The colorful hunting and drinking priest, much like Toby Belch, must have been assigned to Phillips. There is an unusually large number of young men's roles, at least three of sufficient length to prevent doubling, yet none so terribly large as to overshadow any of the full Sharers. Raymond, the romantic lead, must have been taken by Sly, the youngest of the Sharers at the time, with Cooke then as Frank Jerningham, his rival for the hand of the beautiful Milicent. This is one area in which the brevity of the script provides less certainty than most of our previous casting assignments. Sly was not handsome, as his portrait makes clear, and Cooke apparently was, so it seems odd to assign Sly to the romantic lead. However, at this time Cooke had not even a half share, so it is most unlikely he would have played the larger role of Raymond, unless of course the memorial reconstruction reflected a change in balance between these two roles made at a later date. Boys such as Gough and Edmans who had recently graduated from women's roles would have played the remaining young men. One other father role exists, Sir Richard, but it is a very small role that easily doubles with the cowardly Sexton frightened of the dark, a typical comedian's role for Cowley. Condell then would have played the blustery and colorful gamekeeper Brian, who appears in only one scene, probably extending his stage time as Coreb the devil who is tricked by Fabell.

The company also presented the anonymous *Fair Maid of Bristow.* Registered February 8, 1605, it was printed "as it was plaide at Hampton, before the King and Queenes most excellent Maiesties." The only recorded performances at Hampton were in the winter of 1603–04, so the play must have been on the public stages before James's accession and the plague closure in 1603, although it may have been revived during 1604 before printing. An acting company is not specified, but the new King's Men played four times in the King's presence, whereas the Alleyn company did so only once. The principals of the cast fit the King's Men very well, so it was all but certainly a King's Men play. Given that source, the play is almost unique in that it is an extant anonymous Chamberlain's/King's Men play never attributed even in part to Shakespeare.

The surviving text is very brief, barely 1,100 lines, surely a memorial reconstruction and not a very good one at that. With such brevity, we cannot be absolutely certain about the details of each casting assignment, but the basic characters necessary to the two plots make it relatively easy to assign roles. The clown named Frog was obviously intended for Armin, with his straight man Douce played by Cowley, who must have doubled among the masquers and constables. Challener and Vallenger, both in love with the same fair maid, must have been Burbage and Condell, probably in that order. The two fathers must have been Crosse and Shakespeare. The weak-willed young noble Sentloe was most likely Sly, who has played all the other weak-willed young nobles in the previous two seasons and is the only young Sharer left. Richard the Lionheart could have been either Phillips or Heminges, with the other then as the upright friend Harbert who leads Sentloe to a path of honesty. The fair maid herself is a fairly small role, playable by either Burbage's or Condell's younger boy. Sly would not yet have had his own apprentice, so Florence was more likely the boy of the actor playing Harbert, who spends some time converting her to the path of righteousness.

The London Prodigal was printed in 1605 "as it was played by the King's Maiesties servants," and identified as "By William Shakespeare." Given the theater closures to come in 1603–04, it must have been written and first performed in late 1602; although one of the characters is identified as a "commander, under the king,"(II,i,p.201) that is a wording change that would have been easily and automatically made by the text's provider after Elizabeth's death. Although the work may of course have also played in 1604–05, the cast list certainly favors 1602, if not far earlier, for it requires at least three principals old enough to have marriageable children. By 1604–05, when Phillips was replaced by the younger Lowin and Crosse had died, the company would have only Shakespeare and Heminges to play men in that age group. In 1602, however, Shakespeare, Heminges, Phillips, and Crosse were all available if need be for such fatherly roles.

Perhaps the strangest aspect of *The London Prodigal* is its similarity to *All's Well That Ends Well.* In both plays, the principal young woman is wed to a young man unworthy of her, whom she nonetheless pursues in disguise. Matthew is a liar and a scoundrel, almost certainly played by Burbage, who marries young Luce only for her money and is arrested as the couple comes out the church door. She refuses to marry any of the locals, insisting that although unconsummated, the marriage is genuine. She runs off to London where she dons a Dutch dress and accent, only to have Matthew, now a highwayman, tell her his wife has betrayed and bankrupted him. Nevertheless, she throws off her disguise to save Matthew from the gallows when her father charges him with her murder. Rather like Helena and Bertram, Luce and Matthew hardly speak to each other, suggesting that Luce was not Burbage's apprentice. Matthew's only sustained exchange with a woman is the scene in which he robs Delia, Luce's younger sister. It is a small role, although the brevity of the script may have something to do with that, but if we assume the boy who played Lucius in *Julius Caesar* was very young in 1599, then he would be suitable in age for such a young woman's role. Luce was more likely the apprentice of the man playing her father. There are a plenitude of older men in the play; Matthew's father, himself in disguise to find out his son's true nature, must have been Crosse, the oldest man in the company. His brother was probably Shakespeare, who seems to have looked older than his age, which was nearly forty, while Luce's father and the parasite Weathercock would have been assigned to Phillips and Heminges. The country bully Oliver who also wishes to marry Luce was probably Condell, given yet another opportunity to fight with Burbage, whereas the witty city gentleman Civet, described as a very little man, would have been Armin's role.

We have seen almost nothing of Heminges' replacement for Cooke, who should have been quite prominent by now, so he is unlikely to have played Luce. Phillips' boy Gilburne would be a little old by this date, perhaps as old as eighteen, and roles like Maria in *Twelfth Night* hardly seem like preparation for a noble ingenue like Luce. However, we know the name of Phillips' replacement for Gilburne, a boy called James Sands. When Phillips died in 1605, he left a substantial bequest to Gilburne, his "late" apprentice and a similar one to Sands, to be paid when Sands had finished his bonds. We must assume that Sands was relatively close to the end of his term of service in 1605, for if he were only ten or eleven, Phillips would expect the boy to be taken care of by whatever new master he might find, and it would have been awkward for the executors to hold onto the items for many years awaiting the boy's maturity. Thus, Sands probably began his apprenticeship around the time the Globe opened, which would make him about thirteen in 1602 and only a year or so away from freedom when Phillips died in 1605. This in turn would mean he was ready to play some largish roles, and assuming that Phillips played Sir Lancelot, then Sands is the most likely Luce.

The London Prodigal and *The Fair Maid of Bristow* provide a rare glimpse of the company at work in more everyday mode. Although the central characters come from the City, the real focus of the plays is on the variety of characters in the countryside, as is also true of *The Merry Devil of Edmonton.* Of the comic playwrights whose work has survived in any quantity, almost all focused on the City for their comedy. Jonson, Dekker, Marston, and Middleton almost exclusively portrayed London types, whereas Shakespeare's comedies are all but exclusively rural or pastoral.

These plays remind us that Shakespeare was not alone and that *Merry Wives of Windsor*, for example, was not an aberration but rather a sample of what was a very significant strain in the Chamberlain's Men's repertory. (This also provides some support for their apocryphal attributions to Shakespeare.)

Both *Prodigal* and *Fair Maid* deal with London wastrels gone bad, who flee to the countryside and are eventually saved by the love of a good woman; yet, curiously, in both plays, the woman involved is by Shakespearean standards a very small role. If nothing else, this serves to underline Shakespeare's peculiar willingness to trust at least some of the boys to do something out of the ordinary. But it perhaps also indicates the problems all the writers faced when the apprentices and masters did not line up properly for the plots. It is difficult to write more Juliets if you have no boys with the skill or appearance to play such a role; it is even more difficult if the boy's master is not in a position to play her Romeos.

Although these plays provide a sample of company material during these years, Shakespeare's work that had figured so prominently before 1600 is curiously absent. Assuming that the first versions of *Coriolanus* and *All's Well* were in fact written in this period, they would have been finished well before the end of 1601 while Tooley was still young enough to play convincing women. This raises the more than interesting question: What was Shakespeare doing for the rest of 1601–02? If our conjectured early versions of these plays did not in fact appear, that question is even more serious. Since 1594, Shakespeare had consistently provided three plays a year for his company; suddenly, after *Twelfth Night*, his output ground to a halt. But what he was actually doing in this period is a mystery that deserves far more attention than it has previously received from his biographers.

One thing he was almost certainly not doing was writing *Troilus and Cressida*. Somebody wrote a play on the subject, which was registered February 7, 1603, a most curious registration to Roberts "to print when he hath gotten sufficient authority." There is no evidence that this particular text was by Shakespeare. The version we have was registered as a new play in January 1609 and printed shortly thereafter. It may be a revision of an earlier version by Shakespeare or by someone else, or a completely new play written at that later date. But the Shakespearean text that exists under that title could not have been performed with any hope of success during 1602. The fundamental issue is: Who could have played Troilus? Shakespeare took pains to describe Hamlet, unquestionably played by Burbage in 1600, as in his thirties and "fat and scant of breath" (V,ii,290). It is impossible to believe that he would have taken similar pains to describe Burbage in 1602 as "the youngest son of Priam, a true knight/Not yet mature" (IV,v,96–97), who "never saw three and twenty" (I,ii,238) and "has not past three or four hairs on his chin" (I,ii,113–14). The only members of the company likely to have such an appearance are Edmund Shakespeare, who was exactly that age but was never a Sharer, or apprentices or former apprentices like Cooke, Gough, or perhaps Edmans, who were only Hired Men in 1602, if they were in the company at all. One point we have established in detail over the first eight years of the company's existence is that the Sharers did not commission new plays in which Hired Men had larger roles than any, much less all of the Sharers. All of the extant company plays from 1601–02 have followed the same casting patterns as in all previous years. There is no reason to believe that the Sharers would suddenly, for only one play, overturn all their standard practices and all theatrical common sense. If, somehow, we should accept that, just this once, the company reversed all previous practice and cast a young Hired Man as Troilus, we are still left with the question of what to do with Burbage. The "deformed and scurrilous" Thersites, as the editor Malone first called him, would have fallen to Armin, not Burbage, and Nestor of the wandering speeches would have been the actor who played Justice Shallow. We can see Phillips in Ulysses' long, long speeches. Condell, the company's best swordsman, would have been Hector, whereas the middle-aged Agamemnon and Pandarus are both far too old for Burbage. Burbage would have had only Achilles as a viable option. If Burbage played Achilles, at five percent of the lines, it would have been the smallest role he had performed in a new play since he joined the company, and there are not just one or two but seven roles larger than Achilles. Even if somehow Burbage accepted such a negligible role, none of the remaining roles fit the status and ages of the remaining Sharers Crosse and Sly. It is extremely difficult to accept that the Shakespeare who so carefully tailored all his previous work to the talents and the share sizes of the company would have written the play as it exists with such awkward casting assignments in mind. By contrast, as seen in chapter 7, all these practical problems are solved if we date the text to 1607–08, the most plausible date for composition of a play printed in 1609.

Nevertheless, before January 1603, some playwright had written a play about *Troilus and Cressida* for the Chamberlain's Men, and it had been sufficiently popular for someone to think it worth printing. But the nature of that play must have been quite different from Shakespeare's later version.

One Roman work more certainly in this season's repertory was Jonson's *Sejanus*. Although it was registered on November 2, 1604, and published in 1605 in quarto, Jonson in his folio said it was performed in 1603. The theaters were open until February 18, 1603, the beginning of Lent, followed by closures related to Elizabeth's death and then the return of plague, so this is just possible. Many explain Jonson's date as indicating a premiere at a court performance in the following winter of 1603–04, although Jonson gives no such indication. Jonson's own pronounced sycophancy makes it unlikely he would fail to mention such a premiere, while his claim that he was later accused of treason for the contents of the play makes such a court performance even less plausible. There was a public performance at the Globe that was met with "beastly rage" on the part of the audience,[44] but this could not have been its first and only performance or there would have been no interest in the work from a publisher.

The long delay between registration and printing suggests an explanation. The original version of *Sejanus* had been a collaboration; as Jonson stated in the epistle of the first quarto:

. . . this book, in all the numbers, is not the same with that which was acted on the public stage; wherein a second pen had good share; in place of which, I have rather chosen to put

weaker (and no doubt less pleasing) of mine own, than to defraud so happy a genius of his
right by my loathed usurpation. (37–41)

Who this happy genius may have been is another of the points endlessly debated
among theatrical scholars, but for our purposes the significant point is that the play
was on stage long enough before 1604 that Jonson had time to rewrite at least half
of it. That first production then could have come only during the winter of 1602–
03. That first version had enough success to interest a printer, but its run was
interrupted by the theater closures of 1603. During 1604, despairing of a revival,
Jonson sold the play to the printer Blunt, who registered it in November. Then,
rather unexpectedly, the acting company revived the play, where it failed before a
particularly unruly audience. Seeing that response, Blunt decided that there was no
possible market for a printing and, when Jonson at last finished his revisions (and
copious research notes) during the next year, chose to re-assign his rights to Thorpe,
who printed it as a literary play prefaced with as many commendatory verses by
famous literary men as possible in order to counteract the bad publicity of this revival.

Whenever *Sejanus* appeared, the most fascinating aspect in our context is the
likelihood that Shakespeare played Tiberius. In the same often quoted comment in
which Jonson professed his love for Shakespeare "this side idolatry," Jonson added,
"Many times hee fell into those things, could not escape laughter: As when hee said
in the person of Caesar, one speaking to him, 'Caesar, thou dost me wrong.' He
replied, 'Caesar did never wrong but with just cause'; and such like, which were
ridiculous."[45]

It is not clear why such like comments were ridiculous; they seem very much the
kind of thing a character like Caesar would believe and say, often and loudly, particularly when he was being most unjust. Most scholars have interpreted this to apply
to Shakespeare's writing, and most therefore assume Jonson refers to *Julius Caesar's*
"Know, Caesar doth not wrong . . ." (III,i,47), although Caesar does not respond
directly to a challenge. This in turn has led many to assume that Shakespeare's play
must have been revised at some time before printing.[46] However, it is at least equally
reasonable, if not more so, to assume that "said in the person of Caesar" means that
Shakespeare said it while impersonating Caesar, that he was in fact playing the role
of Caesar. It is most unlikely he would have garbled the lines he had written for
himself in his own play, or that anyone else might notice if he did so. There is,
however, an extended scene in *Sejanus* with Silius (III), who charges several times
that Caesar has treated him wrongfully, where such an ad lib would fit nicely. Jonson
would be far more likely to resent and to remember for years a "ridiculous" ad lib
in his own play than in a draft version of Shakespeare's. Perhaps Jonson even har-
bored a grudge, blaming Shakespeare's failure to say the proper lines at least in part
for the failure of *Sejanus* in 1604. All things considered, that Jonson remembered a
Shakespearean performance in a Jonsonian play seems far more likely than that
Jonson remembered a single line in an early draft version of Shakespeare's *Caesar*.
(Alternatively, this might equally refer to lines Shakespeare had written for Tiberius
as Jonson's collaborator and which Jonson then rewrote before printing. As the

collaborator's portion has disappeared, and as there is an unusual shortage of other material by Shakespeare during this period, such a collaboration is certainly a possibility.)

In his later folio, Jonson left a cast list that identified the principal actors in *Sejanus* as Shakespeare, Burbage, Phillips, Sly, Heminges, Condell, Cooke, and John Lowin. As with Jonson's earlier cast lists, this confuses as much as it helps. John Lowin, whose name we have not previously seen, was a member of Worcester's Men with Kemp from 1601 and was still with them at the Rose when the theaters closed for Elizabeth's death in 1603. He did eventually join Shakespeare's company, but he was not on the new patent for Shakespeare's company in May 1603, nor on the list of Sharers in March 1604. Thus, he did not become a Sharer in Shakespeare's company until sometime after March 1604; if he appeared in the play at all, it was only in the revival so poorly received at the Globe. By that time, Phillips had retired, so Lowin could not have appeared in the play with Phillips. Thus, Jonson must have misremembered the cast, probably conflating the two different productions.

In all performances, however, Sejanus, the largest role and a classic over-reacher in the Richard III manner, was obviously played by Burbage. The proud Silius, whose confrontation with Tiberius occupies the core of the first three acts and whose suicide is a traditionally noble Roman death, most likely would have gone to Heminges, with the more military Condell as the Guards Captain Macro. Phillips, who had been playing dissolute men for some time, would seem very likely for Tiberius if not for Jonson's hint that it was actually Shakespeare. Still, with Shakespeare as Tiberius, there is a very large role for an indignant speechmaker, Arruntius, that would have taken advantage of Phillips's rhetorical skills. There are three Sharers left, Crosse, Sly, and Armin, for the three remaining noblemen, Lepidus, Terentius, and Sabinius, who all exceed one hundred lines. No obvious role for Armin leaps out from those three, and Jonson did neglect to mention Armin, so it is possible that the revisions completely eliminated Armin's original role. There does remain a small but significant role for a clown, the lower class barber Eudemus, but this is precisely the size of Cowley's usual roles and more suitable for a Half-Sharer. Women, as is typical with Jonson, hardly appear at all.

At least one significant Hired Man departed the company suddenly during this year, for the company tried to prevent an unauthorized printing of one of their most valuable assets. *Hamlet* was registered July 26, 1602, by the printer James Roberts, the same publisher who had placed the blocking registrations for the plays of August 1600, and who was not the ultimate publisher of Q1. Thus, this Hired Man was probably let go in early July, with the staying registration made as soon as possible to protect the most popular property that he might sell. In August, *Thomas, Lord Cromwell*, was registered and printed in a very short and garbled text, suggesting a quick memorial reconstruction. In early 1603, *Hamlet*'s famous bad quarto appeared in print; the man who played Marcellus is the actor most consistently credited with the memorial reconstruction of that quarto.[47] There are strong suggestions that Kemp participated in the reconstruction of both the *Hamlet* and the *Cromwell* quartos, for the size and clarity of Hodge's scenes stand out from the rest of that text, and the gravedigger's jokes in *Hamlet* are very accurate though in a different order.[48] Thus, it seems likely that the Hired Man concerned went to Worcester's, where he could collaborate with Kemp. When Worcester's company became the Queen's Men during 1603–04, their company lists included four new men who had not been part of the company when they played at the Rose during 1602.[49] Two of these had tenuous ties to the Chamberlain's Men: One was Robert Beeston, whom we have tentatively identified as Condell's boy, now grown up and joining his brother Christopher as an adult. The other was Robert Lee, who around 1590 had been a Hired Man in a company that had also included Richard Burbage.[50] Both names come at the end of a list of ten, which suggests they were Half-Sharers in their new company and thus came in with less capital than usual, further encouraging the idea they had previously been Hired Men in another company. Whether Lee or Robert Beeston in fact provided the text for *Hamlet,* the likelihood that one or both had been fired from the Chamberlain's Men during 1602 indicates belt-tightening within the company due to the intense competition.

The theatrical rivalry of 1601–02 soon took its toll on almost everyone. Derby's Men were on tour in February 1602.[51] To risk such a tour on winter roads indicates a certain amount of desperation, and the fact that they never again appear in any London citations or court records suggests they had given up in London. Although the Blackfriars Boys played three times at court in 1601–02, they were in such serious financial trouble that in April 1602 Henry Evans accepted a deal that he had backed out of in October, giving half the company to new partners in return for some operating capital.[52] Henslowe's diaries are erratic in this period, so we cannot ascertain the daily schedules or income at the Fortune, but that company does not seem to have been particularly prosperous, even with Alleyn performing. They had only one court performance in 1601–02, compared to four for the Chamberlain's Men. Certainly, Alleyn was not happy with the results, for in 1603 he retired again, this time permanently.[53] Despite their belt-tightening, the Chamberlain's Men entered the winter of 1602–03 in the best shape of the London companies. Things would get much worse in 1603.

The King's Men, 1603–06

In January 1603, Elizabeth grew ill, her condition slowly worsening until at last, on the morning of March 24, she died. Four days before her death, a formal "restraint of stage-plaies till other direction be given" was issued by the Privy Council.[1] Theaters should have been closed for Lent some weeks earlier, so this was obviously intended to prevent their reopening during some future period of mourning and perhaps to prevent a replay of the Essex affair, since the succession was still in some doubt.

The new King, James VI of Scotland and now James I of England, took two contradictory public stances toward the theater, as was often his wont in other areas of life. Before he had even arrived in London, he formally banned all Sunday performances.[2] Then he began to bring all the professional acting companies of London under the protection of himself and his family, by issuing on May 19 a patent to the Chamberlain's Men to become the King's Men.[3] It is likely that both acts were intended to bring some centralization to the regulation of theatrical life. The Sunday ban superseded both custom and local regulations that might be bypassed by players under the banner of some powerful lord. At the same time, direct patronage of the acting companies by the royal family made it much simpler to regulate both their activities and the content of their plays. Although this protected the players from more Puritanical local authorities like the Lord Mayor or town councils when on tour, it also eliminated the protections that resulted from the political jockeying of the English nobles.

In a practical sense, neither of the edicts had any immediate impact, because plague returned to London. James in effect sneaked into London for his coronation in July, from which the public was excluded to reduce the risk of infection, and then he immediately left town again, his formal processions and celebrations postponed for nearly a year. The new patent authorized the King's Men to perform only "when the infection of the plague shall decrease." Apparently at least some of the theaters had tried to open before James reached the city, for the Admiral's Men squeezed in two shows at the Fortune on May 4–5, but by May 26, 1603, all London theaters were closed again.[4] They remained closed for almost a year, the longest shut-down since the plague years of 1592–94.

The patent for the new King's Men has encouraged many to theorize unique admiration from the court for these players, and for Shakespeare in particular.[5] There does not seem to be much evidence of this beyond the wishful thinking that continually tries to tie artistry to noble blood. Before granting the patent, James had never seen any of the London acting companies and, as far as can be established, had never seen any of Shakespeare's plays performed by another company. During James' reign, Shakespeare received no awards or personal recognitions, nor did Burbage and his associates. As the King's Men, they received no exemptions from other regulations and were paid no more and no less for court performances than any other company; in fact, they were often paid less than Elizabeth had paid them, for at any court performances James did not personally attend, he neglected to provide the tip that had previously been customary. Given the inflation of the era, by simply continuing Elizabeth's pay schedule, he paid them less than she had ever done. They were invited to perform at court only during the Christmas season, just as during Elizabeth's reign when they were merely the Chamberlain's Men. Their selection as the King's Men rather than the Prince's Men (the old Admiral's) or the Queen's Men (Worcester's), appears to have been merely another example of the luck that had carried them through the crisis years of 1600–01.

However, luck may have had a helper in this case. The 1603 patent lists the Sharers of the company, but the first name on the list is someone new to our history, Lawrence Fletcher. Although probably born in England, Fletcher was a clown who had spent most of his performing life in Scotland, where he had become a favorite of James (but not the court jester; James brought with him an official fool, Archie Armstrong). In 1595, a report reached James that Fletcher had been hanged for some offense. James responded that then he would have to hang all the local justices, but fortunately for them, the report was mistaken. When James came to England, Fletcher left his old company and found a home in Southwark, where he died in September 1608. No one knows how Fletcher came to be associated with Shakespeare's company so quickly, but the addition of James's favorite performer to the company may have been the decisive factor in gaining James's attention.

Nonetheless, "it is generally accepted that Fletcher did not act with the King's Men."[6] Fletcher has always been a problem for Shakespearean scholars because his name does not recur in the Folio list of Principall Actors. However, although we must assume that the names included there were Sharers at some point, there is no reason to believe that this constitutes the complete list of Sharers. One or more may not have satisfied the personal criteria of Heminges and Condell for Principall players, or they may simply have been forgotten; the hardest error to find while proofreading is the omission. Meanwhile, Fletcher's name occurs on all three of the absolutely incontrovertible pieces of evidence of company membership: the 1603 patent, the 1604 livery list for the men who were to march in James's procession, and Phillips' will of 1605. There is no reason whatsoever to think that the names listed on either the patent or the livery list were not Sharers. If Fletcher were not a Sharer and did not act in the company, Phillips a year later would have had no reason to leave him a bequest as a "fellow." If Fletcher were not performing, why did he move to London at all; why not stay with his old company in Scotland? Finally, James surely would expect to see his favorite comic perform when the company played for him at court; how could he not notice that the comedian never performed?

In fact, there is considerable evidence that Fletcher did perform with the new King's Men, and performed regularly. Although the company had Armin as a clown, there was one thing Armin could not do. Being short and funny-looking, he simply could not play the big funny "average guys" that Kemp had played. He certainly could not play Falstaff. Some twenty plays were performed by the King's Men for their new king in the two Christmas seasons of 1603–05. Among those at Hampton in 1603–04 were "Robin Goodfellow," which must have been *A Midsummer Night's Dream*.[7] Among the ten titles recorded for 1604–05 were *Comedy of Errors*, *Love's Labour's Lost*, *Every Man in His Humour*, *Merchant of Venice*, *Every Man Out of His Humour*, and *Merry Wives of Windsor*. According to Burbage himself, the company trotted out *Love's Labour's Lost* only because it had "no new playe that the quene hath not sene."[8] Thus, they must have used up in the 1603–04 performances such obviously suitable material in their repertory as *Much Ado About Nothing* and the play we call *As You Like It*, assuming they had a boy to play Beatrice and Rosalind. All of these plays had major Kemp roles. Armin certainly could not play many of them in any form, although there is an allusion suggesting that he eventually played Dogberry,[9] and modern criticism sees Touchstone as one of his roles. Although it is of course possible that Shakespeare or others revised the plays to fit Armin, no amount of revision would make it possible for Armin to play Jonson's Cob the waterdrawer, nor Costard, and certainly not Falstaff. No matter how much one may rewrite *Merry Wives*, there is no play if Falstaff is not fat and large. Everything points to Fletcher, a professional comic in the Kempean manner, as the man who took over these classic Kemp roles for these court revivals.

Even more tellingly, we can see Fletcher very clearly in at least one of Shakespeare's new plays. Pompey Bum has a great bum—it is in fact the "greatest thing about you" (II,i,214–15). Although modern productions may simply pad an actor's costume, Shakespeare wrote the role for a specific actor. Nothing forced him to call the character Pompey Bum; he could have called him Mouse, or Stubby, or Roach, or simply Pompey. That he chose Pompey Bum must indicate that the role was written for a substantial, large, round, big-bottomed comedian, the physical opposite to Armin. The only possibility is Fletcher.

How Armin felt about this can only be conjectured. We shall have to wait for the details to develop, but it seems obvious from the plays actually performed by the company in 1603–05 that Fletcher was not merely a Sharer on paper but became a very active and regular performing member of the company.

The rest of the patent list is familiar to us: Shakespeare, Burbage, Heminges, Condell, Cowley, Sly, Phillips, and Armin. Crosse's name is missing, indicating that he had retired, or perhaps even had died unexpectedly during the winter. Significantly, some other important names are also missing: John Lowin, whom Jonson listed for *Sejanus*, is not there, as we have previously discussed. Perhaps more surprising is the absence of Cooke, Tooley, Edmans, or Gough. Unlike 1598, when the company needed the older Crosse to replace the older Bryan, the company in 1603 had several Sharers nearing or past age forty—Shakespeare, Heminges, and Phillips—so they could have used Crosse's share to bring in a man much younger than Crosse. In a company with no Sharers under thirty, one would expect the promotion of at least one young man so that there was a dependable young lover on hand. Cooke in particular must have expected at least part of Crosse's share, for he got married sometime shortly before the spring of 1603, almost always a sign of newfound professional stability. If so, he was disappointed, for Crosse's share obviously went to Fletcher instead.

Once the plague arrived in the spring of 1603, most of the acting companies took to the road. The Admiral's Men found this more difficult than in the past and returned to London shortly. The new King's Men apparently were more successful on the road. They left town in late May or June and were recorded in sites as varied and almost random as Bath, Coventry, Shrewsbury, and Mortlake.[10] Performances in Oxford and Cambridge are both mentioned on the title page of the first quarto of *Hamlet*, published at some time during 1603, so they may have been stops on this tour as well.

After his all but secret coronation, James also left plague-ridden London and went into the countryside. In October, he made an extended visit to Wilton House, home of the Earl of Pembroke. On December 2, the Chamberlain's Men were paid for a single performance before James at Wilton. James paid them much more than the usual fee to compensate "for the paynes and expenses . . . in comming from Mortelake."[11] It is unknown why the actors were in Mortelake and whether they made a special trip for this performance or were on tour continuously from June to December.[12]

In 1865, William Cory, on a visit to Wilton House, was told that the family had a letter from Mary Pembroke to her son the Earl, asking him to invite James to Wilton to see *As You Like It* and to meet "the man Shakespeare."[13] Unfortunately, Cory did not see the letter himself, nor has anyone seen it since. A performance of the play we know as *As You Like It* during this tour is most unlikely, for the play itself is not one that might be easily toured. Although it requires little in the way of complex staging, it demands a very large group of Hired Men, the people most likely to be left in London when the company took to the road. As we have seen, even had the Hired Men come with the Sharers, there has been no sign of a strong man to play Charles the Wrestler since John Duke left, and with Bryan retired and Pope and Crosse dead, no one seems available to play the Duke either. Abridgements and revisions are of course possible, but why make awkward revisions in an old play when more suitable current material of a similar nature was already at hand? The play I have suggested was originally called *As You Like It* is at least plausible; we know the company played it at court in 1604, so they had found a way to make it fit the actors available, but the later court performance suggests that it had not yet been seen by the royal party. If we were to guess at a particular play at Wilton, it would be *Hamlet*, which was easily adaptable to a smaller touring company with few or no Hired Men, and which featured the company's greatest star in his most famous role. James went to Wilton in October, but the actors did not come until December, which makes it difficult to believe he was invited expressly, or even as a second thought, to meet the players. Far more likely is that he went to Wilton because the Earl of Pembroke was one of the two or three most powerful English nobles, whose good will James needed to make his crown secure. Once he was at Wilton, the players came to him.

James moved to Hampton Court for the Christmas season, but plague deaths remained high, keeping him out of the city. The new King's Men performed at least eight plays at Hampton Court. One was the Robin Goodfellow play, another *The Fair Maid of Bristow*, according to its quarto. Almost certainly *Hamlet* was performed as well, if it had not already been seen at Wilton, because there were no major plays from the company's active repertoire left in 1604–05 that the queen had not seen. Despite the large number of performances, the new King's Men were no monopoly; the former Admiral's Men performed four times and the former Worcester's played twice. By February 1604, James had at last reached Whitehall, and the King's Men played twice more, the Admiral's once, and there were two shows from the boys' companies. But there were no public performances. On February 8, 1604, Burbage formally petitioned their royal patron for aid, and James granted him thirty more pounds "for the mayntenance and reliefe of himselfe and the rest of his Companye being prohibited to p'sente any playes publiquelie."[14]

James at last made his formal entry into London on March 15, 1604, but Parliament did not open until March 19, so it is unlikely the theaters opened any earlier. When James marched into the city, he authorized the issuance of cloth for the company members to use to make livery for the procession.[15] We do not know if they actually marched. The Herald's office did not list any acting companies in the official order of the procession, and there are several descriptions of that parade, some by theater people like Jonson, Drayton, and Dekker, none of which make mention of the actors.[16] On April 19, after Easter, a new proclamation signed by the Master of Revels, the Lord Chamberlain (patron of the erstwhile Chamberlain's Men), the Earl of Worcester, and three other nobles allowed the Globe, the Fortune, and the Curtain to reopen as soon as plague deaths dropped below thirty a week.[17] The actors thus did not begin public performances until sometime after April 19, 1604.

All of the London companies were damaged by this plague. With modern estimates of deaths ranging as high as 35,000,[18] it would be hard to believe any group escaped unscathed. However, there were no complete collapses of old companies or organizations of new ones such as had occurred in 1593–94. The former Admiral's company, taken under royal patronage as Prince Henry's Men in early 1604 (although not formally licensed until 1607), had once again lost Edward Alleyn, this time to permanent retirement. From April 17, Edward Juby alone accepted all payments for company court performances until 1613. Alleyn stayed in the theatrical business as the landlord of the Fortune, where the Prince's Men continued to perform.

Worcester's Men, now Queen Anne's, felt the worst blow. Will Kemp died during the plague. "Kempe, a man" was buried at St. Saviour's near the Globe on November 2, 1603, and his name is missing from the company's new patent and from the company's 1604 livery list as well. Additionally, one of the company's most promising younger men, John Lowin, left the company to join the King's Men. The reorganized Worcester company, with four new Sharers, surrendered the Rose for the even older Curtain, and references to them show up regularly in provincial records in ensuing years.[19]

Meanwhile, the threat from the boys had all but evaporated. When the plague closed all public gatherings in 1603, Henry Evans tried to give up the Blackfriars lease, but the Burbages refused to let him out of his contract. In January 1604, the group was given a new license as the Queen's Revels company, and the boys were back on stage in the spring. The poet Samuel Daniel somehow became attached to the company and provided *Philotas*, which occasioned some official concern for its allusions to the Essex affair. Daniel almost immediately dropped out of daily operations, removing a layer of respectability that the company sorely needed. The Paul's Boys had similar difficulties, at least financially. Their major artistic voice, Marston, quit writing for them, bought a share of the Blackfriars company, and wrote exclusively for those boys in following years. Although the Paul's Boys continued to perform at court, their audiences steadily declined until mid-1606, when they quit performing.[20]

The plague seems to have had a smaller impact on the King's Men than on the other companies. Crosse's disappearance was probably plague related. We found significant roles for him in all the plays of 1602; thus it seems unlikely he planned a gradual retirement. But as we have discussed, an actor of his age could be replaced relatively easily by older Sharers already in the company. Far more difficult were two other major personnel problems that would have to be dealt with in the coming months. It will help if we pause for a moment, slightly out of chronology, to consider those personnel issues.

The most immediate problem was among the clowns. The addition of Fletcher had been a brilliant strategic move. Fletcher himself had probably been instrumental in gaining the attention of and preferment from the new King. His addition had reopened much of the company repertoire, especially Shakespeare's and Jonson's earlier comedies that depended on a Kemp-like clown. By accident, it had also helped destroy one of their major competitors; with Fletcher in the King's Men, the old Worcester company could not hire him as a clown when Kemp died later that year. The lack of an experienced replacement for Kemp must have been a major factor in that company's decline in the following years. Nor could the old Admiral's Men hire Fletcher to replace John Singer, who retired as company clown around 1603. Nevertheless, as strategically brilliant as the move may have been, it still left the King's Men with two star clowns, a sure recipe for disaster. As a result, within only a few months after the theaters reopened in the late spring of 1604, Armin was squeezed out.

How completely Armin had been eliminated can be seen in the plays performed at court during the winter of 1604–05. During that time, the King's Men played two new Shakespeare plays, *Othello* and *Measure for Measure*, plus revivals of *Comedy of Errors, Love's Labour's Lost, Merry Wives, Henry V,* and *The Merchant of Venice* (so well-received that the King commanded a second performance), as well as Jonson's two Every Man plays and an anonymous *Spanish Maze* that has not survived. One factor all these works have in common is that they have no role for Armin or a clown even minimally like Armin. Fletcher had obviously swept the field.

It may be possible to date Armin's exit with some precision. During 1604, the King's Men produced Marston's *The Malcontent,* which had been earlier performed by the Blackfriars Boys and which was registered for printing on July 5, 1604. Two different editions of the play were published during the year, which we discuss in more detail later, so it is not absolutely clear whether the King's Men production came just before or just after July 5. In either case, *The Malcontent* was definitely one of the earliest new plays presented by the new company. One significant addition to the version made for the adults is a clown called Passarello, which means little sparrow. Armin was the company's little clown. If *The Malcontent* did in fact appear at the Globe at some point between May and July 1604, it indicates that Armin was still performing at that time; as there are no roles for him in any later plays, he thus must have left after *The Malcontent* closed. The company sent twelve men to join James's other servants to impress the Spanish ambassador in August.[21] Although only Heminges and Phillips are named, the unusually large number of men would suggest that the group included both the men on the patent and their potential replacements, already active; if so, then Armin did not officially leave until after August 26.

There is always the possibility that Armin left voluntarily. He had first trained as a goldsmith, so he may have decided to return to a more lucrative trade during the long plague break. Like Bryan and Pope before him, he may have agreed to have himself written out of future company plans while staying on hand until they were ready to drop his old roles from the repertoire. Because the plague lingered, his "retirement" may have been delayed until mid-1604. He may even have been ill. Some years later, Armin published *The Two Maids of Moreclacke,* featuring one of Armin's signature roles, the clown John. But the play had been performed by Paul's Boys, not the King's Men, which must place its performance in 1606 or earlier. Armin's epistle explained that he had not played the role himself because " *Tempora mutantur in illis* etc, I cannot do as I would."[22] The full Latin tag is usually translated, "times change and we are changed with them," suggesting he had grown too old or too frail to perform. Armin had been apprenticed in 1581, so he was only in his mid-thirties in 1604, but illness was always a possibility in this era. There is convincing evidence that Armin was back with the company after 1608, when Fletcher died, but there can be no doubt that he was gone before the winter of 1604.

Armin's retirement left a Share open. Half of it must have gone to William Sly. By 1605–06, Sly was able to buy into the Globe partnership, which means he must have had a major increase in income in order to accumulate so much capital. The most likely source of such income would be an increase in his share of acting company receipts. Sly's early role assignments in the company had been quite variable, as we have seen. As Slender and Aguecheek, for example, his participation was significant, but also curiously truncated, with comparatively few lines for the number of scenes performed; in *Satiromastix*, as Horace, the parody of Ben Jonson, his role was very large, with more lines and comic business than most of the other Sharers. Given the physical characteristics of Horace and Aguecheek, there can be no doubt they were played by the same actor, which would normally indicate that he had moved up to a full Share by January 1602. Yet, in *The Malcontent*, where he plays himself in a prologue, the role is ideal in size for a Half-Sharer, and there are no other later significant roles for him to double. In the other plays of 1602, we likewise found no other large roles he might plausibly have played. Thus, he seems to have retained his half share until at least early 1604. In the later plays, his roles grow significantly in importance. Thus, he must have increased his half share to a full share at about the same time as Armin left the company. The remaining half share then must have gone to Cooke, now a handsome young man in his mid-twenties, who had been waiting for a suitable share for several years already and whose visible roles also increase in future plays.

With Fletcher on hand, Armin's decision to leave was easily dealt with by the other Sharers. The decision of another major player to retire would be dealt with as efficiently, although it would have more long-term effect on Shakespeare in particular. At some time no later than 1604, Augustine Phillips bought a house and land in Mortlake, too far from London for daily commuting. He did not long enjoy his retirement, for he was on his deathbed by May 4, 1605, when his will was made and witnessed in Mortlake. As with the retirement of Bryan and Pope, Phillips probably phased out his participation in the company over some period of time. He was still officially a Sharer in the livery list of 1604 and thus certainly played all the 1603–04 performances for James. He was named among the twelve members who served during the visit of the Spanish Ambassador in August. No record of any performance has been found, despite modern attempts to claim that the Spanish ambassador must have been impressed by the presence of Shakespeare[23]; more than likely, the actors simply bulked up the crowd of liveried servants to impress the ambassador with James's wealth. Thus Phillips may have simply returned from the country for that court service even though he was no longer a regular performer, being technically still a King's Man even in retirement. The purchase of a country house and land indicates he had cashed in some significant city assets. Because he still held his Globe share when he died, he must have sold his acting company share to help pay for his new home.

Phillips was replaced by John Lowin, whose name we have seen in Jonson's cast list for *Sejanus.* Lowin was with Worcester's Men and Kemp in 1601 and was still with them at the Rose as late as the beginning of Lent in 1603. He is in the prologue of *The Malcontent* as himself, but this is a very brief appearance, as it is the only role he might have played later in the play (see p. 132). Thus, he had transferred to the King's Men early in 1604 but had not yet taken over a full share. This addition was certainly prompted by Lowin's obvious talents—as seen later, he could do everything Phillips could do, except swordplay—but it did not hurt that, coming after Kemp's death, the move stripped the old Worcester's Men of another of their most talented and charismatic players. Lowin was of course much younger than Phillips, in fact younger than everyone but Cooke, but the company had plenty of Sharers in their thirties and forties; they needed a replacement who could play roles similar to those Phillips had played in his prime. That he directly replaced Phillips is underlined by Phillips's will, which left bequests to all his old "fellows," including Fletcher, but not including Lowin,[24] indicating that he had not himself acted with Lowin as a regular partner.

Thus, by the fall of 1604, the company had been rebuilt, with full Sharers Burbage, Shakespeare, Heminges, Condell, Sly, Lowin, and Fletcher, and Half-Sharers Cowley and Cooke.

Although the company as a whole coped well with Lowin's replacement of Phillips, for Shakespeare the loss of Phillips was a profound blow. Just as Shakespeare's plays lost their geniality after Kemp left, after Phillips left they lost their color. Over the next three or four years, Shakespeare would rise to great heights as a playwright, but the new plays would be long character studies for Burbage and an exciting new boy. With the single exception of Iago, probably begun with Phillips at least in mind, the rest of the company were reduced to ciphers. After 1603, there are no more Mercutios, no Pistols, no Toby Belch or Puck. There are no more Queen Mabs, no cakes and ale, no characters who overflow with the joy of living and of talking. That colorful energy seems to go missing not only from Shakespeare but from all the writers for the company. Not until Jonson's *Alchemist* will we find another play with the sense of physical energy, verbal pyrotechnics, and simple theatrical excitement that accompanied almost all the plays in the Phillips era. Fashions change, of course, but at least one factor in the many changes that accompanied James' accession to the throne would be the loss of the unique, dynamic, colorful, and very accomplished Augustine Phillips.

Before discussing Shakespeare's new contributions, we should consider one of the first new plays produced by the company in the summer of 1604, John Marston's *The Malcontent.* This was first produced by the Blackfriars Boys in 1602, and there is an open, if joking, admission of the fact that the adults are reviving a play originally intended for the boys (Induction, 94–97). As was seen with *Satiromastix,* the movement of plays between the boys and the adults, though rare, was not unknown. This is the first known between the Blackfriars Boys and the King's Men. To make the play suitable for the adults, however, a number of additions were made, some perhaps by Marston, others apparently by Webster.[25] Both versions were printed in 1604, the only known instance in which we have both adult and boy company versions.

Space precludes a detailed discussion of these changes, which reveal a great deal about the differences between the adult and children's theaters. However, they can be summarized very simply—the additions made the play longer by adding more roles for the larger number of Sharers to play, new scenes to cover the costume changes that were originally made during the musical breaks taken indoors between acts, and more lines for Burbage.

Burbage is identified in the script as Malevole, speaking a third of the lines. The completely new role is a fool, Passarello, which was tailored for the company clown Armin. Even with a number of new scenes, the revisers were unable to provide enough lines and characters for all the Sharers, so they added an Induction in which William Sly and Sinklo meet Burbage, Condell, and John Lowin before they put on their character costumes. In the play proper, Bilioso and the usurper Duke, both of whom are older than Malevole, must have been Phillips and Heminges. Mendoza, the real villain of the piece, roughly the same age and the mirror image of Burbage, thus must have been Condell; since he enters in the play after Malevole/Burbage's re-appearance, he has even longer than Burbage to change into his costume. The "young courtier" Ferneze, with only a handful of lines, must have been Cooke, the senior of the younger players. Lowin then was left with the Captain, who has even fewer lines, indicating that he was not yet the full Sharer he would shortly become, as earlier discussed. Sinklo's brief appearance indicates he was back with the company as a Hired Man, though this is his last mention by name. The largest female role is the bawdy Macquerelle; we would automatically look to the boy who had played Maria in *Twelfth Night*, but Gilburne was nearly twenty by this date. The new scenes include a much expanded role for Bianca, played entirely with Bilioso; this means that the younger apprentice of Phillips, James Sands, was occupied elsewhere. Given the nature of the role, the only likely boy for Macquerelle is Crosse's boy, now about seventeen but without a master (or perhaps taken under the wing of Phillips for his last few months in the company).

A second edition containing the King's Men additions was rushed into print within months. However, it was not presented at court later in the year, perhaps because no one wanted to pay for yet more revisions after Armin and Phillips had left the company.

Despite the major shakeups in personnel, during the 1604 season the new King's Men prospered. The major reason was that Shakespeare once again began to write with his old power and imagination. During the fall of 1604, Shakespeare was represented at court by *The Moor of Venice*, which must have been what we now call *Othello*, and *Measure for Measure*. It is possible that very early in this season, the King's Men also played a version of *Timon of Athens*. There is no generally accepted date for this play. Plutarchian in its source, it suggests proximity to *Coriolanus* or *Antony and Cleopatra*. The bleakness of its tone suggests a close relationship with *King Lear*. Like the romances such as *Pericles* or *Winter's Tale*, it is clearly divided into before and after and reads like a bilious fable, but nonetheless a fable rather than a drama, which has encouraged many to date it around 1608. Some scholars have argued that the version we have is in fact unfinished, and that the play may never have been performed. There is also the possibility that the extant text is either a collaboration or a revision, or both. Wells and Taylor argue, based on computerized studies of language, that Middleton is in fact the second hand.[26]

If we accept Wells and Taylor's argument and their assignment of specific scenes, we find a most unusually bifurcated play. Shakespeare would be responsible for about two thirds of the lines for Timon and Apemantus, and all of the Poet, Painter, Fool, and one of the senators, whereas Middleton would be responsible for almost all of the Steward's scenes and those involving Hired Men. As we have seen in *The Malcontent* and as is seen shortly in *Othello*, the new King's Men, like the Chamberlain's Men in 1594, appear to have begun performing with a much abbreviated complement of Hired Men; even when their number was later expanded, as in *Macbeth* or *Lear*, their dramatic duties were still minimal. But in Middleton's sections, Hired Men play an enormous role, some four hundred lines. Surely, if Shakespeare were writing concurrently with Middleton and such a large number of Hired Men were at hand, Shakespeare would have included some of them in his sections as well. Similarly, Apemantus has a Fool, but the role is curiously truncated, with only twenty-two lines in a single scene ascribed to Shakespeare. As *The Malcontent* illustrates, the company was in the habit of expanding, not contracting, opportunities for Armin (not to mention the question of what to do with Fletcher). This suggests that some other scene or scenes intended for the clown have disappeared. Third, *Timon* is unique among Shakespeare's works in that the women's roles are all but non-existent. Alcibiades has two women who together speak only nine lines, and the characters in the masque have only about twenty lines, the masque is generally agreed to have been the work of Middleton. Although there are no prominent women in any of the probable sources for the play, it seems most unusual that the wealthy and prosperous Timon has no wife or mistress and that later we have no scenes in which he forsakes the company of women as well as of men. These three factors seem to indicate that Middleton's portions came several years later than Shakespeare's, when the company no longer had a competent fool or major woman but did have a large complement of Hired Men or new Half-Sharers (see p. 180). In that case, Middleton would have been revising rather than collaborating, and Shakespeare's original would date some years earlier than the finished version we have in the Folio. Because we are arguing for an earlier performance based on scenes that no longer exist, we cannot of course be certain of that date. However, within the broad range of possible dates suggested by textual analysts, the only time when Shakespeare's company seems to have had a reduced complement of Hired Men is in early 1604.

At that time, Burbage rather obviously would have played Timon, but given that roughly 40% of the play was later replaced by Middleton, our other casting assignments must necessarily be somewhat tentative. The verbosity of Apemantus suggests Phillips, and his retirement during the course of the year encourages our assumption that, if the play appeared at all, it appeared very early in the year. We can perhaps see a company in-joke in casting Shakespeare as the Poet, in which case Heminges would have been the Painter. The bulk of the Alcibiades lines are in the Middleton sections, so we cannot be sure if the role was larger or smaller in 1604, but Condell is the only remaining full Sharer without an assignment. Certainly, such a core cast underscores the plausibility of a performance at this date, but even so, that production must have differed significantly from the text that survives in the Folio.

Much more certainly, Shakespeare's *Othello*, seen at court on November 1, reached the Globe at about the end of summer. The most claustrophobic of Shakespeare's plays, *Othello* could have been performed by this company almost without Hired Men. When placed alongside *The Malcontent*, which also requires almost nothing from the Hired Men, it seems obvious that, just as in 1594, the Sharers had begun performing with only a minimal complement of non-Sharers. *Othello* is also one of the most seriously overbalanced ensembles in Shakespeare's work. Othello and Iago together have 55% of the lines, and with Desdemona included, the three take two-thirds of all the lines. Burbage is known to have played Othello,[27] and Iago has all the marks of a role originally intended for Phillips, much like Cassius to Burbage's Brutus. But if Phillips was in Shakespeare's mind when he began writing, Phillips did not make it to the final draft. Iago clearly states that he has "looked upon the world for four times seven years" (I,iii,311–12), that is, he is twenty-eight years old. Shakespeare rarely mentions a character's precise age, preferring to refer to characters within more generalized age groups. Iago's twenty-eight may be false, of course— Lear's eighty is obviously so—but there would be no dramatic incentive to make an older actor pretend to be younger in order to play Iago. If Shakespeare wanted a false age, it should have been older than Cassio, not younger because Iago's major motivation is resentment at being passed over in favor of the less experienced Cassio. Thus, we have to assume that Iago is twenty-eight because the actor for whom the role was intended appeared to be, or in fact was, twenty-eight years old. This was not Phillips, who was forty or older. Condell, Sly, and Burbage were all about the same age, in their early to mid-thirties. John Lowin, however, left a portrait dated 1640, with the annotation "aged 64." A John Lowin was baptized in St. Giles parish in London on December 9, 1576, the year indicated by the portrait. In that case, in the summer of 1604, Lowin was twenty-seven, about to turn twenty-eight in December. Thus, it seems clear that Iago was originally played by Lowin.

With Burbage as Othello and Lowin as Iago, Condell was obviously Cassio. Although outwardly calm, when he has a little alcohol his temper flares and he draws his sword, just as Condell had been doing since he played Tybalt. Sly, the gullible Aguecheek, was thus the most likely gullible Roderigo. This means that Cooke, the younger swordsman of the company, would have played Montano, a perfectly sized role for a trusted Hired Man about to become a Half-Sharer. That leaves Heminges and Shakespeare, now the right age to play fathers, to sort out the Duke and Brabantio, plus his brother Gratiano and kinsman Lodovico, probably doubled in that order. Fletcher then took the minimal clown, another of those brief clown roles common to the tragedies, and Cowley filled in among the drunkards on Cyprus and probably among the council in Venice during Act I as well.

The women are few in number, but quite striking in their nature. The smallest role, and the most stereotypical, is Bianca; as all her scenes are played with Cassio, this must have been written for Condell's boy who first began to play significant roles in 1602's *Satiromastix*. Emilia is a creation far more complex than usual (or dramatically necessary) for a leading lady's waiting-woman. Her combination of cynicism, bawdiness, meekness, and bravery seems unique in Shakespeare's work, for no similar characters come to mind from any period. We know that Phillips had an apprentice named Sands who would have been about fifteen or sixteen at this date, the right age for such a large role, and if Shakespeare began writing with Phillips in mind for Iago, he would have written with Sands in mind as well. Phillips' retirement may well explain why Emilia, although married to Iago, has only the one brief scene with him. Phillips left a bequest to Sands, payable when he should conclude his bonds. Someone in the company must have taken over those bonds; Heminges, Burbage, and Sly were co-executors of the will, so any of the three is possible. Given that Sly also left Sands a bequest, it seems most likely that Sands finished his bonds with Sly. In that case, he would have continued to act, but there would be no reason to write long complex scenes for Sands to act with Lowin, who was not the boy's master.

As unusual as Emilia might be, Desdemona is something new entirely. With Desdemona, Shakespeare has found a new boy to stimulate his imagination. This is a boy of considerable talent, who also has something we have not seen in previous Shakespearean women, a physical femininity. So convincingly feminine is he that he can even be trusted with long, active, and serious scenes in nightclothes and in bed. Nudity is of course not at issue. The Elizabethan shift or nightgown would have covered the boy's body as completely as did a dress, but it would have required a different sense of movement, a natural "femininity" that would not interrupt the audience's suspension of disbelief. None of the roles for the company's earlier boys has ever hinted at such a physical appearance. This must be a new boy, someone who had not been playing leading roles before the plague break, but it must also be an experienced boy, for Desdemona has almost four hundred lines.

We have only one verified boy's name from the company's first Jacobean decade: John Rice. However, Rice was apprenticed to Heminges. As seen in detail in the following pages, the boy who played Desdemona will continue to play such large roles, almost all of whose stage time involves scenes with Burbage (and almost no one else), and who thus must have been Burbage's apprentice. No apprentice has been identified for Burbage between Tooley's last visible roles in 1602 and the appearance of Richard Robinson around 1610, precisely the period in which this most talented and feminine boy would make his presence felt. In his prime, he will play Desdemona, Isabella, Lady Macbeth, Cleopatra, and probably Imogen and Marina. If he survived into adulthood, he should have become a significant Sharer.

The most plausible candidate is William Ecclestone, who joined the Lady Elizabeth's company in 1611 and then joined (or rejoined) the King's Men in 1613. He is listed as a Principall Actor, despite gaining a share after Shakespeare had stopped writing, and his name also appears in Jonson's cast lists for *The Alchemist* and *Catiline* and in numerous other company plays well into the 1620s. Nothing has been found that ties him securely to an apprenticeship in the King's Men, but his name is also absent from the records of any other company, including the boys' companies. Whoever the Desdemona boy might have been, there is no doubt the company, and Shakespeare, had found a very talented boy who would form a most remarkable partnership with Burbage over the next few years. The most probable name for that boy is William Ecclestone.

Measure for Measure, appearing in the fall, uses the same company as *Othello*. Burbage was surely the Duke and the obvious Angelo, similar in age and experience but with far fewer lines, would have been Condell. Wise, mature Escalus fell to one of the elders of the company, probably the balding Shakespeare, and the Provost to the other, Heminges. Lowin would have been the smart-aleck Lucio, a verbose character similar to those played by his predecessor Phillips, but without the physical energy associated with Phillips. Sly then must have played Claudio, the only remaining role suitable for a full Sharer. Pompey, as we have seen, must have been Fletcher, with Cowley then the clownish policeman Elbow and the other Half-Sharer Cooke as Froth, doubling Abhorson or Fr. Peter, or both. Isabella seems obviously intended for Ecclestone. She has no scenes *en deshabille*, but she does have the ability to stimulate desire in any man she meets. The loyal and loving Mariana may well have been the same boy who played the raucous and bawdy Bianca; her big moment comes in the final scene with everyone on stage, but her marriage to Angelo suggests Condell as the boy's master.

Although critical discussions of the plays themselves are not a major focus of this particular work, one such comment may be in order here. In modern criticism, *Measure for Measure*, *All's Well That Ends Well*, and *Troilus and Cressida* have consistently been grouped as "problem plays." As we have discussed, the chronological connection usually assumed for these plays is more than a little dubious. However, there is no doubt that *Measure for Measure* in particular has been persistently seen as a problem play for modern audiences as well as for critics. As it was sufficiently popular at the Globe to be brought to court, it seems clear that audiences of Shakespeare's day did not find it disturbing or inadequate in any significant way. But then they had an advantage—they *saw* it rather than read it. Most importantly, they saw it with a star, Richard Burbage.

For modern analysts most of the problems of *Measure for Measure* center on the Isabella–Angelo relationship, with the Duke relegated to a rather noisy irritation. But the Duke is in fact the star, the seventh largest role Shakespeare ever wrote (even though he has no soliloquies), almost exactly the same length as Othello and three times the length of Angelo. That comes as a surprise to most readers, for modern stars have unanimously shunned the role. Charles Laughton, Emlyn Williams, James Mason, and John Gielgud, for example, all played Angelo, none the Duke. Thirty-one different name actors turned down the role in the BBC's complete Shakespeare series, forcing them to settle on a capable character actor. Roger Allam, one of the few modern successes in the role, openly admitted that the Royal Shakespeare Company (RSC) offered him the opportunity only because they could find no one else with greater fame willing to take the role.[28] By contrast, Shakespeare's audience saw a play about a witty and dynamic nobleman, played by the charismatic Burbage, who reforms his kingdom and rescues the finest young woman in it from both a hypocritical Puritan and a (Catholic) nunnery. Thus, the audience of 1604 saw no problem when the Duke announced he would marry Isabella. She may have been perfectly willing to let her brother die to protect her chastity from Angelo, but that was different—Angelo was not the star. The heroine always rejects the indecent advances of the hypocritical character actor only to succumb without resistance to the star; when the star offers marriage, wealth, and noble position as well, she doesn't even have to speak to signify her consent, so obvious is it. Shakespeare's audience had never seen Holman Hunt's painting, so they saw a young gentlewoman wearing gentlewoman's clothing, very attractive to men, tricking the villain and ultimately winning the greatest prize of all, the richest, noblest man in the kingdom, not coincidentally played by the greatest star of the age. No audience has ever had a problem with that plot.

There was a new quarto of *1 Henry IV* dated 1604, suggesting that a public performance had stimulated enough new interest to encourage a reprint. The fact that *Merry Wives* was played later at court indicates that Fletcher proved an adequate Falstaff, so a revival of one of the Henry IV plays might be assumed as well during this year. Condell and Burbage, we must assume, continued as Hotspur and Hal, but Heminges and Shakespeare, the only men old enough to play fathers in the company, would have been forced to shift to Henry and Worcester. Sly and Lowin would have played Poins and Mortimer, with Cooke perhaps the young, sword-fighting Douglas.

More certainly, the company was performing *Hamlet* again during late 1604. It was so popular that an anonymous satirist published in 1605 encouraged ambitious young men to "Get thee to London, for if one man were dead, they will have much need of such a one as thou art . . . to play . . . Hamlet with hi for a wager."[29] Burbage of course continued as Hamlet, with Condell still as Laertes. With Phillips and Crosse both now gone, the two eldest actors, Heminges and Shakespeare, moved to Claudius and Polonius, while Sly and Lowin took Horatio and the Ghost, the latter disguising his lack of age with his helmet, much as Shakespeare had done originally.

The court revivals of 1604–05 provide the most detailed picture of the new King's Men at work. In addition to *Othello* and *Measure for Measure*, these included Shakespeare's *Comedy of Errors, Love's Labour's Lost, Merry Wives, Henry V,* and *The Merchant of Venice*, Jonson's *Every Man In* and *Every Man Out of His Humour*, and the anonymous *Spanish Maze*, which has not survived. The practical goal during any revival would have been to make as few cast changes as possible, so as to minimize rehearsal and preparations. Where older actors had left the company, their replacements would move wherever possible directly into the roles of the actor whom they had replaced. Thus, as already discussed, Fletcher would have played Falstaff, Costard, Launcelot Gobbo, Cob, Buffone, and Dromio of Syracuse, all previous Kemp roles. Likewise, Lowin, as the replacement for Phillips, would have covered Bobadilla, Armado, Gratiano, and possibly Macilente, which would require only a minor line change so that he was no longer described as unusually thin.[30] He probably did not play Pistol, however, for both *Merry Wives* and *Henry V* also required someone to replace Crosse. It is of course possible that Evans and Fluellen were rewritten for a different accent, but in any case, the Welsh parson Evans could not be played by Sly (who would have continued to play Slender) or Condell (who played Caius), or Shakespeare (who played Shallow), or Heminges (who played Page), or Fletcher (who must have replaced Kemp as Falstaff). Thus, the priest must have been taken by Lowin. In that case, Lowin would also have played the Welshman Fluellen, leaving Pistol in *Henry V* to Fletcher, available because Falstaff plays no part in that play. It is at least possible, even probable, that Pistol and Bardolph simply disappeared from *Merry Wives*, with Cowley's Nym perhaps augmented to handle all of the scenes in which Ford and Page are informed of Falstaff's designs on their wives. Everyone else who could possibly do so simply repeated previous roles, Burbage playing Henry, Berowne, Bassanio, Ford, and so on (see Chart C).

The only actual movement of roles among remaining Sharers would have occurred in *The Comedy of Errors*, which depends on twins, and *Merchant of Venice*, built around older actors who had retired. Thus, where Heminges and Phillips in 1594 had played the Antipholi, with Bryan as their father, the twins now would have been Burbage and Condell, with Heminges moving to the father role of Egeon. With Fletcher replacing Kemp as one Dromio, and his former twin Pope now retired, the second Dromio must have been Lowin, since he seems to have been much larger than Sly, the remaining new full Sharer. *Merchant of Venice* would also have demanded some significant change. The only plausible Shylock and Antonio would have been Heminges and Shakespeare, the two Sharers senior both in age and experience. Shylock has a grown daughter and Shakespeare's baldness suggests he looked older than his real age; thus, he would have been the more probable Shylock at this time. With Shylock, Polonius in *Hamlet*, and Tiberius in Jonson's *Sejanus*, 1602–04 marked the peak of Shakespeare's performing career. Assuming Lowin replaced Phillips as Gratiano, then Sly would have taken one of "the salads," with the other played by Cooke.

By the time the company finished these 1604–05 court performances, they had re-established themselves as the dominant company of the nation. Later in the year, Shakespeare's reputation as the greatest playwright of the age was cemented by the good quarto of *Hamlet*. "Newly imprinted and enlarged to almost as much againe as it was, according to the true and perfect Coppie," it can have only come from Shakespeare's own papers.[31] Otherwise identical versions dated 1604 and 1605 suggest it was printed around March 25, 1605, the end of the year in the early Jacobean calendar, and that the revival performances had concluded about the same time.

Even so, the company did not enter the new year smoothly. Sometime in late November or early December 1604, the company opened a new play about *Gowry*. In 1600, Alexander Ruthven had tried to assassinate James in Scotland. The plot had been foiled and both Alexander and his apparently innocent older brother, the Earl of Gowry, had been killed in confused circumstances. We have no idea who may have written this play, nor what its specific content might have been, but we do know that shortly after December 18, 1604, the play was suppressed. We must assume this suppression was as complete as the *Isle of Dogs* suppressions, for no copies and no other allusions have survived.[32] If nothing else, the incident serves to remind us that not even (or especially) the King's own company was exempt from political censorship.

It should be noted at this point that we have identified some fourteen plays performed to sufficient acclaim during the first full year of the King's Men to merit either publication or a court performance. Ten were by Shakespeare. Little more need be said about his importance to the company's continued success.

During the following spring, Shakespeare produced two more of his most respected works. One of these was *Macbeth*. Curiously, there has been little argument about the dating of *Macbeth*, despite the lack of registration, a quarto, or any clear contemporary allusions to it before 1611. Chambers suggested 1605–06, which has been generally accepted, with a tendency toward the later date on the assumption that the Porter's jokes refer to the "equivocation" of Father Garnet after the Gunpowder Plot.[33] Although there can be no doubt the term was in the news at that time, there is one very obvious reason why the play must have been written and performed well before rather than after the Gunpowder Plot was discovered: *Macbeth* is a play about the assassination of Scottish kings. In the tense political climate that followed the Gunpowder Plot, no rational acting company, much less one directly in the service of a Scottish King, still relatively insecure on this throne, would stage a play that begins with the successful murder of one Scottish king and ends with the assassination of a second during a coup. James I shared some interesting characteristics with both Duncan and Macbeth. Like the historical Duncan, James was not noted for his warlike manner yet was already famous for his ability to ignore the misdeeds of his friends. James's father, Darnley, was murdered, with the connivance of James' mother, Mary Queen of Scots. James himself was a child at the time and of course could not have participated in this plot in any way, but the manner in which Lady Macbeth manipulated her husband to commit the murder must have reminded some viewers of the way Mary seduced her lover, Bothwell, into murdering Darnley. Given Mary's widely known affairs, there would always be some doubts as to James' true parentage. (James' own claim to the English throne was relatively weak, traced through his mother's great-grandmother, but due to Elizabeth's elimination of the last of the English Dukes, no Englishman could be found with a stronger one.) Although James had not yet had opportunity for serious tyranny, his published theories of the divine right of kings certainly justified any such actions he might wish to take in the future. James was already known as capricious, a profligate, a drunkard, and a king who had favorites with whom he was thought to engage in homosexual as well as political activities, not a combination of public traits likely to endear him to the Protestant gentry and burghers of Parliament and the City of London. Shakespeare curiously retained Holinshed's description of the meeting of Macduff and Malcolm, in a scene that regularly tends to put modern audiences to sleep. The suspicious aspect of this scene is that James himself had a son, Prince Henry, who was already being projected among the more puritanical parts of London society as a young man with all the "king-becoming graces" (IV,iii,91), even at this early date when he was only eleven.[34] The man unfit for kingship whom Malcolm pretends to be fits all too closely the public reputation of James, "luxurious, avaricious, . . . sudden, malicious, . . . voluptuous" (IV,iii,58–62). If we were searching for contemporary political parallels, as audiences often did with *Richard II*, for example, then it would be very easy to read *Macbeth* as a thinly veiled argument for the overthrow of James and his replacement with an (English) regent for his son.

In addition, we should note the following points: First, Shakespeare was personally related to many of the conspirators in the Gunpowder Plot; Robert Catesby, Thomas and John Winter, and Francis Tresham were all cousins related to Shakespeare's mother, and the plot itself was hatched in Warwickshire, primarily in Stratford-upon-Avon. Second, Shakespeare and his associates had had previous treasonous dealings with many of these same plotters: Catesby had arranged the *Richard II* performance before Essex's coup. Third, the plotters in London often met at the Mermaid Tavern, which Shakespeare frequented and whose owner was a personal friend and business associate of Shakespeare. Ben Jonson actually attended at least one of their dinners, but he managed to talk himself out of trouble later by naming names and helping to track down priests in hiding. He may even have been a double agent. That Shakespeare somehow never dropped in on similar discussions seems unlikely; that he was never even questioned about them seems miraculous. Finally, the murder of the grooms, borrowed by Shakespeare from the murder of King Duff in Holinshed rather than of Duncan, rather curiously paralleled the Gowry assassination attempt.[35] James was sufficiently upset by the Gowry play to have it completely banned; he would have been most unlikely to feel flattered by seeing similar scenes reintroduced into *Macbeth*, even before the Gunpowder Plot. Afterward, such scenes were even more inflammatory, because the deaths of the conspirators Catesby and Thomas Percy were suspiciously similar as well.

The dating question is further complicated by the issue of Middleton's hand. It is now generally accepted that, at some point, Middleton participated in some revision that may have included significant cuts and the addition of the two Hecate scenes. The two songs traced to Middleton must have been added after 1613–16, the date currently assumed for *The Witch*, from which they came.[36] This suggests that Middleton's other changes came at that same time, after Shakespeare was no longer active in the company, perhaps already dead, and thus unavailable to make his own modifications. Although no one has yet argued on textual grounds for Middleton's authorship of more than Hecate, it seems most unlikely that the company at any time would go to the expense of a revision simply to add Hecate, a boy's role; Middleton must have made more extensive modifications. Thus, it seems more than likely that Middleton at the very least added not just Hecate's speeches but also the entire scenes in which Hecate appears, one of which (IV,i) includes the vision of the kings. It is this vision that is used by many modern critics to argue that the play was actually written to celebrate James' legitimate claim to the Scottish throne through lineage that could be traced back to Banquo, and may have been inserted for a court performance in 1606.[37] All such arguments lose their point if Middleton's hand extends throughout all of IV,i. Curiously, and I think significantly, Simon Forman's very detailed description of a performance of *Macbeth* in 1611 makes no mention of these visions,[38] a striking omission, given Forman's fascination with astrology and prophecy. He also describes the witches as "feiries or Nimphes," indicating very clearly that they were played by boys, not adult men with beards as in the extant text (I,iii,46), in turn suggesting that Middleton may have modified more than just the speeches for Hecate and two songs. When these points are considered alongside the dangerous political aspects of the play, it seems all but certain that the bulk of the play must predate the Gunpowder Plot and that the text as we have it reflects at least one, possibly two revisions made perhaps by Shakespeare in 1611 and by Middleton around 1616, in an attempt to make a very popular work more palatable to the Stuart government.

Given its basic subject matter, it is remarkable that *Macbeth* should have gotten past the censor and then escaped further public censure at any time. That it might do so immediately after the Gunpowder Plot is all but inconceivable. Given the additional factors implying Shakespearean sympathy for the Guy Fawkes conspirators, it is difficult to find words to indicate the level of bravery (or stupidity) that would have been required to even consider writing or performing the play during 1606, when James and the kingdom as a whole were most sensitive and nervous. Far more likely a scenario is that the play had been on stage during early 1605, well before the Gunpowder Plot. As we have seen, Shakespeare had time for new writing after he finished *Measure for Measure,* so the premiere of *Macbeth* was most likely in the early spring of 1605. In that case, the initial performances of the play would have run their course before the political crises of the autumn.

In those performances, Burbage of course must have played Macbeth, with about a third of the lines (and with a model of his head, already made for *Cromwell,* in the prop room). Macduff would have been Condell, fulfilling his usual role as Burbage's sword-wielding opponent of similar age; unusually, he at last was allowed to win the swordfight, although Burbage apparently insisted they go off-stage to do it. Lowin, with the appearance of a bluff, honest soldier put to such effective use as Iago, would have played the genuinely bluff, honest Banquo. Malcolm was probably Sly, who played younger than his real age in general; certainly, he is the only full Sharer available after other casting who might be youthful enough, and the long Act IV scene with Macduff seems to serve no dramatic function other than to pad a Sharer's part. Shakespeare and Heminges split the significant remainder, one taking the perpetual messenger Ross, who appears throughout, the other playing the noble Duncan and then perhaps returning much later as father Siward. Cooke, the youngest swordsman of the company, was suitable for Siward's brave son in Act V, perhaps doubling Lennox, who is on stage regularly but with few lines for the first half of the play. If the witches' beards were Shakespeare's idea, the hags were played by Fletcher, Cowley, and probably the gaunt Sinklo. There is more than enough off-stage time for Fletcher to change from the witch costume to double the porter. If the beards were part of Middleton's later revision, then the witches were played originally by boys, with Fletcher still as the Porter, perhaps doubling as a murderer as Kemp had done in *Richard III*, with Cowley then as Lennox or the second Murderer. The Hired Men necessary to many of the plays performed at court the previous winter are now obvious in the new play, playing the large number of soldiers, messengers, and servants.

The second largest role, Lady Macbeth, must have been written specifically for the dynamic young Ecclestone. In Holinshed Lady Macbeth makes a most minimal appearance: She "lay sore upon him to attempt the thing, as she was very ambitious,"[39] after which she disappears from the story. (In Holinshed, Macbeth and Banquo, not Macbeth and his wife, commit the murder.) The detail of her plotting, her participation in the murder itself, and the sleep-walking scene are all Shakespeare's invention. She exists only because Shakespeare and the other Sharers had decided to maximize the use of this boy's skill. The other boys have much smaller roles more difficult to assign. Two in particular should be noted for future reference: The Macduff boy is intended to be very young, indicating a most precocious new apprentice, trusted for substantial scenes while still very childish in appearance. Lady Macduff may also mark the first significant appearance for a new boy with the deep voice described for Octavia during 1606.

Despite *Macbeth*'s popularity through the centuries, we can see the hole Phillips left in the company. There is no dramatic balance for Burbage. Macduff makes no real impression until his family is murdered. Malcolm, despite the quantity of his lines, usually makes even less impact on the audience. No one has the fire that seemed to burn inside all of the characters written for Phillips. The play is a brilliant character study much more subtle than *Richard III*, but the brilliant parts never quite add up to a satisfying whole, at least one of the reasons why the play has long been associated with a theatrical curse.

We can also see some significant ways in which Burbage's personal requirements were now shaping the plays themselves. Like the modern movie star, he seems to have insisted on being in every scene the plot would allow and taking all the good lines in those scenes. He also apparently demanded soliloquies. He is not the only one to be given monologues, of course—Lady Macbeth has two famous ones—but the soliloquy in which the character explores his feelings, which we think of as so definingly Shakespearean, is all but completely confined to Burbage's roles. So, too, is a peculiar plot structure that allows the star to leave the stage for a long rest in what we think of as Act IV. Shakespeare had of course written such a break for Romeo, but from the moment Hamlet leaves for England, the pattern was all but set in stone in the serious plays, and even in many of the comedies as well. The Malcolm/Macduff scene is so extensive in part because it provides Burbage with this rest period. So does Desdemona's willow song, and later the blind Glocester/Edgar scenes of *King Lear* and the bucolic scenes of *Winter's Tale*. Much of that off-stage period was needed to allow Burbage to recuperate from another of his signatures, the mad scene, before storming back for physically strenuous and emotionally demanding last acts, like the murder of Desdemona or the battles of *Macbeth*. Insanity had become the Burbage specialty. Hamlet, Othello, Macbeth, Lear, Pericles, Leontes, all get their chance to start in shock and terror, roll their eyes, tear their hair, rant, scream, and howl, or even to faint dead away. *Timon of Athens* is little more than one mad scene after another. Even Antony, in the Thidias scene, goes temporarily insane. This is certainly one of the reasons why the company had revived *The Malcontent:* Malevole feigned madness throughout. The company eventually took up *The Spanish Tragedy* as well, although the specific date is unclear, with its legendary mad scene for Hieronymo. Even in the comedies of this era, Burbage usually goes mad—Ford is mad with jealousy (and then is given a rest while everyone else deals with the confusing Germans of the fourth act), and Malvolio driven mad in his cell. Only the Duke of Venice manages both to escape a comedic mad scene and stay on stage throughout Act IV.

That madness would figure prominently in Shakespeare's second work for the company that year. *King Lear* is dated by almost all scholars in 1605–06.[40] Its quarto was registered in November 1607, noting in the registration itself a court performance the previous December, which would seem to indicate the play had been at the Globe during 1606. The issue is much complicated by *The True Chronicle History of King Leir,* registered May 8, 1605, and printed shortly afterward, "as it hath been diverse and sundry times lately acted." That particular text seems to actually date from 1586 to 1590.[41] Its appearance in print so many years later can only indicate a recent performance of a play about Lear, although the careful avoidance of company identification on the title page suggests that the printer wished to imply he was printing the current version without actually saying so. It is most unlikely that Shakespeare would have written his own version of a Lear play to run immediately after another company had exhausted the audience for the subject. Thus, it would seem very plausible that *King Lear* was actually the Lear play on stage in May 1605, which prompted the publication of the different, older Leir play to take advantage of the publicity.[42] This is somewhat earlier than the play is usually dated. Those modern scholars who place *Lear* in 1605 generally do so only because they are convinced *Macbeth* belongs to 1606, which, as I have argued, seems most unlikely. Many others point to the court performance of *Lear* in December 1606 and to Gloucester's mention of "these late eclipses of the sun and moon" (I,ii,100), an event which did actually occur in September and October 1605, to argue for a date of 1606. Nevertheless, *King Lear* is a historical play, and eclipses were common omens in all periods; there is no more reason to believe that Shakespeare refers here to a specific eclipse than that he refers to a specific storm in *Macbeth* or *Julius Caesar.* In addition, the King's Men were on tour during the months of the eclipses, which means Shakespeare would not have done the writing until December or later. That would make the first few months of 1606 a very crowded composition period, considering that Shakespeare somehow also fit in composition and performances of *Antony and Cleopatra* (see p. 152) before the theaters were closed in the summer for the plague. When Shakespeare was writing regularly in the past, he wrote roughly three plays per year (see Timeline in Chart A). Thus, he usually needed about four months uninterrupted by touring to produce a completely new work. To argue that he rather suddenly increased his writing speed to produce three of his most complex works in less than six months seems unlikely even for a genius. At the same time, such a schedule leaves a large gap after he finished *Measure for Measure* in the early autumn of 1604. Four months per play would provide more than enough time for him to produce both *Macbeth* and *King Lear* between the time he finished *Measure for Measure* in September or October of 1604 and the date the company went on tour in the summer of 1605. Even if *Lear* then followed *Macbeth* in composition, it still could have been on stage by May, when the other *Leir* was registered. If it was on stage before May 1605 and also played at court in December 1606, then it must have been an extremely popular work. We have no record of the court plays of 1605–06, so it is even possible that the December 1606 performance was the play's second appearance at court.

All of this is made even more complicated by the fact that we have two versions of Shakespeare's *King Lear*, but the quarto is not so unlike the Folio as to suggest a memorial reconstruction. One is thus most likely a revision of the other, but scholarly argument as to which may be the earlier version, and its date, is complex and occasionally heated. Fortunately, we need not distinguish between the two at this time because both versions have the same cast and roughly the same proportion of lines per role.

The oddest aspect of *King Lear* at this date, or any other, is Burbage's casting as Lear himself. Lear was one of his signature roles, according to John Fletcher,[43] but it is the *only* Burbage role written by Shakespeare in which Burbage did not play his own age or younger at its premiere. As a rule, stars do not commission material that makes themselves look old. Shakespeare in later years would go to great pains to start even Burbage's fatherly roles with scenes showing him as a younger man only growing older in the course of the play. This suggests that the *Lear* produced at this time was actually a revival of an earlier company play about King Lear and his daughters originally written for Bryan, perhaps visible as one of the extant versions, perhaps much revised by Shakespeare at this time. Because Lear offers not just one but several great mad scenes, Burbage may have wished to essay it, despite the character's ostensible age. Except for the boys' roles, such a revival would have been relatively easy to mount at this time, once Burbage took Lear. Shakespeare and Heminges, both now over forty and the eldest men in the company, would have been Gloucester and Kent, probably in that order. The two youngest full Sharers available, Sly and Lowin, would have played Edmund and Edgar, with Sly more likely as Edgar, who initially seems the weaker of the pair, and Lowin the more Iago-like Edmund. Condell then would have been the mature Albany, and the Half-Sharer Cooke would have taken the much shorter role of Cornwall. The tiny roles of France and Burgundy would have fallen to Gilburne, Gough, Edmans, or Tooley, whereas Cowley probably played the servant Oswald and doubled his specialty, the old country coot who guides Gloucester on the road. As we have indicated, Fletcher was the clown at this time, so he must have been the Fool, despite the general tendency to see this as a quintessential Armin role.

The female roles appear to be a problem, because there were not really three strong experienced boys at this time. Both Regan and Goneril have significant scenes with Lear, so we cannot rely on that factor alone to cast the pair. Ecclestone certainly must have played one, but we must guess to a greater degree than usual about the other. The most experienced one on hand is the boy who played Emilia; Sands was still under his bonds, so this is plausible, although this is a surprising shift of character type for a boy so old. It would have been a large jump for Condell's boy, who only a year or so previously was playing Bianca and Mariana, but with Condell as Albany, his boy is a more plausible choice for Goneril. Regan is usually interpreted as the more sensual, which would encourage our casting of Ecclestone.

Almost all of Cordelia's scenes are also with Lear, which would point to Ecclestone, were he not needed as Regan or Goneril. However, Cordelia is also a very small role in comparison to the others, only about three percent of the total, which points to a less experienced boy. Although Cordelia's big speeches are to Lear, present in all those scenes as well is Kent, who was probably Heminges; thus, one possibility is John Rice. His first mention in the record comes in July 1607, when as Heminges' boy he appeared solo in a pageant before King James, indicating some significant skill at the time. On May 31, 1610, he partnered Burbage in another pageant at court, this time playing Corinea, a "faire and beautiful nymph." He finished his apprenticeship sometime early in 1611, for he signed a bond with Henslowe as a member of the Lady Elizabeth's Men in August of that year. If he was sixteen or seventeen when he played Corinea at court, then he would have been twelve or thirteen in 1605, old enough for visible roles. His later career suggests some precosity, so he might well have taken visible roles from almost the beginning of his training. We have already noted Macduff's son, who was quite small for his age and who was probably played by Heminges' boy. One must assume that, then as now, the one practical casting requirement for Cordelia was that the player be small and light for Lear to carry, so there would certainly be a good reason to advance one of the younger apprentices such as Rice.

As if to demonstrate the immense range required of a repertory company actor, at the same time as the King's Men were coming to grips with *Macbeth* and *King Lear*, they were also playing *A Midsummer Night's Dream* in the Globe. As we have seen, the King's Men performed a play about Robin Goodfellow for the King in 1603–04, but they apparently waited until 1605 to revive it for the general public. There is a joke about Thisbe stabbing herself with the scabbard in *The Fleir*, registered in May 1606, and thus performed by the Blackfriars Boys during 1605–06.[44] This in turn means Shakespeare's work must have been current and popular only slightly earlier, during the summer of 1605. In this new *Dream* production, Shakespeare could have repeated Quince, but Burbage and Condell were both far too old to play Demetrius and Lysander again; if we are to believe *Antony and Cleopatra*, Burbage's hair was actually turning gray (III,xi,13–15). As one of the oldest men in the company, Heminges would have been all but forced to shift to Egeus, which would clear Oberon and Theseus for Burbage and Condell, probably in that order. Lowin, as the replacement for Phillips, would have played Puck. Then Sly and Cooke would have taken the young lovers. Fletcher surely played Bottom. Fletcher had a boy who had been very busy in the court plays of 1604–05 in roles such as Tib and Jacquenetta, but as he was still only eleven or twelve at this time, there would have been little humor in his being forced to play Flute. Thus, Cowley probably moved to Flute; with only the deletion of a line about his beard coming, his increasing age would be an even greater comic effect than an older boy would have provided. The boys' roles are far less clear, because the change in master's roles removes the most likely Hermia and Helena from the picture. Ecclestone's intense femininity suggests that he was comparatively short and thus could play Hermia, but he would automatically have played Titania to Burbage's Oberon. Condell's boy had some experience, but the limited nature of most of his earlier roles makes Hippolyta far more plausible than Helena. Assuming Sands was now apprenticed to Sly, he is the most likely Helena, and his advanced age probably meant he was comparatively tall. Cooke, however, would have had little opportunity to find and train an apprentice in the brief period since he gained his Half Share, and we will see few signs of such an apprentice in later years. Lowin's boy was also short, assuming he had played Moth when the King's Men had revived *Love's Labour's Lost* at court in the previous winter, so he may have been loaned out, so to speak, for the revival; as Puck, Lowin would still be in a position to supervise many of Hermia's scenes.

One other possible revival during 1605 is Marlowe's *Tamburlaine*, both parts of which were reprinted in 1605–06 after a nine-year hiatus. The play had been a part of Edward Alleyn's repertory at the Rose in 1594–95,[45] but Alleyn was long since retired by this time. The Prince's Men, of course, may have staged a revival, although it is not at all clear who among their actors would have been entrusted with such an enormous role. *The Spanish Tragedy* was performed by the Admiral's company in 1597 and 1602, yet Burbage nonetheless eventually played Heironymo (see p. 185). There is no reason to believe he would have had any qualms about portraying Tamburlaine as well. If he did, the King's Men might have used the version printed in 1592, although probably with some significant revisions to adapt the original large cast to the specific circumstances of the King's Men.

Despite their selection as the King's Men, the company had begun performing in 1604 in a precarious position. But in the course of the eighteen months preceding the Gunpowder Plot, they had more than merely survived the replacement of Armin with Fletcher and of Phillips with Lowin. Shakespeare had returned to form, providing new plays as popular as the older works that still formed the bulk of the company's repertoire. Burbage's stardom and domination of company affairs had been turned to advantage, and at least one exciting new boy had come to the fore, allowing Shakespeare (and other new writers) to move into new and more openly sexual subject matter. The successes and all-but-uninterrupted performance schedule of 1604–05 also gave the Sharers a level of financial prosperity not seen since their first full year in the Globe. In July 1605, Shakespeare purchased half of the tithes in three hamlets outside Stratford, at a cost of 440 pounds,[46] an enormous sum of cash for the day, almost all of which must have come from profits earned by his shares in the Globe and the King's Men during these eighteen months. By the summer of 1605, they were truly the King's Men, the dominant force in London theatrical life.

During the summer of 1605, royal displeasure fell on the boys at Blackfriars. Jonson, Chapman, and Marston together had written a London comedy called *Eastward Ho!* that safely passed the censor, played a round of performances in the spring, and was ready to go to the printers in September. The boys apparently revived it in early September, adding some new jokes not in the original script about the flood of Scots who had followed James and were now getting rich in London. James was outraged, the show was shut down, and Marston hot-footed it out of town, but Jonson and Chapman were slow and ended up in jail yet again.[47] Jonson claimed he had not written the offending lines, but nevertheless, he stayed in jail for several months.

Only a few weeks after the *Eastward Ho!* arrests, the Privy Council on October 5, 1605, ordered all the theaters closed.[48] Plague was the reason given, but no records of unusual plague in 1605 have survived and October was very late in the warm season for the cyclical revivals of plague that were to become common in the near future. This was, however, a period of severe political unrest, so plague may have merely provided a handy excuse.

For Shakespeare and the King's Men, this closure turned out to be another piece of unexpected luck. They went on tour and thus were safely out of town on November 5, when Guy Fawkes's gunpowder barrels were discovered. The King's Men were in Oxford on October 9,[49] suggesting they had left town following the *Eastward Ho!* suppressions without waiting for the later official closure. We do not know how long they remained in the provinces, but we must assume they did more than dash to Oxford and return. As we have seen, Shakespeare bought a group of tithes in the Stratford area on July 24, 1605, which would seem to indicate he was in Stratford on that date. Unfortunately, the indenture was signed only by the seller but not by the purchaser or any of his representatives,[50] which leaves open the possibility that Shakespeare's brother Gilbert actually delivered the money, as he had done for a previous deal in 1602. If Shakespeare was in fact present for this transaction, then the company must have closed down in London as early as mid-July. Curiously enough, none of the married members of the company had children during the first half of 1606, suggesting that they all had spent a great portion of 1605 away from their wives.[51] A tour of such length would imply some other crises in London of which we have no other record. Whatever the reason, however, their absence from London meant that Robert Catesby could not arrange an equivalent of *Richard II* on November 4, and that Shakespeare could not drop in on his relatives, even by accident, while they were plotting the King's assassination at Shakespeare's favorite tavern. Thus, the King's Men, and Shakespeare in particular, apparently came under no serious suspicion in the weeks following the arrest of Guy Fawkes.

The decision to tour for such an extended period may have been prompted by a decision to remodel the Globe. This is not the place to enter the arguments about the precise size and shape of the Globe itself. However, it does seem obvious from the extant plays that a major change was made in the nature of the above during late 1605. In 1599, Pindarus went somewhere above in *Julius Caesar* and a woman apparently entered at a window in Jonson's *Every Man Out of His Humour*, but no further mention is made of such a space until Brabantio appears at a window in *Othello*, in 1604. Apparently the original Globe above was very small and thus very rarely used. This is underlined by *Henry V*, which requires men to enter with scaling ladders and then run off stage without scaling the walls, and which has town officials walk out to negotiate rather than stand on the walls as they had done in *King John* at The Theatre. Beginning in 1606, the above is suddenly used a great deal and it is obviously a very large opening, much bigger than a window. Cleopatra and her maids raise up Antony on his chair or cot, and Barnabe Barnes's *The Divil's Charter* sends attacking soldiers up the scaling ladders to fight with other actors in the space. Thus, by that time it had become an opening large enough to hold half a dozen or more actors. In George Wilkins' *Miseries of Enforced Marriage*, there is a long eaves-dropping scene in which we see and hear characters in an "upper chamber" and a lower space simultaneously (11. 1877–2039). The anonymous *Yorkshire Tragedy* has two long scenes played in an upper room from which a maid is thrown "down stairs:/Tumble, tumble, headlong" (v,11–12). *Pericles* has the long pageant of the knights observed from above by Simonides, Thaisa, and others. What had been a small window has rather obviously, and suddenly, expanded into a much larger space.

This modification, and perhaps many others, was apparently paid for by Condell and Sly. By 1606, the Globe partnership had expanded so that one half was still owned by the Burbages but the other half was split among Shakespeare, Heminges, the widow Phillips, Pope's heirs, and Condell and Sly. This addition of two partners is treated rather casually by even the most serious of modern analysts,[52] but it should be taken as a significant change. This was a major property transaction, one which in the long term reduced the equity held by each non-Burbage partner by a third, from 12.5% to about 8.3%. That is not the kind of arrangement casually given as a gift even among close friends, and there is certainly no reason at all why the heirs of Pope and Phillips, who were not actors, should have been happy simply to give away such valuable property. Condell and Sly must have injected a large amount of cash into the partnership to convince the others to reduce their shares so significantly. Thus, Condell and Sly must have bought in at some point before 1606. Sly would not have been in a position to accumulate the necessary capital until a year or so after he had attained his full Share in the acting company, which seems to have occurred in the summer of 1604. Therefore, mid-1605 seems the most likely date for his addition to the Globe partners. At least part of that cash injection would have been used for the remodeling of the Globe. The rest would have been paid directly to the other partners. Interestingly enough, as we have seen, Shakespeare or his representative showed up in Stratford in July with an unusually large amount of cash for his purchase of the tithes. The total paid was far more than he would have received only as his share of Condell and Sly's investment, but their funds may have helped swell the other cash in his money box to allow this surprisingly large invest-ment.

Although Shakespeare and his company seem to have escaped any detailed scrutiny or individualized repression when they returned to London after the Gunpowder Plot, it does not mean that these political events had no impact on the company as a whole or on Shakespeare as a writer. Even without the Gunpowder Plot, the *Eastward Ho!* and *Gowry* affairs must have had what modern artists like to call a chilling effect on all the acting companies. They clearly indicated, even before the

Gunpowder Plot, that James would not tolerate even veiled criticism of his activities or his close friends.

All the theaters must have remained closed after the Gunpowder Plot until December 15, when all the three major companies were once again authorized to perform "at their accustomed places."[53] When the company moved into the remodeled Globe at that time, they apparently expanded the number of Hired Men as well. At least two of the plays of the following year, *Antony and Cleopatra* and *The Divil's Charter*, make demands on company resources in men and in spectacle that would make even East German opera companies of the 1970s think twice about staging them.

One of the first plays in that December must have been *A Yorkshire Tragedy*, one of the oddest of all the King's Men's plays to survive. This is a domestic tragedy in which a Yorkshire gentleman murders his children and tries to murder his wife. It is also what we would today call a one-act, barely seven hundred lines long and identified when printed as "one of the four Plays in one." The other three plays were not printed, but this does demonstrate that on occasion the King's Men staged a mixed bill of shorter entertainments. *A Yorkshire Tragedy* was not printed until 1608, but it undoubtedly was written in the late summer of 1605. Based on a true crime of the day, it contains only the information found in a pamphlet printed shortly after June 12, well before the murderer's execution on August 24.[54] Because of its sustained scenes in the above it must have been written with the remodeled Globe in mind, but as a result of the tour and the closures of autumn 1605, it probably did not actually reach the stage until December or January. The quarto also claims that it is "Written by W. Shakespeare," a claim no modern scholar credits. There is a stark brutality to the play that is less shocking to audiences familiar with David Mamet or Edward Bond than it was to previous generations, but it is completely without the subtlety of language or character we would associate with even Shakespeare's most minor work. Middleton has been suggested, but "with some assistance from others,"[55] which seems far more complex a history than the simple one-act deserves. Its brevity, although part of a bill of several plays, and its simplicity both suggest a memorial reconstruction, which would invalidate all linguistic analyses. Thus, it is not impossible that Shakespeare was involved in the project at some stage, particularly as the play contains a mad scene for Burbage, which was becoming Shakespeare's specialty.

As *A Yorkshire Tragedy* stands, there are really only two major and two minor roles. The Husband is clearly a Burbage role; no age is specified, but he has a mad scene and about half the extant lines. Ecclestone was all but certainly the Wife, with almost as many lines. Based on age, the Master from the University could have been either Shakespeare or Heminges, but the brave and loyal servant could have been anyone in the company. The other Sharers would have had roles in the other plays on the bill. One of the boys is small enough to convincingly play with a top, but his part is dramatically quite demanding. One can easily imagine the same boy as that obnoxious Macduff son, the unusually short apprentice, tentatively identified as John Rice, still able to convincingly play children under the age of ten though he had significant experience and age by this time.

The company may also have revived *Mucedorus*, for a new printing appeared in 1606. The popular old play would have been ideal material to take on tour during late 1605, and such performances would have continued when the King's Men returned to London. How they cast *Mucedorus*, however, is even less clear than it had been in 1602. The printed text includes only the oldest material related to the play, so it gives us no hints of the way the King's Men would have performed the play. Casting turns as usual in this period on the question of Burbage's role, since he was growing quite old for roles like Mucedorus. The best guess is that they simply repeated the casting of 1602. Assuming the production existed, then Fletcher must have played the clown role of Mouse; the company either changed the character's name or revised a few lines to explain Fletcher's size.

At about the same time, Jonson produced another comedy, which many consider his masterpiece. Despite the copious records left by Jonson, the date for *Volpone* is as unclear as that for *Sejanus*. When printed in 1607, it included an epistle dated February 11, 1607, which, given the several different calendars in use at the time, might be our February 1608. Some years later, his folio claimed the play was staged in 1605. Given the company tour and the Gunpowder Plot closures, this would mean it was on stage before July 1605. However, the play mentions porpoises in the river (II,1,40), usually assumed to be an allusion to a porpoise and a whale both seen in the Thames in January 1606,[56] which would seem to indicate *Volpone* was still not yet finished at that time. Lent began in mid-February that year, so despite Jonson's claim that he wrote the play in five weeks, it is hard to see how it could have gone to the censor and then reached the stage before the Lenten closures, after which the year would have been 1606 in all calendars. Thus, it seems likely that, once again, Jonson's memory was a little confused by the time he got around to compiling his folio in 1616. He may in fact have written the play in what he thought of as 1605, but it was most probably produced during the spring of 1606.

Whether in 1605 or in mid-1606, the cast list left to us by Jonson fits the available company well enough. Only six names are listed: Burbage, Condell, Heminges, Lowin, Sly, and Cooke. A hand-annotated copy of Jonson's 1616 Folio has since surfaced, which from the names inscribed must refer to revivals for *Volpone* and *The Alchemist* after 1615, when Nathan Field joined the company, but before Burbage retired or died.[57] To no one's surprise, Burbage is indicated for Volpone and Condell for Mosca, with Lowin as Politic-Would-Be and Heminges as Corbaccio. The most likely casting for Corvino, the jealous husband, and Peregrine would have been Sly and Cooke respectively. Sly died in 1608 and in the revival, his Corvino was played by Tooley, who in 1616 was about the same age Sly had been in 1605. Similarly, Cooke died very early in 1614, his Share almost certainly passing to Gough (see chapter 9) and the name written in for Peregrine in the revival was "Goffe." By process of elimination, that leaves Shakespeare as the original Voltore, for which no name is recorded in the revival. Cowley probably played one of the judges and doubled elsewhere, but the large number of judges, creditors, and the crowd who hear *Volpone*'s mountebank routine indicate some attempts to use the large number of Hired Men on hand for other plays of the date.

Jonson gives no indication of revisions made for printing, as he admitted for several other works, but the delay of as much as two years before *Volpone* was printed at least allows time for such a revision. One oddity of the play, and one that encourages the thought that it may be more revised than Jonson admitted, is that there is no visible role for a clown of any kind. There are the three servants, but none seems likely casting for Fletcher, for they are a dwarf, a hermaphrodite, and a eunuch. As they all sing, one is tempted to think they were actually played by boys. How does one show a hermaphrodite on stage? The early *OED* citations of the term in English indicate merely an effeminate male or obvious homosexual, and the most common theatrical solution has usually been to put a beardless male in a dress—exactly what one of the older boys would do to play a female role—but without a female hairdo. Similarly, a eunuch is usually thought of as a fat, babyish man with a high-pitched voice, again very much like an old boy actor whose voice had refused to break although he was now quite large. And we have of course already identified a boy unusually short for his skill level, who would be a plausible dwarf. (We might also note the three fairies or nymphs that may have been in the original version of *Macbeth* instead of the Witches, implying a set of boys who worked together as a team in this period.) Lady Would-Be is the only female role requiring any skill at all, and she certainly went to Lowin's boy. The lovely Celia's role is so brief it may well have been played by Sly's new boy in his first significant role.

The combination of the newly remodeled Globe and an ever-improving young Ecclestone freed Shakespeare to take on his most ambitious subject. In *Antony and Cleopatra* he pushed the Elizabethan-Jacobean theater to the limits of its capabilities. Covering ten years in forty-two scenes spread across the entire ancient world, with some thirty-nine named speaking characters plus messengers, soldiers, servants, and other assorted participants, it indicates a company at the peak of prosperity. It also makes staggering demands on the acting skills of the performers, leaping from the battlefield to the boudoir, from the most formal of state occasions to the most private and intimate moments, and topping off these demands by killing the star in Act IV and giving the most complex role of all to an apprentice.

No one had ever tried to stage the story of Cleopatra, although she was the most famous woman in history, precisely because she was a she. There had been closet dramas, of course, by Fulke Greville and by Samuel Daniel and perhaps others, but none had appeared on stage, because the demands of the character were assumed to be beyond the capabilities of a boy. Even today, when we have an abundance of fine classical actresses, *Antony and Cleopatra* is staged less often than any of Shakespeare's other major works.[58] That Shakespeare and the King's Men even made the attempt is a tribute to his and the Sharers' faith in the abilities of young Ecclestone. That the final version left him with the long, magnificent solo of Act V is a testament to the validity of that faith. Antony actually has more lines, but that final act makes this *The Tragedy of Cleopatra*, Shakespeare's (and the era's) only female tragedy.

The poet Samuel Daniel had written one of those closet dramas about Cleopatra, first published in 1594. The poem was sufficiently popular to go through as many as eight editions, for most of which Daniel made some minor revisions. But between the 1605 and the 1607 editions, he made major changes that seem to have been influenced by his seeing Shakespeare's play. Thus, *Antony and Cleopatra* must have been at the Globe during 1606–07.[59] Given the plague closures in the second half of 1606, the spring of 1606 seems the most likely performance date.

The death of Antony, written new for Daniel's 1607 edition, deserves some special notice:

> . . . Which when his love,
> His royal Cleopatra understood,
> She sends with speed his body to remove,
> The body of her love imbru'd with blood.
> Which brought unto her tomb, (lest that the press
> Which came with him, might violate her vow)
> She draws him up in rolls of taffaty
> T'a window at the top, which did allow
> A little light unto her monument.
>   There Charmian, and poor Iras, two weak maids
> Foretir'd with watching, and their mistress' care,
> Tug'd at the pulley, having n'other aids,
> And up they hoist the swounding body there
> Of pale Antonius, show'ring out his blood
> On th'under lookers, which there gazing stood.
>   And when they had now wrought him up half way
> (Their feeble powers unable more to do)
> The frame stood still, the body at a stay,
> When Cleopatra all her strength thereto
> Puts, with what vigour love, and care could use,
> So that it moves again, and then again
> It comes to stay. When she afresh renews
> Her hold, and with reinforced power doth strain,
> And all the weight of her weak body lays,
> Whose surcharg'd heart more then her body weighs,
> At length she wrought him up, and takes him in,
>   Lays his yet breathing body on her bed. . . . [60]

Whether this is accurate in detail or simply a poetic embroidery of something played more simply can never be known absolutely. Nevertheless, the rolls of taffeta and the pulley are such unexpected details that Daniel must have seen them in use. Thus, this passage might join Manningham's and Forman's diary entries as our only descriptions of a Shakespearean play in its original performance.

One significant point is that the boys appear to be weak and frail. This is of course exaggerated by Daniel for poetic effect, but it is nonetheless a reminder to a modern reader, for whom the teenaged boy is an image of energy and vigor and often of threat, that the Shakespearean boy was still physically a boy, not a young adult. And

Ecclestone was apparently more frail in appearance than the other boys, given the unusual femininity of his roles and his costumes.

Despite the complexity and power of Ecclestone's role as Cleopatra, Burbage still had the largest role. Antony is one of the ten longest of all Shakespeare's roles, significantly larger than Lear or Macbeth. But unique among Shakespeare's Burbage tragedies, there is no Act IV rest period for Burbage, for all Antony's lines are crammed into the first four acts. Despite the enormous cast, the play is almost as tightly focused on a handful of characters as is *Othello*. Antony, Cleopatra, Octavius, and Enobarbus together have two-thirds of all the lines, the same dominance as Othello, Iago, Desdemona, and Cassio. Normally, Burbage's foil would have been Condell, but Shakespeare often mentions both Octavius's comparative youth and his lack of military bearing, so Sly is more likely, repeating the Macbeth/Malcolm relationship. Enobarbus, then, the old soldier and friend about the same age as Antony would have been Condell's role. Menas is a gruff soldier, so Lowin is more likely than Cooke, who would have then played young Pompey. Lepidus and Agrippa, the two significant older men, would have been the province of Shakespeare and Heminges. Handsome Dolabella might have been any of the young Hired Men. The official clown role is small and distractingly trivial, rather like something thrown in at the last moment to give the clown something to do, but it could have been played by either Fletcher or Cowley.

Barnabe Barnes' only known play, *The Divil's Charter*, was printed in 1607, the title page claiming it had been performed for the king "upon Candlemass night last" (February 2, 1607). It would thus have been playing at the Globe during 1606, concurrent with *Antony and Cleopatra*. It portrays the career of Pope Alexander, who sells his soul to the devil to become an arch-villain. If anything, it requires even more spectacular staging than Shakespeare's play. *The Divil's Charter* opens with a dumb-show including devils, smoke, fire, thunder, and lightning, and that is one of its simpler scenes. Before the show ends, whole armies scale the walls of a city, the Pope appears in full splendor with a college of Cardinals, cannons are fired, "fiery exhalations"(1764) call forth devils, and we see an on-stage tennis match, numerous stabbings, poisoning by asps, by washcloth, and by wine bottle, a shooting, two bodies thrown off a bridge into the river, and finally Hell itself opening up to swallow the Pope. The cast is enormous, with dozens of soldiers, guards, cardinals, and devils. The company must have become very large and very rich.

All but three or four actors must have played devils or soldiers at some point, so we cannot be certain of all the Sharer assignments. But Burbage was certainly Alexander, a composite of Richard III and Doctor Faustus with almost a quarter of all the lines. His military brother, Cesare, with the second largest role, was just as obviously Condell. Lucretia has about two hundred fifty lines, the third largest role, conducted primarily in monologue or scenes with her maids; she has both a nightgown scene in which she murders her husband and a death scene in which she is herself poisoned. The similarities to Cleopatra are so strong that this could only have been Ecclestone, now so highly regarded that he is allowed to work in scenes without Burbage (although Burbage of course could easily have continued to supervise his monologues and death scene, just as he must have done with Cleopatra). There is only one other large role—a murderer named Frescobaldi, who has five percent of all the lines but appears in only one scene. He's a drinker, a brawler, a fine swordsman, and as colorful as Pistol. The best guess is Lowin, who as Phillips' replacement probably played similar characters, but his swordplay might indicate Condell, with Lowin then playing Cesare. After that, we are down among the characters with a hundred lines or less, many of whom must have been doubled by the remaining senior Sharers. Cooke is the likely Barbarossa, with Heminges and Shakespeare sharing Lodovico, Caraffa, King Charles, and Baglioni among them. By process of elimination, Sly was thus most probably the narrator. Once again, there is no single large role for a clown, although the large number of devils and murderers would have kept both Fletcher and Cowley busy.

This is also, I think, the season in which *Cymbeline* first appeared. The dating of *Cymbeline* has always been something of a mystery. Simon Forman saw the play, but his description of its performance is undated; although for many years the diary entry was thought to have been another of Collier's forgeries, it is now generally accepted as genuine and concurrent with productions of *Macbeth* and *The Winter's Tale* in the spring or early summer of 1611. As a result, most scholars date it among the late plays, "from the period of or after *Macbeth*."[61] But 1605–1611 is a rather wide range, which we need to narrow a bit for a history such as this.

One of the many problems posed by *Cymbeline* is that, by almost any criteria, it is not very good. Yet, unlike *Pericles* or *Timon of Athens*, for example, it offers no obvious sign of a likely collaborator to whom the blame can be passed. It is hard to believe that a line like, "Soft, ho, what trunk is here?/Without his top?" (IV,ii,353–4) could ever not have gotten an unintentional laugh, or that Shakespeare could ever have allowed it to stand for any character but Bottom, yet all editors since World War I have found the play to be inarguably by Shakespeare. Only Posthumus' vision in Act V seems atypical, but almost all editors have ultimately accepted that it too is genuinely Shakespearean.

There is nonetheless a great theatrical difficulty that is often ignored in the study but glaringly obvious in the rehearsal hall—there is simply too much play here. There are so many villains at work that they almost trip over each other—the Queen trying to poison Imogen, Cloten trying to rape her, Pisanio trying to assassinate her (in service to two different masters), and Iachimo trying to seduce her or assassinate her character. *Cymbeline* is one of Shakespeare's longest works, longer even than the Folio version of *Hamlet*. When we look at the play itself, we find two plays rather awkwardly jammed together: One deals with Cymbeline's war and his opposition to Imogen's marriage to Posthumous, and another deals with Iachimo's wager with Posthumous. If we were to eliminate Iachimo and the wager plot completely, however, we find a quite coherent romance of about 2,800 lines, Shakespeare's most typical play length. A beautiful young princess secretly marries a man of whom her father disapproves. The man is banished, and to avoid the unwanted advances of the approved suitor, she disguises herself as a boy and runs off to rejoin her true love. On the way, she is befriended by a good-hearted outlaw, whose sons kill the unwanted suitor who has pursued her. Meanwhile, she takes the poison from her stepmother, which she thinks is medicine, but like Juliet, she awakes, to discover that her husband seems to be dead. Her husband, hearing that she is gone from court, thinks she is dead, and mad with grief, tries to get himself killed in battle, but he is captured. England is saved, Imogen is miraculously restored to her husband, and the King relents and approves the marriage. It is a fairy tale, obviously, but one coherent in tone and stagecraft. That play moves along smoothly and coherently, with few temporal or plot confusions and with the scenes still flowing effortlessly in a practical staging sequence. Thus, the present text looks very much like two versions of a play, both of which have been printed together.

Curiously enough, editors have established a significant change in the nature of the manuscript used for the Folio that begins abruptly after II,iv,[62] which happens to be Iachimo's last major scene (until the denouement) and the end of the wager plot. This is not enough to suggest different authors, but it does clearly indicate a text written (or copied) at two different times, with those then copied again by a professional scribe, probably Ralph Crane, to prepare for the printers of the Folio. It is also widely accepted that the scenes involving the Roman invasion are based not merely on Holinshed's description of Cymbeline's reign but also on the same portions that were used for *Macbeth* and *King Lear*, which would suggest initial composition at about the same time as those plays. As we shall see, there would have been good reason to revise in 1611 a *Cymbeline* first performed several years before: By that time *Pericles*, *Philaster*, and a revived *Mucedorus* had made Arcadian romances popular, while Richard Burbage was forty or so and much in need of a major role that at least made allowance for his visible maturity. Thus, what we seem to have is a romance written around 1606, shortly after Shakespeare had composed *Macbeth* and *Lear* and needed new material without political implications, which was then in 1611 revised to provide a new major role (for Burbage). This resulted in a completely new plotline and a complete revision of the first third of the play, almost certainly involving some significant cuts in the later portions for actual performance. As with *Coriolanus* or *Love's Labour's Lost*, the scribe copied and the publisher printed the complete manuscript, considered by Heminges and Condell to be Shakespeare's unabridged version (rather than the performance version).

The casting for this earlier version is necessarily conjectural to some degree. But working on the assumption that the reason for the revision was the invention of Iachimo as a role for Burbage, then we must assume that his earlier role was Posthumus, the only significant character in the romance plot for which he would have been even marginally suitable in 1606. Condell, usually Burbage's mirror image, then must have been Cloten, the distorted mirror of Posthumus who can even wear the same clothes. Cymbeline would have been played by Shakespeare, in appearance the oldest man in the company. Bellarius is not so old as Cymbeline, so Heminges is not necessarily an automatic casting. Arviragus and Guiderius were quite probably played by actual boys, at least one of whom must have been Bellarius' apprentice. Heminges' boy Rice was still young and feminine at this date, so he is unlikely to have played such militaristic boys. Lowin's boy, however, would have been one of the older boys in the company by this time and is quite plausible as one of the sons, which would mean Lowin used his Banquo/Kent mode of bluff camaraderie for the cliché-spouting soldier. In that case, Heminges was probably the Roman general Lucius, leaving Sly as Posthumus' friend Pisanio. Cooke then would have played Philario, a role probably much revised later. Fletcher would have played the Lord who so openly mocks Cloten, with Cowley's half share probably limiting him to the doctor Cornelius or the Jailer. Imogen, who is the largest role in the complete play, was also probably the largest role in the shorter original version, and must have gone to Ecclestone, who was at the very pinnacle of his career in this year, with Imogen's male disguise a sign of his increased age. Because the Queen plays almost all her scenes with Cloten, she was almost certainly Condell's boy, who, as Octavia, had revealed a deeper voice than usual for the boys, suitable for a matron and a villainess.

It is difficult to tell if "Hark, Hark, the Lark" and "Fear no More the Heat of the Sun" were a part of this original version. The boys' song is as implausibly inserted as a musical number in a second feature film of the 1940s. After the serenade, Cloten meets Cymbeline and the Queen as if in the morning, and the scene would play equally clearly whether the audience heard the dawn music or not. Robert Johnson is generally agreed to have composed the music for these songs, and he is assumed to have begun his long association with the King's Men, for whom he wrote a great deal of music, sometime after 1607. Unfortunately, that assumption is in turn based on the presumed dating of *Cymbeline*. Johnson was apprenticed as a musician in 1596 to George Carey, the Lord Chamberlain and patron of Shakespeare's acting company. Carey would not have personally taught music to Johnson, so it is entirely possible, even likely, that he learned his craft from the anonymous composer among the musicians of the Chamberlain's Men who had composed Shakespeare's earlier songs. In June 1604, after his bond concluded, Johnson was formally appointed as a lutenist to King James, which means he may have begun providing music for the King's Men at any time after the company was newly patented.[63] Conjecturally, it seems most probable that the songs were part of the original version and then cut from performances in 1611 to help make room for Iachimo's scenes.

With the available evidence, it is not possible to know if Cymbeline preceded or followed *Antony and Cleopatra*. Imogen's disguise as a boy, however, indicates the role was written for a boy somewhat older than the one who had played Cleopatra but who was growing more boyish, which would point to a somewhat later date. The vision of Jupiter descending and ascending certainly suggests an attempt to use the same rigging that had been used to haul Antony into the Monument, which in turn would mean it was intended to follow the remodeling of the Globe. *Cymbeline* must have had some popularity, for it was revived in 1611, and that popularity must have been far greater than we can imagine today, for if it did first appear in 1606, it was the true initiator of the fashion for the tragi-comic romances and the stimulus for rather than the imitator of Beaumont and Fletcher's *Philaster*.

Despite the insecurities following the Gunpowder Plot, the early part of 1606 was in many ways the most prosperous period of Shakespeare's active career. Never before or later would the company be able to stage plays with the large casts and the visual splendor of *Antony and Cleopatra* or *The Divil's Charter*. The prosperity that allowed the King's Men to do such productions stands in stark contrast to the decline of their competitors. Records of Queen's Men tours grow more extensive during 1606. The Prince's Men, though continuing at the Fortune, would appear at court only three times in 1606–07, compared to nine visits by the King's Men. But the companies in most serious decline were the boys. By the end of 1606, Paul's Boys ceased performing altogether, their last known performance being in July. Over the next two years, a large number of their plays were printed, suggesting that the assets of the company were being sold off. The Blackfriars Boys had both financial and political problems. In February, 1606, their production of John Day's *The Isle of Gulls*, satirizing court figures, had led to new imprisonments and the loss of the Queen's formal patronage. Yet another new partner, Robert Keysar, was brought in. A new syndicate was formed in which the boys were to be held directly responsible for all expenses, paying rent to their masters. Perhaps as a result, the Chapel school and choir severed all ties with the actors, so that there was no pretense that they were anything other than an acting company.[64]

On May 27, James visibly tightened stage censorship for all the companies, forbidding any actor to "jestingly or prophanely speake or use the holy Name of God or of Christ Jesus, or of the Holy Ghoste or of the Trinitie."[65] The actors coped by simply substituting "by Jove" and similar evasions.

More immediately damaging than these legal restrictions was the return of the plague in July 1606. The Prince's Men and the Queen's Men took to the road again,[66] but the King's Men seem to have remained in London for at least a while longer. On July 7, the King of Denmark arrived for a visit, and the King's Men performed twice for him shortly afterward at Hampton Court, returning in early August for a third performance before he left. Most modern biographers assume *Macbeth* was one of these plays, although there is no supporting evidence and no one that I can find has managed to explain its possible interest to a Danish King. It is tempting to envision *Hamlet* there as well, but the choices probably put much less demand on either King's linguistic skill or attention span. The one known production, we assume not by the King's Men, was a masque about Solomon and Sheba in the course of which James jumped up onto the floor to dance with the queen. Too drunk to last more than a few steps, James soon passed out and was carried off to bed, covered in wine and food spilled from the tables.[67] For such a patron, *The Merry Devil of Edmonton* or *Taming of the Shrew*, both seen at the Globe in 1607, are far more likely.

Between the two court appearances, the King's Men went touring, for they were seen in Oxford near the end of July. In September, they were in Maidstone and Dover.[68] When they returned to London, the period of prosperity would be coming to an end.

Replacing Shakespeare, 1607–10

The plague that reappeared in 1606 would haunt London for five years. For most of every summer and autumn until 1611, and often for even more of the year, London would average well over one hundred deaths a week—far below the thousands per week of 1603, but still terrifying, particularly as the plague was accompanied both by another famine and by winters of unusual severity.

For the actors, plague was a double threat. Living in London, they of course were potential victims. But the disease also destroyed their livelihood. With no cure known, the only public health measure open to the authorities in the face of plague was to try to control its spread by limiting crowds in confined spaces, and the largest crowds and most confined spaces were in the theater. Thus, whenever plague threatened, the authorities closed the theaters. Even when the theaters remained open, public fear of continued risk of infection may have reduced the audiences for most performances.

Although we do have records of plague deaths in London at this time, we have no detailed records of the theater closings. When the theaters had reopened in 1604, the proclamation allowed the three principal companies to operate with the proviso that they could play when there were thirty or fewer deaths per week from the plague in London and its immediate environs. We do not know if this figure was used only in 1604 or if it was a convenient benchmark used throughout the decade. Even so, it is the only guideline we have. Although we need not necessarily accept Leeds Barroll's contention that "from 1606 to December 1610 . . . the public playhouses were not likely to have been open for more than a total of nine months,"[1] we should assume that the authorities were likely to act conservatively. The death figure used to determine when public festivities and events might be closed down may have been elastic, but in general, the authorities would have erred on the side of caution. Using the thirty deaths guideline in relation to the known death figures, and keeping in mind that theaters were usually closed during Lent as well, when the cold weather usually suppressed the plague, it does indeed seem likely that during the next five years the theaters were closed more often than they were open (see the timeline in Chart A).

The theatrical season of 1606–07 is one of the most difficult to decipher during these years. Plague deaths began to rise again in the summer and passed the thirty threshold during the week of July 10, 1606. No formal proclamation is known, but all the Prince's Men were on the road by July, the King's Men only shortly afterward. More than one hundred were dying each week by September, so in the fall the actors certainly returned from their tour to find their theater buildings closed. The same pattern recurred in 1607, passing thirty deaths in the first week of July and exceeding one hundred per week in September. The question is whether the theaters opened at all between the two peaks of infection. In 1606, weekly plague deaths dropped below thirty in November. As the normal pattern for plague was to decline when cold weather came—and this was definitely cold weather—the theaters may well have been allowed to reopen, for the authorities would have assumed that the decline signaled the end of the infection. But reported deaths then rose back up to forty-five in the first week of December. This sudden increase would have frightened many officials, precisely because it did not follow the usual pattern, and almost certainly the theaters were closed down again immediately. The King's Men gave nine performances at court during the winter of 1606–07, but that need not mean the Globe was in use as well; court entertainments continued in every winter during this infestation, whether the public theaters were open or closed. From December through March, the death figures fluctuated around thirty, one week going up to thirty-eight, the next dropping to twenty-eight.[2] It is extremely unlikely that the theaters would have been allowed to reopen in such circumstances, at least until there were two consecutive weeks of declining figures. Given that Easter came on April 5, 1607, it would have mattered little if deaths declined during January, for the theaters would have closed again almost immediately for Lent in late February. If the thirty deaths figure was in fact used by local authorities, the theaters probably did not reopen until May 1607, and then stayed open for only two or three months; if thirty was merely an approximate guide, then the theaters probably also were open for about six weeks before Lent.

However brief the 1607 season may have been, one new play can be securely dated to the Globe at this time. George Wilkins' *Miseries of Enforced Marriage* was registered on July 31, 1607, and printed shortly thereafter, so it must have been on stage before that date. The play is generally assumed to be all but contemporary with *A Yorkshire Tragedy* because it seems to share the same source for part of its plot, and because the large number of oaths would appear to predate the ban on such language in May 1606.[3] However, the ban on such oaths did not apply to printed plays and the printed text gives every evidence of being a foul papers text, although perhaps with some revision.[4] Thus, the oaths may indicate only that the play was written before

the summer of 1606. It is extremely unlikely that the King's Men would simultaneously present two plays on the same subject. We must assume that some time
passed after January 1606, when *A Yorkshire Tragedy* was certainly seen, until *Miseries
of Enforced Marriage* was put on stage. Thus, given the tours and plague closures of
late 1606, early 1607 seems the most likely performance date.

The surprise of the play is that of the five largest male roles, three are for actors
under the age of twenty-three: Scarborrow and his two younger brothers. The largest
role, young Scarborrow, who tries to murder his wife, is described as age seventeen
when the play begins (ll. 325–26) and twenty-three when it ends (l. 2521). There
is no way Burbage, now in his late thirties, could have pretended to such youth (nor
could any other previously identified Sharer). This is more than simply a curious
anomaly, for the Yorkshire murderer Calverly, on whom the character was apparently
based, was actually in his late twenties at the time of the murder, much closer to
Burbage's true age. The characterization may have been changed in part to avoid
obvious repetition of *The Yorkshire Tragedy*, but modifications made for that reason
would not require such an extreme reduction of the character's age. Scarborrow's
youth could only have been invented because the role was purposefully designed for
a *young* Sharer, and hence for someone not named Burbage.

This of course does not mean Burbage had no role. There is a subplot, far more
extensive than dramatically necessary, that would become all too common during
the Restoration theater. Ilford, a wastrel gentleman, leads Scarborrow to drink and
gamble away his estate, while Ilford and his friends search for rich widows or heiresses
to marry. Ilford, of unspecified age, with more than five hundred lines and a mad
scene, must have been Burbage's role. Almost as large a role is Butler, the scene-
stealing servant who saves the day. Butler is described as sixty years old, but he is
unusually active for his age. He robs travelers on the highway and climbs trees on
stage, so he must have been played by someone who was far younger than sixty.
Thoughts turn automatically to Cowley, who seems to have made a career of such
colorful old coots, but the role is much larger than any we have been able to trace
to him thus far and far larger than a Half-Sharer has ever played in the company.
Lowin has taken on most of the more colorful or eccentric characters since replacing
Phillips, so he is our best guess for Butler, with powder in his hair. Cowley still has
an old coot to play, Uncle William, whose role is more suitable to his half share.
There is also a role specifically identified as "Clowne" (ll. 24, ff.), so this must have
been Fletcher's assignment, even though he is a servant who does nothing modern
audiences would recognize as clowning. Scarborrow has two brothers younger than
seventeen, so they must have been played by actual boys. Even though they are
among the five largest male roles, their one hundred fifty lines each is not unusual
for experienced boys in women's roles and so not implausible for older boys playing
actual older boys. Due to the large number of scenes with Butler, they were most
probably performed by Lowin's boy and Sands, now at the very end of his bonds.

The remaining roles provide us with a new mystery. Ilford has two companions,
who must be his age or only slightly younger. Given Burbage as Ilford, then these
two must have been played by Condell, Sly, or Cooke. There is only one father, Sir

John Harcop, whose daughter commits suicide when her secret marriage to Scarborrow is voided, but there is also a guardian for Scarborrow who, although he need not be fatherly in appearance must obviously appear to be much older than Scarborrow. We have three actors who might fit the bill, Heminges, Shakespeare, and Condell. No matter how we try to align the casting, one Sharer is left with nothing to play. Logically, Ilford's two friends Wentloe and Bartley, who despite a relative shortage of lines appear in almost every scene with him, must have been Cooke and Sly. In turn, that would imply that Condell played Scarborrow's guardian, simply because he is a guardian; if one of the visibly older Sharers had the role, we could have seen Scarborrow's father. In turn that means either Shakespeare or Heminges played Harcop, and the other was no longer available. As we know that Heminges would continue to be active on stage until at least 1616 (see p. 188) and we find no later references to Shakespeare as an actor, it appears that Shakespeare did not act in this play. In turn, barring a major illness of which there is absolutely no evidence, it means Shakespeare must have decided to retire from the stage during the early summer of 1606, when the play was being written.

None of Shakespeare's biographers have even considered the possibility that Shakespeare retired as a performer long before he stopped writing plays. Most, if they discuss his retirement from acting at all, place it as simultaneous with his writing retirement, usually thought to be in 1611.[5] On the evidence of the extant plays, however, there can be little doubt that Shakespeare was no longer acting after 1607, for there simply are no roles for him in any of the surviving plays dated after *Antony and Cleopatra*. This will be seen more clearly as we examine each of the King's Men productions in detail. However, we can generalize at this point by noting how consistently we have seen two, and only two, clearly middle-aged Sharers in the plays of 1604–06. Of course, in *King Lear* there were three older men, with Burbage playing the elderly Lear, but Gloucester and Kent are both identified as middle-aged men. In the plays of 1607–13, we consistently will see only one such middle-aged man older than Burbage's character. As Heminges continued to act with the company for at least another decade, he must have played that singular older man. If he did, then there can be not the smallest likelihood that Shakespeare made any further on-stage appearances after 1607, even in his own plays. If he did not appear in *Miseries of Enforced Marriage* in the winter of 1606–07, then he did not appear in any other new plays of that season. Given that *Miseries* was probably written during 1606, then Shakespeare planned his retirement far in advance and, like the good company partner he had always been, gave the King's Men plenty of time to write him out of their plans.

I think it is possible to identify the date at which his retirement was finalized. On June 5, 1607, Shakespeare's eldest daughter Susanna married John Hall in Stratford. To the Elizabethans, the ceremony itself was not particularly significant, but the negotiations for the dowry and marriage portion were. In this case, they involved one of the richest families of the town, Shakespeare's, and a doctor who was the son of a doctor and thus a man of considerable substance. Such negotiations would only have been performed face to face. If between Shakespeare and Hall, the negotiations would have been in Stratford; if between Shakespeare and Hall's father, they would have been near Cambridge, where Hall's family lived. In either case, they would have required Shakespeare to travel from London. Susanna's first child was a nine-month baby, so there was no emergency about the wedding, and Hall was a most religious man, so a long clandestine affair requiring sudden legitimization is unlikely. Thus, the timing of the wedding in June can only be explained by the presence of Shakespeare in Stratford or Cambridge (or both) for some extended period during May, with the nuptial agreement reached prior to the first reading of the banns three Sundays before the wedding itself. As we have seen in considerable detail throughout this work, the company could not perform for more than a day or two without the presence of a regular Sharer (see also appendix A). A trip to Stratford in 1607 was no quick visit. In an emergency, using the post horse system, a man might make the trip in two days, assuming he was willing to push the horses hard and to spend about six pounds in each direction (as much as a playwright usually received for two complete plays) in fees, tips, and feed for the post horses.[6] Otherwise, a traveler who owned no horse walked. A good walking speed over even ground is about 2½ miles an hour, but the Elizabethan roads were not even ground. William Harrison in 1587 broke the journey from London to Oxford into six stages, the longest of which was fifteen miles, and Shakespeare would have still had more than thirty to go after he reached Oxford.[7] When Kemp danced a similar distance to Norwich, for example, he needed nine days, not counting the days he did not move at all due to bad weather. Shakespeare could not have simply taken a day or two off from performances to deal with family business. If Shakespeare was in Stratford while the King's Men were performing in London, then during late 1606 he must have started phasing himself out of new material so that he was formally retired no later than May 1607.

The King's Men definitely were in London as late as July, and apparently without Shakespeare. On July 16, 1607, the Merchant Taylor's guild gave a banquet for the King and his family in the City. Ben Jonson was paid for a special speech to welcome the King, which was delivered by John Rice, while Heminges was present to receive further payment and a tip for the boy himself.[8] If Heminges and Rice were still in London, the rest of the company were there as well, and must have been there for some time previously. At the same time, the choice of Jonson to write this speech would certainly suggest that Shakespeare was no longer available to do so himself. He was the company's resident writer and a specialist in material for the company's boys. The Merchant Taylors may, of course, have hired Jonson and the actors independently, but Jonson at this time was not yet the consummate sycophant who would dominate court entertainments in the next decade. His masques were yet to come and Jonson himself had had more than one problem with members of the court, including a recent stint in jail at James's command, so he was hardly an obvious choice to please the King. That they did not turn to Shakespeare would suggest Shakespeare was not in London.

Not only would Shakespeare need to be in Stratford to negotiate Susanna's dowry, he would also need to be able to pay for it. One question not answered in available records is the nature of Susanna Shakespeare's dowry. Hall certainly would have insisted on a substantial settlement. There is some evidence that the Halls expected the property Shakespeare had bought in 1602, but the actual transfer seems not to have occurred until Shakespeare's death, for Shakespeare himself paid a fine on the property in 1610. When the second daughter Judith married later, Shakespeare provided a marriage "porcion" of one hundred pounds,[9] and it seems likely he would have provided at least as much for Susannah, whose new husband he liked far better than Judith's. Due to the interrupted season of 1606, Shakespeare was unlikely to have accumulated much cash since he had purchased the area tithes during 1605. Of course, numerous real estate dealings have disappeared from our records, so we cannot be certain. Nevertheless, it is a more than curious coincidence that the King's Men obviously added a new Sharer at precisely the moment when roles for Shakespeare begin to disappear from play casts and when Shakespeare would have been in need of a substantial sum of cash for his eldest daughter's dowry.

The young actor who played Scarborrow must have been a full Sharer by the time the role premiered, for he has the largest role in the play. He can only have obtained that share from a departing actor, such as Shakespeare. The surprise is not that the King's men added a younger Sharer but that they waited so long to do so. Except for Cooke in his late twenties and with only a half share, all the other Sharers were thirty or older. This all but eliminated any plays with handsome young lovers, which in general eliminated comedy. As it happens, we cannot see this new young man in a comedy, due to the limited number of surviving scripts, but the young lover roles would have been his primary duty. This new Sharer all but certainly was Samuel Gilburne, who is listed as one of the Principall Actors in the Folio. As we have seen, Gilburne was Phillips's apprentice beginning around 1594–95, which in turn would make him about twenty-two in 1607. How he leap-frogged over a half-sharer like Cooke or a former apprentice like Gough, who was slightly older, is difficult to explain. The simplest explanation may well be the best: Somewhere, he found enough capital to buy a share when Cooke or Gough could not. Gilburne's mention in the Folio must indicate that he had played prominent adult roles for some period of time. As he is in none of the later extant cast lists or Sharer lists, the most likely explanation is that he assumed a share shortly after 1605 and then died in 1610–11, before the next play for which we have a cast list first appeared. While not conclusive, his placement in the list of Principall Actors after Cooke, Crosse, Lowin, and Cowley also supports such a chronology. As Chambers noted when discussing the problem, "premature deaths must be expected in plague-time,"[10] so Gilburne's brief career may well be explained by his sudden and unanticipated death around 1610. The best time for his promotion would thus have been the winter of 1606–07, when Shakespeare disappears from casting requirements and the company's plays begin to require a far younger leading man than previously.

More than likely, Shakespeare actually began to think about retirement even before the plague returned in 1606. He was, after all, forty-two years old. Although that seems young to modern eyes, it would have made him possibly the oldest actor in the company (we do not know the precise age of Heminges, who was approximately the same age), perhaps even the oldest actor in the nation.[11] Of the actors he had known of similar age, only Bryan had lived to enjoy his retirement. Phillips, Pope, Kemp, and Crosse had all died by their mid-forties. Edward Alleyn, two years younger than Shakespeare, had already retired twice. The return of the plague, if anything, increased the odds of an early death, particularly if one remained in London. In addition, as a man who had spent most of his life fashioning roles for the company, he more than most would have known his future roles would only grow smaller and less interesting as he aged. Given these factors, it would be shocking if Shakespeare did not begin to ask himself: Why buy the second largest house in his home town if he had no intention of ever living in it? Why remain in plague-infested London risking contamination when he could return a rich man to his old and comparatively safe home? Why risk the loss of everything on the whim of a King who might shut down the company, when he could retire in comfort on his accumulated property?

Having decided to retire, but still present in London to perform at court in the winter and only in his old roles into the spring, Shakespeare had plenty of time to write before moving back to Stratford. One of the plays was almost certainly a work expressly designed for the new Sharer Gilburne—*Troilus and Cressida*. No play in the Folio causes more difficulties for a history such as this, and at times I have felt that I should provide a running footer that says "except for *Troilus*." As discussed in chapter 5, the version performed in 1602–03 must have been quite different from the surviving text and may well not have been by Shakespeare. Our extant version, however, was registered anew on January 28, 1609, underlining the contention that it is in fact a different play. Given the registration date, we would assume it was performed in 1607–08. However, when printed, it was issued with two different title pages, one mentioning performances at the Globe, the other claiming the play was "neuer stal'd with the Stage, neuer clapper-clawd with the palmes of the vulger." Unfortunately, it has been well established that the Globe reference was in the earlier printing. This makes no sense at all—a play that had never been performed might suddenly be staged, prompting a change to the title page in mid-printing, but a play once performed can not be unperformed. Yet the evidence for this sequence of printings seems unassailable.[12]

Whatever the explanation for these curious and frustrating title pages, the printed version is performable by the King's Men as they existed in 1607, something that could not be claimed in 1602. Whether or not it reached the stage before the plague ended performances in the summer of 1607, it was surely crafted for this company at this time. Troilus, not yet twenty-three years old (I,ii,238), must have been intended for the same young man who played Scarborrow. It cannot be an accident that after years in which no young man's age is mentioned, we find two plays printed within eighteen months of each other that specify the largest male role for a man younger than twenty-three years. Gilburne, the newest Sharer, by our computations was almost certainly twenty-two at this time. Perhaps equally significant, we know the company at this time had not one but two potential Cressidas: William Ecclestone, who had already played many sexually attractive women, including Cleopatra, and Heminges' boy John Rice, who was good enough to solo before the King himself and sufficiently feminine in appearance to play beautiful women almost to the day he left the company four years later. Ulysses, the largest of the more mature roles, has almost the same number of lines as Troilus, so it would have been a plausible assignment for Burbage, now in his late thirties. Cowley would have resumed his old man's schtick to play the all but senile Nestor. Hector must be a skilled swords-man, always Condell's role. Heminges was the oldest Sharer, so Cressida's uncle Pandarus must have been played by him, indicating that Rice rather than Ecclestone was the intended Cressida. Lowin would have been Agamemnon. Sly is the remaining Full-Sharer, but Achilles seems all wrong for a man who originated Aguecheek; much more likely is that he would have played the weak-willed Paris, with Cooke, much the better swordsman, as the warrior Achilles. The other significant characters, all small roles, were split among Tooley, Gough, Edmans, or Sands, now at the very end of his bonds, with Ajax intended for a large man among the Hired Men who had probably played the Lion in *A Midsummer Night's Dream* in 1605.

Thersites, the most foul-mouthed and vicious of all Shakespeare's fool roles, has long been thought to be a quintessential Armin role and yet, as we have seen, Armin was not active in the company at this time. However, Thersites presents some un-usual characteristics for a clown, the most notable of which is that he is at one point challenged to a duel by a Trojan stranger (V,vii). This would seem to indicate that he has an appearance similar to the other warriors, not the dwarfish appearance generally associated with Armin that would have made it clear to any Trojan that he was not a soldier. Thus, the role seems to be physically oriented toward Fletcher.

Before leaving for Stratford in May, Shakespeare probably also provided his por-tion of *Pericles*. The play was registered May 20, 1608, in what seems to be a staying registration. A novelization evading that registration appeared shortly afterward, by George Wilkins.[13] Hence, the play must have been "hot" during the first half of 1608, and given the plague closures of the summer and autumn of 1607, must have been written in the spring a year earlier. How much of *Pericles* is by Shakespeare's hand has been the subject of much debate. The consensus now is that Shakespeare wrote the sections after Thaissa went overboard, while someone else wrote the first two acts, with the authorship of Act III still disputed. There have been many nom-inees for the collaborator. The New Arden suggests John Day, Heywood has received many votes, and both Chambers (most grudgingly) and Wells and Taylor suggest Wilkins, the writer of the novelization of the play published in 1608.[14] However, if half of the play was by Wilkins, then it would have been most logical for him to start work in the spring of 1607, when his only other known play, *Miseries of Enforced Marriage*, was a hit for the King's Men. The Venetian ambassador saw *Pericles* but left no specific date, although we know it was no earlier than January 1606, when he arrived in London.[15] If the finished work reached the stage in the early summer of 1607, however, it was for only a very brief run, for the theaters were soon closed and the King's Men went on tour.

The maddest of Burbage's roles would come from another playwright at about this same time. As Vendice in *The Revenger's Tragedy*, from the moment he enters contemplating his mistress's skull to his final soliloquy on a stage littered with bodies, Burbage would walk one of the most demanding tightropes in theatrical history. Although long credited to Tourneur, there is now much argument about the play's authorship,[16] but not much about the dating. Registered and printed in 1607 when the theaters were closed, it must have been performed in 1606–07. That it is a play full of young men indicates a date after Sly, Lowin, Cooke, and Gilburne all progressed to some form of share, and that it requires only one old man indicates a date after Shakespeare had announced his retirement.

With Burbage as the vengeful Vendice, his regular stage mirror Condell would have played Lussurioso, the Duke's eldest and legitimate son. Heminges, as the company elder, must have been the Duke, with his current apprentice Rice as the Duchess and his former apprentice Cooke in the Half-Share role of Spurio, who is sleeping with his stepmother. In age, Sly would have been Ambitioso, the eldest son of the Duchess, with Gilburne as Supervacuo; if cast by character types previously played, then Sly would have been the foppish Supervacuo. Either case would have left Lowin as Vendice's brother Hippolito.

One revival of a popular old play can be traced to the brief playing season of 1607 before the plague returned. *The Merry Devil of Edmonton* was printed in 1607, after an October 2 registration, suggesting it had been recently performed. Middleton's *A Mad World My Masters*, usually dated 1608,[17] alludes to *Merry Devil*, confirming recent performances that perhaps even continued into 1608. Middleton's comments indicate that several Smug scenes were played at this time that are not in the quarto and were thus probably written new for Lawrence Fletcher, replacing Armin who had been the clown in the original in 1602. In such a revival, Burbage, Condell, Cooke, and Cowley simply repeated their earlier assignments, with Lowin replacing Phillips as the drunkard priest (see Chart C). Gilburne would have played young Raymond, the young lover hero. Given the dates when Shakespeare should have been in Stratford, it is unlikely he played in this revival; if new clown scenes were in fact written, then the company intended to perform the play into 1608, when Shakespeare would not be available to play his original father role. Heminges would have moved to Sir Arthur, with Condell now doubling the Gamekeeper and Sir Ralph, and Sly taking over the loquacious Host, a much larger role than when he had had only a half share.

The company also revived *Taming of the Shrew*. A new quarto of *A Shrew* appeared during 1607[18]; the only plausible stimulus for such a new printing after more than ten years must have been a successful production of some *Shrew* play which might trick readers into a purchase of this garbled old text. In *A Whole Crew of Gossips*, Samuel Rowlands stated "The chiefest Art I Have I will bestow/About a worke cald taming of the Shrow."[19] This was published in 1609, indicating that *Shrew* had been visible and popular in the recent past. Both point to 1607 as the date of a revival, which, due to long plague interruptions, probably continued into 1608.

Although it had been almost a decade since its last probable company production, Burbage was still a plausible Petruchio, and Ecclestone would have been more than able to hold the stage with him as Kate, but the alterations in the company would have forced many other changes. Heminges would all but automatically have been Baptista, with his precocious boy Rice as Biondello. Fletcher would have automatically played the chief clown, Grumio, and the company still had a large complement of Hired Men for the comic servants. With young Gilburne as Lucentio, Tranio was most likely Sly, not particularly young but experienced in comedic characters. Gilburne's extreme youth meant either Condell or Heminges would have been plausible as Vincentio, the other then covering Hortensio. Vincentio, however, is a Half-Share role at best, so this casting probably led to the restoration of the Sly scenes where the Lord is a major player. Shakespeare's earlier role of Gremio is a caricature pantaloon who could be played by anyone with powder in their hair, but Cowley was now the company specialist in such characters, which leaves only Cooke with his half share to play Sly. All of this assumes, of course, that no actual revisions were made beyond the restoration of some of the Sly material that probably dated back almost two decades.

By August, plague deaths began to rise sharply and the King's Men went back out on tour, reaching Oxford, on September 7, and nearby Marlborough.[20]

A surprisingly large number of King's Men plays went to the printers in 1607. Between July 31 and November 26, 1607, printers registered *The Merry Devil of Edmonton, The Miseries of Enforced Marriage, The Divil's Charter, The Revenger's Tragedy,* and *King Lear,* and Jonson's *Volpone* was printed about the same time without a registration. As with the large group of printings in 1600, this surely reflects significant turmoil and turnover within the King's Men, but the nature of that turmoil is unclear. All came from different authors and all but *The Merry Devil* were printed in very good quartos. This would certainly suggest that individual authors were trying to forestall the possible appearance of bad memorial reconstructions. Although it is possible that someone among the unusually large group of Hired Men may have threatened to sell reconstructions of these popular works while the Sharers of the King's Men went on tour, it seems unlikely. The one likely memorial reconstruction is *The Merry Devil,* yet it was one of the last to appear in print. Something else must have driven a number of different playwrights to get their own versions of recent big hits safely into print.

The King's Men were back in London by November 1607, and the theaters apparently reopened by early December. Not only had plague deaths declined significantly,[21] but it was also an unusually cold winter, and cold almost always brought a temporary cessation of the plague. The King's Men played at court thirteen times during the Christmas season 1607–08, a rather remarkable feat considering they had had only a few months to develop new plays during the previous year.

Shakespeare's brother Edmund died shortly after Christmas, and someone paid an extra twenty shillings to have the great bell of the church in Southwark rung for his funeral on New Year's Eve. This was a significant sum at the time and must have come from either a wealthy relative or from a group of contributors. Edmund's only such relative was his brother William, so it is possible that William had returned to London to act in whichever of the court revivals might still have required his presence. However, it is also possible that the King's Men themselves paid the fee to mark the passing of one of their own. A similar (and longer) ringing of the bell was later paid for at Fletcher's funeral, and as he had no known London family, the acting company are the most likely underwriters.[22]

The winter of 1607–08 was one of the coldest in history for London. The Thames froze and remained frozen so solid that people could walk on the ice and even build coal fires on it on January 8.[23] That audiences would brave such weather to stand outdoors at a play indicates how important the plays were to the general public of the day. One of the plays that dragged audiences out into the cold open air was *Pericles*, one of the greatest hits of its day, much to the mystification of almost all modern readers. It continued to be popular for years, so that Ben Jonson complained as late as 1631 that people still preferred a "mouldy tale, like *Pericles*" to his new work.[24] Although written earlier, as previously noted, the play was obviously current immediately prior to Wilkin's novelization in 1608, or there would have been little interest in such a novelization.

Despite its large cast, *Pericles* is another of those plays, like *Antony and Cleopatra*, dominated by only a handful of players. Most of the play is actually handled by four performers. Pericles, Marina, and Simonides together have almost 40% of the lines, and the narrator Gower has more than three hundred lines in only eight speeches, a remarkably massive narrator role. Shakespeare (or Wilkins, for that matter) was perfectly capable of writing a sprawling history without narration, so the role must have been written primarily to give stage time to a Sharer. Burbage, of course, played Pericles, a typical late Burbage role complete with mad scene, long break in Act IV, and twice as many lines as the next player. Helicanus, Burbage's noble adviser, who appears throughout the play, is about the same age but has fewer lines, the usual province of Condell. Gilburne, the company's new young Sharer, must have played the handsome young noble Lysimachus. Simonides, a significant father, disappears after Act II, so he must have doubled Cerimon, the wise doctor who rescues Thaissa from the sea in III,2. The thankless role of Cleon, who appears in many scenes although with few total lines, could have doubled as the incestuous Antiochus, who appears only in Act I. We have only Sly, Lowin, and Heminges left to cast these. Given the ages of the characters, Heminges is the obvious choice for Simonides/ Cerimon; both Lowin and Sly are a bit young for Antiochus, but as Cleon begins the play young, either could have taken the role. The other, then, was Gower, the enormous size of his speeches indicating his prominence in both the company and his ability to hold audience interest. Cooke, still a Half-Share man, would have played Leonine, the would-be murderer of Marina, and perhaps doubled as Thaliart, the would-be assassin of Pericles in earlier acts. The clowns are always on stage as a trio of two adults and a boy, as Boult, the Pandar, and the Bawd or as the three fishermen who rescue Pericles, suitable for Fletcher, Cowley, and a clown apprentice.

The second largest dramatic role is once again a very feminine woman. As with Isabella, every man Marina meets wants to sleep with her, and only her own will-power protects her chastity until the right man arrives. Marina splits her scenes fairly evenly among the clowns, Lysimachus, and the final recognition scene with Pericles, which would indicate a mature, experienced boy trusted to work away from his master at times. Thus, although the role is much smaller than Isabella or Cleopatra, it does seem to be designed for the same boy, Ecclestone. He may have doubled as the beautiful incestuous daughter of Antiochus, who appears only in I,1; however, since she is all but silent, this was probably a much less experienced boy.

There are three other women, but only the Bawd actually crosses the hundred line threshold. Thaissa is a stereotype, the typical beautiful daughter of fairy tales, with little of the personality of her daughter, Marina, and as such would have made no particular demands on any of the boys; that Heminges, the oldest actor in the company, was able to carry her away alone while playing Cerimon (III,11,114) indicates the boy was very light, in turn pointing to our short boy of this era, John Rice. If Lowin was Cleon, then his boy was Dionyza, although now very near the end of his bonds.

We should also note the size of the company indicated by the pageant of the five knights in armor and five pages (II,ii). This demonstrates that the company had at the very least nine boys—the five pages plus Marina, Thaissa, Dionyza, and a Clown Boy. There were also at least five young men, all younger than Pericles. One of these may have been Gilburne, since Lysimachus does not appear until much later. The others would have been the young men we have been seeing since they were apprentices—Tooley, Gough, Edmans, and perhaps Sands. With the Marshall and various Lords in attendance in the same scene, followed immediately by the banquet and its servants, the King's men obviously still had a large complement of Hired Men. However, those Hired Men were given very few lines, either individually or as a group.

The company also revived *Richard II* at this time. A new quarto was printed in 1608, the fourth for this immensely popular play but the first in a decade. This quarto now included the deposition scene, as "lately acted by the Kinges Maiesties seruants, at the Globe." That the company thought it safe to revive the play, and to insert the deposition scene, is quite remarkable. Still, a decade earlier it had been one of the company's most successful works, so it must have seemed very attractive to a company trying to fill out a season without Shakespeare on hand to provide new material. Because some seven years had passed since the ill-fated Essex revival, during which time Phillips had died, Burbage of course would have moved to the largest role of Richard himself, for whom Burbage was also now a suitable age, and the rest of the Sharers would have been recast completely (see Chart C). This probably accounted as much as anything for the restoration of the deposition scene, since it both increased Burbage's lines and came as close to a mad scene as the history allowed.

It is also possible that one of the Henry IV plays was also revived in this spring, for a new quarto of *1 Henry IV* appeared in 1608. However, it had been only three years since the previous quarto had been printed, so it is equally plausible that the new printing was a response to reader demand. Fletcher was still in the company to play Falstaff, so a new production is at least possible, but with Burbage and Condell both now approaching forty, wholesale casting changes would have been necessary.

In any case, the plague and a pair of deaths among the Sharers in the summer of 1608 would have made the run very short indeed.

During the winter of 1607–08, the Blackfriars Boys produced Chapman's plays about the Duke de Biron, whose name had provided Shakespeare with Berowne. Unlike Berowne, the real Biron was a scoundrel who was involved in a number of conspiracies against Henri IV in France. The French Ambassador formally complained to James about the plays, in particular about a scene in which the King's mistress slapped the face of the Queen herself. The Ambassador also brought to James' attention that "a day or two before, they had slandered their king [James] . . . portrayed him drunk at least once a day." James ordered the company dissolved so that they "never play more, but should first begg their bread," and ordered the arrest of both authors involved. Chapman somehow escaped, but Marston ended up in jail, so he was apparently the author of the play that had shown James drunk. The French Ambassador's letter about the affair was dated March 11, during the middle of Lent, so the actual events must have transpired before Ash Wednesday, during mid-February. James was so incensed he closed not only Blackfriars but all the adult theaters as well. Easter was on March 27, but on March 29, 1608, the French ambassador reported that "all the London theaters have been closed." All of the adult theater companies paid a large indemnity "about May," in order to get back on stage.[25] This probably happened around May 20, when *Pericles* was registered to prevent its publication because the King's Men had decided to put it back on stage. Thus, the theaters were closed for about two months at the worst possible time, the single portion of the year when plague had not returned, weather was comparatively clement, and performances were likely to draw their largest audiences. As a further result, risky material like *Richard II* would have been taken back out of the repertory, perhaps leading directly to the new printing.

The plague, the weather, and the political repressions combined to keep audience attendance low for all the companies. Paul's Boys had already folded in 1606, with many of their most popular plays sold to the printers. The Blackfriars Boys threw in the towel after the Biron affair, and Henry Evans asked Burbage to release him from the lease. Even without the boys to siphon off audiences, the adults were still desperate. The Prince's Men at the Fortune, the Queen's Men at the Curtain, and the King's Men were all hard pressed. The playwright Dekker predicted that "a deadly war between these three houses will, I fear, burst out like thunder and lightning" during the next summer, for all the players would "wish one another's throat cut for two pence."[26]

The predicted war was prevented by the return of the plague; the theaters were apparently closed in July 1608, when the death rate surged upward yet again. This would turn out to be the worst year of infestation, as a result of which the theaters would remain closed all through the winter and all year of 1609.

The actors of course could not predict this future, so they had to plan as if they would be performing again in the winter at the very latest. Because no reasonable person would look forward to more outdoor performances in winters cold enough to freeze the Thames, Blackfriars must have looked very attractive to the adults. On

August 9, the Burbages put together a new syndicate to take over the lease from Evans. While Richard and Cuthbert retained ownership of the Blackfriars building, they in turn leased it to another set of investors that included as equal partners the two Burbages, Heminges, Condell, Shakespeare, Sly, and Henry Evans. Each put up no lump sum but was to pay one seventh part of the yearly lease of forty pounds, plus an equal share of all improvements and maintenance, until the end of twenty-one years that began with Evans's original lease in 1600.[27] Shakespeare's inclusion means he must have been in London, which may explain why there was such a long gap between the Blackfriar Boys' shutdown before Lent and the lease transfer—to allow Shakespeare to return to town.

Sly immediately fell ill and was buried only a week later, on August 16. This must have been unexpected, or he would never have been included in the Blackfriars partnership. So unexpected was his death that his heir simply allowed the Blackfriars share to revert back to the group and to be split up equally among the others.[28] Given the timing, plague was almost certainly the culprit.

Much has been made of the Blackfriars deal, with many critics seeing it as a watershed event for both the King's Men and Shakespeare. The general tendency has been to assume that the audiences at the Blackfriars, where admission was far more expensive, must automatically have been more sophisticated. This in turn forced the King's Men and Shakespeare to turn away from the vulgar and popular world of the Globe, as reflected in Shakespeare's work in the late romances. Unfortunately for such theories, the extant reports of *Cymbeline*, *Pericles* and *Winter's Tale* indicate they played at the Globe. The boys were in possession of Blackfriars until August 1608, at which point the plague closed the theaters completely. No one played anywhere in London but at court during 1608–09, so the King's Men could not have moved into Blackfriars before the winter of 1609–10. Curiously, two plays were given at court during Christmas 1608–09 by boys who were still referred to as "Children of the blackfriers." This may indicate that the new Blackfriars partners immediately leased the space back to the boys rather than attempting to move in with the adult company. More significantly, when the Globe burned down during 1613, the King's Men did not move to the Blackfriars as a permanent home. Instead, they immediately rebuilt the Globe, at great expense, and in a much improved state. They would hardly have done so if they had not considered the Globe to be their primary home.

The Blackfriars space may have been profitable once the King's Men were able to use it. There was much less audience space, but the audience paid a great deal more. For a company used to the huge playing space of the outdoor stage, however, performances would have been something of a nightmare. The indoor stage was no more than about twenty-five feet wide; the gallants sitting on stools onstage with the actors narrowed it further, leaving only fifteen to eighteen feet of actual performing space, less than half the Globe's width. Although there were three doors and an upper area of some kind, opportunities for crowd scenes and spectacles would have been considerably reduced.[29] Obviously, substantial revisions were needed before much of the repertoire could be staged indoors.

It is also important to remember that the King's Men per se did not take over the Blackfriars; a partnership that included several senior partners from the King's Men took over the Blackfriars. This is a small but important distinction. Half of the six partners in the Blackfriars were non-actors—Henry Evans, Cuthbert Burbage, and William Shakespeare—whereas the three actors—Burbage, Condell, and Heminges—were a minority in the acting company itself. To the remaining majority of the King's Men—Cooke, Lowin, Gilburne, Cowley, the new company clown, and Sly's replacement—the Blackfriars group was merely a landlord in turn fronting for the true owners, the Burbage brothers. One assumes the acting company found them congenial and trustworthy landlords, but none of them could ever have believed that the Blackfriars somehow belonged to the King's Men.

Less than one month after Sly's death, Lawrence Fletcher was buried on September 12. As noted earlier, someone paid forty shillings to have the great bell rung at his funeral: as he had no known relatives, this was probably paid by his fellows from the King's Men, the ring twice as long as that paid for at Edmund Shakespeare's funeral, as befitted Fletcher's Sharer status. The company then went on tour. No precise dates are recorded, but they did perform at some point in Mortlake and Coventry.[30] They would not have toured without a clown. As we saw when Kemp left, finding a replacement for a clown was no simple matter, so the company must have begun looking long before September 13 in order to have one ready to go on the road so quickly. Thus, Fletcher had probably decided to retire earlier in the year and, unluckily, failed to live to enjoy his retirement.

Fletcher's replacement was something of a surprise. Somehow, the Sharers managed to talk Robert Armin out of retirement. Armin's name is in Jonson's folio cast list for *The Alchemist* in 1610, although missing from all the various Beaumont and Fletcher lists, and as we shall see, some of the most typically Armin roles from Shakespeare are datable to late 1608 or later. When Armin published his *Two Maids of Moreclacke* in 1609, it identified the author as "servant to the Kings most excellent Maiesties"[31] although the play itself had been performed by the Paul's Boys. Curiously, Armin took a new apprentice on July 15, 1608, although he registered the boy as a goldsmith,[32] which is almost exactly the date the company would have replaced Fletcher if he had announced his retirement in the spring. Whether as a result of Fletcher's retirement or of his death, there seems little doubt that Armin was the clown on tour with the company that autumn.

Fletcher's share would have gone to Armin, perhaps even without payment to lure Armin out of retirement and compensate for any bruised ego suffered when Fletcher had squeezed him out. The disposition of Sly's share is less obvious. Given Cooke's listing in the Principall Actors, he must have assumed half of it, at last bringing himself up to a full share. The remaining half share seems to have gone to someone whose name began with E, as indicated by the prominent Lord E in *All's Well That Ends Well*. Two names are possible, John Edmans and William Ecclestone, the latter of whose name is also among the Principall Actors and on many later cast lists as well. If, as we have demonstrated, Ecclestone was Burbage's apprentice who had played Cleopatra, then he was still under bonds and could not have held a share at this time. More conclusively, Ecclestone joined the new Lady Elizabeth's company in 1611. He would hardly have abandoned a share in an established and prosperous company such as the King's Men to take a share in one just starting up; hence, it seems clear that Ecclestone did not have a share of any size before 1611. Edmans, on the other hand, was (through his wife) a partner in the Globe and would have had the necessary capital to purchase a half share when it became available. Thus, the company reorganized after the deaths of Sly and Fletcher consisted of Burbage, Heminges, Condell, Lowin, Gilburne, Armin, and Cooke, with two Half-Sharers, Cowley and Edmans.

Sly mentioned none of his acting fellows in his will, leaving a token to Cuthbert Burbage but nothing to Richard or to any of the other actors. One wonders if there were bad feelings. That he had been part of the Blackfriars consortium would seem to indicate that he was respected and trusted, but after ten years in the company, surely he should have left a keepsake to some of his compatriots. The only actor named was James Sands, who had been an apprentice still under articles to Phillips in 1605 but who now seems to have been out of his bonds.

Sly's bequest of his Globe share was even more peculiar, for it passed to the actor Robert Browne, to be administered in his absence by his wife Sisley. Sly's relationship to the couple is unknown, but because Browne spent most of his time acting on the continent, Sly was obviously closer to Sisley than to Robert. Browne had never been associated in any way with the Chamberlain's or the King's Men, nor had he been in the old Admiral's Men before Sly changed companies. The bequest suggests a certain amount of spite on Sly's part, for once the Globe share was in Browne's hands, he retired from the stage and used his Globe money to finance the King's Men's competition, a new company at the Whitefriars in 1610. With Sly's death, the Globe for all practical purposes passed out of the hands of the acting company members. Half of the Globe shares now were held by non-actors who had never been a part of the company—Cuthbert Burbage with 25%, plus Phillips's widow, Browne, and Pope's heir Mary Clarke combined for another 25%. Even had Shakespeare not retired, the actors would have held only half of the shares, although we are working under the assumption that Clarke's husband, Edmans, was still acting in the company; with Shakespeare's retirement, only Heminges, Condell, and Richard Burbage among the acting company continued to hold shares. The Burbages were still the dominant power, so the King's Men were not likely to be harmed in any way as long as Richard continued to perform with them. Nevertheless, in less than ten years, the Kings' Men had reverted to the role of mere tenants in what is usually described as their own building.

While Shakespeare was in London, he hurriedly revised several plays to adjust them to the new company. One of these was all but certainly *All's Well That Ends Well.* As discussed in chapter 5, the extant text is probably a revision of an earlier play that includes many elements unchanged from that earlier version. However, the full text in the Folio can come from only 1608–10 or after 1613, the only periods when both a G and an E could have been Sharers. In 1608, they would have been Gilburne and Edmans, after 1613, Gough and Ecclestone. However, after 1613, the revision would have been made by Middleton or Fletcher, which no modern analysis has even suggested. Thus, 1608 is the only possible date, and Gilburne and Edmans the only possible G and E. As we can see, *All's Well* is clearly designed for a company with a number of relatively young men and very few older ones, which also uniquely fits this era. Burbage, now age thirty-seven to forty, could not possibly have played Bertram. The King, however, is now the largest male role, some 40% larger than Bertram. A King only about forty years old who grew mysteriously ill would have been understood as a major political crisis, requiring measures as desperate as a female doctor, so Burbage's age could have been used there to dramatic effect. Thus, Burbage must have played the King, whose role was certainly expanded as part of the revision. Heminges, the eldest actor, must have played the eldest character, Lafew. Lowin would have taken Parolles, another of the Phillips-like talkers. As the King's role expanded, Bertram's may have shrunk, and the scenes with the young Lords may be completely new at this date. With Gilburne and Edmans as G and E, Bertram then must have been played by Cooke. Condell then would have been left with the principal Soldier not already assigned to G or E, perhaps doubling in the much smaller role of the Duke of Florence. Armin, now back in the company, would have repeated his earlier Lavatch; his reappearance may in fact have been one of the major motivations for such a revival at this time. Cowley then would have played the Steward and doubled soldiers in the Italian scenes. Helena, the largest role in the play, can only have been played by Ecclestone, by far the most experienced boy in the company at this time. By 1608, Ecclestone must have been quite old to be playing women, about seventeen if we have been correct in our description of his career, but this was a rush job, a hurried revision to make an old play fit the current company, and the Sharers may not have projected any future performances beyond the coming winter. Rice more certainly portrayed the Countess, still playing most of his scenes with Heminges. The Widow must have been intended for the Clown Boy. When Sly died, he had a young apprentice of about thirteen, whom we have seen in small roles such as Helen of Troy or *Volpone's* Celia. As Cooke took part of Sly's share, he almost certainly also took Sly's boy, who would have been perfectly suited in age and experience for Diana.

(Placing *All's Well That Ends Well* in this season may well account for the tonal similarities with *Troilus and Cressida*, Shakespeare's last complete work before he left London in 1607. Shakespeare did in fact work on both plays at about the same time, but that time was 1607–08, not 1602–04.)

Shakespeare's other contribution during this visit to London was an equally hasty revision of *Coriolanus*, also apparently designed to deal with Cooke's move into a former Burbage role. As discussed earlier (see p. 113), almost all modern authorities agree on a date shortly after the very cold winter of 1607–08, although all are somewhat tentative in that dating. As it happens, all of the textual allusions suggesting 1608 are in Act I. The long "fable of the belly" told by Menenius in I,i, is usually traced to Camden's *Remaines*, published in 1605. Similarly, the "coal of fire upon the ice" usually thought to refer to the frozen Thames of 1607–08, is in the same scene (I,i,72). Nothing outside this scene can be linked to any specific date, although there are some rather tortured attempts to argue that the man who "wants not spirit to say he'll turn your current in a ditch" (III,i,94–5) applies to a plan for diverting water into London in 1609.[33] As discussed in chapter 5, the casting requirements of the extant script suggest an actual first performance during 1601, which would in turn indicate the 1608 factors were part of a revision confined primarily to Act I.

There is some supporting evidence to suggest a revision at this time. *Coriolanus* is unusually long, 3,836 lines in the Folio. Although no one has previously offered a serious argument for composition and revision at different dates based on textual analyses,[34] the Folio text is famously difficult to edit. Some scholars believe this results from use of the author's foul copy, much confused by multiple typesetters,[35] but there is at least the possibility that some of the anomalies may result from use of the author's foul copy, much confused by revisions superimposed on the original, all of which (as with *Love's Labour's Lost* and probably *Cymbeline*) were included in the Folio without further editing by Heminges and Condell in their attempt to print Shakespeare's complete creative work.

Interestingly enough, the greatest practical problem with new composition during 1608 is the question of Burbage's role assignment. Burbage by 1608 was moving toward forty. Coriolanus has about one quarter of all the lines and thus seems designed for the company star, but he is a stiff-necked, proud, cocky *young* man. Although no specific age is mentioned, he is clearly one of the youngest men in the cast list. Only one character, Titus Lartius, might be thought younger, and even that is questionable because he is an experienced military commander. Even so, that role is so small as to call into question its assignment to even a Half Sharer. At the same time, four major characters—Menenius, Cominius, Sicinius, and Brutus—must be older than Coriolanus, and Aufidius might well be older too. Still, stardom carries its own youth, and we might argue that Burbage played the role anyway, as he must have done in 1602. But to do so, he would need to be surrounded with older actors in contrast to whom he might look younger. In the company after Sly's death in 1608, *everyone* but Heminges was *younger* than Burbage. The only casting that would not have looked ludicrous in 1608 would have been either Gilburne or Cooke, the two youngest Sharers, as Coriolanus, with the other as Aufidius. As Gilburne has had a boy for at least a year, then his apprentice is more plausible as Virgilia, and he then the more likely Coriolanus. Burbage then would have been Menenius, the second largest role but not inconceivable for an actor of his prominence; Menenius has almost the same number of lines as Pericles, for example. Given Burbage's stardom, the role of Menenius would be the one most likely to have been amplified in 1608, and I,i contains almost one hundred lines for him. Nor does this preclude the possibility of other additions to pad the role in scenes that give no hint of date—the more than one hundred lines in II,i, for example, seem on the whole to contribute little to the plot while providing a great deal of stage time for Menenius himself. Curiously enough, the contradictory spellings of Lartius and Latius that have led Honigmann and others to suggest Shakespeare used two different printings of North's Plutarch would seem to support the theory of such a revision; Lartius occurs only in Act I, Latius only in III and a stage direction for II,i, a scene in which he does not actually speak and that revolves around Burbage. Such a large amount of new material for Menenius must have necessarily led to cuts in later scenes, and Coriolanus in particular may have seen his lines much reduced. Lowin, Heminges, and Condell played the other three major mature characters, although it is not quite obvious in what way they assigned the roles. Armin, Cowley, and the Hired Men then played the large number of soldiers and lower class characters.

Volumnia is a problem. When Burbage played Coriolanus, he had an apprentice with a mature presence, Nick Tooley. Neither Gilburne's nor Cooke's boys would have had the experience to take on a role like Volumnia. It is, of course, possible that the role was significantly cut. Outside of the confrontation scene in Act V, Volumnia's scenes are with the women or with Coriolanus and Menenius both present; the confrontation scene is essentially two very long monologues interrupted only briefly by Coriolanus. Thus, it is conceivable that the role might have been played by Burbage's boy Ecclestone, with Virgilia covered by Cooke's boy. In any case, it ultimately did not matter; Shakespeare may have made these hurried revisions in preparation for upcoming winter performances, but as it happened, the plague grew worse and the theaters did not open, and when years later they did at last open, the number of Hired Men was much reduced. It is entirely possible that this version was never performed in Shakespeare's lifetime.

Both of Shakespeare's revisions are designed for a company without Sly or Fletcher, so they can only have been produced after Fletcher's decision to retire and Sly's unexpected death. This further encourages the idea that *Coriolanus* and *All's Well That Ends Well* were revisions of earlier plays, and hasty revisions at that. Sly did not die until August, and the King's Men were on tour by the end of September, so Shakespeare would have been writing very quickly. It seems unlikely that Shakespeare made it back to Stratford by the time his mother died and was buried on September 9. We don't know the details of her final illness, but certainly he would have made every possible effort to reach her on her deathbed, if he had known. On the other hand, if she had been in long-term decline, he would not have left Stratford at the beginning of August to come to London for the Blackfriars deal. However, we do know that he was in Stratford by the end of the autumn. He invited his friend Thomas Greene, the Stratford town clerk, to move into New Place while Greene had some remodeling done on his own home, apparently in October or November. He also instituted a lawsuit against one John Addenbrooke for unpaid debts in December. Shakespeare of course need not have attended all the court sessions, and in fact all the surviving documents were signed by his friend Greene.[36] But Shakespeare would have needed to authorize Greene to begin the suit, so he must have been in Stratford by November.

When the King's Men returned to London after their autumn tour in 1608, they found that plague deaths were not declining with the cold weather. Weekly deaths dropped below fifty only three times during the fifteen months following Sly's death. All the theaters certainly remained closed until at least December of 1609 and probably until January 1610.

There was still much work to be done in the winter of 1608–09, for they performed for the King some twelve times. That same winter, the court also saw five performances from the Queen's Men, three from the Prince's, and three from the Blackfriars Boys, who obviously had stayed together despite the loss of their lease.

After the court performances, the consistently high plague level meant the company had no opportunities to perform at either the Globe or the new Blackfriars. In April 1609, James gave Heminges and his company a gift of forty pounds "for their practice in the time of infeccon that thereby they mighte be inhabled to performe their service before his majestie in Christmas hollidaies."[37] With that money in hand, they were able to limp along until the summer touring season, which began early. They were in Ipswich, Hythe, and New Romney in May 1609.[38] A new quarto of *Romeo* appeared in 1609, which in normal circumstance would indicate a production of some kind. However, the theaters were not open at any time during the year. The Oxford library copy was literally worn away by its readers,[39] so the republication may have been a response to reader demand, despite the passing of ten years since the previously known edition (and perhaps other intervening editions were read so heavily that they have simply disappeared).

Shakespeare was still in Stratford in June, for he sued Thomas Horneby on June 7.[40] Again, he need not have been present in court on that date, but he did need to be present in Stratford to make the decision itself. In October, he told Greene, who was having problems with the builders, that he could stay another year if necessary at New Place until his home was ready. This is usually assumed to mean that Shakespeare would not need New Place because he was still in London. Shakespeare would hardly have turned his own family out on the street while Greene took the large house. Thus, Greene must have been sharing the house with the Shakespeares and Shakespeare merely invited him to stay longer. At that point, Shakespeare may well have thought he had permanently retired from the theatrical life. In London, the King's Men began to prepare for the moment when the theaters would eventually reopen and when they would begin a life without Shakespeare as either actor or author.

The Christmas season of 1609–10 saw another thirteen court performances. So completely had the company exhausted its supply of court plays, they were forced to revive that old chestnut *Mucedorus* as the thirteenth performance, on Shrove Sunday, according to the 1610 edition's title page. How the company actually played *Mucedorus* is a far more complex question, turning as usual in this period on the question of Burbage's role. Most of the 1610 text is identical to the original quarto that long predates the formation of the Chamberlain's/King's Men, while the additions in the 1610 printing almost certainly come from a revision made long before 1610 (see p. 106). Mucedorus is by far the largest role in the play, and one in which Burbage had been a success, but it is intended for a young romantic leading man, and by 1610 Burbage was very near forty, if not past it. In a company of mature actors, he might well continue to play the romantic leading man, but this was not a company full of mature actors. Lowin, Cooke, Gilburne, and Edmans were all significantly younger men, and the revisions had added two additional older, not younger, roles. Logically, Gilburne should have taken Mucedorus, but there is then no plausible role for Burbage but the King. Burbage was clearly moving to fatherly roles in new plays of this era, but this particular one has barely one hundred lines in the existing text. Barring more specific evidence of the text actually used at this time, we can only note the performance and guess at the cast.

The public theaters did at last reopen in this winter, although the precise date is unknown. Lady Arabella Stewart complained on February 10 that she had been insulted in Jonson's *Epicene*, played by a boy company now at the Whitefriars.[41] This was ostensibly a new boys' company, licensed in January 1610 as the Queen's Revels company. Some of the "boys" in the company had been in the Blackfriars group in 1600, so they were now adults. It was supervised by Robert Keysar, one of the final partners in the Blackfriars group. Keysar sued the Burbages for cheating the company out of the Blackfriars, but he seems to have lost the case.[42] One of his partners was Robert Browne, who now held Sly's share in the Globe. Most unusually, the boys went on a tour in February,[43] as noted earlier, indicating they had given up all pretense of being a chapel school.

The adult theaters probably opened at about the same time. The Kings Men, thus, were able at last to move into the Blackfriars for the cold weather before Lent of 1610.

That first Blackfriars season may have included *All's Well That Ends Well* and *Coriolanus*; both would have been new to the general public, and the company of adult actors for whom they had been intended was still intact. If adjustments were made for Sly's absence, *Troilus and Cressida* would have been played as well. Boy casting is not quite so obvious, for the boys for whom Shakespeare had made his hurried adaptations would have been two years older. Rice could have continued as Cressida, but if Ecclestone had been intended for Helena or Volumnia, he certainly could not have played those roles now. All three of the plays might fit into the comparatively cramped space of the Blackfriars, although the crowd scenes in *Coriolanus* would have been a bit congested. To modern eyes, none of these seem likely to have been hits, but if the often argued sophistication of the Blackfriars audience was in fact true, then these plays would have had a far better chance there than in the more rough-and-tumble world of the Globe. On the other hand, we have no evidence that any of these were ever performed in public, whereas the unusual length and the great number of textual problems associated with all three may suggest that the revisions were never put to the test of actual performance.

Wells and Taylor argue for a revision of *King Lear* at this time.[44] This seems most unlikely, even if we were to assume that Shakespeare returned to London otherwise unnoticed. The question of *Lear*'s texts is one of the most vexed in Shakespearean editing, precisely because both extant versions are very good. Hence, it is extremely difficult to see the Folio as a corrected or augmented version of the quarto. This in turn has led to the general assumption that one of these versions is Shakespeare's revision of the other, but there is no general agreement on which came first. The textual questions cannot be resolved here, but the issue must be raised. The only logical reasons for an author to make a major revision of an already popular play would be for a printing or for a new revival with new performers. If the Folio version is a revision of the earlier quarto, it is a literary revision, full of numerous small changes within speeches, similar to the revisions that Jonson, for example, apparently made before many of his printings. However, no known printing of *King Lear* appeared in 1610. Such literary changes are precisely the kind of modifications that actors find most difficult to memorize once they have already learned a role and that they resist most strongly in rehearsal. As we have seen, there certainly had been many changes made in the acting company since *Lear* was presented in 1606, but there is no sign that the assumed revisions were designed to take advantage of those changes. There are no significant new characters in the Folio version that would indicate material for new actors, nor are there any significant cuts. In fact, there are some very serious casting difficulties based on character ages at this date. Heminges is old enough to play Gloucester, but who is to play Kent? Condell is nearing forty but is still some distance from his claim of forty-eight years,[45] and all the other men are younger. Lowin is now thirty-four, more than a bit old for Edmund or for Heminges's son, and apparently growing fatter, making Edmund's sexual charisma a bit hard to understand, even allowing for cultural differences; but if he does not play Edmund, what does he play? Similarly, if Middleton had to be paid to revise *Timon* for a company with no strong boys (see later), why would the same company revise *Lear* and yet retain the three strong female roles? If in fact the Folio text is a revision, it is a revision not made for the King's Men of 1610.

This was, however, the most likely time for Middleton to have provided his portions of *Timon of Athens*, a play very well suited to the Blackfriars space and audience. As Middleton's material seems to be a revision (see p. 132), it must have been provided when the company was in a hurry for a new play: after the membership of the company had significantly changed and when Shakespeare himself was no longer present to make those revisions. This points to either the winter of 1609–10, or after Shakespeare's death. Wells and Taylor argue that Middleton's scenes came no later than 1606,[46] but as the precise dating of Middleton's plays after he left the children's companies is less than solid, the precise nature of the transition between his early and late style must be even more conjectural. Even so, if such analyses have any validity at all, then Middleton's scenes must have been added well before Shakespeare's death. In that case, 1610 is the only plausible date when the company might have wanted Middleton to make such revisions. The simplicity of staging, requiring only a within for Timon's cave, the high proportion of scenes with few characters, and the heavy reliance on talk all make it a plausible work for the smaller Blackfriar's space, which also points to the same date.

The extant *Timon* can be matched to the actors of the adult company of this era with relative ease. Timon rants and raves for five acts—proportionally, only Hamlet talks more—so he was obviously still played by Burbage. Condell was now about forty and thus much less plausible as the handsome Alcibiades than he had been in 1604. The apparently major expansion of the Steward, some 90% of whose lines are in Middleton's scenes, indicates that the role was aimed at a significant full Sharer who either was not present in the earlier version or who had been forced to change roles; Condell, who has most consistently paralleled Burbage, is the most obvious candidate. Cooke or Gilburne, then, would have been Alcibiades, but Cooke is far more likely given the stress on Alcibiades's military experience rather than his historical youth and beauty. The misanthrope Apemantus was probably played by Phillips in 1604; his replacement Lowin seems the most likely casting, with about 30% of his lines new. Middleton's revision of Alcibiades also adds some 50% to the First Senator's role, bringing it up to full Sharer size, suitable for the very mature Heminges. Cowley then probably played the Half-Sharer sized Second Senator, playing his own age. Gilburne and Edmans thus played the Poet and Painter, one a significantly larger role than the other though constantly paired and thus probably similar in age or appearance.

This still leaves the question of Armin. The Fool is assumed to have been written by Shakespeare; as it is the only clown role, we should expect it to be larger, and with Armin returned to the company, Middleton could have added new material to replace older scenes if necessary. Nonetheless, we have seen numerous instances in Shakespeare's previous work in which the Clown role was tiny, so the assignment to Armin is not inconceivable. The large group of Hired Men seems somewhat dubious for a company coming out of a long plague break, but there are no more than six in any given scene; what is remarkable is not the number of Hired Men, but the number of their lines, and their all but complete concentration in scenes by Middleton.

Despite the relative ease with which casting assignments can be made at this time, the lack of any notable female characters is still most unusual. It is most unlike Burbage not to have found a boy he could begin training around 1606 to replace Ecclestone in 1608–09. Of all the actors in the company, Burbage would have realized that a talented apprentice was critical to his own success. One wonders if he, too, had begun contemplating retirement about the same time as Shakespeare did. Or perhaps Burbage's luck merely ran out. He had found three phenomenally capable boys in a row—Saunder, who played Juliet, Portia, and Rosalind; Nick Tooley, who played Gertrude and the first Volumnia; and then the most amazing of them all, William Ecclestone, who introduced Desdemona, Lady Macbeth, and Cleopatra. Finding a fourth consecutive boy of such caliber would have about the same odds as winning the lottery multiple times. One of the oddities of the roles we have seen for Burbage since Pericles is that for the first time in the history of the company, he has no significant scenes with women: Ulysses, Menenius, and Timon have none, and the King in All's Well has only brief scenes with Helena as part of a large group. But ultimately, the lack of a woman for Burbage in Timon may mean nothing at all. As a part of his revisions, Middleton may have been asked to shorten the play—most of the surviving Jacobean plays written for indoor theaters are significantly shorter than those written for the Globe—and it was far more politic to cut a scene for a boy than for a full Sharer. In May, Burbage borrowed Rice from Heminges for the court pageant, but that may mean only that the company wanted to send the very best boy available to play before the King. Rice would finish his bonds in mid-1611, so he certainly would have been the most poised of the boys available; the fact that he could still play believable nymphs in 1610 is in itself remarkable.

In the plays of the following year, not just one but often several boys were closely associated with Burbage, so he clearly had found a usable boy somewhere. He would have begun looking during 1606 for a boy to replace Ecclestone, and we may in fact have seen him as the incestuous daughter of Antiochus who says her only two lines to Pericles and as the Sister of Scarborrow with the minuscule role as Ilford's wife in *Miseries of Enforced Marriage*. Such a boy would have been ready for larger roles in 1610, so the lack of a role for him as Timon's mistress or some similar character is certainly curious; nonetheless, during the plague years there were so few perform- ances, so many changes in company membership, and so few surviving plays we can not conjecture about his early career.

The long plague break had seriously disturbed the normal training system of apprenticeships (see Charts C and D). Sly had taken in Sands in 1604–05, but Sands had finished his service before 1608, when Sly died. Sly probably had found a new apprentice to replace Sands during 1606–07, but when he died the boy would have been masterless. Chances are strong that when Cooke took part of Sly's share, he also took Sly's boy. From the moment Gilburne assumed his full share he seems to have found an apprentice who could go on stage, who played the small role of Scarborrow's wife in *Miseries of Enforced Marriage* and who must have been thirteen or fourteen by 1610. But the plague meant that even Cooke's and Gilburne's boys had had little performing experience. Lowin's own boy began playing young boys more often than women after *Volpone*; assuming he was new when Lowin joined Worcester's Men in 1601, he would have been too old to play women after 1607– 08 and finishing his bonds by 1610 at the latest. Similarly, Condell's second boy should have been nearing the end of his female years in 1606–07, when we saw him in roles like Cymbeline's Queen. Only John Rice among the available boys had any significant skill or experience, and even he must have been old enough to make the company wonder how long he could continue to play women. Heminges thus must have been looking for a replacement who would have been brand new to the com- pany in January 1610. Likewise, Burbage had a boy, Richard Robinson, who was about sixteen in 1616, and thus must have been a new addition at about the same time. All of this meant that when the theaters at last reopened in January 1610, the company had at least four boys with no performing experience at all, and at least two others who, though older, had rarely been on stage.

The best way to give such a group experience would have been to put them on stage singing and dancing. The primary sign of potential talent in young boys is singing, so we should assume that most if not all of the youngest boys were capable young singers. Over the next two or three years, the new King's Men plays almost always included a masque or large group of singing boys. Still, the elimination of all women of any character type in *Timon* is most peculiar, and one cannot help but wonder if some scenes were not cut or lost at an even later date. *Timon* and *Macbeth* are about the same length, both by far the shortest of the Shakespearean non- comedies, and both are all but universally agreed to have been revised by Middleton, so such excisions are not inconceivable. (It is perhaps significant that *Timon* and *Macbeth* are the two shortest of Shakespeare's non-comedic plays. The plays for which Shakespeare appears to have made his own revisions are extremely long and as I have argued elsewhere appear to have been printed with both versions conflated. The only tragedies or histories sufficiently short to play in about two hours are also the only two in which Middleton's hand is visible, suggesting that Middleton not only shortened but also threw away Shakespeare's original scenes after revision.)

At some point in 1610, most probably after Easter, the King's Men moved back into the Globe, where the general public had not seen them play for a very long time. As this was the first time they had played for a Globe audience in almost two years, they must have revived some of their most popular material from the 1607–08 seasons. However, the major changes in company personnel and the peculiar status of the boys make it difficult to determine what plays in particular might have been revived. *Pericles*, their most successful hit of 1608, seems very likely, but there are no corroborating allusions (see Chart D).

With Shakespeare apparently retired, John Fletcher would soon become the company's resident playwright and the most active and popular playwright of the day. In his own time, he would be thought an equal of Shakespeare himself, although that reputation has not survived into the present. Known today as the other half of a writing team with Francis Beaumont, Fletcher wrote part or all of at least fifty plays in a wide range of genres that exceeds the breadth, if not the depth, of Shakespeare's work. He had begun playwriting with Beaumont for the Blackfriars Boys, perhaps as early as 1604, and although he wrote individually during that period, he continued to write with Beaumont until about 1612, when Beaumont married a rich widow and retired from literary life.

It is not clear when Fletcher began to write for the King's Men, with or without Beaumont. During the wedding festivities for the Princess Elizabeth in the winter of 1612–13, the King's Men played *Philaster* and a *Maid's Tragedy*. Similarly, the first quartos of *Philaster* and *The Maid's Tragedy* identified them as King's Men plays.[47] However, these printings did not appear until 1620 and 1619 respectively, long after the wedding celebrations. Thus, it is at least possible that one or both of these plays began life as a boys' company play and, like *The Malcontent* or *Satiromastix* in an earlier decade, were brought to the adult company and perhaps significantly revised by Fletcher after he became associated with them.

The date most often given by scholars for *Philaster*'s composition is 1609.[48] However, the theaters were all closed at that time due to the plague; there is an allusion to it in a poem by John Davies registered in October, 1610, so the play was current before the summer of 1610, when the theaters closed again. Many critics like to see it as a quintessential play for the Blackfriars audience, so it may well have premiered there, but the same factors make it equally plausible for the boys' company at the same time in Whitefriars.

The fundamental difficulty with the existing text as a King's Men original is that, as with the boy version of *The Malcontent*, there are not enough roles to go around. There are numerous commoners, the most positive of whom is a brave country man who knows "not your Rhetorick but . . . can lay it on if you touch the woman" (I,p125), and who in his good-hearted ignorance rescues the princess. This is a shining bit part, but he seems too positive and active for Armin, too muscular for either Cowley or Armin, and is still a bit part, barely twenty lines, small even by Hired Man standards. There are also two brief "Woodmen" who trade quips, but the scenes total less than forty lines, also very brief for such experienced comedians. As Philaster is very young, he could not be Burbage, despite having almost 30% of all the lines. On the other hand, the only plausible Burbage role, the usurping King, is fourth largest, half the size of Philaster, which is possible casting but certainly not typical of the other Burbage roles of the era. The only remaining roles over one hundred lines in a script that is obviously full length, about 2,800 lines, are for one father, suitable for Heminges, and three "women." This is the kind of concentration we would expect to find in a boys' company, where the bulk of the play must be carried by a small handful of older boys, leaving the younger boys to play only very small roles. It is not the apportionment of roles we have seen in any other King's Men play in previous years.

Nor do the women's roles fit as easily as we would expect for a play that eventually would become one of the era's most popular productions. The main plot turns on a woman disguised as a boy, which is of course familiar from many of Shakespeare's early comedies. In this case, however, the audience is not even told the "boy" Bellario is in fact a "woman" until the final scene. It is a *coup de théâtre* that is at once absurd and brilliant, a plot that worked in performance only because the girl was in fact a boy. But it is important to note that the plot also demands an *old* boy. Everyone in the play, Philaster included, believes that Bellario, a page to the Princess Arethusa, is actually sleeping with her. The boy playing her must, like Viola, look and sound old enough to be a plausible sexual being, not a child; among a cast of adult males, this would require a much older and more masculine boy than when played by a company in which all the adults were also played by boys. The King's Men at this time had only one relatively old boy, John Rice, who was very near the end of his apprenticeship in 1610. However, he was still able to play a nymph at court in May, which would seem to indicate he was likely to fool no one in young man's disguise. The other major woman is the bawdy, vulgar Lady Megra, who seems to have no particular ties to any single adult. If Gilburne did have an apprentice on stage in early 1607, the boy would have been old enough for significant roles at this time, but such a large role would have been most unusual, given the lack of experience in the intervening years.

The Beaumont and Fletcher folio lists no cast for *Philaster*, usually (but not necessarily) a sign that the play originated with one of the boy companies. Thus, on balance, it appears that the surviving text also originated with the boys and does not reflect the play as performed by the King's Men.

This does not necessarily mean the King's Men did not also perform the play in 1610; *Philaster's* popularity indicates that one of the adult companies must have produced it eventually, and the King's Men clearly had it in their repertoire by 1613. Rather, it merely means that we cannot determine the complete casting from the extant text. (The play was first printed in 1620, then reprinted in a "corrected and amended" version in 1622, later repeated in the Beaumont and Fletcher folio. Thus, it is also possible the extant text reflects the version performed by the King's Men in 1619–20, after Burbage had died and when the company apparently had an unusually large number of Half-Sharers.)

The Maid's Tragedy, the other Beaumont and Fletcher play usually associated with the King's Men of this year,[49] is even less likely. Like *Philaster*, the surviving text has no roles for clowns and only four adult roles over one hundred lines. The play was published as a King's Men play in 1619, and like *Philaster* was "corrected" in 1622, and thus may in fact be the text used in 1619–22, after Burbage was dead and when the company apparently contained only four full Sharers and eight Half-Sharers (see chap. 9). However, a "proud Mayd's Tragedie" was performed at court in February 1612, by Lady Elizabeth's Men, a new company organized in 1611 with apparently a large number of members. At about the same time, the King's Men were playing a "second" Maid's Tragedy, probably by Middleton (see later). Thus, the latter is the more likely King's Men play *Mayed's Tragedy*, recorded at court in 1612–13.

However, it is probable that during the 1610 season the company added Kyd's *Spanish Tragedy* to their repertoire. The play reappeared in a new quarto in 1610, after a gap of seven years, suggesting recent performances. According to John Fletcher, "Ould Hieronymoe" was one of Burbage's signature roles,[50] which indicates he played the role often after Fletcher began to be associated with the company on a regular basis. There is a joke in *The Malcontent* about the boys playing *Hieronymo* that has led many to assume that Burbage began playing the role even earlier, but this seems unlikely; Alleyn is known to have performed the play in 1602, with additions by Ben Jonson, and it seems most unlikely Burbage would have mounted a simultaneous production. However, by 1610, with no one in the Prince's Men to lay claim to Alleyn's mantle, the King's Men certainly would have been tempted to steal the play with the most famous mad scene in Elizabethan drama for a now middle-aged Burbage.

Unfortunately, the quarto printed in 1610 duplicates the 1602 printing, so we have no idea how closely it matches the King's Men version, if at all. Certain characters are fundamental to the story—Hieronymo, his son Horatio, his murderer Balthazar, the King, and Bel-Imperia, whose love leads to the murders—but the rest of the cast might have been much modified in a revival such as this. Burbage as Hieronymo is certain, and Heminges seems as obvious for the elderly King of Spain. Edmans is the most probable Horatio, whose early death makes this only a Half-Share sized role, and then Gilburne is all but certain as his murderer of the same age, Balthazar. Given the ages of the remaining Sharers, the Viceroy, Balthazar's father, must have been Condell, leaving Cooke as the King's son Lorenzo and Lowin as the Ghost of Andrea and/or the murderer Pedringano.

The lack of an authoritative script for these revivals makes it very difficult to understand how the boys were used. Hieronymo's wife Isabella was, we must assume, Burbage's boy, sufficiently experienced to carry off some very long monologues and an on-stage mad scene and suicide. Lorenzo's page must have been Cooke's boy, the brevity well suited to his lack of experience. But Bel-Imperia is another of those roles which share stage time with a number of different adults and thus would need an experienced and trusted boy. Balthazar does have one significant scene with her, the play within a play in which he is murdered, and with Burbage's more experienced boy already assigned, Gilburne's is the most probable casting.

Plague returned in the summer of 1610, once again closing the theaters, but at about the same time, the company faced an even greater crisis. They lost their two youngest Sharers, Gilburne and Edmans. Because Gilburne is listed in the Folio, he must have played significant roles for some time. As we have seen, his youth meant he could not have taken a share before 1607, and from 1607 to 1610, the theaters were rarely open; in particular, the Shakespearean plays in which he most likely took a principal role could not have seen the public stages until the spring of 1610. Thus, it seems probable that he was the company's young leading man at least through the first half of 1610. In that case, he probably was a casualty of the plague, succumbing without warning in the early summer. Edmans, for whatever personal reason, retired at about the same time. He may have simply decided the life of an actor was not for him and retired to live on the Globe proceeds that he controlled as a result of his marriage to Pope's heir. He was not later listed in the Folio; thus he may not have been highly regarded by his compatriots and, realizing he would never be allowed to increase his half share, he may have merely quit in disgust.

The two new replacements were young men who had never been connected with the King's Men, William Ostler and John Underwood. Both had been in the original Blackfriars troupe, listed in the cast for Jonson's *Poetaster*, so they were apparently among the older original boys in that company, making both in their early twenties when they joined the King's Men, roughly the same age as Gilburne and Edmans had been.

Precisely when this happened is not certain. Cuthbert Burbage indicated no specific date, only that they joined "in processe of time," including their names along with Nat Field, who did not join the company until several years later.[51] However, both names appear in a number of cast lists for plays usually dated during 1610–1614 (although the lists themselves were printed much later), and in 1611 Ostler married Heminges' sixteen-year-old daughter Thomasine. Thus, they both must have been connected with the company by the time the theaters reopened in the winter of 1610–11. The precise date for their admission depends on the date of Jonson's *Alchemist* because they appear in Jonson's folio cast list for that play. However, the date of *The Alchemist* is not so clear as it seems on first glance.

Underwood and Ostler were outsiders with no previous ties to any King's Men plays or performers. We would expect their arrival to cause considerable resentment among the younger members of the King's Men. In fact, during 1611, both Rice and Ecclestone, and perhaps Sands as well, the most obviously talented of the recent apprentices, chose to forgo a life as Hired Men in the King's Men and deserted to another company. Older former apprentices like Gough and Tooley apparently remained, but one wonders why. Gough in particular must have been thirty, and he had been passed over for a Share at least twice previously. The role for which he is listed in *The Second Maiden's Tragedy* in the autumn of 1611 has less than twenty-five lines, clearly a Hired Man role arranged in such a way that he could not double any other roles more befitting a Sharer. Thus, he was not yet even a Half-Sharer when Ostler and Underwood were added.

It is not clear how the shares were apportioned to Ostler and Underwood. We have conjectured a full share for Gilburne and a half share for Edmans. None of the available cast lists tells us enough to know for certain which of the new men took the full share, but Ostler would very shortly own shares in both the Globe and Blackfriars, indicating a much quicker accumulation of capital and thus a full share. Of course, it did not hurt that Heminges was his father-in-law. Still, with no additional evidence to hand, we must assume Ostler had the full share and Underwood the half (see Chart E).

One other new play possible before the theaters closed that summer is Jonson's *The Alchemist*. Jonson's folio said *The Alchemist* premiered in 1610. On the basis of Ananias's calculation of the date when the falsifiers' stone will be ready (III,2,128–32) and the age of Dame Pliant, the play would seem to have been intended for performance in October. Such calculations must be taken with a grain of salt, for obviously Jonson and the company intended for the play to have more than one performance. More importantly in this case, the theaters were closed in October and November due to plague. The play may very well have been intended for October or November but delayed by circumstances until December or January, which under some of the calendars in use at the time was still 1610. Andrew Gurr has argued that the Blackfriars setting indicates it was "explicitly composed for performance" at the Blackfriars theater.[52] Although this is hardly conclusive because most of the audience would not be residents of the Blackfriars neighborhood, it would also place the original performances during the winter of 1610–11. Likewise, Ostler and Underwood are in Jonson's cast list, and since they probably joined the company only in the late summer of 1610, they could not have actually performed the play until the winter. Unfortunately, the play was registered October 3, 1610; no other instance has ever been found for registering a play intended for the professional theater companies before it had been performed (unless of course *Troilus and Cressida* was not performed before early 1609). *The Alchemist* was performed in Oxford in that same October,[53] also indicating the play had been performed in London well before its registration date, for it is unlikely a company would premiere a new play on the road. Despite the 1610 registration, the play did not reach print until 1612. Such a long delay suggests the following scenario: Jonson wrote the play during the spring of 1610, beginning work just after *Epicene* appeared at Whitefriars in January. As usual, it took him some time, so the play was not ready for the stage until just before the plague returned. The King's Men played it before the theaters were closed in the summer, where many now date it.[54] Plague meant that the play had only one or two performances at that time, but the play was so successful the company added it to their tour repertory. In the meantime, in October, believing the plague would keep the theaters closed for a long time, Jonson sold the play to a printer who registered it, just as Jonson had done in similar circumstances with *Sejanus*. But the plague abated, the theaters reopened, the play was revived to great success and played throughout 1611, in Blackfriars and the Globe, with Underwood and Ostler now playing the roles that initially, but only briefly, were played by Gilburne and Edmans. That was the cast Jonson remembered in 1616, when he printed his folio. When those performances at last faded out, Jonson was able to print the play, which appeared in quarto in early 1612.

Jonson's cast list included Burbage, Lowin, Condell, Cooke, Armin, Heminges, Ostler, and Underwood, plus "Nic. Tooly" and "Will. Eglestone." A copy of Jonson's folio survives with handwritten annotations of casting from a performance sometime after Nat Field had joined the company in 1615–16 and before Burbage left.[55] Because this revival was very close to the original and only Kastril and Drugger are age-specific, we can assume the actors of 1616 were playing the same roles they had played in 1610. Burbage is listed as Subtle the Alchemist, Lowin as Epicure Mammon, and Condell as Surly, not Burbage's partner but still a man with a temper and a sword. None of these assignments is surprising in light of the careers we have previously developed. Underwood is assigned Dapper, which would have been an equally plausible assignment for a Half-Sharer in 1610 or 1616. In 1610, Heminges was the oldest man in the company, and as such would have been the only plausible Love-wit, who makes a point of his advanced age. Heminges was still acting, at least in Jonsonian revivals, during 1616, when he also was recorded in *Volpone*. Someone named Bentley is actually assigned by the annotator to Love-wit. It is generally assumed that this was Robert Benfield, who joined the company in 1614, but if so, he would have been a remarkably young Love-wit, for he replaced Ostler as Antonio in the 1623 revival of *The Duchess of Malfi*, according to its quarto. Much more likely is that Bentley/Benfield's name was intended for Drugger, the character without an actor in the space directly above Love-wit's, and the pencil slipped. Drugger is a self-styled "young beginner" (I,iii,7) who also looks as if he has not finished his apprenticeship (I,iii,4). Thus, he must have been one of the youngest men in the company. With Underwood assigned elsewhere, he can only have been Ostler, who was still very young in 1610–11 and who because of his death in 1614 could not appear in the later revival. Benfield joined the company after Ostler's death and replaced him in other roles, further underlining Ostler's original casting. The actor assigned to Face in 1616 was Nat Field, a colorful and handsome actor who joined the company about the same time as Benfield. Field was born in 1587 and thus was about thirty in 1616; the man nearest him in age and experience during 1610–11 in Jonson's list was Cooke, who also had died before Field joined the company. In 1616, Ecclestone played Kastril while Tooley played Ananias, but they may not have played those roles in 1610, when they were not yet Sharers; Jonson's cast list was first printed in 1616, so he may have combined names familiar to his reader from both productions, as he had done with Lowin in his list for *Sejanus*, or may have remembered two minor players who later became more famous. However, there are no other known Sharers from 1610 who are plausible for these roles, so it is at least possible that they were originally played by Ecclestone and Tooley. In that case, Armin played the hypocritical Puritan Wholesome, a most surprising role to modern eyes for the company clown but nonetheless the only role left of any size at all. Baldwin assumed that Armin had played Drugger,[56] but Armin in 1610 was forty or older and had never looked young even when he was young. The tradition that made Drugger the major comic role began with Garrick, who transferred most of the good jokes to the role so that he could play it himself. Interestingly enough, Cowley is not mentioned by either Jonson or the later annotator. He seems not to have retired until 1613–14, but he also seems to have never acquired a full share. Second banana to the very end, he went about his business, made no waves, and made very little impression on anyone.

Despite the multiple shakeups of company personnel and the long plague interruptions of previous years, the King's Men had re-established themselves during the first six months of 1610 as the dominant acting company of London. Even so, the year was not to be without its problems for the King's Men. A new adult company, the Duke of York's, was licensed on March 30, 1610. They seem to have been organized just before the London theaters were closed for plague in 1608, probably incorporating members of the Lenox company that had been touring for some time previously. They performed briefly in London at the Boar's Head after the Queen's Men moved out. There was an expansion of membership shortly after their licensing, and Heminges actually sold them some of the old King's Men costumes, which led to various lawsuits concerning missed payments and disputed ownership of those costumes. This company played at court two or three times a year over the next several years, but almost always only for the Duke of York (Prince Charles) and his sister Elizabeth, not for the King or Queen.[57] They maintained sufficient popularity to still be a regular London company long after Shakespeare died, and eventually the former Chamberlain's Men Robert Pallant and Christopher Beeston were to be found in the company. But for the most part, they seem to have provided no serious threat to the King's Men.

Henry IV, the quasi-Protestant King of France, was assassinated in May, and there were once again rumors of Catholic terrorism, plots, and possible uprisings throughout England. It would have been logical to close the theaters, at least for a week or two until it was clear that there was no English Catholic conspiracy to be coordinated with the one in France. We have no report of such a politically motivated closure, but a temporary one seems very likely.

In July, the plague returned. All of the city's acting companies went out on the road again in the summer and fall. But this would be the last of the significant plague breaks. In the winter of 1610–11, the King's Men would at last enter a period of sustained performance and uninterrupted success. A major factor in that success would be Shakespeare's return to London and to playwriting.

❧ Chapter 8 ❧

Shakespeare Bows Out, 1610–13

Between December 26, 1610, and February 5, 1611, the King's Men presented fifteen plays for James or his family, marking their continued dominance in the London theatrical world. Even more significant, however, would be Shakespeare's return to London that same winter. Within six to nine months, he provided the company with three, possibly four new plays. We do not know why he came back to the city, nor do we know precisely when. Two of his new plays were seen at the Globe in May, so he must have arrived several months earlier. He was physically in London at some time after July 15, 1610, for in *The Tempest* he made detailed use of a unique and unpublished report of the famous Bermuda shipwreck of 1609 that arrived in London after that date.[1] He could only have seen or heard about this report through personal contact with one of the recipients of a copy, none of whom were anywhere near Stratford. He made a deposition in a Stratford lawsuit for which there is no date but to which an answer was recorded in February 1611.[2] This may indicate he made the deposition from London because he was in the city over the winter, or it may mean he left a deposition behind months earlier, knowing he would be away from Stratford when the case finally came to court.

Why he came back to London cannot be determined, but more than likely one factor was a desire to oversee his Globe and Blackfriars shares when the theaters returned to full-time operation. Once there, he would naturally turn his hand to some new writing, if only to help defray his expenses.

The Tempest was probably the first work he provided for his old companions. *The Tempest* contains the only instance in Shakespeare's works where a character exits at the end of one scene and then reappears at the very beginning of the next, the Act IV/V transition. Some scholars have conjectured that a scene is missing,[3] which is of course possible. One other explanation, however, is that the script as we have it was used for a performance at the Blackfriars. On the indoor stage, it was the custom to mark the end of an act by a pause in the action during which music was played.[4] Thus, it was possible for an actor to exit at the end of an act and then re-enter in a new costume, as Prospero does. There are no quartos with which to compare the Folio, but if we accept that Heminges and Condell were trying to print the version closest to their understanding of what Shakespeare actually wrote, then this would be Shakespeare's only work identifiably written for first performance at Blackfriars. Thus, although it was presented at court in November 1611, it was probably written and performed at Blackfriars before Lent of 1611. How it was modified when and if it moved to the Globe after Easter, we cannot know.

Like *Twelfth Night*, *The Tempest* has almost no characters for Hired Men to play. Twelve non-female principal characters appear in multiple scenes and cannot be doubled. Burbage as Prospero and Heminges as kindly but talkative old Gonzalo are the only obvious castings based on age alone. The King of Naples has a grown son and thus must be played by a man of about forty or more; Condell was the only one available. If Condell was Alonso, then the usurping brother must have been Cooke or Lowin, either of whom was significantly younger than Burbage but far too old for Ferdinand. Ferdinand then was probably Ostler, assuming he had the full share, with Underwood and either Tooley or Gough playing the two remaining lords.

At first glance, there are far too many clowns. The automatic assumption for Armin is Trinculo, an official jester, but Trinculo is the smallest of the clown roles by far and does not sing. Thus, Cowley seems the more likely casting. Stephano by contrast does sing a catch, but he is a drunkard, and drunkenness has not played much of a role in Armin's clowning in other plays. We also must ask who plays Caliban and Ariel, both also clown-like roles; Ariel sings often and obviously sings well, which has been one of Armin's strengths. However, in the course of the play, Ariel disguises himself as a nymph, so the performer was still young enough to pass as a beautiful young woman, something altogether implausible for the forty-ish Armin, no matter how short he may have been. This leaves us with Armin as either Caliban or Stephano. Caliban is mis-shapened (V,268), and continually called a "monster." Costume of course was a factor, but even in costume, he would need to be either unusually large or unusually small. None of the Sharers has previously been noted as unusually large, whereas Armin and Cowley were small. Given what we know about Armin's own peculiar proportions and the virulence of his comic personality, he thus seems the only likely Caliban.

In that case, Stephano must have been played by Lowin. In later years outside our study, Lowin would play a succession of rotund older soldiers who are often described as "merrie," a common indication of a man fond of his liquor. He would also later be associated with Falstaff. Lowin had, of course, played comedy before—he was Jonson's Epicure Mammon and Politic Would-be and played all the braggarts and motor-mouths such as Parolles after Phillips retired—but he had never been a clown *per se*. In fact, barely two years after *The Tempest* he would apparently play Henry

VIII and, even more surprisingly, Bosola (see chap. 9). Still, merrie drunkards would eventually become his trademark, so he seems the most probable Stephano.

That still leaves Ariel uncast, and no adult Sharers left to play him. Therefore, he must have been played by Burbage's apprentice added new around 1606 and thus about fifteen years old now, able to play both nymph and boy.

This was also the season of *Catiline*, Jonson's wordiest tragedy. Another of Ben Jonson's tragic disasters, it was roundly hissed at its first performance and may never have seen a second, if we are to believe Jonson. Nevertheless, such failure did not discourage him or a printer, for a quarto appeared all but concurrently. The play was printed without registration, so we cannot be sure of the exact date. However, the same date for printing and performance suggests that the staging came early in the year, and if there were ever a play intended for the supposedly more educated audience of the Blackfriars, *Catiline* must be it.

With more than half of all the lines spoken by only two persons, it is not hard to see why the play was a failure. Even Burbage must have blanched at Cicero's all but uninterrupted 290 lines in the trial scene. The printed text is about 3,600 lines, which means the performance version must have been severely cut (or much expanded for the printer, which again would point to a premiere early in the year). Jonson's folio listed a cast of Burbage, Heminges, Condell, Lowin, Cooke, Underwood, and Ostler, plus Tooley, Ecclestone, and Richard Robinson. Ecclestone's presence lends credence to Jonson's claim that the play failed, for Ecclestone left the company in the summer and could have acted only a very few performances before he was gone. The only physical clues provided by Jonson are that Petreius has been a soldier for thirty years, so he must be in his late forties or older and therefore would have been Heminges. With Burbage as Cicero, Condell is far the most probable Catiline and Lowin is then the obvious Caesar. Underwood, Ostler, and Ecclestone would have played minor Lords (see Chart D).

For the first time in a Jonson play for the King's Men, there are actually scenes for women. There are very few Jonsonian women and even fewer who are memorable in any way, even in plays he wrote for the all-boy companies. From a modern perspective, we might begin to wonder about a writer who wrote such small and simplistic women's roles, but his work serves to remind us yet again how peculiar were Shakespeare's plays in his time. Shakespeare was almost the only playwright to ask his boys to play characters rather than stereotypes, and almost the only playwright to see the potential for complex characterizations in his boys. But the presence of these women in *Catiline* as a greater part of the plot than historically necessary certainly indicates that the company Sharers expected even Jonson to use the senior boys. Aurelia is Catiline's wife and thus surely Condell's apprentice, still so young as to be trusted only with a role of about ten lines. All the other women work as a group, with the most prominent, Fulvia, spending most of her adult scenes with Cicero. This suggests that somehow Burbage had obtained three apprentices, the precise nature of whom is seen more clearly in the discussion of *The Winter's Tale* later.

When the company moved into the Globe, they revived *Cymbeline*, which was seen by Simon Forman during this spring. It had been five years since Shakespeare had written the original version, and the company had been much changed, which would have required some major revisions. As previously discussed, the most likely revision was the invention of the wager plot, which allowed Burbage to move to Iachimo. Forman described all the plot lines, so we cannot be certain which scenes were removed to make room for Iachimo in performance. However, he does not mention the vision nor Jupiter, which we would assume an astrologer would notice, so it is very likely they were cut.[5] If so, then Iachimo would have become the largest male role.

With Burbage as Iachimo, Posthumus would have gone to a young Sharer, either Cooke or Ostler. The other would have played Cloten. Because they are able to share the same costume, the two must have been quite similar in shape and size. Heminges, the company elder, would seem logical for Cymbeline; Lowin would have continued as Bellarius, for whom he was now even more well suited in age. In that case, Condell moved to Lucius. Guiderius and Arviragus may have been played by real boys, as they were in 1606; however, the relative weakness of the current boys at this date suggests that they were in fact played by the same boys as in 1606, even though both were now probably Hired Men. Since the songs are among the most likely material to have been cut to make room for Burbage's new role, the boys may not have sung. Underwood would have taken the Half-Share role of Philario, Armin would have replaced Lawrence Fletcher as the sarcastic Lord who shadows Cloten, where he would have been in position to join the serenaders and sing "Hark Hark, the Lark," assuming it was in fact performed. Imogen, now spending more time with Iachimo or with the other women than with Posthumus, would have been Burbage's boy, while the Queen would have been played by Cooke's boy, who was now about fourteen and ready for some more substantial roles.

Forman also saw *Richard II* on April 30, but his detailed plot summary does not match Shakespeare's play at almost any point.[6] Nor does it match any other known play about Richard, such as *Thomas of Woodstock*. It seems most odd that the company would commission a new play on the subject when they already owned a perfectly good and popular one. Nevertheless, Forman's plot summary is very detailed, which if nothing else serves to remind us that multiple plays on a subject, written by various authors, sometimes appeared even within individual companies.

With *The Tempest, Cymbeline* and *Pericles* among the most recent company successes, it should come as no surprise to find Shakespeare's next play was also set in faraway lands with principal characters separated and years later tearfully reunited after the wife is brought back from the dead. *The Winter's Tale* was immensely popular in its day, with at least seven known court performances before the Civil War, the first on November 5, 1611. Simon Forman saw it at the Globe on May 15, 1611.[7] There is also an allusion in the scene with the dancers (IV,iv,337–38) that is often assumed to mean the scene was written after a masque featuring satyrs was seen at court on January 1, 1611.[8] If that allusion is accurate, then Shakespeare was writing it before Lent in 1611, and it was a very new play when Forman saw it in May.

Leontes has more than one-fifth of all the lines, and the role is full of the Burbage signatures: nobility, jealousy, wild mood swings, fits of rage that border on insanity, and long monologues with both verbal agility and subtlety. There is even a new scene not in the source material to bring him back for the very last scene.[9] Autolycus is clearly tailored to take advantage of Armin's singing skill as well as his clowning. With Armin as Autolycus, Cowley then had another chance at his white-haired routine as the kindly but buffoonish Shepherd, and the Clown Boy played the larger comic role identified simply as Clown. Curiously, Shakespeare eliminated completely the comic shrew wife for the shepherd found in Greene's novella on which the play was based, suggesting that he wanted material more specifically suited to this very old Clown Boy.

With a role such as the large *Winter's Tale* Clown designed expressly for him, this Clown Boy should at least merit a name. We would assume that the company would want to keep him around and perhaps promote him to adult clown after Armin or Cowley retired. Unfortunately, of the Folio's Principall Actors with whom we have not yet dealt, none could have been our Clown Boy. Benfield, Field, Taylor, and Shank are all known to have been in other companies at this time. About three months before Cowley's death in 1619, his daughter married an actor named George Birch. Later in 1619, Birch's name appeared in the manuscript of *Sir John van Olden Barnavelt* assigned to a Hired Man role. Shortly afterward, Birch gained at least a half-share in the King's Men; he is listed in the cast list for several plays in the Beaumont and Fletcher folio which are usually dated to 1619–25, although his first listing as a Sharer is in the list for King James's funeral procession.[10] For Birch to wed Cowley's daughter between the date of his will and his actual funeral suggests a deathbed wish. The most likely personal tie that would have encouraged Cowley to wish his daughter to marry Birch would have been an apprenticeship (e.g., Edmans, Pope's apprentice, married Mary Clark, Pope's heir, Gough married Phillips's sister, and Burbage's apprentice Robinson married Burbage's widow). As this character is old enough to court Perdita in *The Winter's Tale*, then he must have been in his late teens during 1611. In that case, he would have joined the company in 1603–04, just the time to become old enough for prominent roles in 1607, when *Pericles* was being written, where we saw him as the Bawd. This was also the date when Lawrence Fletcher joined the company and would have needed a new London apprentice. Thus, it is altogether likely that Birch actually began as Fletcher's apprentice. When Fletcher died and Armin rejoined the company in 1608, Birch's bond somehow passed to Cowley, even though Cowley held only a half-share.

The old, noble, and considerate Camillo, second largest of the male roles, would have been intended for Heminges, the only Sharer left who was older than Burbage. Polixenes, the noble mirror of Leontes, would have gone to that longtime stage mirror image of Burbage, Condell. Antigonus, the husband of Paulina, then would have been Lowin, now about 35. Ostler must have been the youthful Florizel; Cooke and Underwood would have covered the major Gentlemen and Lords.

Ostler seems to have come to the company fully equipped with an apprentice of some experience, for there can be little doubt that Perdita is the boy of the actor playing Florizel. If so, then that same boy also played Miranda in *The Tempest*, who is very much the same straightforward ingenue type and who splits her time between Ferdinand and Prospero. This boy would eventually have a significant career, probably originating the Duchess of Malfi in 1613–14, when Ostler played her lover/husband Antonio. All the other boys seem to belong to Burbage, who has not two, but three, apprentices visible. One of these is Mamillius, a very young boy indeed, but a boy who speaks only to Leontes and thus must be Burbage's boy. This probably marks the first solo appearance of Richard Robinson. By 1619, he was an adult, for he was listed as a Sharer in the patent of that year and only a few months before he had married Burbage's widow. In *The Devil is an Ass* in 1616, Ben Jonson wrote an extensive and admiring description of Robinson's ability to fool even women off the stage with his female impersonations (although it is his ability to "talk bawdy" (II,viii,64–74), not his delicacy, that is applauded). This was something of an in-joke, since the play was performed by the King's Men and Robinson would most likely have been playing the less than delicate woman the speaker would shortly meet, Lady Tailbush. Nevertheless, it indicates Robinson had not yet stopped playing women and thus must have been about sixteen in 1616. This in turn means he could have been only about eleven in 1611, if not younger, in looks and experience suitable only for little boys with very few lines.

The longest female role (and second largest role in the play) is Paulina, a character not in Greene's original novella. Thus, she was invented by Shakespeare solely because he wanted to give a boy a chance to shine in the great challenges and lectures she delivers to Leontes. The other major role for a Burbage apprentice is Hermione. Both characters appear almost exclusively with Burbage or with other boys. One of these would have been the same boy who played Ariel and, in the revivals, Lady Macbeth and Gertrude, and thus must have been the same boy who had joined Burbage in 1606, now at the height of his powers. The other was also obviously experienced and capable, and since Mamillius is also present, could not have been a precocious Robinson. Where this third boy came from is a mystery like his name. The most logical explanation is that, when Ostler arrived with his own boy, Burbage took Gilburne's boy under his wing for the remaining year or two of his bond, rather than waste an experienced and capable boy. We have no name for either boy, so we will refer to them as the Mature Boy, who played Paulina, and the Noble Boy, who played Hermione. The other young boys in the company, who had appeared only in the masques in *Timon of Athens* and *The Tempest*, now play country girls who sing and dance and may play broadly comic tiny roles like Mopsa and Dorcas.

Macbeth was seen by Simon Forman at the Globe in May 1611. As previously discussed, Middleton's revisions had not yet been made. Forman's description of the Witches as nymphs or fairies indicates they were probably played by the very young boys who were singing and dancing in *The Tempest* and *The Winter's Tale*. Most of the principal adult roles could have been played by the men who had originated them, with Ostler replacing Sly as Malcolm and Heminges, as the oldest member of the company, replacing Shakespeare as Duncan (see Chart D).

It is possible, but not certain, that *Hamlet* may have re-joined the rep about the same time, for a new quarto was printed in 1611. Hamlet was a signature role for

Burbage, so it is hard to believe that anyone else would have dared play the role while he was still performing regularly. Yet the same age problems that had moved Burbage to roles such as Prospero or Pericles make his continued performance of Hamlet problematic. In the present, we are accustomed to forty-year-old Hamlets, but only because they do not perform with younger men playing Claudius, the Ghost, or Polonius. With only Heminges available as an older man, the company would have been forced to recast Condell as Claudius, making Hamlet's uncle the same age or slightly younger than Hamlet, while casting Cooke, Ostler, and Underwood, all ten to fifteen years younger than Burbage, as his old friends Horatio, Rosencrantz, and Guildenstern. Nevertheless, stranger things have happened, and the common practices for casting a revival were necessarily different than for casting newly commissioned work, so a 1611 revival of *Hamlet* is at least imaginable.

During the early part of 1611, John Fletcher seems to have been writing a sequel to *The Taming of the Shrew* called *The Woman's Prize*. The King's Men had the play in their repertoire in 1633, but their decision to send it to the censor at that time suggests that it was the company's first production of the work. The play exists in two versions, one printed in the Beaumont and Fletcher folio and presumed to be the 1633 version, the other a manuscript that seems to predate the folio version and is usually thought to date to 1611.[11] That manuscript is somewhat shorter, with the roles of the two oldest men, Moroso and Petronius, reduced by about a third of their lines. In that form, the play looks much more like one of the boy company plays, with their heavy dependence on a handful of performers, mostly "women" and caricatured old men far more easily portrayed by boy actors than men of other ages. Aside from Petruchio's name, there is little to tie the play to Shakespeare's *Shrew,* and in fact all the other characters are different. Thus, although it seems clear Fletcher had Shakespeare's play in mind, it is most likely that *The Woman's Prize* was not consciously intended as a sequel to be performed in tandem by the same company.

Whether the King's Men or some other company performed *The Woman's Prize*, its very existence at this date indicates a revival only a few months earlier of *The Taming of the Shrew*. There had been many company changes since 1607, when it was last seen in London, but those changes would not have affected the principal casting. Most of the Sharers would have continued in their 1607–08 roles. Ostler would have replaced Sly as Tranio, with Underwood taking the smaller role of Lucentio, and Armin as Chief Clown would have replaced Fletcher as Grumio.

With *The Winter's Tale* on stage by May, Shakespeare had time to contribute to one more play before he returned to Stratford in the summer. That play was probably *The Two Noble Kinsmen*, which is not in the Folio and was not published until 1635, when it was identified as a work written by Fletcher and Shakespeare. Despite the late printing, Shakespeare's participation is all but universally accepted in modern criticism. The dating of this play is usually given as 1613, due to the inclusion of a dance known to have been performed for a masque at court on February 20, 1613.[12] Shakespeare was apparently in London in the spring of 1613 and could have written his portions at that time. Nevertheless, it is curious that scholars rarely, if ever, argue that comic routines such as this might move in either direction. It is always assumed that Fletcher borrowed the routine from the masque, never that he borrowed this surefire, tested comic routine from the play and inserted it into the masque.[13] And of course, there is always the possibility that the comic dance found its way into the text in revivals between 1613 and 1635.

Two factors point to an earlier date of 1611 for the play, with or without the comic dance. First, there is the unusually large role for the Jailer's Daughter, who must have been played by a very experienced apprentice clown. The company had in Birch a most talented and experienced Clown Boy, but Birch was also almost grown up in 1611; by 1613, he would have been visibly an adult and no longer an apprentice. There are no other young "female" clowns visible until John Shank joined the company in 1614 and brought in a new clown apprentice. At the same time, the play requires an unusually large number of unusually brief boys' roles, including the comic dance, which point to the same period as *The Tempest* and *The Winter's Tale*. Those types of scenes decline sharply in company plays during succeeding years, although there is a relative shortage of surviving material on which to judge.

The second factor to consider is the nature of the collaboration itself. Although many Elizabethan and Jacobean plays were produced as collaborations, Shakespeare collaborated rarely, so far as we can tell. Before 1611, we can identify only one surviving collaboration, *Pericles*; the two plays in which Middleton had a hand both appear to be not collaborations but revisions made by him only because Shakespeare was not present to make the alterations himself. In *Pericles*, Shakespeare apparently split the plot with his collaborator, who wrote the first half of the play, while Shakespeare wrote the second. The division of scenes in *Two Noble Kinsmen* is quite different, much more like the pattern we saw in *Timon of Athens*. Without wishing to discuss in detail the nature of period play collaborations, which would require several other books, we can generalize some obvious points. There are three reasons why a company might hire two or more writers to craft a play: speed, inexperience of one of the writers, or unfamiliarity of one of the writers with the current company. In 1611 (or 1613), speed was not an issue; the plague was over, and *Two Noble Kinsmen* is not in any way topical. Neither Fletcher nor Shakespeare would have been thought to be too inexperienced to be trusted with a complete commission. Shakespeare was obviously familiar with the personnel, had in fact just written two major hits for this very company, and even with his long period away in Stratford was still more sensitively attuned to Burbage in particular than any other writer of the day would ever be. That leaves only a fourth possibility, that the collaboration was in fact a revision. The primary reason for a company to spend the money for a revision of an already existing play would be the need to fit an existing script to a company of performers significantly different from the company for which it was originally written.

Two Noble Kinsmen shows some evidence of being such a revision. Its 1635 publication automatically points to a popular production in 1634–35, and some of the marginalia suggest a production in 1625–26. However, since Fletcher died in 1625, all his portions of the play must date from an earlier time. Chambers suggested

1619–20, based on information found on a surviving scrap from the Revels Office, but although possible, this date does not seem very probable. First, by 1619–20, Richard Burbage was dead, replaced as company leading man by the much younger Joseph Taylor (see chapter 9). Taylor would have been cast as Palamon, and any major revision for that production should have reduced rather than expanded Theseus, the only role Burbage could have played in either 1611 or 1613. Secondly, in the one surviving company play of 1619–20, *Sir John van Olden Barnavelt*, the role assigned in the cast list to the clown's boy is only four lines long. This is hardly what we would expect of a boy for whom the Jailer's Daughter was being revised and expanded at the same time. Thus, any revision made in the extant text must have been done much earlier than 1619.

Modern attempts to assign specific portions of the text to Shakespeare and to Fletcher have produced "general agreement regarding the two authors' shares,"[14] something rarely found in any other aspect of Shakespearean studies. This general agreement tends toward the Victorian school of "Everything noble and poetic is Shakespeare's, while everything common or vulgar is someone else's work," but more recent linguistic analyses support this view. Shakespeare's material is almost exclusively confined to scenes for Theseus: the long Act I explaining how the cousins came to be in gaol, and most of Act V that extends Theseus' importance. The only Shakespearean scenes between these bookends are III,i–ii, the argument scene for Palamon and Arcite which repeats information in III,iii but also sets up the mad scene for the Jailer's Daughter, itself a parody of Burbage's typical mad scenes. If those scenes were removed completely, one could easily see a complete play beginning with II,i, and ending with the duel placed at approximately the beginning of Act V, totaling about 2,400 lines. Such a play, however, would have only a minimal role for someone of Burbage's age and status. With Shakespeare's material added, Theseus now becomes the largest nonyouthful role. Thus, assuming these divisions are accurate, it looks suspiciously as if Shakespeare was actually revising an earlier work by Fletcher, rather than Fletcher collaborating on or revising a work by Shakespeare. As it is difficult to believe that Fletcher would write an original work for the King's Men without a role for Burbage, we must assume that the original, so similar to *Philaster* in tone and casting requirements, probably began life in one of the boy companies. When the King's Men somehow came by it, Shakespeare, who had long been something of a specialist in material for Burbage, was paid to revise and expand it.

This scenario offers at least a plausible explanation for the exclusion of *Two Noble Kinsmen* from the Folio. To Heminges and Condell, this was still Fletcher's play. Other collaborations printed in the Folio, such as *Macbeth* and *Timon of Athens*, apparently began as Shakespeare's work and could be honorably included, even though material from later revisions by Middleton could no longer be separated from Shakespeare's original. Because *Two Noble Kinsmen* began as Fletcher's work, it did not qualify in the editors' eyes as one of Shakespeare's plays.

Shakespeare of course could have made these revisions in 1613, where the play is usually dated, as easily as in 1611, except that in 1613, when there was no Clown

Boy available, the Jailer's Daughter should have been cut rather than expanded. Likewise, by 1613, Burbage had released at least one of his boys. Shakespeare's scenes for Theseus/Burbage are almost completely scenes with women, providing about 60% of Emilia's scenes, 75% of Hipolita's, and all of the Queens', and thus indicating that Emilia, Hipolita, and the First Queen were all Burbage apprentices. The only other surviving plays in which three boys seem to be tied to Burbage are *The Winter's Tale* and Jonson's *Catiline*, both of which inarguably belong to 1611.

Palamon and Arcite would have been split between the two youngest full Sharers, Ostler and Cooke. The Wooer is on the cusp between a full Share and a Half-Share role and was probably Underwood, still a Half-Sharer. With Burbage as Theseus, Condell would have been his companion, Pirithous. Lowin would have played the Jailer, Heminges the elderly Schoolmaster, and Cowley the Jailer's Brother, who has a cross-talk scene with the mad Daughter, plus one of the larger countrymen roles. Armin would have been the cynical Doctor, perhaps augmenting his role with the oddly aggressive Prologue/Epilogue, certainly also playing the dancing baboon "with long tail and eke long tool" (III,v,131).

Shakespeare must have been in London until at least August 25, when William Ostler bought a Blackfriars share, for Shakespeare as an active partner would need to have been present in London to approve the deal. The general assumption that the partners simply gave a share to Ostler[15] defies common sense; if they were in the habit of giving shares to acting company Sharers, they would certainly have given one to Lowin or to Cooke, both considerably senior to Ostler. When Ostler died in 1614, Heminges, not the group as a whole, took over his share, suggesting that Ostler had borrowed money for its purchase from his new father-in-law. Only Shakespeare or Henry Evans could have surrendered a share at this time; Evans, however, was named in a lawsuit of 1612 as still a partner in Blackfriars.[16] Thus, the share Ostler bought in 1611 can only have come from Shakespeare. To own and manage property at a distance is not easy, but it is possible. However, to own shares in a business conducted in cash and percentages at a distance is very risky, even when one trusts the other partners. There is no reason to believe that a retired Shakespeare would have been unwilling to sell out of Blackfriars should an opportunity have arisen. Shakespeare's shares in either of the two London theaters are not mentioned in his will, which is not conclusive, of course, because he left his daughter Susanna and her husband, John Hall, everything not specifically enumerated in other bequests. But no mention is made of Hall in later lawsuits involving these shares after Shakespeare's death, implying that the shares were no longer held by the family.

As soon as possible after the Blackfriars deal, Shakespeare returned to Stratford. On September 11, a list of contributors toward a petition to Parliament included his name, added in the margin to the other seventy names.[17] This indicates he was definitely home by then, but only arrived at the last minute, in just about the time it would take to travel from London to Stratford on foot if he left at the end of August. He would make two more visits to London, but for all practical purposes, the King's Men and Shakespeare would now go their separate ways.

The King's Men would also have to do without some of their most talented younger actors. At almost the same moment as Shakespeare left town, Rice and Ecclestone jumped ship. Earlier in the year, on March 27, 1611, a license was given to a new acting company patronized by the Lady Elizabeth, James' eldest daughter, making it the fifth adult company authorized to play in the city. This seems to have begun as a touring company, but by August, they had decided to expand their membership and try to establish themselves in London. On August 29, they signed a bond with Henslowe. The company included John Townsend and Joseph Moore, who had been on the original license, as well as Joseph Taylor, who had been with the Duke of York's as late as Easter 1611, his defection leading to numerous lawsuits concerning the costumes bought from Heminges in 1610 and apparently not yet paid for. Also included in that August list were John Rice and William Ecclestone.[18] Apparently frustrated by the shares taken by Ostler and Underwood, both chose to leave the King's Men at the first opportunity. In one sense, of course, this made no difference to the King's Men. Because their bonds were finished, the two young men would have had no current female roles to play, and any Hired Man could take what they might be assigned in the near future. But it does remind us that the route from apprentice to Sharer was much less simple and regular than is usually depicted.

For the first time in years, during 1611 the King's Men were able to play a full year without interruption. The plague did not return in the summer, and the company had no need to go on tour.

During that summer or autumn, Burbage may have assumed the title role of *Titus Andronicus*. A new quarto appeared in 1611, its title page for the first time crediting the King's Men. Already famous for his Lear and Hieronymo, Burbage would have had no difficulty playing Titus. The renewed company with its large supply of youngish Hired Men and new Sharers would have had no serious problems with the play's large cast of sons. Heminges could easily have played the brother Marcus, who was about Heminges's own age, and Lowin, having played Iago, would have easily portrayed Aaron. Thus, on balance, it is likely that the now middle-aged Burbage encouraged the revival precisely because it was a leading role for a middle-aged star like himself to play. Burbage's Noble Boy certainly would not have found Lavinia beyond his skill level. The Robinson who played Mamillius would have been exactly the right age to play Lucius. Condell's older boy was now old enough for a role the size of Tamora (see Chart D).

A revival of *King John* is also possible but less certain. A new printing of *The Troublesome Raigne* appeared in 1611; coming two decades after its initial printing, it can only have been prompted by a current revival of some play about King John. The new cover identified the play as "Written by W. Sh.," but incomprehensibly claimed it had been "lately acted by the Queenes Maiesties Players," the company listed on the first printing that had been disbanded before 1603. This may mean that the revival was performed by the company patronized by the current Queen, technically Her Highness rather than Her Majesty. They were back in London on a fairly regular basis during these years, playing at the Red Bull. Their production might have been one or both parts of the old *Troublesome Raigne*, which was after all the play actually reprinted, but because that company still included Beeston,

Pallant, and Duke,[19] they may well have performed their own reconstruction of Shakespeare's version. It would also have been possible for the King's Men to have presented Shakespeare's *King John* in 1611, if Ostler took over the Bastard and the forty-ish Burbage shifted to King John. None of the smaller, younger boys of this date had shown the precocity necessary to play a role of Arthur's length or complexity, but there were still some competent, experienced boys who might have been small enough to get by. At this point, a King's Men production must remain somewhat conjectural.

A new quarto of Wilkins's *Miseries of Enforced Marriage* also appeared during 1611, also probably spurred by a successful revival. Since the original production had been as recent as 1607, a revival would have been relatively simple with Ostler taking over Gilburne's role as Scarborrow. The other Sharers would have merely repeated their old roles, with Armin replacing Fletcher in the Clown role and Underwood replacing Sly as one of Ilford's friends (see Chart D).

This was also the season of that strange romance of incest, Beaumont and Fletcher's *A King and No King*. The play is, as Chambers calls it, "a fixed point" in Jacobean stage history, known to have been licensed during 1611 and played at court by the King's Men on December 26, 1611.[20]

Despite his age, there can be little doubt that Burbage played Arbaces, the man who falls in love with the woman he thinks is his sister, a role with three times the lines of any other character and the wild emotional swings that were Burbage's stock in trade. His own obvious age could be explained away by his being at the wars so long that his little "sister" Panthea had grown up. The beautiful Panthea must have been Burbage's Noble Boy, with Robinson in the very brief role of Burbage's mother, Arane, while the lustful Spaconia was played by Cooke's boy. As might be expected from a company that was simultaneously playing *The Winter's Tale* and *The Tempest*, there are quite a large number of very tiny roles for the other boys to play, such as citizen's wives and pageboys, with only one, the Queen-mother Arane, reaching even forty lines.

One other play can be traced to this season. This was the *Second Maiden's Tragedy*, so called by the Master of the Revels "for it hath no name inscribed." It also had no known author, although the weight of most recent scholarship indicates Middleton.[21] The play has been a continual fascination for scholars far beyond its dramatic quality, because it has survived as a full-length manuscript, complete with author's directions, additions, some stage manager prompts, and censor's comments. It was never published, at least in any copy that has survived, and never registered under any recognizable title, so it is known only from this manuscript. Given that the censor cleared it on October 31, it must have received its first performance in the winter of 1611–12.

The play is tied to the King's Men by the fact that the manuscript includes the names of Robinson and Gough. It is shorter than most of Shakespeare's works, at slightly more than 2,200 lines, about the same length as *A Midsummer Night's Dream* or *The Tempest*. Because the manuscript is the fair copy with the censor's comments, the brevity must reflect an acceptable playing length rather than faulty memorial reconstruction. Seven men and three boys speak 95% of the lines, and those men fall easily to the Sharers we have identified at this time. The largest role is the Tyrant, with about 20% of the total. Given his undefined age and the mad scene in the tomb, we would assume this to have been Burbage. However, the Tyrant has only minimal scenes with any women, whereas Govianus needs two apprentices; this seems to indicate clearly that Burbage actually played Govianus, which although slightly smaller than the Tyrant role has his own mad scenes, a more complex personality, and is the hero. In that case, Condell would have played the Tyrant. Only one man, Helvetius, is a father of a grown child, so this would have been assigned automatically to Heminges. The foolish husband Anselmus, only slightly younger than Condell, would thus have been Lowin, the eldest of the remaining Sharers. Ostler would have been the jealous husband Votarius, with Cooke as his mirror Bellarius, who wishes to sleep with Votarius' wife. Underwood would have been left with the first soldier (who is in another scene called the first "fellow"). Cowley, now around forty, would have no need for an old man's wig to play the foolish cuckold and messenger Sophonirus. There are no roles even vaguely comic, and the two songs are both sung by boys, so it is hard to see how Armin fit in. The manuscript identifies one adult actor, "Mr Goughe" (IV,ii,60), and the name is attached to the nobleman Memphonius with about twenty-five lines, about right for a Hired Man, as Gough was at this date.

One of the women is identified as well: "Rich Robinson" plays the Lady's ghost, but this need not prove he played the Lady herself, as is usually assumed.[22] If Robinson had also played the Lady, there would be no reason for an annotator to indicate that he played her Ghost as well; such a notation must indicate the spirit was played by someone unexpected. The spirit and the Lady's body, which the Tyrant has dug up from the grave, both appear in the same scene; it would have been much more practical to have the original Lady play the body than to make a dummy in her likeness. Thus, the Lady herself must have been played by someone who was not Robinson. She proudly resists all blandishments and kills herself rather than surrender her body to the Tyrant, while she plays most of her scenes with Govianus, so Burbage's Noble Boy seems by far the most likely candidate. The faithful Wife of Votarius is almost certainly designed for Ostler's boy, whose roles have been the most stereotypically feminine of all the boys of this period. The maid Leonella, who intrigues with Bellarius, then would have been Cooke's boy.

The King's Men finished their first completely uninterrupted year of playing since 1602 with an astonishing 21 performances at court times during the winter of 1611–12. *The Tempest, The Winter's Tale*, and *A King and No King* were included, as well as plays identified as *The Twins Tragedy* and *The Nobleman*. Written by Cyril Tourneur, *The Nobleman* was registered on February 15, 1612, but all copies have disappeared. The manuscript was owned by John Warburton, but it and fifty-four others were famously destroyed by his cook, who used them to light fires and line pie pans.[23] A *Twynnes Tragedye* by Richard Niccolls was registered in February 1612, but either was not printed or has been lost, and of course may have been the play seen at court, although we have nothing to tie the play to the King's Men. We cannot even guess at the style or contents of such a play, or the company for whom it was intended; no other plays by Niccolls are known, and what little is known about Niccolls' career suggests that it was in fact a literary closet drama not intended for performance. There is at least the possibility that *The Twins Tragedy* performed at court on New Year's Eve 1611, was actually *The Two Noble Kinsmen*. The death of Arcite certainly moves *The Two Noble Kinsmen* outside the common perception of comedy, and even with its dancing bumpkins, Shakespeare and Fletcher's play could easily be thought a tragedy. Palamon and Arcite are actually cousins, but their persistent pairing as mirror images of each other might easily lead most audience members to think of them as twins, and as we saw in *Cymbeline*, Ostler and Cooke were close enough in appearance to trade clothes, which might further encourage such a misunderstanding.

Court records for that winter season also record a curious joint payment to the King's Men and the Queen's Men for *The Silver Aiedg* and *Lucrecia*. These are generally assumed to have been Heywood's *Rape of Lucrecia* and *Silver Age*, but how the King's Men came to be involved is not clear. Heywood was a Sharer as well as a principal playwright for the Queen's Men, and all of his works from this period must have been written for that company without any help from outside companies. *The Rape of Lucrecia* was in fact registered and printed in 1608 as a play performed at the Red Bull. The latest scholarly edition dates the original to 1594, with a major revision for Robert Browne to star in during 1607. *The Silver Age* was part of a trilogy of plays on classical mythology that are "not so much play as dazzling spectacle," and thus might have been treated for courtly purposes as a masque-like entertainment. Yet, according to the epistle of *The Golden Age*, printed in 1611, both *The Silver Age* and *The Brazen Age* had already "adventured the stage." Thus, the Queen's Men must have been able to produce any of them without additional cast from other companies. How or why the King's Men were involved in the court revivals is a complete mystery.[24]

On February 10, 1612, William Ostler bought a share in the Globe partnership. It has never been explained where he got the share. The share dealings inside the Globe partnership are necessarily murky at this distance, and no one explanation has ever been made that was entirely consistent. Heminges and Condell together appear to have bought out Browne at some point well before 1612, most probably around early 1610 when the Globe had yet to return a cent of income to Browne and when Browne would have needed capital to buy into the Whitefriars company partnership. The half not owned by the Burbages consisted of six shares, three held by Shakespeare, Pope's heirs, and Phillips's heirs, with Heminges and Condell each holding a share and a half (see Chart F). Heminges in various later lawsuits indicated merely that Ostler had obtained a share, not how he did so. Scholars thus generally assume Ostler simply was added to the existing partnership, his presence reducing the overall value of shares held by all the partners not named Burbage. Curiously enough, in his later lawsuit defending against Witter, Heminges identified Witter's share in 1613 as one sixth of the half, not the one seventh he should have held had Ostler merely been added in during 1612. Chambers (and almost everyone else) considers this nothing more than "a slip" on Heminges' part.[25] Why all the shareholders would consent to such a deal has never been explained, and it seems more than merely likely that the contentious John Witter in particular, now married to Anne Phillips and using this as his sole source of income, would have refused to blithely give away (or even sell) part of his share. Heminges and Condell could have given up portions of their larger shares—Ostler was, after all, Heminges's son-in-law—but when Ostler died in 1614, Heminges alone took over his share, indicating Condell had not been involved in any such grant in 1612. The simplest and therefore most reasonable hypothesis is that, as with the Blackfriars share in 1611, Ostler actually bought out someone (probably with money borrowed from his father-in-law).

Shakespeare had returned to London in early 1612, for he was present for a trial at Westminster in May. He left the city almost immediately and did not appear when recalled on June 19,[26] indicating he had not made the trip to London merely to testify. Other business had brought him to London before May. That business must have been related to his Globe share. Neither Heminges nor Cuthbert Burbage mentions Shakespeare's having previously sold out, but such information was not necessarily relevant in the question of Witter's share, which traced back to Phillips.

It is not easy to live a hundred miles away from your source of income, even today. In 1612, there was no way to transfer cash on a regular basis from the Globe to Stratford except to have someone carry it. As far as we can tell today, the King's Men kept no books; the Sharers simply gathered together at the end of the day and divided up the admissions money. The portion then paid to the landlords would itself be divided among them as quickly as possible, so that each could be sure he had received his fair share. If Shakespeare could not be present when that division was made, he could never know if he was in fact being paid what he was owed. It seems obvious that Heminges in particular was a friend and that he was thought to be trustworthy, but when money is concerned, even friends are trusted only so far. Assuming that Shakespeare's friends did faithfully put aside his share, the cash piling up in the strongbox or carried in a heavy purse on the road between London and Stratford would always be a temptation to burglars and bandits. Given these difficulties, the surprise is not that Shakespeare sold out his Globe share but that he held his share for so long. Then again, between 1607 and 1611, the Globe share had not been worth all that much, for there had been plays on its stage only rarely. Perhaps it was not until after the building had managed to stay open for an uninterrupted year that Shakespeare was able to find a willing purchaser. Ostler must have acquired his share of the Globe from someone. Heminges, Condell, and the heirs of Pope and Phillips were still in possession of their shares at the time of the 1613 fire, so the only sharer likely to have sold out in 1612 is Shakespeare.

The King's Men seem to have had a peaceful and prosperous year throughout most of 1612. No significant plague is recorded, so the theaters remained open on a regular basis all year long. One of the very few new plays that can be dated to performance that year is John Fletcher's *The Captain*, one of his most lively comedies for the company, which also provided one of Burbage's most successful comic roles. *The Captain* was played at court during 1612–13, so there can be little doubt that it was new during 1612. The folio identifies only Burbage, Condell, Ostler, and Cooke. The largest role is Jacomo, a bluff, verbal, and stiff-necked misogynist, perfectly suitable for Burbage, with Lowin as his friend Fabritio, one of the earliest of the many "merry souldier" roles Lowin would play in the next decade. There is only one father, who must have been played by Heminges. Cooke and Ostler would have been the two young men Angelo and Julio, paired again as competitors for the beautiful Lelia, with the other young man of the company, Underwood, in the smaller but significant role of Frederick.

Burbage still seems to have had two boys, for Frank, the beautiful and sincere young woman whom even Jacomo cannot resist, and her friend Clora play almost all their scenes together. Frank was probably the Noble Boy, but the large size of Clora's role indicates that Robinson must have matured a great deal during the previous year. Lelia, the largest female role, is a sexy, dominating woman who could have been either Cooke's or Ostler's boy, as she plays significant scenes with both. Cooke's boy has played more dominating females in the past and is thus slightly more likely to have played the part. Ostler's boy would have been Lelia's waiting woman. The company still showed a large complement of less-experienced boys, with several different waiting women and maids, as well as two serving boys. Curiously, two songs are associated with Lelia, but not sung by her—for "Away Delights," they "bid the Boy go sing/That song above," and "Come hither you that love" is sung by an unidentified singer(s) while they prepare her banquet and Lelia is off-stage (V, pp. 273, 295–96). With no obvious clown role, and songs sung by boys rather than by Armin, it looks as if Armin had chosen to retire once again.

One of their more significant revivals of 1612 may have been *Edward II*. A new quarto appeared that year, identical but for its date with the 1598 edition, but the fourteen years between editions suggests that something more than reader interest had led to the printing. There is nothing that positively ties the play to the King's Men; the earliest editions were credited to Pembroke's Men, long since gone from the scene, while a later 1622 edition would be credited to the Queen's company at the Red Bull. Nonetheless, as in 1597–98, the actor most likely to be both able and willing to play a gigantic role such as Edward would have been Richard Burbage. Without further information, we can only assume a possible production and, beyond Burbage's casting as Edward, guess at the nature of the other roles, who might have been much modified without such changes appearing in print.

If we are to judge from the plays produced at court during the winter, most of the company's successful productions during 1612 were revivals of old material. Of the eighteen titles presented, only *The Captain* and perhaps three other plays that have since disappeared can be tentatively identified as new plays actually written during 1612. Although Shakespeare was no longer active, the King's Men were still dependent on his work for their continued success.

Curiously, the King's Men seem to have gone on tour in the spring rather than the late summer. They visited Winchester and New Romney on the Channel, some hundred miles apart, which suggests a fairly extensive tour.[27] On the other hand, the New Romney performance was April 21, during Lent, something we have seen no sign of in previous years. The company also played at court on April 16 and April 26, which would have made the trip to New Romney something of a mad dash. Thus, it seems likely that there has been some confusion in the records, which would hardly be unique in this era.

In the autumn, there were crowd control problems at the Fortune, which the authorities blamed on the jigs rather than the plays themselves. Thus, on October 1, "all Jigges Rymes and Daunces after their plays" were banned in London and all its liberties by the Middlesex justices of the peace.[28] How effectively this law was enforced is unclear, for the King's Men would shortly add a new Chief Clown who was famous for his jigs. However, it does indicate that the authorities still were keeping a close eye on the theaters, and on the comedians in particular.

The long period of uninterrupted performances that began in the winter of 1610–11 at last came to an end when Prince Henry died on November 6, 1612. Henry had been a very popular prince and in many ways he had been the hope of the nation, an unequivocally Protestant male heir, so the official period of mourning was accompanied by a significant national outpouring of grief.[29] The theaters were almost immediately closed. But the period of mourning that could have been expected to go on for several months was cut short when, on December 27, 1612, the court announced the betrothal of Princess Elizabeth to the Elector Palatine. Mourning turned into celebration, with numerous new masques, dances, and musical performances augmented by an unusually large number of plays performed at court. In the winter of 1612–13, the King's company alone performed twenty times at court. (It was as part of these celebrations that the masque including the dancing baboon of *Kinsmen* was performed.)

Fortunately for the company, not every play in the marriage festivities needed to be new. The company performed a number of their greatest hits from the past, many if not most of which may have been in the active company repertory during 1612. These included such romantic comedies as *The Tempest, The Winter's Tale*, and *Much Ado About Nothing*, apparently called back for a second performance.[30] Not all the productions were romantic material, for among the plays known to have been presented were *Julius Caesar* and two Falstaff plays, one listed only as *Falstaff*, the other as *Hotspur*, probably meaning *Merry Wives of Windsor* and *1 Henry IV*. They also played *Othello*, a rather odd choice for a young wife about to embark on a life overseas with a new and unfamiliar husband. Also seen were Beaumont and Fletcher's *Philaster* (apparently twice, the second appearance called *Love Lies A-Bleeding*, the subtitle of the play in a later printing), *The Captain*, and *A King and No King*, plus a *Maid's Tragedy* that may have been either Middleton's or Beaumont and Fletcher's. Jonson's *The Alchemist* and the anonymous *Merry Devil of Edmonton* were seen as well. *The Knot of Fools, The Twins Tragedy, The Nobleman, Cardenio*, and *A Bad Beginning Makes a Good End* were also performed but have all disappeared.

There are a number of interesting points about these plays, not least of which is the high proportion of works by Shakespeare. Obviously, the company still considered his work to be the core of their repertory. The primary focus, however, was on current material. Only six of these plays dated in any way to a time before Sly died and Shakespeare retired from acting. That means that the adults who had been in the premieres were still playing the same roles they had always played (see Charts C and D).

Of the revived plays too old to be played by their original casts, all but *Othello* were *very* old. *Othello* would have been performable even on short notice, for Burbage, Lowin, and Condell, as Othello, Iago, and Cassio, were still available; so easily could the work be revived, we must assume it had been played at court during the plague years as well, when we have no records listing play titles. The five other plays known to predate Lowin's entrance all seem in some way to have been chosen to provide significant roles for Lowin. He would later be famous for his Falstaff, so the two Falstaff plays almost certainly mark his assumption of that character, last played by Lawrence Fletcher, long since dead. By this time, Lowin was thirty-six and his barrel chest had almost certainly dropped to his waistline or he could not have played Falstaff. As a large man, he could not have played Cassius without major line revision, but his suitability for Julius Caesar probably encouraged that revival as well.

It seems clear that these court performances were Armin's last round with the company. We have of course assigned Armin prominent roles in *The Winter's Tale* and *The Tempest*, and Dogberry and Mouse would have been assigned to him as well. But we have seen no clearly defined roles for him in the Beaumont and Fletcher material or in *The Second Maiden's Tragedy*. This can only mean that the Sharers had been preparing for his retirement for some time. The shortage of surviving new plays during 1612–13 make it impossible to determine when he officially left the stage, and a ballad upon the burning of the Globe mentions "the Foole and Henry Condye" running out of the flames together, so he may have stayed on for a very long time while the company hunted for a replacement.[31] The shortage of new roles for him in plays as early as *A King and No King* indicates that this took the Sharers a very long time.

Cardenio has occasioned some modern interest, even though no script exists, for it was registered in 1653 as the work of Shakespeare and Fletcher. If it was printed, all copies have disappeared, although Lewis Theobald claimed that his *Double Falsehood* in 1727 was based on a manuscript of Shakespeare's work.[32] *Cardenio* was played for the Ambassador from Savoy on June 8, 1613, so it was still popular months after its winter court performance.

Because no copy of *Cardenio* exists, we can make no reliable assumptions about Shakespeare's contribution to it or about its company casting. Although Cervantes's work did not reach print until sometime in 1612, it was registered in January 1611, and such was the fame of Cervantes' work that Shakespeare may have read proofs or manuscripts before the printing was finished. This means a collaboration is at least possible. The Cardenio story in Cervantes concerns one young man who forsakes his promised love to steal away the beauty loved by his friend, kidnapping her with the aid of a set of outlaws. A final reunion forces the false young man to realize his true nature, forsake the friend's betrothed, and return to his original love, who has meantime followed him in male disguise.[33] This is so much like *Two Gentlemen of Verona* that Shakespeare would hardly have needed to be present to collaborate.

Fletcher's contribution may have been no more than adding new character names and a new scene or two to change *Two Gentlemen of Verona* into "Two Gentlemen of Spain."

Aside from *Cardenio*, little is known about King's Men activity in the Globe during the first half of 1613. *1 Henry IV* must have continued in some public performances, for a new quarto appeared during 1613. One other possibility should be mentioned. During the wedding celebrations, the company presented a play identified in Chamber Accounts as "a badd beginninge makes a good endinge." This is usually thought to have been a play by John Ford which has disappeared, another of the manuscripts burned by Warburton's cook, but the various citations are confusing to say the least.[34] Ford could have written a play at this time—he would have been twenty-six—but his earliest surviving play is *The Witch of Edmonton* in 1621, almost a decade later. One alternative is that this was in fact *All's Well That Ends Well.* The list of titles in the Chamber Accounts can hardly be called precise, and "a bad beginning makes a good ending" certainly means the same thing as "all's well that ends well." The Noble Boy had now become the company's most experienced leading lady, able to play even the largest role in a play, and in other roles he has shown a great deal of the uprightness and nobility of character that lie at the core of Helena's stubbornness. The rest of the cast would fit the company easily; with the simple substitution of Ostler and Underwood for Gilburne and Edmans, every one else could still play the same role he had been intended to play in 1608–09. Only the Countess presents any problems; we have seen little sign of a replacement for Rice, although we must assume Heminges did find another boy. We know that the second Jacke Wilson was about seventeen at this time, but he was a musician, not an actor. Heminges seems to have been the master of record for several musicians, including one or both Wilsons and William Tawyer, but that was in addition to his acting apprentices. However, if we assume Heminges did add a new boy around 1610, when so many new boys were added, then he could have been plausible for the Countess by early 1613; if he was not ready, then Burbage's Mature Boy was still able to act and could be trusted in scenes with other masters.

On June 29, the Globe caught fire and burned to the ground. This was a major news event in the life of London and many contemporary reports survive. The damage was not as bad as it might have been; the fire took an hour to burn the building down, which allowed time to evacuate the audience without injury and to save most company props, playbooks, and all but "a few forsaken cloaks; only one man had his breeches set on fire [but] a provident wit put it out with a bottle of ale."[35] The King's Men were certainly more fortunate than the company in the Fortune when it burned down in 1621, who lost everything,[36] which accounts in part for the vast gap in our knowledge of the plays performed by the Admiral's company and its successors. The Globe conflagration began when the firing of some cannons set the thatch roof ablaze during a performance of a play about Henry VIII called *All is True* and assumed by all to be the play included in the Folio as *Henry VIII.*

Shakespeare, as it happens, made a trip to London in early 1613, during which he bought the gatehouse to the Blackfriars, which he apparently then leased out as housing, on March 10, 1613. He and Burbage together designed an emblem and motto for the Earl of Rutland's shield worn on March 24, Shakespeare devising the motto, Burbage painting the emblem.[37] With plenty of time on his hands between property negotiations, he certainly could have written one more play; English history had always been one of his specialties. Despite the inclusion in the Folio, the play is rarely accepted by modern scholars as being completely Shakespeare's work. Most now see it as a collaboration between Shakespeare and Fletcher, although Beaumont's hand is sometimes mentioned as a third participant.[38] Although the history of the acting company itself does not require we settle the authorship question, the nature of the extant text does require some more detailed attention before we can fit the play into the company history.

The most recent scholarship has divided the play into three portions, roughly two-fifths by Shakespeare, a quarter by Fletcher, and the remaining third, in Wells and Taylor's phrase, "Shakespeare, touched up by Fletcher." Such a phrase conjures up Anthony Dawson's scene with Condell and Heminges, heads in hands while reading over Shakespeare's first draft:

Heminges: Good lord, it's getting worse, isn't it?

Condell: How are we going to handle this? We can't just cashier the dear fellow, can we?

Heminges: I've talked to Fletcher—he's willing to work with him. That might keep him straight. How much of this has he done?[39]

Although we might sympathize when trying to wade through some of Shakespeare's knottiest verse, the idea of Fletcher touching up Shakespeare's work seems as ludicrous on its face as this imaginary conversation. It is unlikely Shakespeare's old friends would have thought it necessary for Fletcher to somehow fix his work; if the work needed fixing, Shakespeare was actually present and the company could easily require him to make the changes himself. In fact, given that it had been years since Shakespeare wrote any new material, it is unlikely they would have even asked him to write at all, if they intended for Fletcher to finish and fix it. Most importantly, if they had thought Shakespeare needed fixing, then surely Fletcher would have touched up *all* of Shakespeare's material, not merely a few scenes here and there.

Even if we assume the disputed scenes are in fact all by Shakespeare, there is still the question of why there are two writers to begin with. As we discussed in relation to *The Two Noble Kinsmen*, there are only three usual reasons to pay two writers rather than one (see p. 198), and none of those three seem to apply in this case. Shakespeare was in London as early as February 1613 and still there in late March, and the play did not premiere until June, so the company was obviously not in a hurry to get the play on stage. Both Shakespeare and Fletcher were very experienced playwrights and the company had little need to worry that either might not provide playable material on deadline. We might argue that Shakespeare was relatively unfamiliar with the company, except that the Sharers were unchanged since he had written several plays for them in 1610–11. If he were unfamiliar with any performers in particular, it would have been the boys, whom he had not seen in almost two years. Yet the scenes attributed to him include almost all the material for the boys. This eliminates all the usual reasons for a collaboration. Thus, the most sensible explanation for Fletcher's hand is a revision made to adapt the material to a new company (much as Middleton apparently did for *Timon* during 1609–10, when Shakespeare was in Stratford or for *Macbeth* after 1616, when Shakespeare was dead).

According to reports of the day, the Globe was packed with spectators on the day it burned down in the middle of *Henry VIII*, which had had few if any previous performances. Thus, we can be all but certain that when the Globe was at last rebuilt in 1614, the King's Men would have revived this popular (and now notorious) work. What better way to show off the remodeled Globe than to restage the same spectacular piece that had led to the destruction of the old Globe? The place would be packed again if for no other reason than to see if the cannons would set fire to the place this time around. However, there had been major changes in company membership during the time when the Globe was closed. Cooke died, Armin was replaced by John Shank, Ecclestone and Rice returned to the company, and Ostler's influence had greatly expanded. In those circumstances, all older material would have required some revision. Shakespeare was most definitely not available. At that point, and only at that point, it would have made sense to turn to John Fletcher.

The extant text is among the longer Shakespearean plays, more than 3,400 lines in the Folio, which with the masque and the processions would have taken almost four hours. This at least suggests that, like *Coriolanus*, for example, it includes material not actually performed and is perhaps even a "complete" version containing both original and revision. The text is generally agreed to be a scribal copy of foul papers, which could have been necessitated by the comparative illegibility of revisions made directly on those foul papers.

Shakespeare's undisputed portion contains almost all of the lines for Buckingham, Norfolk, and Anne Bullen. The sections currently assigned to Fletcher include all of the Porter clown scene and almost all of Cranmer, the Lord Chamberlain, Cromwell, and the various Gentlemen. The "touched up" scenes contain almost all the rest of Cranmer, the Lord Chamberlain, Cromwell, and Gentlemen. Almost none of Wolsey and the Queen are in Fletcher's scenes, with four-fifths of Wolsey's material and two-third's of Katherine's either in undisputed Shakespeare scenes or scenes thought to be predominantly Shakespeare's, and almost none of Cranmer, the Chamberlain, Cromwell, and the Gentlemen are in Shakespeare's solo scenes.[40] Curiously enough, the most probable casting for Buckingham in 1613 is Cooke, who died in January 1614. Similarly, the most likely Porter is John Shank, who did not join the company until some time in 1614. Even more curiously, the play has two beginnings and two endings; it could easily begin with I,iii, leaving out Shakespeare's scenes with Buckingham, just as it could end with the procession moved up immediately after Elizabeth is born in V,i, skipping all the defeat of Cranmer written by Fletcher. In either case, the play would be about 2,700 to 2,800 lines, close to the median length of Shakespeare's Folio plays. Thus, the most likely scenario is that the 1613 production was written completely by Shakespeare, but that it contained little or no material about Cranmer's plot. During 1614, the play was revised by Fletcher, reducing Buckingham to a Hired Man role and expanding Cranmer's plot, with Cromwell inserted for Wolsey to talk to in III,ii, and a new clown scene. When preparing the copy for the Folio, both versions were combined by the scribe. There is no way, of course, to prove this uncontestably, but it does make better sense of the textual analyses than current theories of face-to-face collaboration.[41]

Reports during the Restoration indicated that Lowin had played Henry, and that Shakespeare was on hand to teach him the role.[42] Burbage then would have played Wolsey, a role almost exactly as long as Henry's and one of Burbage's characteristic tragic overreachers. Cooke in his thirties would have been the probable Buckingham, with Heminges a best guess as Norfolk, and Condell thus probably the Lord Chamberlain. Ostler then was Suffolk, the other Lord in multiple scenes, perhaps doubling the Surveyor. Underwood would have been left with another Lord and perhaps Campeius, significant but still small enough for a Half-Sharer. Cranmer's position in this first version was so small that he might have been played by a Hired Man. The Noble Boy repeated his Hermione trial demeanor as Katherine, with beautiful young Robinson as Anne Bullen and the clownish Mopsa boy as the bawdy Old Lady.

However the final division of compositional labor was sorted out, it seems clear that *Henry VIII* was a great hit. It continued to be very popular well into the nineteenth century, when Spedding decided it was mostly by Fletcher; only at that point did it turn literally overnight into a terrible play that no one wanted to perform. This tells us far more about attitudes to Shakespeare than it tells us about the play itself, which on those rare occasions when it is performed always seems to surprise reviewers and audiences with how interesting it is.[43] Whether he wrote it all or only in part, Shakespeare's final play was a hit. He went out as he had come in, a successful commercial playwright writing for a company of specific actors. After that London visit in 1612–13, Shakespeare quit writing, except perhaps for the doggerel on his tombstone. He went back to Stratford and settled down to the lawsuits and speculations that constituted the life of a wealthy provincial retiree until his death in 1616.

Epilogue

The Globe fire marks the end of an era, not merely because most modern interest in the drama of the time ends with Shakespeare's final play. While the Globe was being rebuilt, the King's Men were also being rebuilt into a company with quite a different shape, which we can only briefly sketch here.

Armin certainly retired after the fire, if he had not done so much earlier. If *The Valiant Welshman*, a play printed in 1615 as the work of "R. A. Gent.," was by Armin, then he was certainly gone from the King's Men, for the play was performed by the Prince of Wales' Men sometime in 1614, if not earlier. However, Armin's authorship is generally discounted,[1] and no other mention of him has ever been found. Thus, Armin may even have died at about this time. Cowley, too, seems to have chosen this moment to leave the company. The seasons of 1610–11 had been something of a high point in his career; his roles in *The Tempest* and *The Winter's Tale* were the largest and most memorable we have been able to trace in his twenty years of company service, followed by his assumption of Justice Shallow in 1612–13. However, Cowley was well past forty in 1613, and there was little in the company's history to suggest he would even continue to find interesting roles in the future. Given his age, there was no likelihood at all that he might fill Armin's shoes. The company found a completely new clown, John Shank, before the Globe reopened in 1614. Cowley's will is dated January 1618, although it would be another year before he died, but there is no hint of his name in any of the Beaumont and Fletcher cast lists for plays usually dated 1614–18. Thus, it seems clear he also retired, or was squeezed out, during the period when the Globe was rebuilding.

During that winter, Alexander Cooke took ill, so ill that he made out his will on January 3. Holding no share in either the Globe or the Blackfriars, he in effect threw his wife and children on the mercy of Heminges and Condell. He was buried on February 25, so his illness lingered for many weeks.

After Armin and Cowley's retirement and Cooke's death, the company had two and a half shares available. They used at least two half shares to bring Tooley and Gough into the company at last. Their names appear in both the patent and the livery list of 1619, and Tooley is listed in *Bonduca*, from 1614. The remaining three half shares, however, went to men from other companies.

One of these new men was a former apprentice, William Ecclestone, who in 1611 had defected along with John Rice to the Lady Elizabeth's Men. Ecclestone's name is in a cast list for *The Honest Man's Fortune*, dated in its surviving manscript as performed by the Lady Elizabeth's Men in 1613,[2] but after that point both his name and John Rice's disappear from that company's records and reappear in various King's Men lists. Thus, about the same time as the Globe was being rebuilt, they must have left the Lady Elizabeth's Men and gone back to their old company. Robert Benfield, who is among the Folio Principall Actors, probably came with them. Also listed in *The Honest Man's Fortune*, Benfield cannot have joined the King's Men before the Globe fire at the earliest. Rice is not listed as a Sharer until 1621, while Ecclestone is in the cast list for *Bonducca* and a Sharer list of 1619. Benfield does not appear in the cast list for *Bonducca* but is in all the other lists that also include Ecclestone, plus *The Knight of Malta*, and it is in the 1619 Sharer list. Thus, Benfield and Ecclestone probably joined at the same time and probably split a share.

The final half share went to John Shank. He was later remembered as a "Comedian," and one other reference indicates he sang "his rhymes," so he was apparently a professional clown. Shank's career had been checkered, to say the least, but there was no doubt he was experienced. He was on patent lists for Prince Henry's (and the Elector's) Men, the former Admiral's Men now playing at the Fortune, in 1610 and 1613. Why he chose to change companies when he already had a Share is unclear, but there is no doubt that he did so. He was on the King's Men Sharer list of 1619, but his name in later cast lists hints that he specialized in the "hungry knave," the first of whom in this company's plays is Judas in *Bonduca*. This means he was thin, which may help explain Lowin's casting as Falstaff despite the presence of a company clown.

Before the year was out, the company faced another shock. Ostler died quite suddenly on December 16, 1614. This was potentially cataclysmic, for Ostler was a full Sharer in the acting company and a partner in both the Globe and Blackfriars. Heminges took over the Globe share, for which his daughter, Ostler's widow, sued him. Heminges also took over the Blackfriars share, but Thomasine did not sue about this until 1629.[3] As Ostler's replacement, the King's Men eventually lured away Nathan Field. As a child, he began his career in the Blackfriars Boys, and Jonson in particular praised his talent and listed him in casts for plays as early as *Cynthia's Revels* in 1600; Jonson also claimed that he had helped educate the boy in Latin. As a young adult, Field was the leading man of the company when it moved to Whitefriars and when it combined with the Lady Elizabeth's Men during 1613. He was still there until mid-1615, after which he moved to the King's Men.

The addition of Benfield, Shank, and Field is yet another reminder that the acting shares demanded both skill and capital, and that company loyalty rarely was a factor in their apportionment. The company already had two competent clowns on hand, for example, when they began to look for Shank. That Cowley was once again passed over for promotion may be explained by his age, and may also explain his retirement. But there was also a young and very talented clown in the shape of the Clown Boy who had played Ariel. The Clown Boy was not promoted, nor given a share, even when a slot opened for his specialty. Once again, the Sharers went outside, as they had done in almost every previous instance.

The Globe partners went through a similar shake-up in 1613–14. They immediately began the reconstruction of the space, apparently using the same foundation footprint but erecting a much more grand and impressive building over it at the cost of some 1,400 to 1,680 pounds, with a tile roof replacing the thatch that had burned. It was open again by June 1614. Heminges and Condell appear to have taken advantage of the crisis to consolidate their financial position. John Witter was unable or unwilling to pay for his share of the theater's reconstruction, and the pair squeezed him out by paying his share of the costs. They do not seem to have paid Witter anything, which led to later lawsuits, but Heminges and Condell won the case.[4] Nat Field had a share shortly after he joined the company. Most probably, he bought out either Pope's heirs or Sly's; when Field died in 1619–20, Underwood bought out his share. Heminges and Condell gradually absorbed almost all the rest of the shares not held by the Burbages, at some point buying out the heirs of Pope and/or of Sly not purchased by Field. After Underwood's death in 1624, Heminges and Condell held his shares as well, in trust for his children. By 1635, the theater was owned by only four people, Cuthbert Burbage, Heminges, Condell's widow, and Richard Burbage's widow, now married to Richard Robinson.[5]

The Blackfriars partnership was similarly condensed. Ostler's share was taken back by Heminges in 1614. Underwood apparently bought out Evans, for Underwood held a share at his death in 1624. After he died, Heminges and Condell administered it as a trust, as they did Underwood's Globe share. Thus, by 1624, Blackfriars was operated by Cuthbert Burbage, Richard Burbage's widow, Heminges and Condell, with Heminges in effect controlling three of the six shares.[6]

No one knows for certain how the King's Men coped with the loss of their primary performing space in the Globe. Because Burbage and some of the active Sharers also owned the lease at the Blackfriars, it is assumed that the company simply moved operations indoors, but we have no documentary evidence of such a move. The initial response seems to have been to go on tour. They visited Oxford, Shrewsbury, and possibly Coventry in the west and Folkestone on the Channel,[7] so they must have been out of London for either a very long trip or, more likely, two separate tours with a pause in London in between. They were certainly back in London by November 1, 1613, when they played at court, the first of sixteen performances that season. Most likely, then, they began performing at Blackfriars around the beginning of November.

The new material the Sharers commissioned reflects this short-handed company.

The major new play of that winter was Webster's *Duchess of Malfi*, the only King's Men play not by Shakespeare or Jonson to maintain a place in the modern repertoire. Not printed until 1623, the precise date of the first production is not certain. However, the 1623 quarto included a cast list in which two names were listed for several roles, suggesting a conflation of both the original cast and their replacements in a revival performed shortly before the printing. Assuming that to be an accurate interpretation, the original cast would have been Lowin as Bosola, with Burbage as the jealous Duke, Condell as his brother the Cardinal, and Ostler as Antonio. This means the original performance came before Ostler's death in December 1614. There is no role suitable for Cooke; the only other role of even Half-Sharer size is Delio, for which Underwood is the only name assigned, implying that he played the same role in both original and revival. The absence of Cooke's name, and more importantly the absence of any significant role for an actor of his age and standing, would thus place the play's commission after Cooke's illness. The rest of the casting is not so clear. Minor roles are indicated for Nick Tooley and John Rice, who probably was back in the company as a Hired Man in 1614 and a Half-Sharer in 1623. On the other hand, Ecclestone's name is not present, although he should have joined at the same time as Rice and was certainly a Sharer by 1619. He was certainly alive and active in the company when the revival was performed. Only one role, Malateste, might have been suitable for a Half-Sharer like Ecclestone in 1614, and curiously no one is assigned that role in the quarto, so Ecclestone may have played it in both productions. Likewise, four other names appear that could not have been part of the original cast: One of these, T. Pollard, was a Sharer of some kind by 1625, but in 1614 he was an apprentice of John Shank and would not have played an adult role.

The other three names are boys: R. Sharpe, R. Pallant, and J. Tomson. Richard Sharpe ultimately became a company Sharer, listed in 1625 records and in a large number of Beaumont and Fletcher plays in their folio. Pallant appears to have been the son of the Robert Pallant who began as a Hired Man in the Chamberlain's Men and then acted in the Queen's and Lady Elizabeth's companies. The elder Pallant died in 1619, which would explain his son's apprenticeship in a different company during 1621–23. John Tomson was somehow connected with, perhaps apprenticed to, John Shank, and is specified in women's roles as late as 1630–31, so he too could have played only in the revival. Thus, all three names seem to belong to the revival, whereas the original boys were thought too insignificant to mention a decade later. In that case, the original Duchess was played by Ostler's boy, for whom we have no hint of a name, the Cardinal's beautiful mistress by Condell's boy, and the maid Cariola by the boy specializing in lusty maids.

This Blackfriars provenance may help explain some of the claustrophobia of Webster's play as well. The quarto is very clear that the work had been seen both in the Blackfriars and in the Globe, although "diverse things . . . that the length of the Play would not beare in the Presentment" had been cut in both venues, and no suggestion of dates is made.[8] Still, the tight progression of scenes for only two or three people and the shortage of spectacle scenes (the madmen revealed in the within) would suggest that it was originally designed for the much smaller Blackfriars stage in this period before the new Globe was opened.

With the rebuilding of the Globe and the death of Ostler, "Shakespeare's Company" comes to its end. Shakespeare's plays continued to be a significant part of the company's repertoire, of course, although perhaps not as large a part as we might think. Revivals before 1625 are known for *Hamlet, Henry IV, Pericles, Twelfth Night,* and *The Winter's Tale.*[9] New quartos of *Richard II* in 1615 and *Richard III* in 1622 suggest they too had been recently revived, as does *Othello*'s first quarto in 1622. *Macbeth* must have been performed between 1616 and 1623, or Middleton's revisions borrowed from *The Witch,* which failed in 1616, would not have been available for the Folio. Fletcher eulogized Burbage for his Lear, which suggests *King Lear* had been performed after Fletcher became closely associated with the company and before Burbage's death in 1619. Other productions must have existed but were not recorded. In 1619, Henry Jaggard issued reprints of *Henry VI (Parts II & III), Pericles, Merry Wives of Windsor, Merchant of Venice, King Lear, Henry V,* and *A Midsummer Night's Dream,* apparently intending an unauthorized complete Shakespeare that was stopped by legal action from Heminges.[10] These may have been selected by Jaggard simply because he could find earlier quartos to duplicate, or they may have been chosen because they were the most popular of Shakespeare's works during the previous few years. The brevity of this list of revivals—as few as nine plays, perhaps no more than fifteen in a decade—is something of a surprise, for Shakespeare had been the foundation on which the company had been built and on which its popularity in London and at court had rested for twenty years. Perhaps it was not merely literary hyperbole that led Heminges and Condell in 1623 to call Shakespeare's plays "his Orphanes" and to insist that they only wished "to keepe the memory of so worthy a Friend, & Fellow alive."[11] On the other hand, it is perhaps not so surprising at all. Shakespeare's plays had been carefully tailored to specific actors in a specific company organization, and those actors and that company had ceased to exist. In particular, Shakespeare's leading roles had been built on the specific age and skills of Richard Burbage. Burbage's increasing age made most of his old roles unplayable, while his very presence would have made it difficult to assign the roles to others. The company's immediate future lay primarily with John Fletcher, who seems to have written exclusively for the King's Men after the Globe was rebuilt.[12] Middleton, too, provided a number of popular works, although not exclusively writing for the company. Other playwrights, of course, provided material as well, but Fletcher and Middleton were the regulars.

The King's Men as an organization continued until Cromwell closed down all the theaters, but the individuals with whom Shakespeare had lived and worked and for whom he had written no longer dominated the company. When the new Globe reopened, only three of the original Sharers with Shakespeare still remained from 1594. Of these, Heminges had already begun phasing himself out of performance; there is no role for him in *The Duchess of Malfi,* for example, as we have seen, although he continued to appear in revivals until at least 1616. He remained active in company business affairs, however, until his death in 1630. Richard Burbage continued to act until just before his death in 1619. Condell retired shortly afterward, before 1621. Condell was one of the few to live long enough to fully enjoy his retirement, buying a country house near Fulham where he lived until his death in December 1627.

Of the next wave of Sharers, the men whom Shakespeare knew well but who had not been part of the original company, Sly, Crosse, and Cooke were already dead. John Lowin lasted into the last decade of the company, possibly still performing in his sixties; after the Civil War he kept an inn in Brentford, but the date and place of his death are uncertain, because two men with his name dying a decade apart have been found. Robert Armin simply disappeared from the record.

As for the apprentices who had played such an important role in the company's life, and in particular in Shakespeare's plays, few went on to significant careers as adult actors. Tooley, Rice, Ecclestone, and Gough all eventually obtained shares in the acting company, but only Ecclestone seems to have found any real success. Tooley, the first Gertrude, probably continued to act until he died, unmarried and still living with Cuthbert Burbage, in June 1623, but none of the cast citations suggest he ever increased his half-share. Gough was in company patent lists of 1619 and 1621, although surviving records suggest a half-share at best. He was buried in 1624, at which time his son Alexander was apprenticed to someone in the King's Men; the boy appeared in company cast lists for women's roles from the age of twelve to seventeen, and then apparently became a Hired Man but never a Sharer. Ecclestone, the first Cleopatra and Lady Macbeth, seems to have been the most successful, for his name is on the 1619 and 1621 patent lists and all the surviving cast lists for Fletcher's plays between 1614 and 1622. He is not on the new patent issued in 1625, but tradition says he lived to a ripe old age, suggesting he retired with considerable wealth after 1622. The beautiful John Rice, who had so impressed King James, found no prominent adult roles. He soon gave up the stage and became a clergyman. As noted earlier, Richard Robinson, so much admired by Ben Jonson, married Burbage's widow after the old star's death and continued to perform until the outbreak of the civil war; Robinson did not take over Burbage's roles, however, for the company's new Hamlet was Joseph Taylor.

The company's most famous playwright had nothing more to do with the company. We know Shakespeare made at least one more visit to London in November of 1614, accompanied by his son-in-law John Hall, but no one knows exactly why. He also was involved in some legal questions about the Blackfriars gatehouse and arranged a trust that kept it until 1618.[13] The papers are dated April 26, 1615, which suggests that Shakespeare spent the entire winter in London. If he used the time to collaborate on other theatrical material, none of it has survived. After April, he returned to Stratford, where he grew ill about a year later and died. He was buried in the local church with the prominence expected for a very rich local man on April 25, 1616.

Appendix A: Doubling Roles

There can be no doubt that the doubling of roles for Elizabethan actors was common; however, it seems probable that the practice was not nearly so common as is often assumed. Since William Ringler's influential study arguing that *Julius Caesar* could be played by sixteen men, there has been significant research on this question.[1] However, almost all of this research has been concerned with establishing minimum sizes of cast, which may not have been all that important to the Elizabethans. In the modern theater, actors play more than one role in a production for one and only one reason: to reduce the payroll. As demonstrated in the main text in some detail, this was rarely a problem for the Elizabethan companies. The company preceded the play; new plays were written to fit the company, and old plays were revised to fit the company. This gave the writer great freedom and flexibility in the history plays, for example, where he could present large casts and cover many years, because he knew that there were actors available for anything he might write. But in comedies or tragedies, where the subject matter required a focus on a small number of characters, this presented serious difficulties. The most practical solution was a play with two or three alternating plots, designed more than anything to use up all the available actors. Thus, the careful research of King and Bradley, in particular, which has established the minimum company size necessary for any given play, is helpful only so far; it tells us the minimum size of the company. But that does not mean the company held itself to this level of efficiency. The only list we have of what seems to be a full company, rather than merely the Sharers, is the list of King's Actors to be protected from arrest on December 27, 1624, which includes twenty-one names, all of whom seem to be adults and none of whom are Sharers.[2] Some are musicians and some apparently work around the theater and are not regular Hired Men, but it seems clear that the company did not consist of the most efficient minimum. It is not necessarily obvious that, because a play could be performed by a certain minimal number of actors, it was performed by a certain minimal number of actors. If there were twenty actors on the payroll, it would be difficult to believe the company continued to pay some for doing nothing while others played three, four, or six roles.

In addition, many roles may be double-able on paper but still be impractical to double in performance. It is the very essence of the theatrical experience that the audience must always be able to understand who is doing what at every moment. Audiences must be able to identify significant characters immediately, without confusion and without hesitation. They may make this identification by face, by costume, by voice, or some combination of the three, but the identification must occur immediately and remain consistent from scene to scene. Anything that interferes with this identification process endangers the dramatic success of a production. Hence, we need to distinguish two types of characters. Some characters are "significant," either critical to the plot or likely to have a memorable impact on the audience, usually both. These almost always would have been the province of the Sharers. Others are "forgettable," by which I mean they have no impact on audience consciousness. They may momentarily provide important information—someone has to tell Macbeth and the audience that Birnham Wood is on the march—but they make no impression as a character. To the audience, a messenger is a messenger, a soldier a soldier, a servant a servant, and it matters not if they are shown in the cast list under a specific name. To audiences without a playbill, they are all one. If an actor playing a significant character reappears in a different costume, audiences will assume it is the earlier character in a different costume rather than a new character, and be confused; if a forgettable character returns several times in different costumes (or even in the same costume), no one will be bothered at all.

As discussed in chapter 1 and illustrated throughout the following chapters, there are three fundamental indicators of Sharer roles: number of lines, multiple scenes, and significance of character. Although lines and scenes are important, the most important factor is significance. Some Sharers were willing to accept roles much smaller than others, particularly than Burbage, but only if the roles they did have were significant and potentially memorable. After all, it is only through memorable roles that an actor even has a career. But the more memorable an actor's impact, the less practical is it for him to double another role. If somehow he does double, this actor who plays memorable and significant roles must not be recognized by the audience. Polonius, for example, dies in Act III of *Hamlet*.[3] There is nothing practical to prevent his doubling as the Gravedigger.[3] Or he could double Osric, or the English Ambassador. If he wishes, he could double at least two of those. But should Polonius double as the Grave-digger, some significant portion of the audience will recognize him and as a result be confused, wondering why this man they thought was dead now has such a terrible lower class job. This confusion, or dissonance, is not so strong in modern Shakespearean productions, where most of the audience already knows the play and treats it as a study text rather than a theatrical experience. But for people coming to the play for the first time, such confusion can be so distracting as to destroy the scene. Such confusion would be even greater if the Polonius actor played Osric or the Ambassador, because his costume would be similar to that worn by Polonius.

This is not merely a question of appearance. Many scholars have commented on the way many Elizabethans wrote of hearing a play, arguing that the audience was much more aware of the spoken lines than the physical spectacle. But audiences attuned to vocal patterns would spot voices even more easily than they would recognize faces. It is, after all, possible to change a costume or to put on a false beard. It is much harder to disguise a voice, and even in modern productions, we usually spot the doubling actor by his or her voice before we recognize the face. An actor might put on an accent, but there are surprisingly few requirements for funny accents in Shakespeare's work, or those of others writing for the same company. Almost all of the various lower class accents are in scenes that were obviously intended for either the clowns or the Hired Men. The roles that might plausibly be doubled by Sharers, as suggested in King's numerous charts, for example, rarely offer any practical opportunities for disguising the voice.

Disguises were themselves minimal. The technology for what we think of as "character makeup" today simply did not exist. Greasepaint was not invented until the nineteenth century, and latex of course was inconceivable until the late twentieth. Any primitive makeup used at the time, such as burnt cork smeared to play Morocco or Aaron or white powder imbedded in a layer of grease for a Ghost, would take far longer to remove than to apply. The actors were fundamentally left with their own faces. Any wigs and false beards worked in only one direction—Burbage might wear a white wig for Lear or a false beard for Benedick before he shaved, but Bryan could not put on a false beard to play Romeo. Even costume was limited—the actor doubling as Poins and Vernon in *1 Henry IV* might be understood as Poins in armor rather than as Vernon. And costume change itself had very real limitations. The Elizabethans had no velcro, no zippers, and only limited use of buttons. Most items of clothing came in multiple pieces which had to be laced together on the body of the wearer. Armor, when used, was real armor, which meant that each piece had to be tied or hammered into place. A "fast change" was impossible.[4] Any doubling that required a change of costume demanded that the actor spend a long time off stage to make the change.

Thus, we can offer five general guidelines to Sharer doubling:

1. Such doubling should stay within the same general age as the performer, except when a young actor might also play a much older character. Cowley as Old Gobbo in his old coot disguise might later play Balthasar in *Merchant of Venice* in his own face, but Bryan in his own grey hair and beard could not come back from Shylock to play Balthasar.

2. One of the appearances must disguise the actor as completely as possible within the technology of the time. It is possible for Lowin to play Banquo and then to come back as the Doctor, for example, because the Doctor's hat and gown might hide most of his head, but he could not come back as Siward, who in his armor would look exactly like Banquo in his armor. Similarly, Hamlet's Ghost might take off his helmet and appear as the Player King, since no one saw his face clearly in the Ghost scene.

3. The more memorable role should come last. Mercutio cannot double as Paris, but it is certainly plausible that one of the Lords in *Taming of the Shrew* might double as Vincentio.

4. There must be ample time for the Sharer to assume the disguise of the second role. There is no hard and fast rule here, either, but in general, there should be sufficient time for the Sharer to be sure he will be ready without panic and also to give the audience time to forget the earlier appearance. As a rule of thumb, it should be several scenes, ideally a full act or longer.

5. The doubling must increase the Sharer's stage time in a way that befits his status in the company. With eight or ten Hired Men standing around backstage, there is no reason why a Sharer should struggle through two costume changes to tell Macbeth that Birnham Wood is moving.

Given these five limitations, we have to assume that doubling of roles by Sharers occurred much less often than is generally believed.

However, there is one kind of doubling that may have occurred fairly often. This is the elimination of a character and the absorption of his lines by another character. For example, in *Macbeth*, Angus has lines in two scenes separated by four acts. Shakespeare, writing with Holinshed to hand, knew there was an Angus, but the audience, having no printed cast list, would not have known Angus from Lennox, or from Adam for that matter. In performance, the role of Angus might well have been eliminated while his lines would still have been heard on stage. There are two approaches the company could have taken: one would be to expand a Sharer's part, not by asking him to change costumes and pretend to be two different people but rather by simply picking up those lines in scenes when he is on stage already. Lennox, for example, might have spoken Angus' lines as Lennox. This seems to have been what happened in a case we know about in *Sir John van Olden Barnavelt*, played by the King's Men in 1619. In the surviving manuscript, John Rice is written in for a substantial role as a captain, but in one scene also plays a servant; this comes in between two appearances as the captain, an awkward and rather pointless costume change, as Rice already has the fourth largest role in the play. Far more likely is that Rice said the servant's lines, a substantial scene of almost fifty lines, but in his guise as the captain. Similarly, Robinson plays a Dutch captain and a Dutch Ambassador; most likely, though written as separate characters on the page, they were treated as the same character on stage. This casual assignment of lines and characters is evident in some of Shakespeare's surviving work. In *All's Well That Ends Well*, for example, the court scene gives lines to four Lords, although the stage directions say only "three or four" enter (F944); the specific lines might have been taken by almost any one of the Lords on stage, and in any order. Similarly, at the wars, we have variously Captain E, Captain G, Lord E, with "five or sixe other souldiers" (F1911), one of whom serves as an interpreter, plus a later separate Interpreter. In one scene, we have both Captain E and Lord E (modern IV,iii). All modern editors combine the two, and we can assume that the King's Men did as well, and that the Soldier who interprets probably also spoke the lines of the Interpreter without any attempt to portray a separate character.

A second alternative would be to assign Angus' lines in each scene to different actors, who do not trade costumes to make Angus always look like Angus but who simply say Angus' lines in their guise as a soldier or lord. This seems to have happened in the surviving manuscript of Massinger's *Believe as You List* in 1631, somewhat outside our period, complete with stage manager's annotations and role assignments. In this document, some half-share men or Hired Men play as many as six different roles, often changing characters in back-to-back scenes too close together to make a costume change. Rowland Dowle and Thomas Hobbs even play two characters each on stage at the same time in one scene. One character, Demetrius, is assigned to three different actors.[5] This is clearly a case not of doubling as we understand it but of character compression. As long as the lines were said, it would not matter to the company, or to the audience, whether they were said by the nobleman Demetrius or the senator Favius or the Second Messenger. Thus, the assignment of three actors to Demetrius, for example, who has six lines total, simply indicates that three different actors picked up those lines, depending on the scene. But it need not indicate that the three actors ran around in the tiring room trading costumes, each trying to develop a characterization for Demetrius. We must assume that this was in fact a quite common practice among the smaller Hired Man roles, and that where we struggle mightily to distinguish Reynaldo from "Servant," for example, or Margarelon from Helenus, or Angus from "Lord," Shakespeare's company made little or no such effort, simply assigning the lines to whichever Hired Man happened to be convenient.

Appendix B: Charts

Chart A
Timeline of Productions for Shakespeare's Company

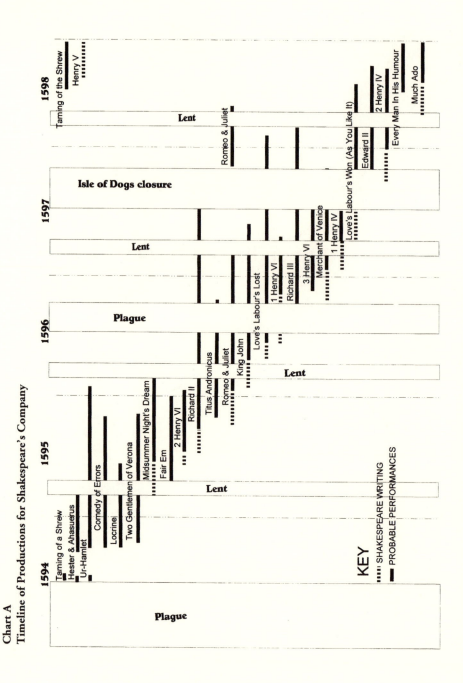

224

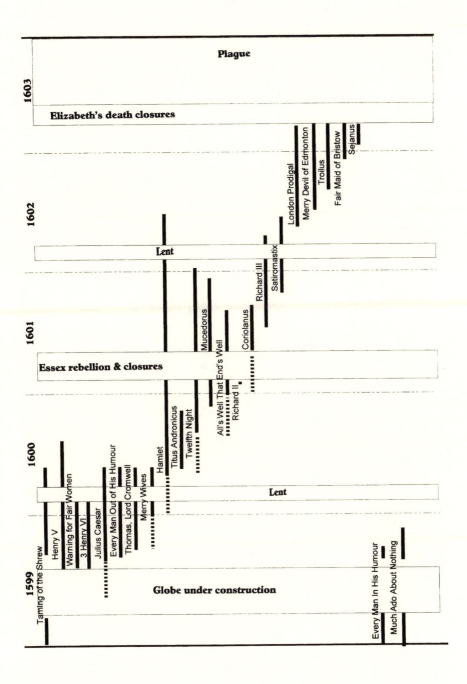

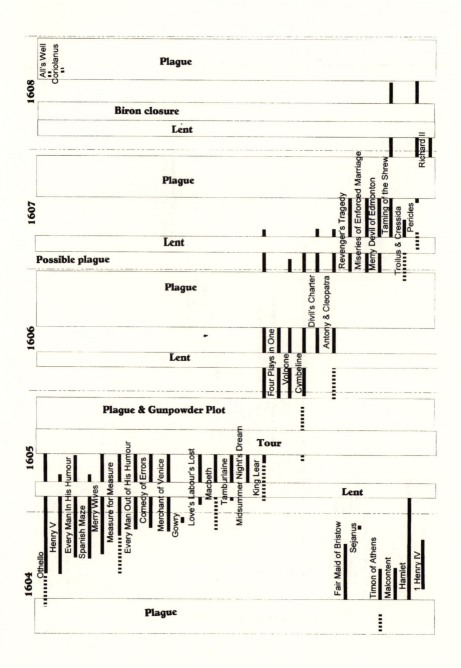

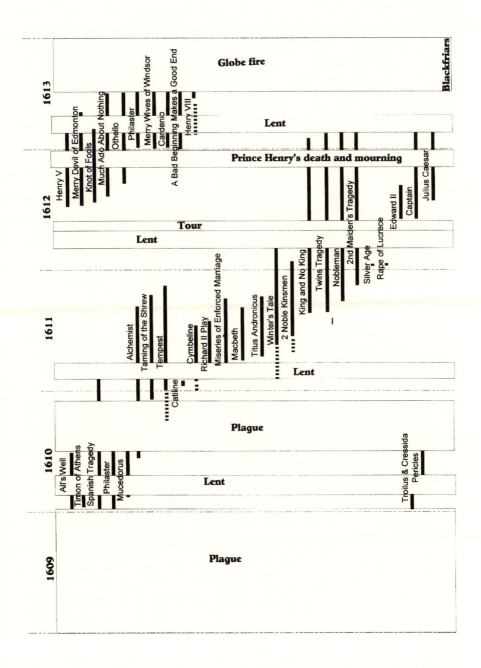

Chart B
Probable Casting of Chamberlain's Men Plays

	BEE?	C. BEESTON	R. BEESTON?
COMEDY OF ERRORS (1594)	Luce?	Boy	Boy
TWO GENTLEMEN OF VERONA (1594)	Speed	Boy	Boy
LOCRINE (Corrected by WS) (1594-95)	Dorothy/Margery	Boy	Madan
MIDSUMMER NIGHT'S DREAM (1595)	Flute	Fairy	Helena?
2 HENRY 6 (1595)	Peter	Company	Boy
FAIR EM (Anon) (1595)	Boy	Mariana	Boy
RICHARD2 (1595)	Gardener	Boy	Boy
TITUS ANDRONICUS (1595)	Company	Boy	Boy
ROMEO & JULIET (1596)	Nurse	Boy	Boy
KING JOHN (1596)	Boy	9 Arthur	Boy
LOVE'S LABOUR'S LOST (revised? 1596)	Boy	Moth	Katherine
1 HENRY 6 (new? 1596)	Boy	Margaret	Boy
RICHARD 3 (revived 1596)	Boy	Margaret	Boy
3 HENRY 6 (revived? 1596-97)	Boy	Elizabeth	Rutland
MERCHANT OF VENICE (1596-97)	Boy	Nerissa	Jessica
1 HENRY 4 (1597)	Company	Boy	Lady Percy
LOVE'S LABOUR'S WON (AS YOU LIKE IT) (1597)	William	Boy	Phebe
EDWARD II (Marlowe) (revival 1597)	Company	Isabella	Boy
2 HENRY 4 (1597-8)	Company	Doll	Boy
EVERY MAN IN HIS HUMOUR (Jonson) (1598)	Company	Lorenzo Junior	Boy
MUCH ADO ABOUT NOTHING (1598)	Company	Watch	Hero
TAMING OF THE SHREW (revised? 1598)	Servant	Company	Bianca
HENRY 5 (1599)	Company	Company	Boy
3 HENRY VI (revived 1599)	Company	Company	Boy
WARNING FOR FAIR WOMEN (Anon) (1599)	Carpenter?	Company	Anne Sanders
JULIUS CAESAR (1599)	Company	Company	Boy
THOMAS LORD CROMWELL (Anon) (1599)	Company	Company	Boy
EVERY MAN OUT OF HIS HUMOUR (Jonson)(1599)	Company	Company	Fallace
MERRY WIVES (1600)	Company	Company	Boy
TITUS ANDRONICUS (revived 1600)	left company	Company	Boy
HAMLET (1600)		left company	Ophelia
TWELFTH NIGHT(1600)			Viola
MUCEDORUS (revised 1600-01)			Envy?
RICHARD II (revived 2/7/1601)			Company
ALL'S WELL THAT ENDS WELL (first version 1601)			Company
CORIOLANUS (first version 1601)			Company
RICHARD III (revived 1601)			Company
SATIROMASTIX (Dekker) (1601)			Company
LONDON PRODIGAL (Anon) (1602)			Company
MERRY DEVIL OF EDMONTON (Anon) (1602)			Company
FAIR MAID OF BRISTOW (Anon) (1602)			Company
SEJANUS (Jonson) (1602-03)			Company

BELT?	BRYAN	BURBAGE	CONDELL	COOKE
Abbess	Egeon	Angelo	Merchant	Luciana
Boy	Milan	Panthino/Eglamour	Outlaw	Julia
Boy	Brutus	Albanact	Hubba	Gwendolen
Hippolyta	Theseus	Lysander	Demetrius	Titania
Duchess Gloucester	Humphrey	Henry	Warwick	Young Clifford
Elnar	Danish King	Valingford	Manville	Blaunch
Duchess York	York	Bolingbroke	Aumerle	Harry Percy
Lavinia	Titus	Demetrius	Chiron	Tamora
L Capulet	Capulet	Romeo	Tybalt	Company
Boy	Pandulph	Bastard	Lewis Dauphin	Constance
Boy	Holofernes	Berowne	Dumaine	Princess
Young Talbot	Talbot	York	Dauphin	La Pucelle
Company	Hastings	Richard III	Richmond/Tyrrell	Duch York
Company	Warwick	Richard Gloucester	Clifford	Prince Edward
Company	Shylock	Bassanio	Lorenzo	Company
Company	Henry IV	Hal	Hotspur	Prince John
Company	Duke Sr	Orlando	Silvius	Jaques de Boys
Company	Kent	Edward	Gaveston	Company
Company	Henry IV	Hal	Prince John	Company
Company	retired	Thorello(Kitely)	Musco	Company
Company		Benedick	Claudio	Company
Company		Petruchio	Lucentio	Company
Company		Henry	Dauphin	Company
Company		Richard Gloucester	Clarence	Prince Edward
Company		Browne	Roger	Company
Company		Brutus	Antony	Octavius
Company		Cromwell	Bedford	Company
Company		Brisk	Deliro	Company
Company		Ford	Caius	Fenton
left company		Titus	Demetrius	Martius
		Hamlet	Laertes	Fortinbras
		Malvolio	Orsino	Sebastian
		Mucedorus	Segasto	Company
		Bolingbroke	Aumerle	Harry Percy?
		Bertram	Company	Company
		Coriolanus	Aufidius	Lartius
		Richard III	Richmond	Company
		Tucca	Terrill	Company
		Matthew	Oliver	Daffodil
		Peter Fabell	Coreb/Brian/Hild	Frank Jerningham
		Challener	Vallenger	Company
		Sejanus	Macro	Drusus Sr/Caligula

	COWLEY	DUKE
COMEDY OF ERRORS (1594)	Company	Company
TWO GENTLEMEN OF VERONA (1594)	Host	Outlaw
LOCRINE (Corrected by WS) (1594-95)	Trompart	Company
MIDSUMMER NIGHT'S DREAM (1595)	Snout	Snug/Lion
2 HENRY 6 (1595)	Simpcox	Iden
FAIR EM (Anon) (1595)	Citizen	Company
RICHARD2 (1595)	Company	Scroop?
TITUS ANDRONICUS (1595)	Martius	Goth
ROMEO & JULIET (1596)	Gregory/Balthasar	Company
KING JOHN (1596)	Melun?	Austria
LOVE'S LABOUR'S LOST (revised? 1596)	Nathaniel	Dull
1 HENRY 6 (new? 1596)	Somerset/Shepherd	Bastard
RICHARD 3 (revived 1596)	2nd Murderer	Citizen/Company
3 HENRY 6 (revived? 1596-97)	Company	Company
MERCHANT OF VENICE (1596-97)	Old Gobbo	Jailer
1 HENRY 4 (1597)	Gadshill	Westmoreland
LOVE'S LABOUR'S WON (AS YOU LIKE IT) (1597)	Adam	Charles
EDWARD II (Marlowe) (revival 1597)	Company	Company
2 HENRY 4 (1597-8)	Silence?	Peter Bullcalf
EVERY MAN IN HIS HUMOUR (Jonson) (1598)	Matheo(Matthew)	Giuliano(Downright)
MUCH ADO ABOUT NOTHING (1598)	Verges	Watch
TAMING OF THE SHREW (revised? 1598)	Servant	Servant
HENRY 5 (1599)	Nym	Gower
3 HENRY VI (revived 1599)	Company	Company
WARNING FOR FAIR WOMEN (Anon) (1599)	Company	Executioner
JULIUS CAESAR (1599)	Plebeian/Poet	Plebeian
THOMAS LORD CROMWELL (Anon) (1599)	Old Cromwell	Company
EVERY MAN OUT OF HIS HUMOUR (Jonson)(1599)	Mitis	Company
MERRY WIVES (1600)	Nym	John
TITUS ANDRONICUS (revived 1600)	Clown	Company
HAMLET (1600)	Guildenstern/Gravedigger	left company
TWELFTH NIGHT(1600)	Curio/Officer	
MUCEDORUS (revised 1600-01)	Rumbelo	
RICHARD II (revived 2/7/1601)	Company	
ALL'S WELL THAT ENDS WELL (first version 1601)	Company	
CORIOLANUS (first version 1601)	Citizen	
RICHARD III (revived 1601)	2nd Murderer	
SATIROMASTIX (Dekker) (1601)	Demetrius	
LONDON PRODIGAL (Anon) (1602)	Artichoke	
MERRY DEVIL OF EDMONTON (Anon) (1602)	Sir Richard/Sexton	
FAIR MAID OF BRISTOW (Anon) (1602)	Douce	
SEJANUS (Jonson) (1602-03)	Eudemus	

GOUGH	HEMINGES	KEMP	'NED'	PALLANT	PETER?
Courtesan?	Antipholus Syr	Dromio Syr	Adriana	Company	Company
Lucetta?	Proteus	Launce	Sylvia	Outlaw	Serenader
Boy	Thrasimacus	Strumbo	Elstrid	Company	Company
Boy	Oberon	Bottom	Boy	Company	Company
Margery	York	Jack Cade/Armorer	Margaret	Commoners	Commoner
Boy	Mountney	Trotter	Mariana	Company	Company
Duchess Gloucester	Northumberland	Gardener	Queen	Company	Company
Young Lucius	Saturninus	Clown	Company	Quintus	Company
Boy	Paris/Chorus	Sampson/Peter	Company	Company	Peter
Blanche	John	Austria	Company	Company	Company
Boy	Navarre	Costard	Company	Company	Winter or Summer
Boy	Gloucester	Reignier	Company	Vernon	Company
Elizabeth	Edward IV	1st Murderer	Company	Citizen/Company	Company
Boy	Clarence	Company	Company	Company	Company
Boy	Solanio/Duke	Launcelot Gobbo	Company	Company	Singer
Boy	Mortimer/Archbishop	Falstaff	Company	Carrier	Company
Boy	Frederick	Touchstone	Company	Company	Amiens
Company	Lancaster	Company	Company	Company	Company
Company	Archbishop	Falstaff	Company	Company	Silence
Company	Lorenzo	Cob	left company	Company	Company
Company	Don John?	Dogberry		Watch	Balthasar
Company	Tranio	Grumio		Servant	Peter
Company	Exeter	'ill'		Williams	Company
Company	Edward	ill'		Company	Company
Company	James	Carpenter		Company	Company
Company	Messala/Decius	Cobbler/Plebeian		Plebeian	Company
Company	Gardiner	Hodge		Company	Company
Company	Sogliardo	Buffone		Company	Company
Company	Page	Falstaff		Robert	Peter Simple?
Company	Lucius	Clown		Company	Company
Company	Horatio	Clown/left company		left company	left company
Company	Antonio				
Company	King				
Company	Northumberland				
Company	Company				
Company	Cominius				
Company	Edward IV				
Company	Crispinus				
Company	Weathercock				
Company	Sir Ralph/Prologue				
Company	Richard Lionheart				
Company	Silius				

	PHILLIPS	POPE	ROWLEY?
COMEDY OF ERRORS (1594)	Antipholus Eph	Dromio Eph	Apprenticed
TWO GENTLEMEN OF VERONA (1594)	Valentine	Antonio/Host	Boy
LOCRINE (Corrected by WS) (1594-95)	Locrine	Corineus	Boy
MIDSUMMER NIGHT'S DREAM (1595)	Puck	Egeus/Philostrate	Fairy
2 HENRY 6 (1595)	Suffolk	Beauford/Clifford	Simpcox's Wife
FAIR EM (Anon) (1595)	Lubeck	Miller	Boy
RICHARD2 (1595)	Richard II	Gaunt	Boy
TITUS ANDRONICUS (1595)	Aaron	Marcus	Boy
ROMEO & JULIET (1596)	Mercutio	Fr. Lawrence	Servant
KING JOHN (1596)	Hubert/Citizen	King Phillip	Company
LOVE'S LABOUR'S LOST (revised? 1596)	Armado	Boyet	Jaquenetta
1 HENRY 6 (new? 1596)	Suffolk	Winchester	Boy
RICHARD 3 (revived 1596)	Buckingham	Stanley	Company
3 HENRY 6 (revived? 1596-97)	Edward	York	Boy
MERCHANT OF VENICE (1596-97)	Gratiano	Antonio	Boy
1 HENRY 4 (1597)	Douglas	Worcester	Hostess
LOVE'S LABOUR'S WON (AS YOU LIKE IT) (1597)	Jaques	Corin	Audrey
EDWARD II (Marlowe) (revival 1597)	Mortimer	Warwick	Boy
2 HENRY 4 (1597-8)	Pistol	Chief Justice	Hostess
EVERY MAN IN HIS HUMOUR (Jonson) (1598)	Bobadilla	Clement	Tib
MUCH ADO ABOUT NOTHING (1598)	Borachio	Leonato	Boy
TAMING OF THE SHREW (revised? 1598)	Hortensio	Baptista	Servant
HENRY 5 (1599)	Prologue/Pistol	King of France	Hostess
3 HENRY VI (revived 1599)	Clifford	York	Boy
WARNING FOR FAIR WOMEN (Anon) (1599)	Barnes	Old John	Boy
JULIUS CAESAR (1599)	Cassius	Caesar	Boy
THOMAS LORD CROMWELL (Anon) (1599)	Bagot	Frescobaldi	Joan
EVERY MAN OUT OF HIS HUMOUR (Jonson)(1599)	Macilente	Sordido	George
MERRY WIVES (1600)	Pistol	Host	Mrs. Page
TITUS ANDRONICUS (revived 1600)	Aaron	retired	left with Kemp
HAMLET (1600)	Claudius		
TWELFTH NIGHT(1600)	Belch		
MUCEDORUS (revised 1600-01)	Bremo		
RICHARD II (revived 2/7/1601)	Richard II		
ALL'S WELL THAT ENDS WELL (first version 1601)	Parolles		
CORIOLANUS (first version 1601)	Menenius		
RICHARD III (revived 1601)	Buckingham		
SATIROMASTIX (Dekker) (1601)	King		
LONDON PRODIGAL (Anon) (1602)	Sir Lancelot		
MERRY DEVIL OF EDMONTON (Anon) (1602)	Sir John (Priest)		
FAIR MAID OF BRISTOW (Anon) (1602)	Harbert		
SEJANUS (Jonson) (1602-03)	Arruntius		

'SAUNDER'	SHAKESPEARE	SHAKESPEARE'S BOY	SINKLO	JEFFES?
Company	Duke Ephesus	Apprenticed	Dr. Pinch	
Boy	Thurio	Boy	Outlaw	
Sabren or Ate	Humber	Boy	Company	
Hermia	Quince	Fairy	Starveling	
Boy	Salisbury	Spirit	Simpcox	Richard P
Em	Cooke	Boy	Company	Company
Boy	Mowbray	Boy	Company	Green
Boy	Lucius	Boy	Company	Company
Juliet	Benvolio/Friar John	Boy	Apothecary	Company
Queen Elinor	Salisbury	Boy	Robert F.	Chatillon
Rosaline	Longaville	Maria	Company	Company
Prince Henry	Mortimer	Boy	Company	Warwick
Anne	Clarence	Prince	Scrivener/Company	Tyrrell
Margaret	Henry	Boy	Company	Nothumberland
Portia	Salerio	Boy	Company	Judge
Boy	Poins/Vernon	Francis	Carrier	left company
Rosalind	Oliver	Company	Martext	
Company	Company	Boy	Company	
Company	Poins/Shallow	Davy	Beadle/Feeble	
Company	Prospero/Wellbred	Hesperida	Company	
Company	Don Pedro?	Boy	Watch	
Company	Grumio	Boy	Tailor	
Company	Canterbury/Chorus	Boy	Company	
Company	Henry	Boy	Company	
Company	Sanders	Dumb Show	Company	
Strato	Casca/Titinnius	Boy	Plebeian	
Company	Hales	Boy	Company	
Company	Puntarvalo	Puntarvalo's Wife	Tailor	
Company	Shallow	Boy	Company	
left company?	Saturninus	Boy	Company	
	Ghost	Boy	left company	
	Fabian	Boy		
	Anselmo	Boy		
	Gaunt	Boy		
	King	Boy		
	Sicinius	Boy		
	Clarence	Boy		
	Sir Qunitillian	Boy		
	Flowerdale Jr			
	Host			
	Sir Eustace			
	Tiberius			

	LEE?	HOLLAND?	SPENSER?
COMEDY OF ERRORS (1594)			
TWO GENTLEMEN OF VERONA (1594)			
LOCRINE (Corrected by WS) (1594-95)			
MIDSUMMER NIGHT'S DREAM (1595)			
2 HENRY 6 (1595)	Hume	Holland	Lieutenant
FAIR EM (Anon) (1595)	Company	Company	Company
RICHARD2 (1595)	Bushy	Company	Bagot
TITUS ANDRONICUS (1595)	Company	Company	Company
ROMEO & JULIET (1596)	Company	Company	Company
KING JOHN (1596)	Bigot	Company	Pembroke
LOVE'S LABOUR'S LOST (revised? 1596)	Company	Company	Company
1 HENRY 6 (new? 1596)	Exeter	Company	Bedford
RICHARD 3 (revived 1596)	Ratcliff	Company	Catesby
3 HENRY 6 (revived? 1596-97)	Prince	Company	Somerset
MERCHANT OF VENICE (1596-97)	Judge	Company	Aragon
1 HENRY 4 (1597)	Northumberland	Company	left company
LOVE'S LABOUR'S WON (AS YOU LIKE IT) (1597)	Lord #1	Company	
EDWARD II (Marlowe) (revival 1597)	Company	Company	
2 HENRY 4 (1597-8)	Warwick	Company	
EVERY MAN IN HIS HUMOUR (Jonson) (1598)	Company	Company	
MUCH ADO ABOUT NOTHING (1598)	Company	Company	
TAMING OF THE SHREW (revised? 1598)	Company	Company	
HENRY 5 (1599)	Mountjoy	Company	
3 HENRY VI (revived 1599)	Company	Company	
WARNING FOR FAIR WOMEN (Anon) (1599)	Company	Company	
JULIUS CAESAR (1599)	Company	Company	
THOMAS LORD CROMWELL (Anon) (1599)	Company	Company	
EVERY MAN OUT OF HIS HUMOUR (Jonson)(1599)	Company	Company	
MERRY WIVES (1600)	Company	Company	
TITUS ANDRONICUS (revived 1600)	Company	Company	
HAMLET (1600)	Marcellus	left company	
TWELFTH NIGHT(1600)	Company		
MUCEDORUS (revised 1600-01)	Company		
RICHARD II (revived 2/7/1601)	Company		
ALL'S WELL THAT ENDS WELL (first version 1601)	Company		
CORIOLANUS (first version 1601)	left company		
RICHARD III (revived 1601)			
SATIROMASTIX (Dekker) (1601)	Company		
LONDON PRODIGAL (Anon) (1602)			
MERRY DEVIL OF EDMONTON (Anon) (1602)			
FAIR MAID OF BRISTOW (Anon) (1602)			
SEJANUS (Jonson) (1602-03)			

TOOLEY	CROSSE	CROSSE'S BOY	GILBURNE	SLY	EDMANS
Apprenticed					
Boy	Montague				
Lady Falconbridge	Company				
Boy	Company	Apprenticed			
Boy	Company	Boy			
Prince	Rivers	Boy			
Boy	Louis	Lady Bona			
Boy	Morocco	Boy	Apprenticed		
Company	Glendower	Lady Mortimer	Boy		
Celia	Company	Hymen	Boy		
Boy	Company	Boy	Prince Edward		Apprenticed
Boy	Northumberland	Lady Percy	Boy	Shadow/Morton	
Biancha(Mrs. K)	Matheo	Boy	Boy	Stephano/Stephen	Boy
Beatrice	Antonio	Ursula	Margaret	Conrade	Boy
Kate	Vincentio	Boy	Widow	Pedant	Biondello
Katherine	Fluellen	French Gentlewoman	Pistol's Boy	Constable	Isabel
Margaret	Warwick	Boy	Elizabeth	Company	Boy
Anne Drury	Justice	Dumb Show	Tragedy	John Beane	Joan
Portia	Murellus	Company	Boy	Flavius/Pindarus	Calpurnia
Boy	Bannister	Mrs. Bannister	Boy	Suffolk/Chorus	Boy
Saviolina	Cordatus?	Boy	Boy	Fungoso	Boy
Mrs. Ford	Evans	William Page	Quickly	Slender	Anne Page?
Boy	Marcus	Lavinia	Tamora	Chiron	Boy
Gertrude	Polonius	Boy	Boy	Rosencrantz	Boy
Olivia	Captain/Priest	Boy	Maria	Aguecheek	Boy
Comedy?	Valencia	Boy	Amadine	Tremelio	Boy
Boy	York	Duchess York	Queen	Mowbray	Boy
Helena	Lafew	Countess	Boy	Company	Boy
Volumnia	Brutus	Boy	Boy	Senator/Roman	Boy
Anne	Stanley	Elizabeth	Margaret	Catesby	Boy
Company	Ap Vaughan	Mrs. Miniver	Boy	Horace	Boy
Delia	Flowerdale Sr	Luce	Company	10 Greenfield	Boy
Company	Sir Arthur	Millicent	Company	Raymond	Boy
Company	Sir Godfrey	Mother	Company	Sentloe	Boy
Company	6 Sabinius	Boy	Company	7 Terentius	Boy

	POCK-MARKED MAN	ECCLESTONE
COMEDY OF ERRORS (1594)		
TWO GENTLEMEN OF VERONA (1594)		
LOCRINE (Corrected by WS) (1594-95)		
MIDSUMMER NIGHT'S DREAM (1595)		
2 HENRY 6 (1595)		
FAIR EM (Anon) (1595)		
RICHARD2 (1595)		
TITUS ANDRONICUS (1595)		
ROMEO & JULIET (1596)		
KING JOHN (1596)		
LOVE'S LABOUR'S LOST (revised? 1596)		
1 HENRY 6 (new? 1596)		
RICHARD 3 (revived 1596)		
3 HENRY 6 (revived? 1596-97)		
MERCHANT OF VENICE (1596-97)		
1 HENRY 4 (1597)		
LOVE'S LABOUR'S WON (AS YOU LIKE IT) (1597)		
EDWARD II (Marlowe) (revival 1597)		
2 HENRY 4 (1597-8)	Bardolph	
EVERY MAN IN HIS HUMOUR (Jonson) (1598)	Company	
MUCH ADO ABOUT NOTHING (1598)	Company	
TAMING OF THE SHREW (revised? 1598)	Company	
HENRY 5 (1599)	Bardolph	Apprenticed
3 HENRY VI (revived 1599)	Company	Boy
WARNING FOR FAIR WOMEN (Anon) (1599)	Company	Boy
JULIUS CAESAR (1599)	Company	Lucius
THOMAS LORD CROMWELL (Anon) (1599)	Company	Young Cromwell
EVERY MAN OUT OF HIS HUMOUR (Jonson)(1599)	Company	Cinedo
MERRY WIVES (1600)	Bardolph	Anne Page?
TITUS ANDRONICUS (revived 1600)	Company	Boy
HAMLET (1600)	left with Kemp	Boy
TWELFTH NIGHT(1600)		Boy
MUCEDORUS (revised 1600-01)		Boy
RICHARD II (revived 2/7/1601)		Boy
ALL'S WELL THAT ENDS WELL (first version 1601)		Boy
CORIOLANUS (first version 1601)		Virgilia
RICHARD III (revived 1601)		Prince
SATIROMASTIX (Dekker) (1601)		Tucca's Boy
LONDON PRODIGAL (Anon) (1602)		Citizen's Wife
MERRY DEVIL OF EDMONTON (Anon) (1602)		Boy
FAIR MAID OF BRISTOW (Anon) (1602)		Annabelle?
SEJANUS (Jonson) (1602-03)		Livia

CONDELL'S BOY #2	T. SLYE?	SANDS	ARMIN	E SHAKESPEARE	SHAKESPEARE'S 2ND BOY
Apprenticed					
Rutland					
Boy					
Boy	Apprenticed	Apprenticed			
Boy	Seely	Boy			
Boy	Boy	Boy			
Boy	Robin	Boy			
Boy	Boy	Boy			
Boy	left with Kemp	Boy			
Boy		Boy	Feste		
Boy		Ariena	Mouse	Company	
Boy		Boy	Gardener	Company	Apprenticed
Boy		Boy	Lavatch	Company	Boy
Boy		Boy	Citizen	Company	Boy
Boy		Boy	Citizen	Company	Prince
Celestine		Boy	Asinius Bubo	Company	Boy
Boy		Boy	Civet	Company	Boy
Dorcas?		Prioress	Smug	Company	Boy
Annabelle?		Florence	Frog	Company	Boy
Boy		Boy	Lepidus	Company	Boy

Chart C
Probable Casting of King's Men Plays 1604–08

	ARMIN	BURBAGE	CONDELL
TIMON OF ATHENS (first version 1604)	Clown	Timon	Alcibiades
MALCONTENT (Marston) (revised 1604)	Passarello	Malevole	Mendoza
OTHELLO (1604)	retired	Othello	Cassio
MEASURE FOR MEASURE (1604)		Duke	Angelo
1 HENRY IV (revived 1604)		Hal	Hotspur
HAMLET (revived 1604)		Hamlet	Laertes
COMEDY OF ERRORS (revived 1604-05)		Antipholus Syr	Antipholus Eph
LOVE'S LABOUR'S LOST (revived 1604-05)		Berowne	Dumaine
EVERY MAN IN HIS HUMOUR (revival 1604-05)		Thorello(Kitely)	Musco
EVERY MAN OUT OF HIS HUMOUR (revived1604-05)		Brisk	Deliro
MERCHANT OF VENICE (revived 1604-05)		Bassanio	Lorenzo
HENRY V (revived1604-05)		Henry	Dauphin
MERRY WIVES OF WINDSOR (revived 1604-05)		Ford	Caius
MACBETH (1605)		Macbeth	Macduff
MIDSUMMER NIGHT'S DREAM (revived1605)		Oberon	Theseus
TAMBURLAINE (Marlowe) (revived, revised? 1605)		Tamburlaine	Company
KING LEAR (1605-06)		Lear	Albany
YORKSHIRE TRAGEDY (Anon) (1605-06)		Husband	Other play
VOLPONE (Jonson) (1605-06)		Volpone	Mosca
CYMBELINE (first version 1606)		Posthumus	Cloten
DIVIL'S CHARTER (Barnes) (1606)		Pope Alexander	Frescobaldi
ANTONY & CLEOPATRA (1606)		Antony	Enobarbus
MISERIES OF ENFORCED MARRIAGE (Wilkins) (1607))		Ilford	Falconbridge
MERRY DEVIL OF EDMONTON (revised 1607)		Peter Fabell	Brian/Sir Ralph
REVENGER'S TRAGEDY (Middleton?) (1606-07)		Vendice	Lussurioso
TAMING OF THE SHREW (revived, revised? 1607)		Petruchio	Hortensio
TROILUS & CRESSIDA (1607)		Ulysses	Hector
PERICLES (1607-08)		Pericles	Helicanus
RICHARD II (revived 1607-08)		Richard II	York
CORIOLANUS (revised 1608))	Citizen	Menenius	Brutus
ALL'S WELL THAT ENDS WELL (revised 1608))	Lavatch	King of France	Duke/Soldier #

Chart C   239

CONDELL'S BOY #2	COOKE	COWLEY	CROSSE'S BOY	ECCLESTONE
Masquer	Company	Old Athenian	Company	Masquer
Aurelia	Ferneze	Guerino	Macquerelle	Maria
Bianca	Montano	Company	Company	Desdemona
Mariana	Claudio	Elbow	Company	Isabella
Lady Percy	Douglas	Nym	Company	Boy
Ophelia?	Rosencrantz	Guildenstern		Gertrude?
Adriana	Company	Company		Luciana
Katherine	Longaville	Nathaniel		Rosaline
Boy	L. Junior	Mattheo		Biancha
Fallace	Company	Sordido?		Saviolina?
Jessica	Salerio	Old Gobbo/Stephano		Portia
Boy	Company	Nym		Katherine
Quickly	Fenton	Nym		Mrs Ford
Lady Macduff?	Young Siward	Lennox		Lady Macbeth
Hippolyta	Demetrius	Flute		Titania
Boy	Company	Company		Zenocrate
Goneril	Cornwall	Oswald		Regan
Other play	Other play	Other play		Wife
Hermaphrodite?	Peregrine	Judge		Herm?
Queen	Philario	Jailer		Imogen
Boy	Barbarossa	Bernardino		Lucretia
Octavia	Pompey	Eros?		Cleopatra
Katherine	Bartley	Uncle William		Boy
Boy	Frank Jerningham	Sir Richard/Sexton		Boy
Boy	Spurio	Antonio?		Gratiana
Widow	Sly	Gremio		Kate
Cassandra	Achilles	Nestor		Boy
	Leonine/Thaliart	Pandar/Fisher		Marina
	Aumerle	Gardener		Boy
	Aufidius	Citizen		Volumnia?
	Bertram	Steward		Helena?

	EDMANS	GILBURNE	GOUGH
TIMON OF ATHENS (first version 1604)	Company	Boy	Company
MALCONTENT (Marston) (revised 1604)	Company	Boy	Company
OTHELLO (1604)	Company	Emilia	Company
MEASURE FOR MEASURE (1604)	Company	Boy	Company
1 HENRY IV (revived 1604)	Company	Boy	Company
HAMLET (revived 1604)	Company	Boy	Company
COMEDY OF ERRORS (revived 1604-05)	Company	Boy	Company
LOVE'S LABOUR'S LOST (revived 1604-05)	Company	Boy	Company
EVERY MAN IN HIS HUMOUR (revival 1604-05)	Company	Boy	Company
EVERY MAN OUT OF HIS HUMOUR (revived 1604-05)	Company	Boy	Company
MERCHANT OF VENICE (revived 1604-05)	Company	Boy	Company
HENRY V (revived 1604-05)	Company	Boy	Company
MERRY WIVES OF WINDSOR (revived 1604-05)	Company	Boy	Company
MACBETH (1605)	Company	Company	Company
MIDSUMMER NIGHT'S DREAM (revived 1605)	Company	Company	Company
TAMBURLAINE (Marlowe) (revived, revised? 1605)	Company	Company	Company
KING LEAR (1605-06)	Company	France	Company
YORKSHIRE TRAGEDY (Anon) (1605-06)	Company	Company	Other play
VOLPONE (Jonson) (1605-06)	Company	Bonario	Bonario
CYMBELINE (first version 1606)	Company	Company	Company
DIVIL'S CHARTER (Barnes) (1606)	Company	Company	Company
ANTONY & CLEOPATRA (1606)	Company	Dolabella	Company
MISERIES OF ENFORCED MARRIAGE (Wilkins) (1607))	Company	Scarborrow	Company
MERRY DEVIL OF EDMONTON (revised 1607)	Company	Raymond	Company
REVENGER'S TRAGEDY (Middleton?) (1606-07)	Company	Supervacuo	Company
TAMING OF THE SHREW (revived, revised? 1607)	Company	Lucentio	Company
TROILUS & CRESSIDA (1607)	Patroclus	Troilus	Aeneas
PERICLES (1607-08)	Company	Lysimachus	Company
RICHARD II (revived 1607-08)	Company	Bolingbroke	Company
CORIOLANUS (revised 1608))	Company	Coriolanus	Company
ALL'S WELL THAT ENDS WELL (revised 1608))	Lord E	Lord G	Company

Chart C   241

HEMINGES	LOWIN	LOWIN'S BOY	PHILLIPS	RICE
Painter	Senator	Apprenticed	Apemantus	Apprenticed
Pietro	Lowin/Captain	Boy	Billioso	Boy
Lodovico/Duke	Iago	Boy	retired	Boy
Provost	Lucio	Nun		Boy
Henry IV	Mortimer/Archbishop?	Lady Mortimer		Boy
Claudius	Ghost/Player	Player Queen		Boy
Egeon	Dromio Eph	Boy		Boy
Boyet	Armado	Boy		Boy
Lorenzo	Bobadilla	Boy		Boy
Sogliardo	Mascilente/Asper	Boy		Boy
Antonio	Gratiano	Nerissa		Boy
Exeter	Fluellen	Boy		Boy
Page	Evans	William Page		Boy
Ross	Banquo	Fleance	dead	Young Macduff
Egeus/Philostrate	Puck	Hermia		Fairy
Company	Company	Boy		Boy
Kent	Edmund	Boy		Cordelia
Master	Other play	Boy		Son
Corbaccio	Would-Be	Lady Would-Be		Waiting Woman
Lucius	Bellarius	Arviragus		Boy
Lodovico/Caraffa?	Cesare Borgia	Katherine		Boy
Agrippa	Menas	Boy		Iras
Harcop	Butler	John Scarborrow		Clare
Sir Arthur	Sir John (Priest)	Prioress		Millicent
Duke	Hippolito	Castiza		Duchess
Baptista	Vincentio/Lord	Boy		Biondello
Pandarus	Agamemnon	Boy		Cressida
Simonides/Cerimon	Cleon	Dionyza		Thaissa
Gaunt	Mowbray			Duchess Gloucester
Sicinius	Cominius			Boy
Lafew	Parolles			Countess

	E SHAKESPEARE	W SHAKESPEARE
TIMON OF ATHENS (first version 1604)	Company	Poet
MALCONTENT (Marston) (revised 1604)	Company	Celso
OTHELLO (1604)	Company	Brabantio/Gratiano?
MEASURE FOR MEASURE (1604)	Company	Escalus
1 HENRY IV (revived 1604)	Company	Worcester
HAMLET (revised 1604)	Company	Polonius
COMEDY OF ERRORS (revived 1604-05)	Company	Duke Ephesus
LOVE'S LABOUR'S LOST (revived 1604-05)	Company	Holofernes
EVERY MAN IN HIS HUMOUR (revival 1604-05)	Company	Prospero/Wellbred
EVERY MAN OUT OF HIS HUMOUR (revived1604-05)	Company	Puntarvalo
MERCHANT OF VENICE (revived 1604-05)	Company	Shylock
HENRY V (revived1604-05)	Company	Canterbury
MERRY WIVES OF WINDSOR (revived 1604-05)	Company	Shallow
MACBETH (1605)	Company	Duncan
MIDSUMMER NIGHT'S DREAM (revived1605)	Company	Quince
TAMBURLAINE (Marlowe) (revived, revised? 1605)	Company	Company
KING LEAR (1605-06)	Company	Gloucester
YORKSHIRE TRAGEDY (Anon) (1605-06)	Company	Other play
VOLPONE (Jonson) (1605-06)	Company	Voltore
CYMBELINE (first version 1606)	Company	Cymbeline
DIVIL'S CHARTER (Barnes) (1606)	Company	Charles/Baglioni?
ANTONY & CLEOPATRA (1606)	Company	Lepidus
MISERIES OF ENFORCED MARRIAGE (Wilkins) (1607))	Company	
MERRY DEVIL OF EDMONTON (revised 1607)	Company	retired
REVENGER'S TRAGEDY (Middleton?) (1606-07)	Company	
TAMING OF THE SHREW (revived, revised? 1607)	Company	
TROILUS & CRESSIDA (1607)	dead	
PERICLES (1607-08)		
RICHARD II (revived 1607-08)		
CORIOLANUS (revised 1608))		
ALL'S WELL THAT ENDS WELL (revised 1608))		

Chart C   243

SHAKESPEARE'S BOY #2	SINKLO	TOOLEY	SANDS	SLY	FLETCHER
Boy	Company	Company	Masquer	Steward	
Boy	Sinklo	Ferrardo	Bianca	Sly	
Boy	Company	Company		Roderigo	Clown
Boy	Company	Company	Overdone	Froth/Friar Peter	Pompey
Boy	Carrier	Company	Francis	Poins/Vernon	Falstaff
Boy	Company	Fortinbras		Horatio	Gravedigger
Boy	Dr. Pinch	Company	Adriana	Angelo	Dromio Syr
Boy	Company	Company	Princess	Navarre	Costard
Hesperida	Company	Company		Stephano/Stephen	Cob
Puntarvalo's Wife	Company	Company	Saviolina?	Fungoso	Buffone
Boy	Company	Company		Solanio/Duke	Launcelot Gobbo
Boy	Company	Company		Constable	Pistol
Boy	Company	Company	Mrs Page	Slender	Falstaff
Boy	Witch	Company	Company	Malcolm	Porter
Boy	Starveling	Company	Helena	Lysander	Bottom
Boy	Company	Company		Company	Company
Boy	Company	Burgundy?		Edgar	Fool
Boy	Company	Other play	Maid	Servant	Other play
Boy	Company	Company	Castrato?	Corvino	?
Boy	Company	Company	Guiderius	Pisanio	Cloten's Lord
Boy	Apothecary	Astor	Company	Prolog/Guicchiardine?	Devils
Boy	Company	Company	Company	Octavius Caesar	Clown
	Company	Company	Thomas S	Wentloe	Clown
Boy	Company	Suitor	Company	Host	Smug
	Company	Lord	Company	Ambitioso	Dondolo(Clown)
	Tailor	Company	Company	Tranio	Grumio
	Company	Company	Company	Paris	Thersites
	Company	Company	Company	Gower	Boult/Fisher
	Company	Company	Company	Northumberland	Gardener
	Citizen	Company	Company	dead	dead
	Company	Company	Company		

	BIRCH
TIMON OF ATHENS (first version 1604)	
MALCONTENT (Marston) (revised 1604)	
OTHELLO (1604)	Boy
MEASURE FOR MEASURE (1604)	Bawd
1 HENRY IV (revived 1604)	Hostess
HAMLET (revived 1604)	Boy
COMEDY OF ERRORS (revived 1604-05)	Luce
LOVE'S LABOUR'S LOST (revived 1604-05)	Jaquenetta
EVERY MAN IN HIS HUMOUR (revival 1604-05)	Tib
EVERY MAN OUT OF HIS HUMOUR (revived1604-05)	George
MERCHANT OF VENICE (revived 1604-05)	Boy
HENRY V (revived1604-05)	Boy
MERRY WIVES OF WINDSOR (revived 1604-05)	Robin
MACBETH (1605)	Witch
MIDSUMMER NIGHT'S DREAM (revived1605)	Fairy
TAMBURLAINE (Marlowe) (revived, revised? 1605)	Boy
KING LEAR (1605-06)	Boy
YORKSHIRE TRAGEDY (Anon) (1605-06)	Boy
VOLPONE (Jonson) (1605-06)	Dwarf?
CYMBELINE (first version 1606)	Boy
DIVIL'S CHARTER (Barnes) (1606)	Boy
ANTONY & CLEOPATRA (1606)	Charmian
MISERIES OF ENFORCED MARRIAGE (Wilkins) (1607)	Boy
MERRY DEVIL OF EDMONTON (revised 1607)	Company
REVENGER'S TRAGEDY (Middleton?) (1606-07)	Boy
TAMING OF THE SHREW (revived, revised? 1607)	Sly Boy/Servant
TROILUS & CRESSIDA (1607)	Company
PERICLES (1607-08)	Bawd/Fisher Boy
RICHARD II (revived 1607-08)	Gardener
CORIOLANUS (revised 1608))	Citizen
ALL'S WELL THAT ENDS WELL (revised 1608))	Widow

Chart C 245

SLY'S BOY	CONDELL'S BOY #3	MATURE BOY	NOBLE BOY	LOWIN'S BOY #2
Apprenticed				
Boy				
Boy				
Boy				
Boy				
Celia				
Boy	Apprenticed	Apprenticed		
Boy				
Boy				
Boy	Boy	Sister		
Boy	Dorcas?	Boy		
Boy	Boy	Boy		
Bianca	Boy	Boy		
Helen	Andromache	Boy		
Boy	Boy	Diana	Apprenticed	
Boy	Duchess York	Anne	Boy	
Boy	Boy	Valeria	Virgilia	Apprenticed
Diana	Boy	Boy	Boy	Mariana

Chart D
Probable Casting of King's Men Plays, 1610–14

	ARMIN	BURBAGE	CONDELL
MUCEDORUS (revived, revised? 1610)	Mouse	King	Valencia
ALL'S WELL THAT ENDS WELL (revived? 1610)	Lavatch	King of France	Duke/Soldier #1
TROILUS & CRESSIDA (revived? 1610)	Thersites	Ulysses	Hector
TIMON OF ATHENS (revised, revived 1610)	Fool	Timon	Steward
PERICLES (revived 1610)	Boult/Fisher	Pericles	Helicanus
SPANISH TRAGEDY (Kyd) (revived, revised? 1610)	Pedrignano	Hieronymo	Viceroy
ALCHEMIST (Jonson) (1610)	Tribulation	Subtle	Surly
TAMING OF THE SHREW (revived 1611)	Grumio	Petruchio	Hortensio
ALCHEMIST (revived 1611)	Tribulation	Subtle	Surly
TEMPEST (1611)	Caliban	Prospero	Alonso
CYMBELINE (revived 1611)	Cloten's Lord	Iachimo	Pisanio
MISERIES OF ENFORCED MARRIAGE (revived 1611)	Clown	Ilford	Falconbridge
MACBETH (revived 1611)	Porter	Macbeth	Macduff
CATILINE (Jonson) (1611)	?	Cicero	Catiline
WINTER'S TALE (1611)	Autolycus	Leontes	Polixenes
TITUS ANDRONICUS (revived 1611)	Clown	Titus	Saturninus
KING & NO KING (Beaumont & Fletcher) (1611)	?	Arbaces	Mardonius
TWO NOBLE KINSMEN (Shakesepare & Fletcher) (1611)	Doctor/Prolog?	Theseus	Pirithous
SECOND MAIDEN'S TRAGEDY (Middleton)) (1611)	?	Govianus	Tyrant
CAPTAIN (Beaumont & Fletcher) (1612)	Piso	Jacomo	Lodovico
PHILASTER (Beaumont & Fletcher) (revived 1612-13)	?	King	Captain
2ND MAIDEN'S TRAGEDY (revived 1612-13)	?	Govianus	Tyrant
OTHELLO (revived 1613)	?	Othello	Cassio
MERRY WIVES OF WINDSOR (revived 1613)	?	Ford	Caius
1 HENRY IV (revived 1613)	Gadshill?	Hotspur	Westmoreland
MUCH ADO ABOUT NOTHING (revived 1613)	Dogberry	Benedick	Don Pedro
JULIUS CAESAR (revived 1613)	Plebeian	Brutus	Antony
TEMPEST (revived 1613)	Caliban	Prospero	Alonso
WINTER'S TALE (revived 1613)	Autolycus	Leontes	Polixenes
ALCHEMIST (revived 1613)	Tribulation	Subtle	Surly
MERRY DEVIL OF EDMONTON (revived 1613)	Smug	Peter Fabell	Brian/Sir Ralph?
ALL'S WELL THAT ENDS WELL (revived? 1613)	Lavatch	King of France	Duke/Soldier #1
HENRY VIII (first version 1613)	Fool?	Wolsey	Chamberlain
DUCHESS OF MALFI (1614)	retired?	Duke	Cardinal
HENRY VIII (revised Fletcher) (1614)		Wolsey	Chamberlain?

COOKE	COWLEY	ECCLESTONE	EDMANS	GILBURNE	GOUGH
Mucedorus	Rumbelo	Company	Tremelio	Segasto	Company
Bertram	Steward	Company	Lord E	Lord G	Company
Achilles	Nestor	Company	Paris	Troilus	Company
Alcibiades	Second Senator	Company	Painter	Poet	Company
Gower	Pandar/Fisher	Company	Leonine/Thaliart	Lysimachus	Company
Lorenzo	Bazulto	Company	Horatio	Balthazar	Company
Face	Company	Company	Drugger	Dapper	Company
Lucentio	Sly	Company	Company	dead	Company
Face	Company	Kastril	Left company		Company
Antonio	Trinculo	Company			Company
Cloten	Jailer	Company			Company
Wentloe	Uncle William	Company			Company
Malcolm	Lennox	Company			Company
Cato	Company	Company			Company
Gentleman/Lord	Shepherd	Company			Company
Lucius	Company	Company			Company
Tigranes	Lygones	left company			Company
Arcite	Jailer's Brother				Company
Votarius	Sophonirus				Memphonius
Angelo	Host				Company
Cleremont	Citizen/Countryman				Company
Bellarius	Sophonirus				Memphonius
Duke	Gratiano				Company
Evans	Shallow				Company
Mortimer/Blunt	Worcester				Company
Don John	Verges				Company
Cassius	Plebeian				Company
Antonio	Trinculo				Company
Gentleman/Lord	Shepherd				Company
Face	Company			dead	Company
Raymond	Sir Richard/Sexton				Company
Bertram	Steward				Company
Buckingham	Commoner				Company
dead	retired	rejoined company			Company
					Company

	HEMINGES	LOWIN	RICE
MUCEDORUS (revived, revised? 1610)	Anselmo	Bremo	Boy
ALL'S WELL THAT ENDS WELL (revived? 1610)	Lafew	Parolles	Countess
TROILUS & CRESSIDA (revived? 1610)	Pandarus	Agamemnon	Cressida
TIMON OF ATHENS (revised, revived 1610)	First Senator	Apemantus	Boy
PERICLES (revived 1610)	Simonides/Cerimon	Cleon	Thaissa
SPANISH TRAGEDY (Kyd) (revived, revised? 1610)	Spain	Ghost	Boy
ALCHEMIST (Jonson) (1610)	Lovewit	Epicure Mammon	Boy
TAMING OF THE SHREW (revived 1611)	Baptista	Vincentio/Lord	Biondello
ALCHEMIST (revived 1611)	Lovewit	Epicure Mammon	Company
TEMPEST (1611)	Gonzalo	Stephano	Company
CYMBELINE (revived 1611)	Cymbeline	Bellarius	Company
MISERIES OF ENFORCED MARRIAGE (revived 1611)	Harcop	Butler	Company
MACBETH (revived 1611)	Duncan	Banquo	Company
CATILINE (Jonson) (1611)	Petreius	Caesar	Company
WINTER'S TALE (1611)	Antigonus	Camillo	Company
TITUS ANDRONICUS (revived 1611)	Marcus	Aaron	left compan
KING & NO KING (Beaumont & Fletcher) (1611)	Gobrias	Bessus	
TWO NOBLE KINSMEN (Shakesepare & Fletcher) (1611)	Schoolmaster	Jailer	
SECOND MAIDEN'S TRAGEDY (Middleton)) (1611)	Helvetius	Anselmus	
CAPTAIN (Beaumont & Fletcher) (1612)	Father	Fabritio	
PHILASTER (Beaumont & Fletcher) (revived 1612-13)	Dion	Pharamond	
2ND MAIDEN'S TRAGEDY (revived 1612-13)	Helvetius	Anselmus	
OTHELLO (revived 1613)	Brabantio	Iago	
MERRY WIVES OF WINDSOR (revived 1613)	Mr. Page	Falstaff	
1 HENRY IV (revived 1613)	Henry IV	Falstaff	
MUCH ADO ABOUT NOTHING (revived 1613)	Leonato	Boracchio	
JULIUS CAESAR (revived 1613)	Messala/Decius	Caesar	
TEMPEST (revived 1613)	Gonzalo	Stephano	
WINTER'S TALE (revived 1613)	Antigonus	Camillo	
ALCHEMIST (revived 1613)	Lovewit	Epicure Mammon	
MERRY DEVIL OF EDMONTON (revived 1613)	Sir Arthur	Sir John (Priest)	
ALL'S WELL THAT ENDS WELL (revived? 1613)	Lafew	Parolles	
HENRY VIII (first version 1613)	Norfolk	Henry VIII	
DUCHESS OF MALFI (1614)	Forobosco	Bosola	rejoined co
HENRY VIII (revised Fletcher) (1614)	Norfolk	Henry VIII	

SINKLO	TOOLEY	SANDS	BIRCH	SLY'S BOY	CONDELL'S BOY #3	MATURE BOY
Company	Company	Company	Boy	Amandine	Boy	Boy
Company	Company	Company	Widow	Helena?	Boy	Helena?
Company	Company	Diomedes	Company	Helen	Andromache	Cassandra?
Company	Lord	Lucullus	Flaminius	Masque	Masque	Boy
Company	Company	Company	Bawd/Fisher Boy	Boy	Boy	Diana
Company	Alexandro	Company	Company	Page	Boy	Isabella
Company	Ananias	Company	Company	Boy	Dame Pliant	Doll
Tailor	Company	Company	Sly Boy	Boy	Widow	Kate
	Ananias	Company	Company	Boy	Dame Pliant	Doll
	Francisco	Company	Masque	Masque	Masque	Ariel
	Philario	Guiderius	Company	Queen	Boy	Imogen
	Company	Company	John S	Boy	Katherine	Boy
	Company	Company	Witch?	Witch?	Lady Macduff	Lady Macbeth
	Company	Company	Company	Boy	Aurelia	Sempronia
	Company		Clown	Boy	Boy	Paulina
	Company		Company	Boy	Tamora	Boy
	Company		Philip	Spaconia	Boy	Boy
	Company		Jailer's Daughter	Boy	Queen #1	Hippolita
	Company		Company	Boy	Boy	Boy
	Company		Company	Lelia	Boy	Boy
	Company		Company	Lady	Boy	Bellario
	Company		Company	Leonella	Boy	Boy
	Company		Company	Boy	Bianca	Emilia
	Company		Company	Boy	Quickly	Mrs. Page?
	Peto		Carrier/Servant	Boy	Boy	Boy
	Company		Company	Boy	Boy	Beatrice?
	Company		Company	Boy	Boy	Plebeian
			Masque	Boy	Boy	Ariel
	Company		Clown	Boy	Boy	Paulina
	Ananias		Doll Common	Boy	Dame Pliant	Doll
	Suitor		Company	Boy	Dorcas	
	Company		Widow	Diana	Boy	
	Company		Company		Boy	
	Madman		Madman		Julia	
	Buckingham		Company		Boy	

	NOBLE BOY	LOWIN'S BOY #2	ROBINSON
MUCEDORUS (revived, revised? 1610)	Boy	Ariena	
ALL'S WELL THAT ENDS WELL (revived? 1610)	Boy	Mariana	Apprenticed
TROILUS & CRESSIDA (revived? 1610)	Boy	Cassandra?	Boy
TIMON OF ATHENS (revised, revived 1610)	Masque	Masque	Masque
PERICLES (revived 1610)	Marina	Dionyza	Daughter?
SPANISH TRAGEDY (Kyd) (revived, revised? 1610)	Bel-Imperia?	Boy	Boy
ALCHEMIST (Jonson) (1610)	Boy	Boy	Boy
TAMING OF THE SHREW (revived 1611)	Boy	Boy	Boy
ALCHEMIST (revived 1611)	Boy	Boy	Boy
TEMPEST (1611)	Boy	Masque	Masque
CYMBELINE (revived 1611)	Boy	Arviragus	Lady Helen
MISERIES OF ENFORCED MARRIAGE (revived 1611)	Boy	Thomas S	Sister
MACBETH (revived 1611)	Witch	Fleance	Witch?
CATILINE (Jonson) (1611)	Fulvia	Boy	Galla
WINTER'S TALE (1611)	Hermione	Boy	Mamilius
TITUS ANDRONICUS (revived 1611)	Lavinia	Boy	Boy
KING & NO KING (Beaumont & Fletcher) (1611)	Panthea	Boy	Arane
TWO NOBLE KINSMEN (Shakesepare & Fletcher) (1611)	Emilia	Boy	Queen #2
SECOND MAIDEN'S TRAGEDY (Middleton)) (1611)	Lady	Boy	Lady's Ghost
CAPTAIN (Beaumont & Fletcher) (1612)	Frank	Boy	Clora
PHILASTER (Beaumont & Fletcher) (revived 1612-13)	Boy	Megra	Galatea
2ND MAIDEN'S TRAGEDY (revived 1612-13)	Lady	Boy	Ghost
OTHELLO (revived 1613)	Desdemona	Boy	Boy
MERRY WIVES OF WINDSOR (revived 1613)	Mrs. Ford	Mrs. Page?	Boy
1 HENRY IV (revived 1613)	Boy	Hostess	Lady Percy
MUCH ADO ABOUT NOTHING (revived 1613)	Boy	Margaret	Ursula
JULIUS CAESAR (revived 1613)	Portia	Calpurnia	Lucius
TEMPEST (revived 1613)	Masque	Masque	Boy
WINTER'S TALE (revived 1613)	Hermione	Masque	Mamilius
ALCHEMIST (revived 1613)	Boy	Boy	Boy
MERRY DEVIL OF EDMONTON (revived 1613)	Millicent	Prioress	Boy
ALL'S WELL THAT ENDS WELL (revived? 1613)	Helena	Mariana	Boy
HENRY VIII (first version 1613)	Katherine		Anne Bulleyn
DUCHESS OF MALFI (1614)	Boy		Boy
HENRY VIII (revised Fletcher) (1614)	Katherine		Anne Bulleyn

HEMINGES' BOY #4	CONDELL'S BOY #4	OSTLER	OSTLER'S BOY	UNDERWOOD	SHANK	POLLARD
Apprenticed	Apprenticed					
Boy	Boy					
Masque	Masque					
Boy	Boy					
Boy	Boy					
Boy	Boy					
Boy	Boy	Tranio	Bianca	Gremio		
Boy	Boy	Drugger		Dapper		
Masque	Masque	Ferdinand	Miranda	Adrian		
Boy	Boy	Posthumus		Philario		
Boy	Boy	Scarborrow	Clare	Bartley		
Macduff boy?	Boy	Malcolm		Lennox		
Boy	Lady	Cethegus		Curius		
Mopsa	Dorcas	Florizel	Perdita	Lord/Gentleman		
Boy	Boy	Demetrius		Chiron		
Dula	Boy	Bacurius		Gentleman, etc		
Dancer	Queen #3/Dancer	Palamon	Dancer	Wooer		
Boy	Boy	Bellarius	Leonella	Soldier #1		
Boy	Boy	Julio	Lelia's Woman	Frederick		
Boy	Boy	Philaster	Arethusa	Company		
Boy	Boy	Votarius	Wife	Soldier #1		
Boy	Boy	Roderigo		Montano		
Boy	Boy	Slender	Anne	Fenton		
Boy	Boy	Hal		Poins		
Boy	Boy	Claudio	Hero	Conrade		
Boy	Boy	Casca/Titinnius		Octavius		
Boy	Boy	Ferdinand	Miranda	Adrian		
Mopsa	Dorcas	Florizel	Perdita	Lord/Gentleman		
Boy	Boy	Drugger		Dapper		
Boy	Boy	Frank		Brother		
Countess	Boy	Lord G		Lord E		
Old Lady	Boy	Suffolk		Campeius/Lord		
Cariola	Julia	Antonio	Duchess	Delio		
Old Lady	Boy	Suffolk		Lovell	Porter	Boy

Chart E
Acting Company Shares

1594	1597-98	1600	1603-04	1607-08	1611	1613-14
Burbage						
Heminges						
Shakespeare				Gilburne	Ostler	Taylor
Phillips			Lowin			
Condell						
Kemp		Armin	Cooke	Cooke		Tooley
						Gough
Bryan	Sly		Sly	Edmans	Underwood	
	Crosse	Crosse	Fletcher	Armin		Shank
Pope		Cowley				Ecclestone
						Benfield

252

Chart F
Globe Partnership Shares

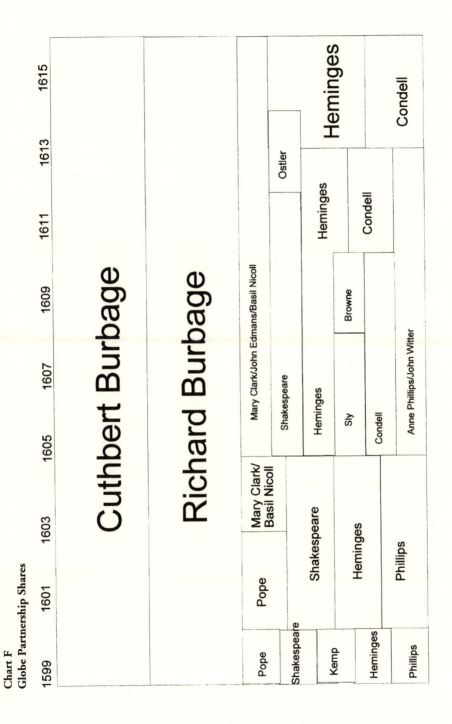

1599 · 1601 · 1603 · 1605 · 1607 · 1609 · 1611 · 1613 · 1615

Cuthbert Burbage

Richard Burbage

Pope | Pope | Mary Clark/Basil Nicoll | Mary Clark/John Edmans/Basil Nicoll

Shakespeare | Shakespeare | Shakespeare

Kemp | Hemings | Hemings | Hemings | Ostler

Heminges | | | Hemings | **Heminges**

Phillips | Phillips | Sly | Browne

| | Condell | Condell | **Condell**

Phillips | Anne Phillips/John Witter

253

Notes

Unless otherwise noted, actors' biographical information is drawn from E. K. Chambers, *The Elizabethan Stage*, 4 vols. (Oxford: Clarendon, 1923), II; Edwin Nungezer, *A Dictionary of Actors and of Other Persons Associated with the Public Representation of Plays in England before 1642* (New Haven: Yale University, 1929); and Gerald Eades Bentley, *The Jacobean and Caroline Stage*, 7 vols. (Oxford: Oxford University, 1941–68), II. Datings for all registrations and printings of plays and of court performances are from Chambers, *Elizabethan Stage*, III–IV. Line counts and percentages for Shakespeare's plays are based primarily on figures in Martin Spevack, *A Complete and Systematic Concordance to the Works of Shakespeare* (Hildesheim: Georg Olms, 1968–70), which is based on the Riverside Edition, with additional reference to T. J. King, *Casting Shakespeare's Plays: London Actors and Their Roles, 1590–1642* (Cambridge: Cambridge University, 1992), which counts the First Folio and significant quarto editions; for all other playwrights, the counts are the author's own. The citation of (edn) indicates the cited editor's edition of the play under discussion, more fully listed in the bibliography. Folio indicates Shakespeare's First Folio in the edition indicated in the bibliography.

INTRODUCTION

1. T. W. Baldwin, *The Organization and Personnel of the Shakespearean Company* (Princeton, NJ: Princeton University, 1927).

CHAPTER 1: PROLOGUE

1. David Bradley, *From Text to Performance in the Elizabethan Theatre: Preparing the Play for the Stage* (Cambridge: Cambridge University, 1994), 50; in his chart of all surviving plays (230–43), the earliest to require more than eight men is *The Famous Victories*, 1586, which

requires an absolute minimum of twelve adults; it is known to have been played by the Queen's Men, which had twelve Sharers. After that date, almost all surviving plays require at least twelve men, usually sixteen or more, and the exceptions all have first performance dates of 1590 or earlier.

2. The patent issued May 6, 1593, listed "Edward Allen, servaunt to the right honourable the Lord Highe Admiral, William Kemp, Thomas Pope, John Heminges, Augustine Phillips, and George Bryan" (Chambers, *Elizabethan Stage*, II, 123).

3. W. W. Greg, *Henslowe's Diary*, 2 vols (London: Bullen, 1904–08), II, 126–27; Gerald Eades Bentley, *The Profession of Dramatist in Shakespeare's Time, 1590–1642* (Princeton, NJ: Princeton University, 1986), 88–110.

4. Gerald Eades Bentley, *The Profession of Player in Shakespeare's Time, 1590–1642* (Princeton, NJ: Princeton University, 1984), 64–70.

5. Greg, *Henslowe's Diary*, I, 16–17.

6. John Singer of the Admiral's Men was also so designated, but he could trace his roots back to the old Queen's Men and may have simply claimed the honor for the remainder of his life.

7. Baldwin, *Organization and Personnel*, 233–36, argues that Pope played Falstaff, inventing a temporary absence for Kemp for which there is no other evidence.

8. This plot is much discussed in the standard sources; particularly valuable among newer works are Bradley, *From Text to Performance*, 98–105, and King, *Casting Shakespeare's Plays*, 29–30, 97, 259.

9. Robert Greene, *Groats-Worth of Witte, bought with a million of Repentance*. Ed. G. B. Harrison (London: Bodley Head, 1926. Reprinted New York: Barnes & Noble, 1966), 45–416.

10. Chamber Accounts, in Chambers, *Elizabethan Stage*, IV, 164.

11. The dating of most of these are discussed later, when the individual works enter the repertory of the Chamberlain's Men. For *Arden*, cf. Wine (edn), xliii–xlv; for *Ironside*, cf. Sams (edn), 9–40, or E. B. Everitt, *Six Early Plays Related to the Shakespeare Canon* (Copenhagen: Rosenkilde & Bagger, 1965), 103.

12. Cf. Charles Nicholl, *The Reckoning: The Murder of Christopher Marlowe* (Chicago: University of Chicago, 1992).

13. Cf. charts in Bradley, *From Text to Performance*, 232–39. Exceptions are discussed in the text.

14. W. W. Greg, *The Henslowe Papers* (London: Bullen, 1907), 120; *Henslowe's Diary*, I, 29.

15. The most detailed single modern analysis of typical acting company organization is Bentley, *Profession of Player*. Cf. also Baldwin, *Organization and Personnel*, and Andrew Gurr, *The Shakespearean Stage, 1574–1642*, 3rd ed. (Cambridge: Cambridge University, 1994), 67–118.

16. Bentley, *Profession of Player*, 113–26.

17. King, *Casting Shakespeare's Plays*, 28–36, 117–25.

18. The evidence on this is most confusing, for Trigg swore in court that he had been apprenticed on December 20, 1626, when he was probably about fourteen (Bentley, *Profession of Player*, 122), but his name is in the cast list for a small woman's role in Massinger's *The Roman Actor*, licensed for performance two months earlier, on October 11, 1626 (King, *Casting Shakespeare's Plays*, 53–54).

19. Greg, *Henslowe's Diary*, I, 73.

20. Much quoted and extracted in all the literature, the spellings here are from Chambers, *Elizabethan Stage*, IV, 246.

21. Bentley, *Profession of Dramatist*, 62–79.

22. Greg, *Henslowe Papers*, 52–55; 113–22.

CHAPTER 2: FROM CROSS KEYS TO THE THEATRE, 1594–97

1. Greg, *Henslowe's Diary*, I, 17.

2. Letter to the Lord Mayor, Chambers, *Elizabethan Stage*, IV, 316.

3. E. K. Chambers, *William Shakespeare: A Study of Facts and Problems*. 2 vols. (Oxford: Oxford University, 1930), I, 310; Sidney Thomas, "The Date of *The Comedy of Errors*," *Shakespeare Quarterly*, VII (1956), 377–84; Stanley Wells and Gary Taylor, *William Shakespeare: A Textual Companion* (Oxford: Clarendon, 1987), 117–18; Leeds Barroll, *Politics, Plague, and Shakespeare's Theater: The Stuart Years* (Ithaca, NY: Cornell University, 1991), 202.

4. Chambers, *William Shakespeare*, I, 331; James G. McManaway, "Recent Studies in Shakespeare's Chronology," *Shakespeare Survey 3* (1950), 25; Peter Levi, *The Life and Times of William Shakespeare* (New York: Holt, 1991), 124–25; Foakes (edn), xxvi–xxxv; Wells and Taylor, *Textual Companion*, 109; E. A. J. Honigmann, *Shakespeare: The Lost Years* (Manchester: Manchester University, 1985), 128.

5. "To the great Variety of Readers" and the Principall Actors page in Folio.

6. Greg, *Henslowe's Diary*, I, 17.

7. Richard Simpson (ed.), *The School of Shakespeare*, 2 vols. (London: Chatto & Windus, 1878), I, 356–58; II, 12.

8. Robert Greene, "Preface," *Menaphon*, and Thomas Lodge, *Wit's Misery*, both quoted in Jenkins (edn), 83.

9. Theories of the dating for *Taming of the Shrew* are discussed in chapter 3, note 36.

10. Everitt, *Six Early Plays*, 7, 252; A. R. Braunmuller and Michael Hattaway (eds), *The Cambridge Companion to English Renaissance Drama* (Cambridge: Cambridge University, 1995), 425, list it as "Anon"; Ure (edn), xxxix.

11. Gooch (edn), 8–10, 32–34.

12. Henslowe's journals are sadly lacking in this information; the early sections record play performances, but no payments to writers; once he begins to record payments, he stops listing performance dates. Thus, he does not tell us how far in advance of performance the actors actually commissioned a new play.

13. Brooks (edn), xxxiv–xxxix; Holland (edn), 110; Foakes (edn), 1; Wells and Taylor, *Textual Companion*, 118–19; Chambers, *William Shakespeare*, I, 358–60; Levi, *Life and Times*, 135; Sir Sidney Lee, *A Life of William Shakespeare* (New York: Macmillan, 1931, Reprinted New York: Dover, 1968), 231–32.

14. Cf. Wells and Taylor, *Complete Works*, 332; *Textual Companion*, 286; Brooks (edn), 126. In performances, I have never heard this speech sung.

15. Cairncross (edn), *II*, xlvi–xlvii.

16. King, *Casting Shakespeare's Plays*, Tables 31 and 32.

17. Wells and Taylor, *Textual Companion*, 137.

18. Lapides (edn), 37.

19. Chambers, *Elizabethan Stage*, IV, 9–10; Lapides (edn), 31; Wells and Taylor, *Textual Companion*, 136–37.

20. Barroll, *Politics, Plague*, 231–32.

21. Chambers, *Elizabethan Stage*, IV, 318.

22. R. A. Foakes and R. T. Rickert (eds.), *Henslowe's Diary, with Supplementary Material, Introduction, and Notes* (Cambridge: Cambridge University, 1961), 93.

23. For several of the actors, parish records have been found of the baptism of their children in London, which usually occurred within less than a week of birth. Although not all gestation periods are precisely nine months, this does provide a probable time in which we can establish the presence of the husband in London. Likewise, we cannot guarantee that all the wives were absolutely faithful, but must work under the assumption that they were, or at the very least that any illegitimate pregnancies were begun in such circumstances that the husband might plausibly think the child was his, again establishing his presence in London roughly nine months before the baptism. This, in turn, can indicate times when the actors were definitely not on tour. These, and all succeeding, children's baptismal dates are from Chambers, *Elizabethan Stage*, II.

24. Ure (edn), xliii; Wells and Taylor, *Textual Companion*, 117–18; Ian Wilson, *Shakespeare: The Evidence* (New York: St. Martin's, 1999), 200–01; Chambers, *William Shakespeare*, I, 351–55; *Elizabethan Stage*, IV, 385.

25. Chambers, *William Shakespeare*, I, 354.

26. Letter of Jacques Peti, in Gamini Salgado, *Eyewitnesses of Shakespeare: First Hand Accounts of Performances 1590–1890* (New York: Barnes & Noble, 1975), 16–17.

27. Longleat manuscript; the picture is reproduced in almost all editions of *Titus Andronicus* and studies of Shakespearean staging or biography too numerous to list. The attribution of the manuscript to Henry Peachum is all but universally identified as another of Collier's forgeries. Charles Hamilton, *In Search of Shakespeare: A Reconnaissance into the Poet's Life and Handwriting* (San Diego: Harcourt Brace, 1985), 147–60, argues the date is a forgery as well, leading him to conclude that the manuscript is actually a costume sketch for the original production. This interpretation seems most unlikely, for a drawing made for such a purpose would clearly identify each figure. If such designs were common, we should surely have had at least one example in the extensive surviving papers of Edward Alleyn. The private dinner makes clear there was a company production of the play in 1595–96, which makes the date of the drawing at least plausibly from the same season.

28. Charles Edelman, *Brawl Ridiculous: Sword Fighting in Shakespeare's Plays* (Manchester: Manchester University, 1992), 31.

29. Gibbons (edn), 31; Wells and Taylor, *Textual Companion*, 118, and Chambers, *William Shakespeare*, 345, both favor early 1595, before *A Midsummer Night's Dream*, which for reasons of practicality discussed under *Dream* I find unlikely. Cf. also Levi, *Life and Times*, 151–52. Lee, *A Life*, 111–12, argued for 1591–92, but he has had few followers.

30. Arthur Brooke, *The Tragicall Historye of Romeus and Juliet*, (l. 697), in Geoffrey Bullough, *Narrative and Dramatic Sources of Shakespeare* (London: Routledge, 1957), I, 304.

31. William Kemp, *Kemp's Nine Daies Wonder*, ed. G. B. Harrison (London: Bodley Head, 1926), 1.

32. Chambers, *William Shakespeare*, I, 367; Wells & Taylor, *Textual Companion*, 119; Peter Alexander, *Shakespeare's Life and Art* (New York: NYU, 1964), 85; Braunmuller (edn), 2–15. Honigmann (edn), xlv–lviii. Levi, *Life and Times*, 162–63, dates it even later, in late 1596.

33. Letter of Johann de Witt, translation in S. Schoenbaum, *William Shakespeare: A Compact Documentary Life* (Oxford: Oxford University, 1978), 138–39.

34. Fleay argued from versification that it was Shakespeare's first play: cf. chart in Oscar

James Campbell and Edward G. Quinn, *The Reader's Encyclopedia of Shakespeare* (New York: MJF, 1997), 932; T. W. Baldwin, *Shakspere's Five-Act Structure: Shakspere's Early Plays on the Background of Renaissance Theories of Five-Act Structure from 1470* (Urbana: University of Illinois, 1963), 626–64, and Lee, *A Life*, 102–03, agreed but on different grounds. David (edn), for example, dates it in the summer of 1593 (xxviii), revised in 1597. Hibbard (edn), 45, opts for 1594–95, while Wells and Taylor, *Textual Companion*, 117, and Chambers, *William Shakespeare*, 335, cite 1595–96.

35. Cf. charts of the measurements of various scholars in Campbell and Quinn, *Reader's Encyclopedia*, 932; Wells and Taylor, *Textual Companion*, 112–13.

36. Edelman, *Brawl Ridiculous*, 56–57.

37. Chambers, *Elizabethan Stage*, IV, 319; Greg, *Henslowe's Diary*, II, 329; John Tucker Murray, *English Dramatic Companies, 1558–1642* (Boston: Houghton Mifflin, 1910), I, 109.

38. Chambers, *Elizabethan Stage*, IV, 319–20.

39. Foakes and Rickert, *Henslowe's Diary*, 94–98.

40. Hammond (edn), 61; Chambers, *William Shakespeare*, I, 270; Wells and Taylor *Textual Companion*, 115–16.

41. Cf. Chambers, *William Shakespeare*, I, 281–85; Wells and Taylor, *Textual Companion*, 197–99; Cairncross (edn), III, xv–xl; Hattaway (edn), I, 41.

42. Brown (edn), xxv–xxvii; Halio (edn), 27–29; Wells and Taylor, *Textual Companion*, 117–8.

43. The story is translated in full in Brown (edn), 140–153.

44. Schoenbaum, *Compact Documentary Life*, 232–237.

CHAPTER 3: THE CRISIS YEARS, 1597–98

1. Schoenbaum, *Compact Documentary Life*, 206–07.

2. Cf. for example, Baldwin, *Organization and Personnel*, 241, who in order to exclude Kemp from the role invents "one of his foreign jaunts" to explain his absence. David Wiles, *Shakespeare's Clown: Actor and Text in the Elizabethan Playhouse* (Cambridge: Cambridge University, 1987) feels it necessary to devote a full chapter, 116–35, to a demonstration that Kemp played the role.

3. Richard Hosley (ed.), *Shakespeare's Holinshed* (New York: Putnam, 1968), 98–142.

4. Richard James to Sir Harry Bourchier, Chambers, *William Shakespeare*, II, 241–42.

5. *Shakespeare versus Shallow* (Boston: Little, Brown, 1931), 114–121.

6. Bevington (edn), *H4*, 9, and Weis (edn), *H4*, 15, both accept Hotson and argue *1 Henry IV* was written late in 1596; Craik (edn), *MW*, 1–12, accepts Hotson's date, and Oliver (edn), *MW*, liii–lviii, recognizes some of the problems but nevertheless accepts Hotson and argues that Shakespeare actually interrupted the composition of *2 Henry IV* to write *Merry Wives*. Wells and Taylor, *Textual Companion*, 120, consider Hotson still "conjectural" and date *Merry Wives* during the winter of 1597–98, in order to leave room for both Henry IV plays.

7. Leslie Hotson, *Shakespeare's Sonnets Dated and Other Essays* (New York: Oxford University, 1949), 37–43, offers *Troilus and Cressida*; Chambers, *William Shakespeare*, I, 273, suggested *Taming of the Shrew*, finally discredited by T. W. Baldwin, *Shakspere's "Love's Labor's Won": New Evidence from the Account Books of an Elizabethan Bookseller* (Carbondale: Southern Illinois, 1957); Robert Fleisner, "*Love's Labour's Won* and the Occasion of *Much Ado*" (*Shakespeare Survey* XXVII, 1974), revives old arguments favoring *Much Ado*; and Lee, *A Life*, 233–34, offers *All's Well That Ends Well*.

8. Oldys noted the anecdote, crediting the story to one of Shakespeare's brothers after the Restoration; Capell in 1779 retailed the story in almost the same words, credited to an anonymous old relative. Unfortunately, as Schoenbaum points out (*Compact Documentary Life*, 201–02), none of the brothers survived into the Restoration, nor would have any more distant relations who had been adults during Shakespeare's performing career. By the time Oldys noted the story, it would have been in its fourth or fifth generation, assuming it had not been invented in a coffeehouse that week.

9. The only editors I have found to even suggest this connection are Knowles and Mattern (edn), who consider that *Love's Labour's Lost* may have been a source for *As You Like It* but make no further connection with *Won*.

10. The most detailed and sophisticated modern explication is Wiles, *Shakespeare's Clown*; cf. esp. 61–72.

11. Chambers, *Elizabethan Stage*, II, 131.

12. Greg, *Henslowe's Diary*, I, 54.

13. Chambers, *Elizabethan Stage*, IV, 322–23.

14. Chambers, *Elizabethan Stage*, II, 132–34.

15. Greg, *Henslowe's Diary*, II, 100.

16. G. L. Hosking, *The Life and Times of Edward Alleyn* (London: Jonathan Cape, 1952. Reprint, New York: AMS, 1970), 97.

17. Cf. chart in Braunmuller and Hattaway, *Cambridge Companion*, 426–34.

18. Campbell and Quinn, *Reader's Encyclopedia*, 13; Chambers, *Elizabethan Stage*, II, 382–83; Foakes and Rickert, *Henslowe's Diary*, charts pp. 98–100.

19. Murray, *English Dramatic Companies*, I, 109.

20. Ure (edn), xv.

21. Gibbons (edn), 3.

22. Greg, *Henslowe's Diary*, I, 82; II, 287.

23. Cf. for example, Greg, *Henslowe's Diary*, I, 54, 68.

24. *Scourge of Villainie*, 1598, in Chambers, *William Shakespeare*, II, 195–96.

25. Humphreys (edn), lxviii; Wells and Taylor, *Textual Companion*, 351.

26. Nathan Field was still making them in *Amends for Ladies*, a play printed in 1618 and generally dated 1611.

27. Hotson, *Shakespeare's Sonnets Dated*, 148

28. *An Apology for Actors*, extract in Chambers, *Elizabethan Stage*, IV, 252.

29. Murray, *English Dramatic Companies*, I, 14

30. Greg, *Henslowe's Diary*, II, 100.

31. Bentley, *Profession of Player*, 36–38.

32. "Articles of [ ]uance Against M[ ] Hinchlowe" in Chambers, *Elizabethan Stage*, II, 249.

33. It seems unlikely the Anglicized version was made for Jonson's folio in 1615–16, simply because it would have been unnecessary; although it makes sense to change the setting for a stage production intended for a London audience, it provides little or nothing for a reading audience and is hardly worth the effort. Chambers, *Elizabethan Stage*, III, 360, and Lever (edn), xi–xii, argue the revision was made for the revival played at court in 1605. This seems unlikely for a simple reason: The revisions make the play longer, a most implausible modification for King James, whose predilection for short works was so well known that it is often used as an argument that *Macbeth*, for example, was actually written for a court performance. Similarly, the additions not directly related to name and place are of a kind most difficult for actors to deal with, mostly small modifications within existing speeches that many of the actors already had memorized, particularly for Bobadilla but occurring to varying extent among

nearly all the characters. What seems far more likely is that the English setting was the original. Fearing political repercussions after *The Isle of Dogs*, Jonson changed the setting before sending it to the censor, at the same time making a large number of small cuts to make the play a bit less speechy. This version was learned by the actors and published in his quarto. For his folio, he simply restored his original, although he carefully excised all the oaths and religious allusions that might disturb James I, who by 1616 had become a personal patron of Jonson. (The one datable reference in the folio is to the seige of Strigonium, but Bobadilla is a braggart and a liar, so that may have been merely a late, minor modification to make his lie more obvious.)

34. Letter from Tobie Matthew to Dudley Carleton, in David Riggs, *Ben Jonson: A Life* (Cambridge, MA: Harvard University, 1989), 45.

35. For a discussion of this, see Humphreys (edn), 14–21.

36. Morris (edn), 65, says 1589; Wells and Taylor, *Textual Companion*, 109–11, favor 1590–91; Thompson (edn), 3, opts for 1592; Wilson, *The Evidence*, 169–70, places it as originally a private play for Lord Strange in 1593–94, and Chambers, *William Shakespeare*, I, 270, chose 1594. Russell Fraser, *Young Shakespeare* (New York: Columbia University, 1988) and *Shakespeare: The Later Years* (New York: Columbia University, 1992) ignores it in both volumes.

37. Oliver (edn), 10–13, details a number of these, which he identifies as "signs of change of mind."

38. The earliest recorded excision of Christopher Sly was in 1667, when John Lacy changed Grumio to the play's principal character and a Scotsman; Garrick restored Petruchio and Kate to the center, but again left out Sly, and his version held the stage for more than a century, with very rare exceptions, and of course Franco Zefferelli eliminated Sly from the extremely popular film version (Kenneth McClellan, *Whatever Happened to Shakespeare?* (New York: Barnes & Noble, 1978), 38, 72).

39. Schoenbaum, *Compact Documentary Life*, 207.

40. Schoenbaum, *Compact Documentary Life*, 198–99.

41. February 19, 1598, in Chambers, *Elizabethan Stage*, IV, 325.

42. Chambers, *Elizabethan Stage*, II, 365.

43. Chambers, *Elizabethan Stage*, II, 127.

44. Schoenbaum, *Compact Documentary Life*, 208.

45. C. W. Wallace, "The First London Theatre: Materials for a History," *Nebraska University Studies*, xiii (1913), 275–76.

CHAPTER 4: THE GLOBE AND KEMP'S EXIT, 1599–1600

1. Author's figures drawn from charts in Foakes and Rickert, *Henslowe's Diary*, 85–100. Expenses are computed on the assumption of regular maintenance costs of 100 pounds (less than the 120 per year indicated in Henslowe's later Fortune records), plus the 105 pounds known to have been spent on remodeling the Rose.

2. Chambers, *Elizabethan Stage*, II, 417.

3. Schoenbaum, *Compact Documentary Life*, 210.

4. Chambers, *Elizabethan Stage*, II, 417.

5. Walter (edn), xxxv.

6. Schoenbaum, *Compact Documentary Life*, 209. Even this is a disputed point in Shakespearean studies: Campbell and Quinn, *Reader's Encyclopedia*, 82–83, for example, identify this not as the Globe but as a house in which Shakespeare lived.

7. Chambers, *Elizabethan Stage*, II, 436–40; John Orrell, "Designing the Globe," *Shakespeare's Globe Rebuilt*, ed. J. R. Mulryne and Margaret Shewring (Cambridge: Cambridge University, 1997), 56.

8. *Shakespeare's Mystery Play, The Opening of the Globe Theatre, 1599* (Manchester: Manchester University, 1999).

9. Gurr (edn), 1, argues that Shakespeare "wrote the draft . . . in the early summer of 1599," which would make the production later; however, it seems far more plausible that the play was written earlier, with the Prologue/Chorus a last minute addition used only on a special occasion.

10. Walter (edn), xxxiv–v; Wells and Taylor, *Textual Companion*, 375.

11. Cf. Walter (edn), xxxiv–xxxix, for a detailed discussion.

12. Cannon (edn), 43–48.

13. Cf. Chambers, *Elizabethan Stage*, II, 203; Campbell and Quinn, *Reader's Encyclopedia*, 420; Gurr, *Shakespearean Stage*, 88; Wiles, *Shakespeare's Clowns*, 35–6.

14. Translation in Chambers, *Elizabethan Stage*, II, 365. Platter's summary of the Curtain play describes a clown servant who got drunk and threw a shoe at his master. The significant point is that the Curtain company still had a clown, used significantly; Armin was still known as the Clown of the Curtain in 1600, so he must have been the clown there in September 1599 as well and thus cannot have also been dancing the jig at the Globe.

15. Armin, *Collected Works*, I, title pages.

16. This very brief summary is based on the detailed, extensive analysis of Wiles, *Shakespeare's Clowns*.

17. Riggs, *Ben Jonson*, 53–57.

18. In the epilogue, the actor playing Macilente states that he had also played Asper, seen only in the prologue, so some of the prologue was at least intended for performance.

19. Jonson's Introductory comments, ll. 22–25.

20. Wiles, *Shakespeare's Clowns*, 145–47, argues that this must have been Armin because he is also called a "profane jester." This seems to me to treat a very generalized common term as specialized professional vocabulary, a distinction dealt with in the earlier "clown/fool" discussion. The assumption of such precision of terminology would require us to place Armin in the company as early as 1597 so that he could play Falstaff, whom Hal calls a "fool and jester" as well (Part II, V,v,47).

21. Baldwin Maxwell, *Studies in the Shakespearean Apocrypha* (New York: Columbia University, 1956), 102–05.

22. The story first appeared in the dedication to John Dennis' 1702 play, *The Comical Gallant*, but found wider distribution through Charles Gildon's "Remarks" in Rowe's 1710 edition of Shakespeare's works.

23. Chambers, *Elizabethan Stage*, II, 204.

24. Even though Kemp became famous from this stunt, the actual date is open to some debate. Alexander Dyce, the first modern editor of Kemp's pamphlet, thought the dance took place during Lent of 1599 (edn, vii). The temptation to accept that date is strong, for a temporarily out-of-work clown who had just invested all of his savings in a new theater building might attempt such a stunt to make enough money to last him until the theater could open. It also should have required several months for ballad-mongers to write and publish the insulting ballads Kemp complains about and for him to track down the various culprits, one of whom also had time to grow ill and die. On the other hand, it is hard to explain why Kemp should have waited more than a year to print his report of the exploit, and the April 22, 1600 registration and the title page date of 1600 are irrefutable. Fortunately,

either date for the dance results in the same Chamberlain's Men scenario proposed in the preceding pages. If Kemp went to Norwich in 1600, events happened exactly as described; if he went to Norwich in 1599, he returned long before the Globe opened and company events still happened as described. Thus, it seems prudent to adopt the generally accepted date of February 1600 for the dance.

25. Kemp, *Nine Daies Wonder*, ed. Harrison; quotations from 29, 33.

26. *Witter v. Heminges & Condell*, 1619, in Chambers, *William Shakespeare*, II, 52–57.

27. Walter (edn), xii, xxxv; Wells and Taylor, *Textual Companion*, 375; Oliver (edn), *Merry Wives*, xxi.

28. Chamber Accounts, Chambers, *Elizabethan Stage*, IV, 180. It may be significant that both *Much adoe aboute nothinge* and *Benedicte and Betteris* are listed in the same season. All have assumed they were the same play, performed once for the royal family without the King and once with the King present, but the payments are sequential and there is no obvious, or even subtle, reason why the accountant should have given them different titles. It is thus at least possible that the company was using the "Much Ado" title for a different play, despite its earlier publication.

29. Dekker was paid for new additions to *Oldcastle* in August 1602, when Worcester's Men were at the Rose (Foakes and Rickert, *Henslowe's Diary*, 214). Drayton's two-part play had been originally staged by the Admiral's Men, who were by 1602 in the Fortune. Chambers, *Elizabethan Stage*, III, 308, assumed this meant that Drayton's play "had been transferred to Worcester's Men." Wiles, *Shakespeare's Clowns*, 134–35, accepts this, on the assumption that Kemp was to play the role of Sir John of Wrotham because Oldcastle himself is as dull and unfunny as we might expect a strict Protestant martyr to be. Why the Admiral's Men would choose to sell away only Oldcastle and no other works is not explained by either. Nevertheless, it seems far more logical to me that Kemp would rather play the original Falstaff he already knew and had gone to considerable effort to reconstruct for a printer than to play a pseudo-Falstaff in a different play. Henslowe, of course, should have known the difference, but he was always more than a little casual about names and titles.

30. W. W. Greg, *The Shakespeare First Folio: Its Bibliographical and Textual History* (Oxford: Clarendon, 1955), 59.

31. *Shakespeare at the Globe, 1599–1609* (New York: Collier, 1962), ix.

CHAPTER 5: LIFE WITHOUT KEMP, 1600–03

1. Chambers, *Elizabethan Stage*, II, 437.

2. Greg, *Henslowe's Diary*, II, 61–63.

3. Chambers, *Elizabethan Stage*, IV, 329–31.

4. So helpful was this order to the Chamberlain's Men, and so damaging to the Admiral's Men and to Henslowe in particular, and so great the authority invoked, that one wonders if it were more a matter of political infighting among the great nobles than of Puritanical attempts to regulate the theaters, as is usually assumed.

5. Murray, *English Dramatic Companies*, I, 142, 109.

6. Chambers, *Elizabethan Stage*, II, 311, 322.

7. Cf. in particular Alfred Harbage, *Shakespeare and the Rival Traditions* (New York: Macmillan, 1952), to which most of these arguments can usually be traced.

8. Chambers, *Elizabethan Stage*, II, 43.

9. Andrew Gurr, *Playgoing in Shakespeare's London* (Cambridge: Cambridge University, 1994), 26–34.

10. Chambers, *William Shakespeare*, I, 423–24; Wells and Taylor, *Textual Companion*, 122; Rowse, *A Biography*, 317–8. Jenkins (edn), 1–13, suggests some material was added in 1601, but that the bulk was written in 1599–1600. Fraser, *Later Years*, 118–21, and Levi, *Life and Times*, 217, both assume 1601, as a response to the Essex affair, which requires an analysis of the text unusually subtle even by the standards of modern Shakespearean criticism and at the same time postdates *Twelfth Night*, raising the question of what Shakespeare wrote during the now empty 1600 and making it even more difficult to explain the lack of a role for Armin in *Hamlet* itself.

11. The tradition can be traced to Nicholas Rowe's "Life" in his 1709 edition of Shakespeare's works (Chambers, *William Shakespeare*, 264–69), by which time it was already third- or even fifth-hand legend.

12. Bertram and Kliman (edn), 170.

13. Margaret in *Richard III* and Cassandra in *Troilus and Cressida* are of course traditionally understood to be mad, but their madness is expressed through prophecy, a different kind of madness than Ophelia's or Lady Macbeth's. This is more on the order of Burbage's typical roles—sudden mood shifts, apparent nonsequiturs, and loss of physical control.

14. Leslie Hotson, *The First Night of "Twelfth Night"* (New York: Macmillan, 1954). Quotations pp. 180–81, 202. Hotson tries to get around the problem of *Twelfth Night*'s small cast by suggesting that the other companies actually performed different plays in other rooms (16), providing something of an excess of splendor for the kitchen help while keeping all the fancy show hidden from Elizabeth and her guest and rather defeating the point of the whole affair.

15. Chambers, *Elizabethan Stage*, 363–64, has "little doubt" that this was the Twelfth Night play, and G. A. Wilkes lists it as a firm date in his chronology in *The Complete Plays of Ben Jonson*, I, xii; W. David Kay, *Ben Jonson: A Literary Life* (New York: St. Martin's, 1995), 52–54, also is certain it was seen at court that winter, but believes it was not well received. The masques are all in scenes that appear only in Jonson's folio but not in the quarto published in 1601; as there is no reason to believe Jonson revised the play to insert the masques in 1616, then the full text would seem to represent the text used at court, which was then simplified for performance when the boys were on their own at Blackfriars later in the year.

16. Excerpted in Chambers, *William Shakespeare*, II, 327–28.

17. Harbage, *Rival Traditions*, 109.

18. Jupin (edn), 8–9.

19. Testimony quoted in Chambers, *Elizabethan Stage*, II, 205.

20. J. E. Neale, *Queen Elizabeth I* (London: 1934; Repr. Chicago: Academy Chicago, 1999), 388.

21. Privy Council Minute, Chambers, *Elizabethan Stage*, IV, 332.

22. Chambers, *William Shakespeare*, I, 450–51; Hunter (edn), xxiii–xxvi; Wilson, *The Evidence*, 292–94; Levi, *Life and Times*, 239; Ted Hughes, *Shakespeare and the Goddess of Complete Being* (London: Faber, 1993), 116–57. Wells and Taylor, *Textual Companion*, 126–27, and Fraser (edn), 1–5, are unusual in that they place it just after *Measure* and *Othello*, in late 1604 or early 1605.

23. Cf. charts summarizing various analyses in Campbell and Quinn, *Reader's Encyclopedia*, 932; Wells and Taylor, *Textual Companion*, 126–27.

24. Revisions of *Spanish Tragedy, Jew of Malta, Dr. Faustus*, plus Jonson's new *Richard Crookback*, which must have been a new Richard III play, were all noted. The alterations were probably not for Alleyn per se, who would have preferred to play his old roles as he already

knew them, but rather would have been designed to modify the old plays for the many new actors added to the company since Alleyn had last performed.

25. Chambers, *Elizabethan Stage*, II, 127.

26. Chambers, *Elizabethan Stage*, II, 225–26, IV, 334–35; Wiles, *Shakespeare's Clown*, 39–40; Gurr, *Shakespearean Stage*, 139–40.

27. Gurr, *Shakespearean Stage*, 49–55.

28. *Jack Drum's Entertainment*, quoted in Chambers, *Elizabethan Stage*, II, 20.

29. Chambers, *Elizabethan Stage*, II, 45–46.

30. Foakes and Rickert, *Henslowe's Diary*, 182, 203.

31. Chambers, *Elizabethan Stage*, III, 293.

32. Brockbank (edn), 24–29; Chambers, *William Shakespeare*, I, 479–80; Rowse, *A Biography*, 394; Wells and Taylor, *Textual Companion*, 131.

33. Cf. T.J.B. Spencer (ed.), *Shakespeare's Plutarch* (London: Penguin, 1968), 354–57.

34. Chambers, *William Shakespeare*, I, 479.

35. Brockbank (edn), 29–30.

36. Cf. charts in Campbell and Quinn, *Reader's Encyclopedia*, 932; Wells and Taylor, *Textual Companion*, 96, 98–99.

37. Chambers, *William Shakespeare*, II, 212.

38. Greg, *Henslowe's Diary*, I, 149.

39. Chambers, *William Shakespeare*, II, 107–13.

40. Bullen (edn), *Works of Middleton*, VIII, 36.

41. Abrams (edn), 28–36.

42. *The Devil Is an Ass*, Prologue, 1, 22.

43. Abrams (edn), 38–39.

44. Kay, *Ben Jonson*, 68; Chambers, *Elizabethan Stage*, III, 367; Ben Jonson, *Conversations with William Drummond*, Ed. G. B. Harrison (London: Bodley Head, 1923), 14; "Ev. B," in *Sejanus*, 11, 1–5.

45. *Discoveries, 1641*, Ed. G. B. Harrison (London: Bodley Head, 1923), 29.

46. Cf. Dorsch (edn), 65n.

47. Jenkins (edn), 20.

48. Cf. Bertram and Kliman (edn), 224–37. Almost all of the jokes are in Q1, although their order is quite different. This suggests the memory of a clown who in such a stand-up routine would need to remember only the punchlines, leaving the order to the "straight man," who feeds him the questions.

49. Greg, *Henslowe's Diary*, II, 108.

50. King, *Casting Shakespeare's Plays*, 258.

51. Norwich, February 27, and then again in June, plus Ipswich. Chambers, *Elizabethan Stage*, II, 127.

52. Gurr, *Shakespearean Stage*, 52–53.

53. Hosking, *Life and Times*, 143.

CHAPTER 6: THE KING'S MEN, 1603–06

1. Chambers, *Elizabethan Stage*, IV, 335.

2. Chambers, *Elizabethan Stage*, IV, 335.

3. Chambers, *Elizabethan Stage*, II, 208.

4. Murray, *English Dramatic Companies*, I, 133, 207.

5. Alvin Kernan, *Shakespeare, the King's Playwright: Theater in the Stuart Court, 1603–1613* (New Haven, CT: Yale University, 1995) develops the thesis at length; cf. also Levi, *Life and Times*, 255; Dennis Kay, *Shakespeare: His Life, Work, and Era* (New York: William Morrow, 1992), 290–91; Fraser, *Later Years*, 138–39, Rowse, *William Shakespeare: A Biography* (New York: Harper & Row, 1963), 358; Schoenbaum, *Compact Documentary Life*, 251.

6. Beckerman, *Shakespeare at the Globe*, 133; for the range of this acceptance, see also Schoenbaum, *Compact Documentary Life*, 251; Campbell and Quinn, *Reader's Encyclopedia*, 234; Charles Boyce, *Shakespeare A to Z* (New York: Dell, 1990), 196; Peter Thomson, *Shakespeare's Theatre*, 2d ed. (London: Routledge, 1992), 74; Chambers, *Elizabethan Stage*, II, 318, etc. Cf. also Wiles, *Shakespeare's Clown*, who in a most detailed, sophisticated, and extensive study does not mention Fletcher's name even once.

7. Letter from Dudley Carleton to John Chamberlain, January 15, 1604, in Roslyn Lander Knutson, *The Repertory of Shakespeare's Company, 1594–1613* (Fayetteville: University of Arkansas, 1991), 202–02.

8. Letter from Sir Walter Cope to Robert Cecil, in Chambers, *William Shakespeare*, II, 332.

9. Dedication to *Phantasma*, 1609, in Chambers, *Elizabethan Stage*, II, 300.

10. Murray, *English Dramatic Companies*, I, 183, 207.

11. Chamber Accounts, Chambers, *Elizabethan Stage*, IV, 168.

12. Heminges fathered a child baptized February 12, 1604, and thus must have left town no earlier than mid- to late May; Burbage fathered a child baptized September 16, 1604, which indicates the company returned to London by mid-December, after the visit to Mortelake. No records of children of other company members have been found to suggest they were in London before December, so the company probably toured for a very long time this year.

13. Extract in Chambers, *William Shakespeare*, II, 329.

14. Chamber Accounts, Chambers, *Elizabethan Stage*, IV, 168.

15. Chambers, *Elizabethan Stage*, II, 211.

16. Lee, *A Life*, 381.

17. Chambers, *Elizabethan Stage*, IV, 336.

18. Fraser, *Later Years* (New York: Columbia, 1992), 137.

19. Murray, *English Dramatic Companies*, I, 186–93.

20. Gurr, *Shakespearean Stage*, 51–55.

21. Chamber Accounts, Chambers, *Elizabethan Stage*, IV, 169–70.

22. Robert Armin, *Collected Works*, II, unpaged.

23. Thomson, *Shakespeare's Theatre*, 77.

24. Chambers, *Elizabethan Stage*, II, 334.

25. Both names are on the Q2 title page; for assignments of various scenes, see Jackson and Neill (edn), 190–94, 513–35.

26. Oliver (edn), xli; Chambers, *Elizabethan Stage*, III, 488; Chambers, *William Shakespeare*, I, 482; Una Ellis-Fermor, "*Timon of Athens*: An Unfinished Play," *Review of English Studies*, sviii (1942), 270–83; Oliver (edn), xl; Wells and Taylor, *Textual Companion*, 127–28, 501–02.

27. John Fletcher(?), "Elegie . . .". in Chambers, *Elizabethan Stage*, II, 309.

28. Susan Willis, *The BBC Shakespeare Plays: Making the Televised Canon* (Chapel Hill: University of North Carolina, 1991), 19; Roger Allam, "The Duke in *Measure for Measure*," *Players of Shakespeare*, ed. Russell Jackson and Robert Smallwood (Cambridge: Cambridge University, 1996), 22.

29. *Ratseis Ghost,* 1605, in Chambers, *William Shakespeare,* II, 215.

30. In later life Lowin would become quite large, with Falstaff one of his signature roles. He may of course have been a thin actor still in 1604, but chances are he had already begun to round out a bit.

31. Chambers, *William Shakespeare,* I, 412; Jenkins (edn), 37.

32. Letter of John Chamberlain, December 18, 1604, quoted in Thomson, *Shakespeare's Theatre,* 78.

33. Chambers, *William Shakespeare,* I, 475; Muir (edn), xx–xxii. Wells and Taylor, *Textual Companion,* 128–29, also favor 1606 due to the porter scene and various metrical tests, but with some hesitation due to the involvement of Middleton.

34. Alan Haynes, *The Gunpowder Plot* (London: Grange, 1994), 137.

35. Wilson, *The Evidence,* 314–15; Fraser, *Later Years,* 175–78; Hosley, *Shakespeare's Holinshed,* 11–12; Riggs, *Ben Jonson,* 127–28; Haynes, *Gunpowder Plot,* 136.

36. Greg, *Shakespeare First Folio,* 389–90; Wells and Taylor, *Textual Companion,* 543; David J. Lake, *The Canon of Thomas Middleton's Plays* (Cambridge: Cambridge University, 1975), 26.

37. Levi, *Life and Times,* 256. Fraser, *Later Years,* 181; Rowse, *A Biography,* 380–81; Kernan, *King's Playwright,* 75–80. The most extreme argument for a royal performance is Henry N. Paul, *The Royal Play of Macbeth: When, Why, and How It Was Written by Shakespeare* (New York: Macmillan, 1950).

38. Diary entry reprinted in Chambers, *William Shakespeare,* II, 337–38.

39. Hosley, *Shakespeare's Holinshed,* 18.

40. Wells and Taylor, *Textual Companion,* 128; Chambers, *William Shakespeare,* I, 467–69; Muir (edn), xxi.

41. Everitt, *Six Early Plays,* 11; Wells and Taylor, *Textual Companion,* 128.

42. W. W. Greg, "The Date of *King Lear* and Shakespeare's Use of Earlier Versions of the Story," *The Library,* xx (1939), 377–400.

43. Chambers, *Elizabethan Stage,* II, 309.

44. J. Munro, *The Shakspeare Allusion Book: A Collection of Allusions to Shakspeare from 1591 to 1700* (London: Oxford University, 1932), I, 174.

45. Greg, *Henslowe's Diary,* II, 167.

46. Schoenbaum, *Compact Documentary Life,* 246–47.

47. Petter (edn), xiii–xxvi.

48. Chambers, *Elizabethan Stage,* IV, 338.

49. Murray, *English Dramatic Companies,* I, 183.

50. Chambers, *William Shakespeare,* II, 119–122.

51. The only known company child of 1605 was Cooke's, baptized on October 27 and thus conceived during February; the next was Sly's illegitimate child, baptized in late September 1606, followed shortly by Condell's daughter about a month later, both conceived between Christmas 1605 and Lent 1606.

52. *Witter v. Heminges and Condell,* 1619, in Chambers, *William Shakespeare,* II, 55. For other discussion of this exchange, cf. Gurr, *Shakespearean Stage,* 46; Schoenbaum, *Compact Documentary Life,* 210–11.

53. Chambers, *Elizabethan Stage,* IV, 338.

54. Maxwell, *Studies in the Shakespeare Apocrypha,* 141.

55. Lake, *Canon of Middleton's Plays,* 173.

56. Brockbank (edn), xxvii.

57. Bentley, *Profession of Player,* 292–93; This also indicates that Heminges was still per-

forming at least occasionally after the Globe fire, eliminating the theory that he had retired much earlier.

58. Richard Madelaine, *Shakespeare in Production: Antony and Cleopatra* (Cambridge: Cambridge University, 1998), lists only eighteen productions in England since World War II—three with the same actress, Vanessa Redgrave—although three others have since appeared (to lukewarm or awesomely bad notices), in one of which a man played Cleopatra. None have been presented in the United States with a star actress since Katherine Hepburn at the Stratford, Connecticut, festival in 1960. In the first half of the century, almost half of the twelve English productions were played by the same actress, Dorothy Green.

59. Chambers, *William Shakespeare*, I, 477–78, favors early 1607 due to an additional allusion in *The Divil's Charter*; Wells and Taylor, *Textual Companion*, 129, opt for 1606; Ridley (edn), xxv–xxviii, seems to agree.

60. The 1607 additions are quoted in full in Rev. Alexander B. Grosart (ed.), *The Complete Works in Verse and Prose of Samuel Daniel* (New York: Russell & Russell, 1963), III, 3–19; the modern English spelling here is from Salgado, *Eyewitnesses of Shakespeare*, 27–28.

61. Wells and Taylor, *Textual Companion*, 131.

62. Wells and Taylor, *Textual Companion*, 604.

63. Stanley Sadie (ed.), *The New Grove Dictionary of Music*, IX, 681.

64. Chambers, *Elizabethan Stage*, II, 22, 51–53; III, 286.

65. Chambers, *Elizabethan Stage*, IV, 338–39.

66. Murray, *English Dramatic Companies*, I, 202.

67. Thomson, *Shakespeare's Theatre*, 83–84.

68. Chambers, *Elizabethan Stage*, II, 212.

CHAPTER 7: REPLACING SHAKESPEARE, 1607–10

1. Barroll, *Politics, Plague*, 177.

2. Bell's *London Remembrancer*, 1665, table in Murray, *English Dramatic Companies*, II, 185–86.

3. Blayney (edn), vii; Maxwell, *Studies in the Shakespeare Apocrypha*, 176.

4. Blayney (edn), viii.

5. The association of Prospero's breaking staff and Shakespeare's retirement apparently began with the poet Thomas Campbell in 1838, but it is now one of the standard parts of the mythos, to be found in program notes for every production of *The Tempest*. Hughes (*Shakespeare and the Goddess*, 379–500), for example, reads *The Tempest* as a conscious summation of all Shakespeare's previous works; cf. also Wilson, *Evidence*, 355–56. The idea is unchallenged even by the meticulous Schoenbaum (*Compact Documentary Life*, 278), accepted with minor reservations by Fraser (*Later Years*, 238, 251). Honan (*Shakespeare: A Life*, 372) does notice that there were other plays after *The Tempest*, but seems to believe that Shakespeare stopped writing several years before he stopped acting (381).

6. John Dover Wilson, *Life in Shakespeare's England* (Hammondworth: Pelican, 1944), 108.

7. William Harrison, *The Description of England* (1587), ed. George Edelen (New York: Dover, 1994), 403.

8. Bentley, *Profession of Player*, 126.

9. Honan, *Shakespeare: A Life*, 355–56; Schoenbaum, *Compact Documentary Life*, 246. Shakespeare's will can be found in Chambers, *William Shakespeare*, II, 170–80, or in modern spelling in Wilson, *The Evidence*, 476–79.

10. *William Shakespeare*, II, 79.

11. The oldest actor still active in London when James took the throne was apparently John Singer, clown at the Fortune, who had been in the original Queen's Men in 1583. His name is found in no further records of Henslowe and no company cast lists, so he appears to have retired during the plague break of 1603–04.

12. Palmer (edn), 1–2.

13. *The Painfull Adventures of Pericles, Prince of Tyre* (1608), ed. Kenneth Muir (Liverpool: Liverpool University, 1967).

14. Hoeniger (edn), lxii–lxiii; Chambers, *William Shakespeare*, I, 526; Wells and Taylor, *Textual Companion*, 130. Although Heywood is the critical favorite, he seems the least likely, on the obvious grounds that he was a Sharer in a different company, the Queen's Men, and even assuming he did write a play for another than his own, he could not have done so at this time, as his own company was touring away from London.

15. Chambers, *William Shakespeare*, II, 335.

16. Chambers, *Elizabethan Stage*, IV, 42, settled for "Anonymous"; Lake, *Canon of Middleton's Plays*, 136–62, marshals a large body of linguistic arguments that seem to settle the matter in favor of Middleton.

17. Abrams (edn), 38–39.

18. Chambers, *Elizabethan Stage*, IV, 48.

19. Quoted in Morris (edn), 64.

20. Murray, *English Dramatic Companies*, I, 184.

21. *London Remembrancer*, table in Murray, *English Dramatic Companies*, II, 187.

22. Chambers, *William Shakespeare*, II, 18; Wilson, *The Evidence*, 334.

23. Chambers, *William Shakespeare*, I, 479.

24. *The New Inn*, "Ode to Himself," ll, 21–22, in Wilkes (edn), IV.

25. Translation from Gurr, *Shakespearean Stage*, 54; Chambers, *Elizabethan Stage*, II, 50–53, 213.

26. *Raven's Almanac* (1608), in Murray, *English Dramatic Companies*, I, 152.

27. Schoenbaum, *Compact Documentary Life*, 267. There is some confusion about who precisely owned the Evans share. The name actually used was Thomas Evans, but Henry Evans was named as a partner in lawsuits of 1610 and 1612 (Chambers, *William Shakespeare*, II, 64–65; *Elizabethan Stage*, II, 509), so it is generally understood that he used Thomas, a relative of some kind, as a front man for this particular transaction.

28. Chambers, *Elizabethan Stage*, II, 214.

29. Gurr, *Shakespearean Stage*, 157–60.

30. Murray, *English Dramatic Companies*, I, 184.

31. Armin, *Collected Works*, II, unpaged.

32. Bentley, *Profession of Player*, 125.

33. Wells and Taylor, *Textual Companion*, 131; Chambers, *William Shakespeare*, I, 479–80; Brockbank (edn), 24–29; Parker (edn), 2–7.

34. E.A.J. Honigmann, *The Stability of Shakespeare's Texts* (London: Arnold, 1965), 146–47, does argue that the scenes were composed out of order, but he does not suggest there was a difference of years involved.

35. Brockbank (edn), 2–24.

36. Eccles, *Shakespeare in Warwickshire*, 131–8; Chambers, *William Shakespeare*, II, 114–8. Greene's diary notation is actually in October 1609, when Shakespeare extended the invitation for a second year. However, Greene could not have stayed a second year if he had not stayed the first, so Shakespeare must have invited him about a year earlier, around October or

November 1608. Nor was Shakespeare likely to have turned out his entire family, so Greene must have been sharing space in the house, and thus Greene's presence does not establish that Shakespeare must have returned to London. It does, however, indicate that Shakespeare must have been in Stratford in order to make the offer. Had he written, the good lawyer Greene would have retained the letter and had no need to make a diary entry.

37. Chamber Accounts, Chambers, *Elizabethan Stage*, IV, 175.

38. Chambers, *Elizabethan Stage*, II, 214.

39. Campbell & Quinn, *Reader's Encyclopedia*, 714.

40. Chambers, *William Shakespeare*, II, 115–16.

41. Letter of the Venetian Ambassador, February 2, 1610, in Beaurline (edn), xiii–xiv.

42. Chambers, *William Shakespeare*, II, 64–65.

43. Chambers, *Elizabethan Stage*, II, 56–59.

44. *Textual Companion*, 131.

45. This age is present in both Q1 and the Folio; cf. Wells and Taylor, *Complete Works*, 915, 949. Surely a revision intended for performance would have modified this age at least.

46. *Textual Companion*, 128.

47. Glover and Waller (edn), I, 389, 399.

48. Chambers, *Elizabethan Stage*, II, 222–3; Andrew Gurr (edn), xxvi–xxix.

49. Chambers, *Elizabethan Stage*, II, 215; Braunmuller and Hattaway, *Cambridge Companion*, 432.

50. "Elegie . . . ," in Chambers, *Elizabethan Stage*, II, 309.

51. Answer to a petition of Robert Benfield, 1635, in Chambers, *William Shakespeare*, II, 66.

52. Andrew Gurr, *Playgoing in Shakespeare's London* (Cambridge: Cambridge University, 1994), 162.

53. Mares (edn), lxiii.

54. Cf. Chambers, *Elizabethan Stage*, III, 371; Brown (edn), xi; Mares (edn), lxiii.

55. Bentley, *Profession of Player*, 292–93.

56. Baldwin, *Organization and Personnel*, 437.

57. Murray, *English Dramatic Companies*, I, 229–35; Chambers, *Elizabethan Stage*, II, 242–45.

CHAPTER 8: SHAKESPEARE BOWS OUT, 1610–13

1. A detailed discussion of the relationship between the play and the report can be found in Rowse, *A Biography*, 430–34. Although challenged by committed Oxfordians, the connection is accepted as widely as any piece of evidence in Shakespearean dating; cf., for example, Chambers, *William Shakespeare*, I, 491–93; Kermode (edn), xxvi–xxxiii; Wells and Taylor, *Textual Companion*, 132.

2. Chambers, *William Shakespeare*, II, 122–27.

3. Cf. Wilson and Quiller-Couch (edn), 85.

4. Gurr, *Shakespearean Stage*, 178.

5. There are a number of aspects of Heywood's *The Golden Age* that seem to be borrowed from *Cymbeline* (cf. Warren [edn], 65–67). Unfortunately, the date of *The Golden Age* is even less clear than the date of *Cymbeline*. Heywood's epistle claims it as the first play of a completed trilogy that had all been performed, which, assuming *Cymbeline* was an influence, would seem to indicate knowledge of a version of *Cymbeline* long predating 1611, such as I have suggested earlier.

6. Chambers, *William Shakespeare*, II, 339–40.

7. Chambers, *William Shakespeare*, II, 340–41.

8. Pafford (edn), xxii–xxiii; Wells and Taylor, *Textual Companion*, 131, regard this as a later interpolation.

9. Robert Greene, *Pandosto. The Triumph of Time* (1588), in Bullough, *Narrative and Dramatic Sources*, IV, 1973, 156–99.

10. Bentley, *Jacobean & Caroline Stage*, II, 377, 532–33; King, *Casting Shakespeare's Plays*, 38, 108–09.

11. Ferguson (edn), 25–35, Bradley, *From Text to Performance*, 239.

12. Chambers, *William Shakespeare*, I, 530; Wells and Taylor, *Textual Companion*, 134; Potter (edn), 34–35.

13. It should be noted that this routine is not actually included in the published text of the masque; it was described in a separate pamphlet reporting the affair (Glover and Waller [edn], X, 383), at least allowing the possibility that it was an insertion from another source.

14. Wells and Taylor, *Textual Companion*, 625.

15. Cf. for example, "On 25 August 1611 [a share] was transferred to William Ostler" (Chambers, *Elizabethan Stage*, II, 510); "the incorporation of Ostler" (Schoenbaum, *Compact Documentary Life*, 211). "granted to Ostler" (Campbell and Quinn, *Reader's Encyclopedia*, 596); etc.

16. Chambers, *Elizabethan Stage*, II, 509n.

17. Chambers, *William Shakespeare*, I, 152–53.

18. Chambers, *Elizabethan Stage*, II, 243–48.

19. Murray, *English Dramatic Companies*, I, 185–201.

20. *Elizabethan Stage*, III, 225.

21. Lancashire (edn), 15–23; Lake, *Canon of Middleton's Plays*, 185–91. Charles Hamilton, *Cardenio, or the Second Maiden's Tragedy* (Lakewood, CO: Glenbridge, 1994), argues that the handwriting of *The Second Maiden's Tragedy* is in the same handwriting as Shakespeare's will, and thus must be by Shakespeare. I am unable to judge the handwriting question, despite his copious examples, but having read *The Witch*, for example, I have no difficulty accepting Lake's stylistic arguments for Middleton's authorship of *The Second Maiden's Tragedy*. The play's similarity to Cervantes' story of the "Curious Impertinent" is well known, but it is a tale within a tale within a tale, the story of Lothario, not of Cardenio. Similarly, it is used as the subplot of the *Tragedy*, not the Maiden's story that the censor recognized as the central plot.

22. King, *Casting Shakespeare's Plays*, 35; Chambers, *Elizabethan Stage*, II, 336.

23. Chambers, *Elizabethan Stage*, III, 500.

24. Holaday (edn), *Lucrece*, 5–19; Barbara J. Baines, *Thomas Heywood* (Boston: Twayne, 1984), 142; Chambers, *Elizabethan Stage*, III, 344.

25. Chambers, *Elizabethan Stage*, II, 418–19, 423n.; Schoenbaum, *Compact Documentary Life*, 211. Even Chambers seems to have been confused at this point, for Sly's share is here identified as "left . . . to his son Robert," where all previous discussion had clearly identified Robert as the very adult and married Robert Browne, who was if anything older than Sly himself.

26. Eccles, *Shakespeare in Warwickshire*, 131.

27. Chambers, *Elizabethan Stage*, II, 216–17.

28. Chambers, *Elizabethan Stage*, IV, 340–41.

29. David M. Bergeron, *Royal Family, Royal Lovers: King James of England and Scotland*

(Columbia: University of Missouri, 1991), 107–09; Letter from Privy Council to Lord Mayor, November 8, 1612, Chambers, *Elizabethan Stage*, IV, 341–42.

30. The play was recorded under two titles, *Much adoe aboute nothinge* and *Benedicte and Betteris*. No one I have found has argued that they were two different plays, but it seems most unusual that on the same day the court clerk would have recorded two different titles for the same work.

31. "A Sonnett upon the pittiful burneing of the Globe playhowse in London," in Chambers, *Elizabethan Stage*, II, 420–22.

32. Chambers, *Elizabethan Stage*, III, 489–90.

33. Miguel de Cervantes, *Don Quixote*, tr. Ozell (New York: Modern Library, 1930), Part I, Book III, Ch. IX-Book IV, Ch. IX.

34. Bentley, *Jacobean & Caroline Stage*, III, 444–46.

35. Letter of Sir Henry Wotton to Sir Edmund Bacon, July 2, 1613. Cf. letters of Thomas Lorkin and John Chamberlain, and numerous poems, all in Chambers, *Elizabethan Stage*, II, 419–23.

36. Chambers, *Elizabethan Stage*, II, 442.

37. Schoenbaum, *Compact Documentary Life*, 272–75; Chambers, *William Shakespeare*, II, 153.

38. Multiple authorship was first proposed by James Spedding, "Who Wrote Shakespeare's Henry VIII?" *The Gentleman's Magazine*, 34, (August 1850), 115–23, and since concurred by numerous others, such as Chambers, *William Shakespeare*, I, 496, and Wells and Taylor, *Textual Companion*, 618–19. Spedding suggested Beaumont as a probable third hand, which now has some support from Wells and Taylor, but this seems most unlikely, as Beaumont had married his rich widow by 1613, although the exact date of the marriage is uncertain. There are yet those who believe it was all done all by Shakespeare: cf. Foakes (edn), xv–xxvii; Levi, *Life and Times*, 317; Rowse, *A Biography*, 437–41.

39. "*Tempest* in a Teapot: Critics, Evaluation, Ideology," *Bad Shakespeare: Revaluations of the Shakespeare Canon*, ed. Maurice Charney (Rutherford, NJ: Fairleigh Dickinson University, 1988), 63.

40. Cf. assignment of scenes in Wells and Taylor, *Textual Companion*, 618; line counts are the author's.

41. It is even possible that *Henry VIII* began its life much earlier than 1613. It seems most odd that a play about Henry VIII written during the reign of James I should have as its dramatic climax the birth of Elizabeth I. One would think that such an ending would have been far more appropriate before 1603. If so, the "third hand" sometimes detected might be someone writing an original ten to fifteen years earlier, possibly but not necessarily a younger Shakespeare (e.g., we have no new plays in 1602), which Shakespeare revised in 1613, probably to expand Wolsey for Burbage (who had originally played Henry), and which Fletcher then again revised as discussed in 1614.

42. John Downes, *Roscius Anglicanus* (1708), in Chambers, *William Shakespeare*, II, 264.

43. See, for example, the widespread critical reaction to the production in the BBC-TV Complete Shakespeare series, which generally thought it not only surprisingly interesting but one of the most successful of that much maligned series of productions (Willis, *BBC Shakespeare*, 53–54).

CHAPTER 9: EPILOGUE

1. Chambers, *Elizabethan Stage*, IV, 51; Braunmuller and Hattaway, *Cambridge Companion*, 433.

2. Chambers, *Elizabethan Stage*, II, 248–50, III, 227.

3. Chambers, *Elizabethan Stage*, II, 424, 510.

4. Chambers, *William Shakespeare*, II, 56–57.

5. Chambers, *Elizabethan Stage*, II, 424–25.

6. Chambers, *Elizabethan Stage*, II, 510.

7. Chambers, *Elizabethan Stage*, II, 217–18.

8. *The Duchesse of Malfy*, title page.

9. Bentley, *Jacobean & Caroline Stage*, I, 127–30.

10. Greg, *Shakespeare First Folio*, 11–17.

11. "Epistle Dedicatorie," Folio, unpaged.

12. Bentley, *Jacobean & Caroline Stage*, III, 308.

13. Eccles, *Shakespeare in Warwickshire*, 113, 131; Schoenbaum, *Compact Documentary Life*, 274–75.

APPENDIX A: DOUBLING ROLES

1. William A. Ringler, Jr., "The Number of Actors in Shakespeare's Early Plays," *The Seventeenth Century Stage: A Collection of Critical Essays*, ed. Gerald Eades Bentley (Chicago: University of Chicago, 1968), 110–36; see also King, *Casting Shakespeare's Plays*; Bradley, *From Text to Performance*; Stephen Booth, "Speculations on Doubling in Shakespeare's Plays," *Shakespeare, The Theatrical Dimension*, Ed. by Philip McGuire and David Samuelson, New York, AMS, 1979, 103–31. Arthur Colby Sprague, *The Doubling of Parts in Shakespeare's Plays* (London: Society for Theatre Research, 1966) examines the traditional doubling patterns in productions since the early eighteenth century.

2. King, *Casting Shakespeare's Plays*, 267; Bentley, *Jacobean & Caroline Stage*, I, 14–16.

3. Sprague, *Doubling of Parts*, 23, finds this to be the most common double in Shakespearean productions since the eighteenth century; it can still be seen, for example, in the 2000 production at the Royal National Theatre in London.

4. The only "fast change" indicated in all of Shakespeare's work is Jessica's change to boy's clothes in *Merchant of Venice* in twenty-eight lines while simultaneously running upstairs (F896–924). As written, this change is all but impossible today, even with velcro, suggesting that the masquers on stage while she makes the change in fact inserted a song or dance that is not included in the surviving text. If such quick changes were the standard, as Ringler argues, then we should see more of them. Rosalind's change from boy to woman is given eighty lines plus music (F2601–81), and a more pointless set of eighty lines would be hard to find in all of Shakespeare. If the costume change could have been done in twenty-eight lines, then it certainly should have been done so there.

5. King, *Casting Shakespeare's Plays*, 43–48, 111.

Bibliography

EDITIONS OF SHAKESPEARE'S PLAYS

Allen, Michael J. B. and Kenneth Muir (eds.). *Shakespeare's Plays in Quarto: A Facsimile Edition of Copies Primarily from the Henry E. Huntington Library.* Berkeley: University of California, 1981.

Bawcutt, Nina (ed.). *Measure for Measure.* Oxford: Clarendon, 1991.

Beaurline, L. A. (ed.). *King John.* Cambridge: Cambridge University, 1990.

Bertram, Paul and Bernice W. Kliman (eds.). *The Three-Text Hamlet: Parallel Texts of the First and Second Quartos and First Folio.* (New York: AMS, 1991).

Bevington, David (ed.). *Henry IV, Part I.* Oxford: Clarendon, 1987.

Braunmuller, A. R. (ed.). *King John.* Oxford: Clarendon, 1989.

Brockbank, Philip (ed.). *Coriolanus.* London: Methuen, 1987.

Brooks, Harold F. (ed.). *A Midsummer Night's Dream.* London: Routledge, 1988.

Brooks, Nicholas (ed.). *Macbeth.* Oxford: Clarendon, 1990.

Brown, John Russell (ed.). *The Merchant of Venice.* London: Routledge, 1988.

Cairncross, Andrew (ed.). *King Henry VI, Part I.* London: Mehtuen, 1969.

Cairncross, Andrew (ed.). *King Henry VI, Part II.* London: Methuen, 1985.

Cairncross, Andrew (ed.). *King Henry VI, Part III.* London: Methuen, 1985.

Craik, T. W. (ed.). *The Merry Wives of Windsor.* Oxford: Clarendon, 1990.

David, R. W. *Love's Labour's Lost.* London: Methuen, 1985.

Dorsch, T. S. (ed.). *The Comedy of Errors.* Cambridge: Cambridge University, 1988.

Dorsch, T. S. (ed.). *Julius Caesar.* London: Methuen, 1986.

Evans, G. Blakemore (ed.). *The Riverside Shakespeare.* Boston: Houghton Mifflin, 1974.

Foakes, R. A. (ed.). *The Comedy of Errors.* London: Methuen, 1984.

Foakes, R. A. (ed.). *King Henry VIII.* London: Methuen, 1986.

Foakes, R. A. (ed.). *A Midsummer Night's Dream.* Cambridge: Cambridge University, 1984.

Fraser, Russell (ed.). *All's Well That Ends Well.* Cambridge: Cambridge University, 1985.

Gibbons, Brian (ed.). *Measure for Measure.* Cambridge: Cambridge University, 1991.

Gibbons, Brian (ed.). *Romeo and Juliet.* London: Routledge, 1988.

Gurr, Andrew (ed.). *The First Quarto of Henry V.* Cambridge: Cambridge University, 2000.

Gurr, Andrew (ed.). *King Henry V.* Cambridge: Cambridge University, 1992.

Gurr, Andrew (ed.). *Richard II.* Cambridge: Cambridge University, 1984.

Halio, Jay L. (ed.). *King Lear.* Cambridge: Cambridge University, 1992.

Halio, Jay L. (ed.). *The Merchant of Venice.* Oxford: Clarendon, 1993.

Hammond, Antony (ed.). *King Richard III.* London: Methuen, 1986.

Hattaway, Michael (ed.). *The First Part of King Henry VI.* Cambridge: Cambridge University, 1990.

Hibbard, G. R. (ed.). *Love's Labour's Lost.* Oxford: Clarendon, 1990.

Hoeniger, F. D. (ed.). *Pericles.* London: Methuen, 1986.

Holland, Peter (ed.). *A Midsummer Night's Dream.* Oxford: Clarendon, 1994.

Honigmann, E. A. J. (ed.). *King John.* London: Methuen, 1973.

Hughes, Alan (ed.). *Titus Andronicus.* Cambridge: Cambridge University, 1994.

Humphreys, A. R. (ed.). *King Henry IV, Part 2.* London: Methuen, 1987.

Humphreys, A. R. (ed.). *Much Ado About Nothing.* London: Methuen, 1988.

Hunter, G. K. (ed.). *All's Well That Ends Well.* London: Methuen, 1985.

Jenkins, Harold (ed.). *Hamlet.* London: Methuen, 1986.

Kermode, Frank (ed.). *The Tempest.* London: Methuen, 1986.

Knowles, Richard and Evelyn Joseph Mattern, IHM. *A New Variorum Edition of Shakespeare: As You Like It.* New York: MLA, 1977.

Latham, Agnes (ed.). *As You Like It.* London: Methuen, 1987.

Leech, Clifford (ed.). *The Two Gentlemen of Verona.* London: Methuen, 1986.

Lever, J. W. (ed.). *Measure for Measure.* London: Routledge, 1988.

Lothian, J. M. and T. W. Craik (eds.). *Twelfth Night.* London: Routledge, 1988.

Mahood, M. M. (ed.). *The Merchant of Venice.* Cambridge: Cambridge University, 1987.

Mares, F. H. (ed.). *Much Ado About Nothing.* Cambridge: Cambridge University, 1988.

Margeson, John (ed.). *King Henry VIII.* Cambridge: Cambridge University, 1990.

Maxwell, J. C. (ed.). *Titus Andronicus.* London: Methuen, 1987.

Morris, Brian (ed.). *The Taming of the Shrew.* London: Methuen, 1988.

Moston, Doug (ed.). *The First Folio of Shakespeare, 1623.* New York: Applause, 1995.

Muir, Kenneth (ed.). *King Lear.* London: Methuen, 1987.

Muir, Kenneth (ed.). *Macbeth.* London: Methuen, 1986.

Muir, Kenneth (ed.). *Troilus and Cressida.* Oxford: Clarendon, 1981.

Neill, Michael (ed.). *Antony and Cleopatra.* Oxford: Clarendon, 1993.

Nosworthy, J. M. *Cymbeline.* London: Methuen, 1980.

Oliver, H. J. (ed.). *The Merry Wives of Windsor.* London: Methuen, 1987.

Oliver, H. J. (ed.). *The Taming of the Shrew.* Oxford: Clarendon, 1982.

Oliver, H. J. (ed.). *Timon of Athens.* London: Methuen, 1986.

Orgel, Stephen (ed.). *The Winter's Tale.* Oxford: Clarendon, 1996.

Pafford, J. H. P. (ed.). *The Winter's Tale.* London: Routledge, 1988.

Palmer, Kenneth (ed.). *Troilus and Cressida.* London: Methuen, 1982.

Parker, R. B. (ed.). *Coriolanus.* Oxford: Clarendon, 1994.

Pollard, A. W. (ed.). *King Richard II: A New Quarto.* London, 1916.

Potter, Lois (ed.). *The Two Noble Kinsmen.* London: Nelson, 1997.

Ridley, M. R. (ed.). *Antony and Cleopatra.* London: Methuen, 1986.

Ridley, M. R. (ed.). *Othello*. London: Methuen, 1984.

Schlueter, Kurt (ed.). *The Two Gentlemen of Verona*. Cambridge: Cambridge University, 1990.

Spevack, Marvin (ed.). *Julius Caesar*. Cambridge: Cambridge University, 1988.

Spevack, Marvin, Michael Steppat, and Marga Munkelt (eds.). *Antony and Cleopatra*. New York: MLA, 1990.

Thompson, Ann (ed.). *The Taming of the Shrew*. Cambridge: Cambridge University, 1984.

Ure, Peter (ed.). *King Richard II*. London: Routledge, 1988.

Waith, Eugene M. (ed.). *Titus Andronicus*. Cambridge: Cambridge University, 1984.

Walter, J. H. (ed.). *Henry V*. London: Methuen, 1987.

Warren, Roger (ed.). *Cymbeline*. Oxford: Clarendon, 1998.

Warren, Roger and Stanley Wells (eds.). *Twelfth Night*. Oxford: Clarendon, 1994.

Weis, René (ed.). *Henry IV, Part II*. Oxford: Clarendon, 1998.

Wells, Stanley and Gary Taylor (eds.). *William Shakespeare: The Complete Works, Compact Edition*. Oxford: Clarendon, 1990.

Wilson, John Dover and Arthur Quiller-Couch (ed.). *The Tempest*. Cambridge: Cambridge University, 1921.

Zitner, Sheldon P. (ed.). *Much Ado About Nothing*. Oxford: Clarendon, 1993.

EDITIONS OF PLAYS BY OTHER PLAYWRIGHTS

Abrams, William Amos (ed.). *The Merry Devil of Edmonton, 1608*. Durham, NC: Duke University, 1942.

Armin, Robert. *Collected Works of Robert Armin*, 2 vols. Introductions by J. P. Feather. New York: Johnson Reprint Corp, 1972.

Barnes, Barnabe. *The Divil's Charter*. Ed. R. B. McKerrow. Louvain: Uystpruyst, 1904. Reprinted Vaduz: Kraus, 1963.

Beaumont, Francis and John Fletcher. *A King and No King*. Ed. Robert K. Turner, Jr. Lincoln: University of Nebraska, 1963.

Beaumont, Francis and John Fletcher. *Philaster, or Love Lies a-Bleeding*. Ed. Andrew Gurr. London: Methuen, 1969.

Beaumont, Francis and John Fletcher. *Philaster, OR, Love lies a Bleeding*. The Second impression, corrected, and amended. London, 1622. Reprinted Menston, Eng: Scolar, 1970.

Bowers, Fredson (ed.). *The Complete Works of Christopher Marlowe*. Cambridge: Cambridge University, 1981.

Brooke, C. F. Tucker (ed.). *The Shakespeare Apochrypha: Being a Collection of Fourteen Plays which Have been Ascribed to Shakespeare*. Oxford: Clarendon, 1967.

Bullen, A. H. (ed.) *The Works of Thomas Middleton*. 8 vols. Boston: Houghton, Mifflin and Co., 1886.

Cannon, Charles Dale (ed.). *A Warning for Fair Women: A Critical Edition*. The Hague: Mouton, 1975.

Cawley, A. C. and Gaines, Barry (ed.). *A Yorkshire Tragedy*. Manchester: Manchester University, 1986.

Dekker, Thomas. *Satiro-Mastix, or the Untrussing of the Humourous Poet*. Ed. Hans Scherer. Louvain: Uystpruyst, 1907. Reprinted Vaduz: Kraus, 1963.

Everitt, E. B. (ed.). *Six Early Plays Related to the Shakespeare Canon*. Copenhagen: Rosenkilde & Bagger, 1965.

The Faire Maide of Bristow. London: 1605. Reprinted 1912. Reprinted New York: AMS, 1970.

Fletcher, John. *The Woman's Prize; or, The Tamer Tamed.* Ed. George B. Ferguson. The Hague: Mouton, 1966.

Gibbons, Brian (ed.). *The Revenger's Tragedy.* London: Benn, 1967.

Glatzer, Paula. *The Complaint of the Poet: The Parnassus Plays.* Saltzburg, Austria: Universitat Salzburg, 1977.

Glover, Arnold and A. R. Waller (eds.). *The Works of Francis Beaumont and John Fletcher.* 8 vols. Cambridge: Cambridge University, 1906–10. Reprinted New York: Octagon, 1969.

Gooch, Jane Lytton (ed.). *The Lamentable Tragedy of Locrine.* New York: Garland, 1981.

Hazlitt, William (ed.). *The Doubtful Plays of William Shakespeare.* London: Routledge, 1887.

Holaday, Allan (ed.). *Thomas Heywood's The Rape of Lucrece.* Urbana: University of Illinois, 1950.

Jackson, Macdonald P. and Neill, Michael (eds.). *The Selected Plays of John Marston.* Cambridge: Cambridge University, 1986.

Jonson, Ben. *The Alchemist.* Ed. Douglas Brown. London: Benn, 1966.

Jonson, Ben. *The Alchemist.* Ed. F. H. Mares. London: Methuen, 1967.

Jonson, Ben. *Catiline.* Ed. W. F. Bolton and Jane F. Gardner. Lincoln: University of Nebraska, 1973.

Jonson, Ben. *The Devil Is an Ass.* Ed. Peter Happé. Manchester: University of Manchester, 1994.

Jonson, Ben. *Poetaster.* Ed. Tom Cain. Manchester: Manchester University, 1995.

Jonson, Ben. *Sejanus His Fall.* Ed. Philip J. Ayres. Manchester: Manchester University, 1990.

Jonson, Ben, George Chapman, and John Marston. *Eastward Ho!* Ed. G. B. Petter. London: Benn, 1973.

Jupin, Arvin H. (ed.). *A Contextual Study and Modern-Spelling Edition of* Mucedorus. New York: Garland, 1987.

Kozlenko, William (ed.). *Disputed Plays of William Shakespeare.* New York: Hawthorn, 1974.

Kyd, Thomas. *The First Part of Hieronimo and The Spanish Tragedy.* Ed. by Andrew S. Cairncross. Lincoln: University of Nebraska, 1967.

Kyd, Thomas. *The Spanish Tragedy.* Ed. by J. R. Mulryne. London: Black, 1995.

Lancashire, Anne (ed.). *The Second Maiden's Tragedy.* Manchester: Manchester University, 1978.

Lapides, Fred (ed.). *The Raigne of King Edward the Third: A Critical, Old-Spelling Edition.* New York: Garland, 1980.

Lever, J. W. (ed.). *Every Man in His Humour: A Parallel-Text Edition of the 1601 Quarto and the 1616 Folio.* By Ben Jonson. Lincoln: University of Nebraska, 1971.

The London Prodigal, "by William Shakespeare." London: 1605. Reprinted New York: AMS, 1970.

MacArthur, John Robertson (ed.). *The First Part of Sir John Oldcastle, a Historical Drama by Michael Drayton et. al.* Chicago: Scott, Foresman, 1907.

Marlowe, Christopher. *The Complete Plays.* Ed. Irving Ribner. New York: Odyssey, 1963.

Marlowe, Christopher. *Edward II.* Ed. Charles R. Forker. Manchester: Manchester University, 1994.

Munday, Anthony, and others. *Sir Thomas More.* Ed. Vittorio Gabrieli & Giorgio Melchiori. Manchester: Manchester University, 1990.

Proudfoot, G. R. (ed.). *A Knack to Know a Knave.* Oxford: Malone Society, 1964.

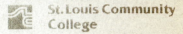
St. Louis Community College

Current Check-Outs summary for GARNER, A
Thu Feb 23 13:33:10 CST 2006

BARCODE : 300030005461035
TITLE: The best actors in the world : Sh
DUE DATE: Mar 16,2006
STATUS:

The Puritan; or, The Widow of Watling Street. London: 1607. Reprinted New York: AMS, 1970.

The Return from Parnassus. A Select Collection of Old English Plays, 4th ed., vol. VIII. Ed. W. Carew Hazlitt. London, 1876, Reprinted New York: Benjamin Blom, 1964, 97–217.

Sams, Eric (ed.). *Shakespeare's Lost Play, Edmund Ironside.* London: Fourth Estate, 1985.

Sider, J. W. (ed.). *The Troublesome Raigne of John, King of England.* New York: Garland, 1979.

Simpson, Richard (ed.). *The School of Shakspeare* (2 vols.). London: Chatto & Windus, 1878, Reprinted New York: AMS, 1973.

The Taming of a Shrew. Narrative and Dramatic Sources of Shakespeare, I, ed. Geoffrey Bullough. London: Routledge and Kegan Paul, 1964, 68–108.

Thomas of Woodstock, or 1 Richard II, ed. E. B. Everitt, *Six Early Plays Related to the Shakespeare Canon* (Copenhagen: Rosenkilde, 1965), 253–307.

Tourneur, Cyril. *The Revenger's Tragedy.* San Francisco: Chandler, 1962.

The Troublesome Raigne of King John. (1591) ed. Geoffrey Bullough, *Narrative and Dramatic Sources of Shakespeare,* IV. London: Routledge and Kegan Paul, 1962, 72–151.

The True Chronicle History of King Leir and His Three Daughters. (1605) ed. Geoffrey Bullough, *Narrative and Dramatic Sources of Shakespeare,* VIII. London: Routledge and Kegan Paul, 1973, 337–402.

Warnke, Karl and Ludwig Proescholdt (eds.). *Pseudo-Shakespearean Plays.* Halle: Niemeyer, 1883–88. Reprinted New York: AMS, 1973.

Webster, John. *The Duchess of Malfi.* Ed. John Russell Brown. Manchester: Manchester University, 1997.

Webster, John. *The Tragedy of the Duchesse of Malfy.* London, 1623. Reprinted Menston, Eng: Scholar, 1968.

White, M. (ed.). *Arden of Faversham.* London: New Mermaids, 1982.

Wilkes, G. A. (ed.). *The Complete Plays of Ben Jonson,* 4 vols. Oxford: Clarendon, 1981.

Wilkins, George. *The Miseries of Enforced Marriage.* Ed. Glenn H. Blayney. Oxford: Malone Society, 1963.

Wine, M. L. (ed.) *The Tragedy of Master Arden of Faversham.* London: Methuen, 1973.

A Yorkshire Tragedy. London: 1608. Reprinted New York: AMS, 1970.

OTHER WORKS CONSULTED

Alexander, Peter. *Shakespeare's Life and Art.* New York: New York University, 1964.

Allam, Roger, "The Duke in *Measure for Measure,*" *Players of Shakespeare 3.* Ed. Russell Jackson & Robert Smallwood. Cambridge: Cambridge University, 1996.

Baines, Barbara J. *Thomas Heywood.* Boston: Twayne, 1984.

Baldwin, T. W. *On Act and Scene Division in the Shakespeare First Folio.* Carbondale: Southern Illinois University, 1965.

Baldwin, T. W. *On the Literary Genetics of Shakespeare's Plays, 1592–94.* Urbana: University of Illinois, 1950.

Baldwin, T. W. *The Organization and Personnel of the Shakespearean Company.* Princeton, NJ: Princeton University, 1927.

Baldwin, T. W. *Shakespeare's Five-Act Structure: Shakspeare's Early Plays on the Background of Renaissance Theories of Five-Act Structure from 1470.* Urbana: University of Illinois, 1963.

Baldwin, T. W. *Shakspeare's 'Love's Labor's Won': New Evidence from the Account Books of an Elizabethan Bookseller.* Carbondale: Southern Illinois, 1957.

Barroll, Leeds. *Politics, Plague, and Shakespeare's Theater: The Stuart Years.* Ithaca, New York: Cornell University, 1991.

Beckerman, Bernard. *Shakespeare at the Globe, 1599–1609.* New York: Collier, 1962.

Bentley, Gerald Eades. *The Jacobean and Caroline Stage,* 7 vols. Oxford: Oxford University, 1941–68.

Bentley, Gerald Eades. *The Profession of Dramatist in Shakespeare's Time, 1590–1642.* Princeton, NJ: Princeton University, 1986.

Bentley, Gerald Eades. *The Profession of Player in Shakespeare's Time, 1590–1642.* Princeton, NJ: Princeton University, 1984.

Bergeron, David M. *Royal Family, Royal Lovers: King James of England and Scotland.* Columbia: University of Missouri, 1991.

Berry, Ralph (ed.). *The Methuen Book of Shakespeare Anecdotes.* London: Methuen, 1992.

Bevington, David (ed.). *Shakespeare: The Poems.* New York: Bantam, 1988.

Boas, F. S. *Shakspere and His Predecessors.* New York: Scribner's, 1910.

Booth, Stephen, "Speculations on Doubling in Shakespeare's Plays," *Shakespeare, The Theatrical Dimension,* Ed. Philip McGuire and David Samuelson, New York, AMS, 1979, 103–31.

Booth, Stephen (ed.). *Shakespeare's Sonnets.* New Haven CT: Yale University, 1977.

Boyce, Charles. *Shakespeare A to Z.* New York: Dell, 1990.

Bradley, David. *From Text to Performance in the Elizabethan Theatre: Preparing the Play for the Stage.* Cambridge: Cambridge University, 1994.

Braunmuller, A. R. and Michael Hattaway (eds.). *The Cambridge Companion to English Renaissance Drama.* Cambridge: Cambridge University, 1995.

Bullough, Geoffrey. *Narrative and Dramatic Sources of Shakespeare.* 8 vols. London: Routledge and Kegan Paul, 1957–75.

Campbell, Oscar James and Edward G. Quinn (eds.). *The Reader's Encyclopedia of Shakespeare.* New York: MJF, 1997.

Carson, Neil. *A Companion to Henslowe's Diary.* Cambridge: Cambridge University, 1988.

Cervantes, Miguel de. *Don Quixote.* Tr. Peter Motteux, revised Ozell. New York: Modern Library, 1930.

Chambers, E. K. *The Elizabethan Stage.* 4 vols. Oxford: Clarendon, 1923.

Chambers, E. K. *William Shakespeare: A Study of Facts and Problems.* 2 vols. Oxford: Oxford University, 1930.

Chute, Marchette. *Shakespeare of London.* New York: E. P. Dutton, 1949.

Cook, Judith. *The Golden Age of the English Theatre.* London: Simon & Schuster, 1995.

Dawson, Anthony, "*Tempest* in a Teapot: Critics, Evaluation, Ideology," *Bad Shakespeare: Revaluations of the Shakespeare Canon.* Ed. Maurice Charney. Rutherford, NJ: Fairleigh Dickinson University, 1988.

Dessen, Alan C. *Recovering Shakespeare's Theatrical Vocabulary.* Cambridge: Cambridge University, 1995.

Eccles, Christine. *The Rose Theatre.* London: Nick Hern, 1990.

Eccles, Mark. *Shakespeare in Warwickshire.* Madison: University of Wisconsin, 1961.

Edelman, Charles. *Brawl Ridiculous: Sword Fighting in Shakespeare's Plays.* Manchester: Manchester University, 1992.

Edwards, Philip. "An Approach to the Problem of *Pericles,*" *Shakespeare Survey* V, 1952, 25–49.

Ellis-Fermor, Una, "*Timon of Athens*: An Unfinished Play," *Review of English Studies,* xviii (1942), 270–83.

Fleisner, Robert, "*Love's Labour's Won* and the Occasion of *Much Ado*," *Shakespeare Survey*, XXVII, 1974.

Foakes, R. A. and R. T. Rickert (eds.). *Henslowe's Diary, with Supplementary Material, Introduction, and Notes*. Cambridge: Cambridge University, 1961.

Fraser, Russell. *Shakespeare: The Later Years*. New York: Columbia University, 1992.

Fraser, Russell. *Young Shakespeare*. New York: Columbia University, 1988.

Gilson, Joy Leslie. *Squeaking Cleopatras: The Elizabethan Boy Player*. Phoenix Mill, Eng: Sutton, 2000.

Greene, Robert. *Groats-Worth of Witte, Bought with a Million of Repentance*. Ed. G. B. Harrison. London: Bodley Head, 1926. Reprinted New York: Barnes & Noble, 1966.

Greene, Robert. *Pandosto. The Triumph of Time* (1588). ed. Geoffrey Bullough, *Narrative and Dramatic Sources of Shakespeare*. London: Routledge and Kegan Paul, VIII, 1973, 156–99.

Greg, W. W. *A Bibliography of the English Printed Drama to the Restoration*. 4 vols. London: Bibliographical Society, 1939–59.

Greg, W. W. "The Date of *King Lear* and Shakespeare's Use of Earlier Versions of the Story," *The Library*, xx (1939), 377–400.

Greg, W. W. *The Henslowe Papers*. London: Bullen, 1907.

Greg, W. W. *Henslowe's Diary*, 2 vols. London: Bullen, 1904–08.

Greg, W. W. *The Shakespeare First Folio: Its Bibliographical and Textual History*. Oxford: Clarendon, 1955.

Grosart, Rev. Alexander B. (ed.). *The Complete Works in Verse and Prose of Samuel Daniel*, 5 vols. New York: Russell & Russell, 1963.

Gurr, Andrew. *Playgoing in Shakespeare's London*. Cambridge: Cambridge University, 1994.

Gurr, Andrew. *The Shakespearean Stage, 1574–1642*, 3rd ed. Cambridge: Cambridge University, 1994.

Halliday, F. E. *A Shakespeare Companion, 1550–1950*. New York: Funk & Wagnalls, 1952.

Hamilton, Charles. *Cardenio, or the Second Maiden's Tragedy*. Lakewood, CO: Glenbridge Publishing, 1994.

Hamilton, Charles. *In Search of Shakespeare: A Reconnaissance into the Poet's Life and Handwriting*. San Diego: Harcourt Brace Jovanovich, 1985.

Harbage, Alfred. *Shakespeare and the Rival Traditions*. New York: Macmillan, 1952.

Harrison, William. *The Description of England*. Ed. George Edelen. New York: Dover, 1994.

Hart, Alfred. *Stolne and Surreptitious Copies: A Comparative Study of Shakespeare's Bad Quartos*. 1942. Reprint, Folcroft, PA: Folcroft Library, 1970.

Haynes, Alan. *The Gunpowder Plot*. London: Grange, 1994.

Heywood, Thomas. "An Apology for Actors (1612)," *The Seventeenth Century Stage: A Collection of Critical Essays*. Ed. by Gearld Eades Bentley. Chicago: University of Chicago, 1968, 10–22.

Hickson, Samuel, "Who Wrote Shakespeare's *Henry VIII?*" *Notes and Queries* (Aug. 24, 1850), 198.

Hinman, Charlton. *The Printing and Proofreading of the First Folio of Shakespeare*, 2 vols. Oxford: Oxford University, 1963.

Hodges, C. Walter. *The Globe Restored: A Study of the Elizabethan Theatre*, 2nd ed. New York: Norton, 1973.

Holmes, Martin. *Shakespeare and His Players*. New York: Scribner's, 1972.

Honan, Park. *Shakespeare: A Life*. Oxford: Oxford University, 1998.

Honigmann, E. A. J. *Shakespeare: The "Lost Years."* Manchester: Manchester University, 1985.

Honigmann, E. A. J. *The Stability of Shakespeare's Texts.* London: Arnold, 1965.

Hosking, G. L. *The Life and Times of Edward Alleyn.* London: Jonathan Cape, 1952. Reprint, New York: AMS, 1970.

Hosley, Richard (ed.). *Shakespeare's Holinshed: An Edition of* Holinshed's Chronicles *(1587).* New York: Putnam, 1968.

Hotson, Leslie. *The First Night of "Twelfth Night."* New York: Macmillan, 1954.

Hotson, Leslie. *Shakespeare's Sonnets Dated and Other Essays.* New York: Oxford University, 1949.

Hotson, Leslie. *Shakespeare versus Shallow.* Boston: Little, Brown, 1931.

Hughes, Ted. *Shakespeare and the Goddess of Complete Being,* rev. ed. London: Faber, 1993.

Jonson, Ben. *Discoveries, 1641. Conversations with William Drummond of Hawthornden, 1619.* Ed. G. B. Harrison. London: Bodley Head, 1923.

Kawachi, Yoshiko. *Calendar of English Renaissance Drama 1552–1642.* New York: Garland, 1986.

Kay, Dennis. *Shakespeare: His Life, Work, and Era.* New York: William Morrow, 1992.

Kay, W. David. *Ben Jonson: A Literary Life.* New York: St. Martin's, 1995.

Kemp, William. *Kemps Nine Daies Wonder.* London: 1600. Ed. G. B. Harrison. London: Bodley Head, 1926. Reprinted New York: Barnes & Noble, 1966.

Kemp, William. *Kemps Nine Daies Wonder.* Ed. the Rev. Alexander Dyce. London: Camden Society, 1840, Reprinted New York: AMS, 1968.

Kernan, Alvin. *Shakespeare, the King's Playwright: Theater in the Stuart Court, 1603–1613.* New Haven, CT: Yale University, 1995.

King, T. J. *Casting Shakespeare's Plays: London Actors and Their Roles, 1590–1642.* Cambridge: Cambridge University, 1992.

Knutson, Roslyn Lander. *The Repertory of Shakespeare's Company, 1594–1613.* Fayetteville: University of Arkansas, 1991.

Lake, David J. *The Canon of Thomas Middleton's Plays: Internal Evidence for the Major Problems of Authorship.* Cambridge: Cambridge University, 1975.

Lee, Sir Sidney. *A Life of William Shakespeare.* London: Macmillan, 1931. Reprinted New York: Dover, 1968.

Levi, Peter. *The Life and Times of William Shakespeare.* New York: Henry Holt, 1991.

Lodge, Thomas. *Rosalynde.* (1591). Ed. Geoffrey Bullough, *Narrative and Dramatic Sources of Shakespeare,* II. London: Routledge and Kegan Paul, 1958, 158–256.

Madelaine, Richard. *Shakespeare in Production: Antony and Cleopatra.* Cambridge: Cambridge University, 1998.

McManaway, James G. "Recent Studies in Shakespeare's Chronology," *Shakespeare Survey,* 3 (1950): 22–33.

Maxwell, Baldwin. *Studies in the Shakespearean Apocrypha.* New York: Columbia University, 1956.

McClellan, Kenneth. *Whatever Happened to Shakespeare?* New York: Barnes & Noble, 1978.

Michell, John. *Who Wrote Shakespeare?* New York: Thames & Hudson, 1996.

Mulryne, J. R. and Margaret Shewring (eds.). *Shakespeare's Globe Rebuilt.* Cambridge: Cambridge University, 1997.

Munro, J. *The Shakespeare Allusion Book: A Collection of Allusions to Shakespeare from 1591 to 1700.* 2 vols. London: Oxford University, 1932.

Murray, John Tucker. *English Dramatic Companies, 1558–1642.* 2 vols. Boston: Houghton Mifflin, 1910.

Neale, J. E. *Queen Elizabeth I.* London, 1934; Reprinted. Chicago: Academy Chicago, 1999.

Nicholl, Charles. *The Reckoning: The Murder of Christopher Marlowe*. Chicago: University of Chicago, 1995.

Nungezer, Edwin. *A Dictionary of Actors and of Other Persons Associated with the Public Representation of Plays in England before 1642*. New Haven CT: Yale University, 1929.

Paul, Henry N. *The Royal Play of Macbeth: When, Why, and How It Was Written by Shakespeare*. New York: Macmillan, 1950.

Pollard, Alfred W. *Shakespeare's Fight with the Pirates and the Problems of the Transmission of his Text*. 2nd ed. Cambridge: Cambridge University, 1937.

Riggs, David. *Ben Jonson: A Life*. Cambridge, MA: Harvard University, 1989.

Ringler, William A., Jr, "The Number of Actors in Shakespeare's Early Plays," *The Seventeenth Century Stage: A Collection of Critical Essays*. Ed. by Gearld Eades Bentley. Chicago: University of Chicago, 1968, 110–136.

Rowse, A. L. *Sex and Society in Shakespeare's Age: Simon Forman the Astrologer*. New York: Scribner, 1974.

Rowse, A. L. *William Shakespeare: A Biography*. New York: Harper & Row, 1963.

Sadie, Stanley (ed.). *The New Grove Dictionary of Music & Musicians*, 20 vols. London: Macmillan, 1995.

Salgado, Gamini. *Eyewitnesses of Shakespeare: First Hand Accounts of Performances 1590–1890*. New York: Barnes & Noble, 1975.

Schoenbaum, S. *William Shakespeare: A Compact Documentary Life*. Oxford: Oxford University, 1978.

Shapiro, Michael. *Children of the Revels: The Boy Companies of Shakespeare's Time and Their Plays*. New York: Columbia University, 1977.

Shapiro, Michael. *Gender in Play on the Shakespearean Stage: Boy Heroines and Female Pages*. Ann Arbor: University of Michigan, 1994.

Skura, Meredith Anne. *Shakespeare the Actor and the Purposes of Playing*. Chicago: University of Chicago, 1993.

Smith, Irwin. *Shakespeare's Blackfriars Playhouse: Its History and Its Design*. New York: New York University, 1964.

Sohmer, Steve. *Shakespeare's Mystery Play: The Opening of the Globe Theatre, 1599*. Manchester: University of Manchester, 1999.

Spedding, J. "Who Wrote Shakespeare's *Henry VIII?*," *Gentleman's Magazine* (Aug. 1850) NS 34, 115–23.

Spencer, T.J.B. (ed). *Shakespeare's Plutarch*. London: Penguin, 1968.

Spevack, Martin. *A Complete and Systematic Concordance to the Works of Shakespeare*. Hildesheim: Georg Olms, 1968–70.

Sprague, Arthur Colby. *The Doubling of Parts in Shakespeare's Plays*. London: Society for Theatre Research, 1966.

Stow, John. *A Survey of London Written in the Year 1598*. Ed. Henry Morley. London, 1912. Reprint: Stroud, Eng.: Sutton, 1997.

Thomas, Sidney. "The Date of *The Comedy of Errors*," *Shakespeare Quarterly*, VII (1956), 377–84.

Thomson, Peter. *Shakespeare's Professional Career*. Cambridge: Cambridge University, 1994.

Thomson, Peter. *Shakespeare's Theatre*, 2nd ed. London: Routledge, 1992.

Tillyard, E.M.W. *Shakespeare's Problem Plays*. Toronto: University of Toronto, 1949.

Trewin, J. C. *Going to Shakespeare*. London: George Allen & Unwin, 1978.

Tucker, T. G. (ed.). *The Sonnets of Shakespeare*. Folcroft, PA: Folcroft Library, 1970.

Wallace, C. W., "The First London Theatre: Materials for a History," *Nebraska University Studies*, xiii (1913), 275–9.

Wells, Stanley (ed.). *Shakespeare: A Bibliographical Guide*, new ed. Oxford: Clarendon, 1992.

Wells, Stanley and Gary Taylor, with John Jowett and William Montgomery. *William Shakespeare: A Textual Companion*. Oxford: Clarendon, 1987.

Wiles, David. *Shakespeare's Clown: Actor and Text in the Elizabethan Playhouse*. Cambridge: Cambridge University, 1987.

Wilkins, George. *The Painfull Adventures of Pericles, Prince of Tyre*. Ed. Kenneth Muir. Liverpool: Liverpool University, 1967.

Willis, Susan. *The BBC Shakespeare Plays: Making the Televised Canon*. Chapel Hill: University of North Carolina, 1991.

Wilson, Ian. *Shakespeare: The Evidence*. New York: St. Martin's, 1999.

Wilson, John Dover (ed.). *Life in Shakespeare's England*. Hammondsworth, Eng: Pelican, 1944.

Index

About the Author

DAVID GROTE has been involved in theatrical activities for 40 years in Texas and California, where he has acted, produced, and written plays and directed more than 120 productions for school, amateur, and professional theatre companies. He is the author of more than a dozen plays and of 7 previous books, including *Common Knowledge* (Greenwood, 1987) and *British English for American Readers* (Greenwood, 1992).

canned